CARY GRANT

The Lonely Heart

CHARLES HIGHAM
and
ROY MOSELEY

CARY GRANT

The Lonely Heart

HARCOURT
BRACE
JOVANOVICH

San Diego   New York   London

HBJ

Requests for permission to make copies of
any part of the work should be mailed to:
Copyrights and Permissions Department,
Harcourt Brace Jovanovich, Publishers,
Orlando, Florida 32887.

Library of Congress Cataloging-in-Publication Data

Higham, Charles.
Cary Grant: the lonely heart.

1. Grant, Cary, 1904–1986.
2. Motion picture actors and actresses—United States—Biography.
I. Moseley, Roy. II. Title.
PN2287.G675H54   1989   791.43′028′0924 [B]   88-34801
ISBN 0-15-115787-1

Designed by Michael Farmer
Printed in the United States of America
First edition
A B C D E

Roy Moseley wishes to dedicate
this book to his mother and father,
with all his love and gratitude,
and to Jane, Glen, and Gavin Kern

Charles Higham wishes to dedicate
this book to Pamela, Madeleine,
and Philippe Mora

Special acknowledgment
to Victoria Shellin

"What can one say about Cary Grant?—
He went from rags to riches in one short jump—
and filled us all with love and laughter."

—*Katharine Hepburn*

"As a child I wished I was a member of the Secret Service."

—*Cary Grant*

"He was the last of the great gentlemen."

—*Timothy Hutton*

PREFACE

In 1987, *People* magazine named Cary Grant, along with Greta Garbo, the greatest of the stars. Certainly, no actor, except possibly Clark Gable, has equaled Grant's romantic appeal; he had few peers in the art of romantic comedy. Despite the occasional news story suggesting some collision or other with a wife or girlfriend, his life appeared enviably smooth, and marked by a virtually unbroken chain of successes. Among the wealthiest of all performers, he owned houses in Beverly Hills, Malibu, and Palm Springs; in London, he stayed at the Connaught; he was the owner of two Rolls-Royces; his clothes and shoes were hand-made for him.

For many of his contemporaries, and for subsequent generations, he was the nonpareil of elegance and style. Men like Frank Sinatra and Ronald Reagan, George Burns, Bob Hope and Jack Benny envied his sophistication, his poise and his air of breeding. Even the women who suffered through marriage to Grant—most notably his first wife Virginia Cherrill and his fourth wife Dyan Cannon—could find warm things to say about him when time had almost healed their wounds. One could conjecture that the pain they feel in discussing him stems in part from the fact that they are still, after many years, in love with him.

To many young men, Grant was a surrogate father, giving them tender and considerate advice. Among those who benefited from his guidance and consideration were Ted Donaldson, the gifted child star of Grant's admirable comedy *Once Upon a Time,* Barbara Hutton's son, Lance Reventlow, and Timothy Hutton, one of the best young contemporary actors, brilliant in *Ordinary People,* whose father, Jim Hutton, Grant had befriended during the shooting of his last film, *Walk Don't Run.* For Phyllis Brooks, the exquisite, half-forgotten blonde actress of the 1930s, most memorable in *Rebecca of Sunnybrook Farm* and *The Shanghai Gesture,* he was the love of her life; even today, in her mid-seventies, widowed and with a happy family of grown children, she smiles, and the tears start in her eyes, as the memories reemerge.

Yet Cary Grant cannot be said to have enjoyed the comfortable, glowing existence that his multitude of admirers imagined. Much of his life was painful, even tortured; his spirit was ambiguous, deeply compulsive, at times almost insane in its obsessiveness. Like so many actors, he was a mass of contradictions: he could be generous to a fault and unholy in his stinginess; passionately devoted and loving, yet unthinkably cruel, sadistic and destructive. He could be meticulous in his punctuality, letter perfect on a movie set, giving no trouble to producer, director or co-stars, or maddeningly emphatic over pointless details, holding up work for hours or even days on end over the position of a light or the cut of a coat or the material used in a doorknob. Casual and careless to the point that his home would be the most disheveled, poorly repaired and messy in the whole of Beverly Hills, he could be so maddened by the presence of a trademark on a window that he would have the glass panel removed at vast cost and replaced. He would fuss over the ironing of his shirts by a housekeeper, sending them back repeatedly for new pressing, yet his neighbors would notice him hanging out his washing on a line with clothes pegs.

Sometimes, he took a pixieish pleasure in confusing everyone through his personal contradictions; often he was tormented by the conflicts in his nature. He was puzzled and disturbed all through his life by the mystery of his origins. He was circumcised in 1904 when circumcision was almost unknown in Britain, except for extreme medical reasons. The operation had to be performed by a mohel, a special surgeon appointed by a rabbi through a local synagogue; and yet exhaustive research in Bristol, Grant's birthplace, shows no trace of anyone Jewish on either side of his family.

Documentary proof is lacking, but the authors believe strongly that Grant's true mother, whose name was almost certainly Lillian, was of Jewish birth. They believe that she was a seamstress, working in the same clothing factory as Grant's father. His closest friends, including Ray Austin and William Curry McIntosh, have confirmed that his visits with Elsie Leach, his supposed mother, were artificial and strained, that she never seemed to recognize him as her son, that she appeared to be indifferent to his career and to his life in California, and that she refused to visit Los Angeles.

Certainly she was, in the early years, a cruel and despotic human being, whom the boy Archie resented as he grew up. One quasi-Freudian belief is that sons of mothers who have ill-treated them tend to wreak vengeance upon the women who love them for the rest of their lives. Whether or not this psychiatric explanation makes sense, the fact is that Grant tormented certain of the women with whom he became involved or whom he married. His actions against them went beyond mere verbal punishment: he physically abused them, beating them and sometimes injuring them.

It has been stated, with some glibness, that bisexuality or homosexuality is the result of a dominating female presence in the life of a growing man. We have made no attempt, in the text of this book, to explain why, throughout his life, Cary Grant became sexually involved with certain men, two of them of great prominence, others totally obscure. When he ceased to enjoy a liaison with Howard Hughes (testified to by three of Hughes's lieutenants and his publicist, it can only have been brief and superficial) or, far more seriously, with Randolph Scott, he remained a good and true friend of these men throughout their subsequent relationships with women, and he owed much of his fortune to Hughes's skilled guidance.

Bisexuality is a subject that, even today, makes many people feel uncomfortable. To them, a human being who moves, comfortably or not, between the poles of sexual experience is something alien and unsettling: a creature beyond understanding. Hence the fact that, when books or articles imply or state that an idol of the world is sexually ambiguous, the resentment seems almost as fierce as if he were disclosed as being purely homosexual.

Yet the honest biographer cannot shirk the painful truth, even at the risk of being called deliberately sensationalist; in an area in which even compassion is suspect, the facts are unavoidable. And for a star of Cary Grant's magnitude, the pressure towards invention and deceit, cover-up and confusion, can be terrifying. Forced to be an actor in private and public life as well as on the screen itself, a famous performer can suffer intolerably; he is forced to satisfy the fantasies of millions, live out a complex mythology and deny himself any utterance of the "love that dares not speak its name." Even today, in this supposedly liberal age, actors of note feel compelled to disguise their true natures, so that autobiographies have appeared, seemingly exhaustive, written with expert ghosts, in which not an inkling of a true sexual orientation emerges.

The stress of uncertainty over his parentage (Grant identified strongly with his father, whom he loved, and who died early in the actor's career), the agony of hiding his sexual nature from the world, created much of the tension from which Grant suffered. Conflict and stress provoked this charmer's manic and violent temper, his sudden moods of neurotic, deeply self-absorbed solitariness, his unreasoning hatreds and drastically consuming loves. Nothing for Grant was tepid or halfhearted; he flew to extremes; he was never really at ease.

A consistently devouring passion of his was for vaudeville, for knockabout comedy, the excitement and glitter of the musical theater. He learned at the feet of the masters: George Burns and Eddie Foy, Sr. among them. For all of his polished manners, acquired as an actor acquires them, as it were phonetically, Grant remained at heart a working-class boy, with all of the moodiness and darkness of his West Country forebears. Family rumors hint that he might have been of gypsy or Spanish blood, intermingled in the eras before genealogical records were taken. Be that as it may, he was British working class to the end of his life: in his cockiness, obstreperousness, love of vulgar humor, fondness for fish and chips, sausages and mash, and tripe and onions, and in his affection for old music hall songs. His rare moments of happiness would find him banging away at a grand piano in his Beverly Hills living room, shouting such once popular refrains as "Yes, We Have No Bananas!" or "Up In a Balloon, Boys." It was his proletarian charm that endeared him to men and women alike; behind the perfectly tailored suits, the immaculately groomed hair, the perfect tan and flashing teeth of the ultimate matinee idol there was a tough, brash, sardonically humorous West Country lad screaming to be let out.

In exploring the story of a remarkable life, which encompassed triumph after triumph, as well as secret intelligence work in World War II, the authors have not attempted to smooth out the many bumps with slick explanations, or paper over the cracks with convenient invented detail. The acknowledgments and source notes pages will indicate the range of opinion, for, against, and in the middle, of over 150 people who loved, hated, slept or worked with this great star. The record is presented plainly, for the reader to interpret as he chooses. Our conclusion, for what it is worth, was that Cary Grant, despite his many very human failings, did his best to be a good and decent man. Let others argue if they will.

CARY GRANT

The Lonely Heart

ONE

Archibald Alec Leach was born at 1:00 A.M. on Sunday, January 18, 1904, at 15 Hughenden Road, Horfield, Bristol. King Edward VII was on the throne and Theodore Roosevelt was in the White House; the Russian-Japanese War was about to erupt; automobiles and films were in the teething stage, and the blazing red of the British Empire covered most of the world map. Night workers were toiling in the factories and coal mines and cleaning the streets, but most of England was asleep; the pale flicker of gaslight gleamed in glass globes over Bristol's streets, and from the harbor, dominated still by the tall masts of sailing ships, there was the toot of a whistle, the sudden blare of a funnel signaling departure, and the powerful scent of the sea.

The house in which the child was born was on the northern edge of the city, where there were green hills and beekeepers' gardens and clumps of bare oak trees. Number 15 was one of a newly constructed row of narrow terrace houses fashioned of gray Gloucester stone. Proliferating in drab monotony, these cheerless semi-detached homes would soon swallow up the lush countryside like a dark pestilence. Renumbered from 8 Hughenden Road the week before the boy's birth, the house had a front parlor of twelve by sixteen feet; the back parlor was twelve by twelve, the kitchen seven by ten feet. A narrow staircase rose from the hall to a landing, onto which opened three small bedrooms. There was an outside toilet, and a pump for bathing in the back garden that sloped up to a stone wall.

The weather was unseasonably mild in Bristol that January. While London was swathed in a yellow sulfur fog that choked the throat and burned the eyes, turning passers-by into barely glimpsed phantom figures shivering in the cold, Bristol air was clear, swept with a fine wind from the Channel, and the temperature was a tolerable 48 degrees.

Elias Leach, Archie's father, was thirty-two years old, delicately and weakly handsome, with light brown curly hair, soft, dark, reflective eyes, chiseled cheekbones, and a sensual mouth decorated with a neat mustache. He had a slight cleft in his chin and a wistful, captivating smile few could resist.

He was the son, grandson and great grandson of earthenware potters. He had followed his unlettered mother Emily's calling by working at Todd's Clothing Factory, where he was a suit presser, receiving the garments off the assembly line and steaming in creases with hot irons for an average of ten hours a day. He found release from the monotony of the work by indulging in affairs with numerous young women and drinking himself into a pleasant stupor night after night in the local pubs.

Elias's wife Elsie Maria, whom he had married on May 30, 1898, was the daughter of a family of brewery laborers, laundresses and ships' carpenters. Her first child, John William Elias, had died on February 6, 1900, a few days short of his first birthday, in the violent convulsions of tubercular meningitis. It had been a terrible way to start the new century, and Elsie had become neurotic and tortured as a result of her bereavement.

The couple behaved strangely after Archibald Alec was born. He was baptized three weeks later, but his birth was not registered until three weeks after that. Still more oddly, the Leaches had him circumcised, a procedure almost completely unknown outside the Jewish community in England in 1904. It is possible that the reason for the circumcision was medical: a closing of the foreskin which would have rendered urination impossible. Cary Grant believed later that the reason for the circumcision was that his father was partly Jewish, but, in fact, there is no record of anything in the family tree to suggest such a possibility. We believe that he was the illegitimate child of a Jewish woman, who either died in childbirth or disappeared. His own attitude to his possible Jewishness was extraordinarily complex throughout his life. He declined the leading role in the anti-racist film *Gentleman's Agreement* because the hero was a gentile posing as a Jewish person, and he felt that as a Jew he could not satisfactorily play the part. He gave substantial sums to Jewish causes on several occasions; in 1939, he presented $25,000 to the Jewish actor Sam Jaffe to give to the United Jewish appeal with the understanding that his Jewishness would not be disclosed. In 1947, he gave an identical sum to the new state of Israel, announcing that it was in the name of his dead Jewish mother. He told some friends and the actress Mary Brian, to whom he almost became engaged, that he was Jewish; he told many others, including Clifford Odets, that he was not. The mystery remains.

Perhaps because of trouble in paying the rent, perhaps because of Elias's bad local reputation, the Leaches moved twice before their son was five: to two subsequent addresses in the suburb of Bishopston, which was only a few streets away from Horfield. These drab, semi-detached houses huddled together on narrow streets which ran directly into open country. Dominating the neighborhood was the looming Bristol Prison, into which, day after day, night after night, the Black Marias trundled behind government horses, carrying convicts into a place where hope was rapidly abandoned. The only other building of consequence was the equally depressing orphanage, which housed the innumerable illegitimate children whose unhappy existence was Dickensian and dark.

The familiar sounds of Bishopston were the chop of horses' hooves and the grinding of wheels as conveyances, ranging from enormous, top-heavy furniture vans to simple two-wheel flies, trundled along the streets to the nearby Gloucester Road, the main artery in and out of the city. Counterpointed with these constant reminders of a now industrialized Bristol were the occasional sounds of nature emanating from the rural districts: the hum of bees from hives in a neighboring estate, the cawing of crows and the lowing of cattle.

The Leaches' existence was cheerless and depressing. Elsie was a harsh woman, who rapped Archie's knuckles at the slightest opportunity and docked his sixpence-a-week pocket money if he marked a table or upset a cushion. She served basic British food—thick, lumpy porridge, kippers, bread and lard, sausage and mash, suet pudding of a gelatinous consistency—and made pots of too-strong tea which were covered by woolen cosies knitted in the shape of animals or birds.

Elsie resented Archie for taking the place of the child who had died; Elias was feckless and irresponsible, disappearing for long periods of time to a mistress or mistresses in the port of Southampton. In later years, Cary Grant tried to belie the ugly truth of his upbringing by writing of his father carrying him into a chandeliered drawing room to recite a poem. But there was no drawing room and there were no chandeliers in the pinched houses he occupied in these first years of his life.

He wrote that he was kept in dresses until he was several years old:

> It seemed to me that I was kept in baby clothes much longer than any other child, and perhaps, for a while, wasn't sure whether I was a boy or a girl. I wonder why little boys are ashamed to be mistaken for little girls. Why do they take such pride in being little boys? Do little girls take similar pride in their sex and not wish to be mistaken for little boys?

He made too much of this, disturbed as he was in later life by his ambiguous sexual nature. In fact, it was characteristic of all Victorian and early Edwardian parents to dress their infant male children in girls' clothing.

Another memory of those earliest days of life was the emphasis, in family conversations, on money. Elsie nagged his father over the insufficiency of funds for the housekeeping. The butt of clichés like so many children, told repeatedly that money "didn't grow on trees," and that one must "waste not, want not," he would be almost painfully tight with money to the end of his life. For years he kept in his pocket a length of twine of mysterious significance. Was it to remind him of the days when he and his family had nothing?

Even when, one night during a storm, he woke and saw his parents holding each other around the waist for once, resting from their many quarrels as they looked out into the rain, he didn't feel a sense of happiness or belonging. He wrote in his middle age, "And now, today, as I think of it, I recall the intense feeling of being shut off from [my parents'] unfamiliar unity."

He seems to have found consolation with his Uncle John (Jack) Leach, the fourth child of Elias's parents and the eldest son, who worked in a department store. He liked his elderly grandmother Elizabeth, who could neither read nor write. Her ugly house on Picton Street may, like his own, have had no bathroom, and was cold and damp in winter, but he felt at home there, and objected only to being bathed naked in front of his grandmother in a copper placed in the kitchen, ashamed even at that four-year-old stage of exhibiting his genitals to a woman.

At four and a half, Archibald Alec was sent to Bishop Road Infant School. A short walk from the Bishopston house in which the family was living, the gray stone establishment clung to the shadow of the prison on Victoria Road, and was scarcely more appealing in its featureless, almost windowless blankness. The child was frightened from his first day at school. Rendered nervous and introspective by Elsie's cruelty and neurotic instability, and by the fact that he had no father to depend on, he was a classic example of a misfit in the rough-and-tumble of young boys and girls. As long as he lived, he never forgot the threat of the cane, the smell of the chalk dust, the aroma of varnish on yellow desks with their hinged tops, the squeak of an inscription on a blackboard, or the fearsome demeanor of the spinster teachers. But gradually he got used to the other children, and he grew stronger through constant exercise that ranged from compulsory physical training in the morning in a damp or freezing yard, to playing football with no more than the outline of a goal in chalk drawn on the brick wall behind him. His success as goalkeeper earned him the grudging admiration of his lustier fellow pupils, and laid the groundwork for his lifelong hunger—the hunger that consumes all performers—to be loved by the crowd.

There were some moments of relief from the misery of his existence at home. He managed to slip away to meet his father at the Todd Clothing Factory on Saturdays and walk home with him and

Elias's cribbage-playing friends. He would search in his father's pockets for candies and joyfully fish one up, munching it hungrily. At Christmas, he had a consolation: the pantomimes. Elias, who liked to sing music hall songs while Elsie pounded away at the piano, loved the theater and took Archie to these annual Christmas presentations. A tradition in England since the 1830s, pantomimes were uniquely English: colorful and bizarre entertainments involving cross-dressing, with the hero or Principal Boy played by a woman. There were transformation scenes of magical beauty in which the figures of old legends would form into exquisite and colorful patterns. The spectacular lighting effects and sumptuous costumes of the dancers and singers contrasted with the heavy-weight antics of the crude and vulgar music hall clowns who provided the comedy relief. *Babes in the Wood, Aladdin, Cinderella, Jack and the Beanstalk,* and *Puss in Boots* were notable among the entertainments seen in Bristol during Archie's first five years, at such gilt-and-gingerbread palaces as the Prince's and the Empire-and-Hippodrome Theatre.

The boy loved pantomimes: he found escape from his gloomy existence in the multicolored dancing world of the theater. Elias was a stage-door Johnny, addicted to actresses, and it is possible that Archie's true mother was a member of that profession. Elias was often backstage, flirting in dressing rooms with the attractive chorus girls. He also formed a friendship with the well-known troupe of acrobatic dancers and stilt walkers known as the Penders. Starting on the week of August 8, 1910, when Archie was six and a half, the Penders were at the Empire-and-Hippodrome in a show entitled *The Long and the Short of It: A Screaming Absurdity.* The Penders' real names were Robert and Margaret Lomas. Working at the time under the banner of Howard and Wyndham, Booking Agents, they appeared with their ten-year-old daughter Doris, and Robert's brothers, performing a Harlequinade. Robert Lomas was to become the dominant influence in Archie Leach's life, and would be far more of a father to him, albeit a stern one, than his own parent.

Born of yeoman stock in Bury, Lancashire, in 1872, Lomas was the son and grandson of traveling players. The Lomas family had for thirty years criss-crossed the British Isles and continental Europe with a collapsible stage and props, and a canvas tent, alternating Shakespearean performances with a knockabout music hall act. Until the turn of the century, the family had appeared in a popular "turn," "Fun and Antics in Monkeyland," in ape, gorilla and chimpanzee costumes, dancing and singing and pulling their heads off at the end of the act to disclose their grinning faces. Now they also provided an eccentric routine dressed as policemen, which was later echoed by the silent movie comedy ensemble the Keystone Cops.

In 1908, they had had a narrow escape when the Theatre Royal, Drury Lane, caught fire at the end of a performance and burned many of their props. Under the aegis of the genial Arthur Collins, a distant relative of the actress Joan Collins and general manager of Drury Lane, they had appeared year after year in Christmas pantomimes, scoring a triumphant success in *Aladdin* in the 1909 season.

Robert Lomas was five feet eight, muscular from years of acrobatic training, handsome and olive-skinned, with slicked-down black hair and strong, aquiline features. Archie Leach resembled him strongly, and imitated him in later years. Despite his broad Lancashire accent and somewhat coarse, aggressive character, Lomas was very much a dapper man-about-town. He chain-smoked expensive cigars, sported smart suits, and boasted fancy hand-painted ties. He was flashy, a "toff"; he was "theatre" all the way down to his smart, fashionable spats. But he was also despotic, cruel, and a severe taskmaster.

Archie was enthralled by the Lomases in their *The Long and the Short of It.* He laughed and clapped and jumped up and down as Robert Lomas, in a grotesque mask of an old woman's face, wearing a Mother Hubbard dress, dropped his hat on the stage and the shortest of the nine dancers, ten-year-old Doris Pender, picked up the hat and passed it up the line. He was delighted by the Harlequinade, with Robert Lomas as Harlequin and Margaret Lomas as Columbine, in scenes that included the explosion of a steam train and a commotion in which the half-nude toweled figures of a Turkish bath ran helter-skelter all over the stage. He loved the police act, in which the family, in their tall black helmets that kept falling off, ran across scenery rooftops, plunged down chimneys, shot up through trap doors, exploded through windows and hung perilously from fire escapes. At one stage a horse pulled a fire wagon across the proscenium as the entire family hung from its ladder. The Lomases tumbled and danced in the Russian manner, with their knees bent and their feet kicking high; they tangled themselves in human pretzels of limbs, and then disentangled and danced again; miraculously fluid and limber, they became the focus of the child's dreams.

At home, there was the pallid, gray light of day and the flickering gaslight at night; the smell of cooking, especially of cabbage; his father coming home drunk; his mother's hysteria and stinginess; her constant mourning for her lost elder son. The Empire-and-Hippodrome Theatre was full of laughter and gilt and bronze, polish and red velvet and dazzling lights and sparkling, spinning acrobatic dancers. Seeing his son's happiness, Elias Leach saw a way out for both of them. He gave Archie to Robert Lomas as an extra member of his troupe; and, since his wife, according to the laws of the time, would have no say in the matter, he signed the necessary paper himself. He must have lied that the boy was ten: the authorities did not permit children of six to work.

For all his life, protecting both his father and Robert Lomas, Cary Grant decently lied that he joined the troupe at sixteen. Robert Lomas's decision to adopt the boy at this tender age was both surprising and daring: if the true facts had emerged, he could have been fined or possibly even imprisoned for the offense, but he was a fellow Mason of Elias's. Lomas needed an extra player because so great was the demand for his troupe that it frequently had to split up; the Christmas before, augmented by outsiders, a splinter group had appeared at the Prince's Theatre Edinburgh, in a pantomime. Although he could barely dance or do more than perform amateurish somersaults learned in the school gym, the six-year-old boy, so far as can be determined, joined the Pender ensemble in their second week at the Bristol Empire-and-Hippodrome in two shows a night at 6:30 and 8:50, from August 15–20, in "Bob Pender's Little Dandies," described in the programme as "an expert dancing scena [sic] à la Russe." The Bristol *Times and Mirror* in its edition of August 16, 1910, reviewed the performance as follows:

> Bob Pender's Little Dandies, half a dozen lads and one little lassie—Doris Pender—daintily attired, present a rather unique

dancing scene, combined with acrobatic feats. . . They do their work briskly and skillfully, especially the damsel, whose terpsichorean feats are graceful and facile. . .

When the show closed, the troupe took off on an extraordinary journey. They were booked to appear at the Wintergarten Theater of Varieties in Berlin. Since the Berlin show was to open on the 27th, they barely made it to the destination in time via train, ship, and train again. It is easy to imagine the excitement of the six-year-old boy as he was propelled from dreary Bristol to a steamship, and thence to a new culture.

The Wintergarten was the largest and most extravagant music hall in Germany. Cavernous, luxurious, a riot of red plush and gilt, with motifs of angels blowing trumpets and heroic male nude athletes carved into the walls and ceiling, decorated with six massive crystal chandeliers, the theater was situated in the rambling old Central Hotel opposite the Friedrichstrasse Railroad Station. Run by the genial, mutton-chop-mustached impresario Franz Steiner, it could accommodate as many as 750 performers on the stage and over 1,800 in the audience.

Since there is no way that Archie Leach could have learned to stilt walk in the time allowed, he had to sit upon the shoulders of Robert or Margaret Lomas as they paraded up and down on stilts in their comedy routines. Among the enthusiastic first-night audience were the sharp-witted, thirty-year-old New York entrepreneur Jesse L. Lasky, and the jolly, twenty-two-year-old Leo Maase, chief European representative of the H. B. Marinelli Agency, which numbered Sarah Bernhardt, Réjane, and Anna Held among its galaxy of famous clients. The two young men from New York were hunting for talent for the Folies Bergère Theater, which was under construction at Forty-sixth and Broadway and was scheduled to be opened the following April under the management of Lasky and his able partner, Henry B. Harris. Captivated by the Pender Troupe of Giants, they made their way backstage to append Robert Lomas's signature to a contract. He signed without hesitation, despite the fact that he was now under contract to the Moss-Stoll theater circuit in England. Somehow, given the loose laws of the time, he got away with this.

The troupe had a triumphant two weeks at the Wintergarten, and Leo Maase secured them an October engagement at the equally famous Olympia in Paris. Meanwhile, they returned to England for a less inspiring tour of the music halls. Though rocking with audience laughter night after night for twelve performances a week, the "halls" were ugly and depressing, seldom clean, and usually in need of a fresh coat of paint. There was a great deal of drunkenness backstage, and fornication in the seedy dressing rooms. Stage-door-keepers allowed in a motley collection of friends and relatives, barmaids, soldiers and sailors. The air behind the scenes was thick with smoke, alive with bawdy conversation and the constant smacking of buttocks and frequent pinching of female flesh followed by loud, raucous giggles. The music hall managers, who spent the day washing the windows and posting the bills, would turn up at night in tie and tails and make futile attempts to bring some measure of control to the bedlam backstage.

Travel was by train and, as members of the Music Hall Artists Railway Benevolent Association, the Lomases traveled first class for third-class fares. The windows were pulled up tight no matter what the season, and cigarette and cigar smoke filled the air. The Lomas family and outside members of the troupe were housed in "digs."

The music halls had appreciative, noisy audiences. But people in the galleries would scream out ribald comments during the show or let out "raspberries," greatly upsetting untried performers. The tradition was to shout back at the gallery "birds" with equal vigor, and sometimes there would be confrontations in the alley outside the theater: a free-for-all in which several men might wind up in the gutter with teeth missing.

Learning to stilt walk must have been an ordeal for Archie Leach. The stilts were 1⅜-inches square, with "steps" inside, cut from a block of the same thickness as the ash or oak stilt. They were fastened by carriage bolts and washers. A two-inch wooden screw inserted near the bottom prevented the stilt from turning on the bolt. The stilts were tied around the waist with rope, and the feet which were also tied rested on the steps. Stages in England sloped from the back to the footlights and it was almost impossible to keep balance. Again and again the boy would tumble, only to be expertly caught by one or another of the Lomases. Occasionally, he would crash through their reaching hands and hurt himself on the hard wooden boards.

The Pender Troupe appeared successfully at the Paris Olympia in October; they were booked that Christmas for the Theatre Royal, Drury Lane, pantomime, *Jack and the Beanstalk,* starring the great vaudevillean George Graves. The Penders, of course, played the giants. Archie was among them, as the smallest performer, and he also appeared in a routine as a stork, wearing a bird mask. He celebrated not only Christmas but his seventh birthday in the show, and the Penders were warmly reviewed, singled out from the cast for their marvelous antics.

TWO

On March 15, 1911, Archie sailed for New York with several of the Pender Troupe aboard the *Lusitania.* Robert and Margaret Lomas, and some of the boys, went on the S.S. *Oceanic;* Doris traveled with Archie. Both vessels suffered rough crossings through turbulent, windswept seas, and the *Lusitania,* destined to be sunk by a German torpedo years later, was top-heavy and rolled alarmingly in the swell. The seven-year-old boy's excitement must have been extreme as the troupe docked. The Lomases checked into rooms on West Forty-ninth Street, and began rehearsing at the Hudson Theater, while the finishing touches were being put to the *Folies Bergère.* The city was alive with over thirty major theatrical spectacles. Mrs. Fiske, the reigning star of Broadway, was a sensation in *Mrs. Bumpstead-Leigh* at the Lyceum. Hazel Dawn was the star of *The Pink Lady* at the New Amsterdam; Nora Bayes and Jack Norworth were the sweetly singing duo in *Little Miss Fix-It* at the Globe; and *Get-Rich-Quick Wallingford* was a comedy riot at the George M. Cohan Theater. Broadway in 1911 was still authentically the dazzling Great White Way, and everyone was saying that the *Folies Bergère* of New York would offer a spectacle that even the colossal show at the Winter Garden and the dramatic epic *Thaïs* at the Criterion could not hope to equal. At first rehearsal, the Lomases met the robust and dynamic R. H. Burnside, one of the great theatrical

The present little act might indicate that the Pender Troupe is capable of giving a pleasing and regular number. The ten people, one by one, appear on stilts. . . . Each wears a large hooded mask with comedy face, while little hands are seen from the arms up in the air. The close is the grouping of the ten figures, in step one behind the other.

The Penders were especially popular in an antic encore to the "Down the Strand" number in *Gaby*, in which they wore London costermonger's costumes, and they closed both the main performance and the midnight cabaret in costumes composed partly of Stars and Stripes and partly of Union Jacks.

In spite of its razzle-dazzle, cheerful vulgarity, and richness of production values, the *Folies Bergère* flopped—chiefly because the price, at $2.50 a ticket, was too high for the masses of theatergoers, who couldn't manage more than a dollar a seat. The show was for the rich, and the rich who went to the theater were limited in number and had many other entertainments to distract them. What was more, the show lacked the touch of genius that Florenz Ziegfeld was already bringing to his celebrated Follies. Whereas Ziegfeld integrated dance, comedy (the latter never to his complete satisfaction), ballet, and light-operatic effects into a stunningly complete whole, Lasky and Harris simply threw one act after another into the melting pot, and failed to produce pure gold. Worse, they panicked, and the moment the show began to lose money, they chopped some of their best French acts, made the entire company take salary cuts totaling $1,000, and put so much pressure on Ethel Levey to revise her performance that she found an excuse and left for London, to appear with great success at the Alhambra. R. H. Burnside resigned in a fury because of too much interference.

The Penders left before the show completed its run, victims of another economy purge. Apparently, the decision was made to send Archie back to Bristol. He returned to his home and to the drab and humdrum Bishop Row Infant School that September, undoubtedly in a state of severe disappointment, while the Lomases went on to do another pantomime, *Hop O' My Thumb,* at the Theatre Royal, Drury Lane. It must have been painful for the boy to miss this show and to have to make up stories explaining his absence; more painful still to suppress the exciting truth and to show no hint of his newly acquired acrobatic skills on the school playground.

He found some consolation in attending Saturday matinees at the Metropole, Pringle's Picture Palace, and Claire Street Cinemas, where he could see the Keystone Cops imitating the Lomases, along with such comedians as John Bunny, who had a face like moldy cheese, and the beautiful comedienne Mabel Normand. He loved knockabout comedy more than ever, and seeing these actors on the screen, racing in fire wagons or souped-up 1911 jalopies down the rambling, interminable suburban streets of Los Angeles, past palm trees and scrub and telephone poles, stirred longings in him for a distant world.

On September 30, 1912, the Lomases were back in Bristol, performing at the Empire Music Hall as Bob Pender and his Dandies. In January 1914, Archie's father took him to see the great American star Fanny Brice in the revue *Hello, Ragtime,* at the Prince's Theatre. That same year, Archie won a scholarship to Fairfield Grade and Secondary School. His father could barely find enough money to buy his cap, blazer, and trousers in secondhand stores.

Then Archie received a shock: he returned home from a walk one day to be told that Elsie had died suddenly of a heart attack and been buried immediately. His repeated inquiries about the location of the grave were never answered. It was only years later that he learned she had been admitted to Fishponds Lunatic Asylum—much the worse of the two existing institutions for the insane in Bristol. It cost only one pound a year to put someone into this bedlam. Conditions were filthy and disgusting, and the patients wandered about, dirtying themselves, screaming, and tearing at their hair. Elias's apparent reason for signing papers committing his wife was revealed when he installed a mistress, Mabel Bass, sometimes known as Meg, in his house. Though neurotic and disturbed, Elsie Leach was no more insane than he was. Perhaps she was less so—considering the appalling wickedness of his incarcerating her.

Archie began his career at Fairfield Grade and Secondary School on September 2, 1915. The school was a grim Victorian pile surrounded by a large playground. Poorly heated in winter and almost airless in the summer, it was a bare, stark place, serving wretched food. However, Archie, who had learned much from his months in the music hall world, mixed well. His good looks, and sturdy physique—improved by stilt walking and acrobatic training—and long-lashed eyes captivated many of the young girls and earned him the admiration of his fellow pupils. The headmaster of Fairfield, the Mr. Chips-like Augustus Smith, was a delight. Almost everyone loved the glorious "Gussie." It is true that he would rap certain students over the knuckles, among them Archie Leach, for such innocent offenses as eating an apple between classes, and, like many head teachers of his time, he was a little too handy with a birch rod. But few resented even his strictest punishments. He was a benign despot, striding through the corridors of the school with his mortarboard and floating black gown, dressed in tweeds, his cheeks flushed with excitement. Archie was also very fond of George Stockwell, the science master, with whom he kept in touch for the rest of his life, giving him a five-pound note on his retirement in the 1960s. There was the mustachioed Henri Audcent, the French teacher, the robust "Maps" Madkins, who taught geography, the music teacher J. D. Arnold, and the chemistry teacher Henry H. Howett, known by the name of one of his famous formulae, as H3. And there was the vigorous Miss Truscott, who taught brisk gymnastics, in which, of course, Archie Leach was supreme.

Archie was a mischievous boy, whose chief offense, according to a schoolmate, the present Mrs. Lillian Pearce, was that "he wouldn't do his homework at night. Instead, he would go to the Prince's or the [Empire-and-] Hippodrome." Mrs. Pearce adds, "He was a very popular boy, he was clever at most subjects and expert at all sports."

Another classmate, who later assisted the art teacher, was Ellen Kathleen Hallett. She remembers:

Archie was average in art, good-looking, but you can't tell from the acorn what the oak will be. The room in which I taught Archie was divided in half. The boys on the left next to the corridor, and the girls on the right. I can still see Leach halfway down the classroom. He always said he wanted to join the circus. He wasn't troublesome. He was just a nice, ordinary boy. But I must admit I was annoyed in 1947 when I saw the film *Bachelor*

Girl [*The Bachelor and the Bobby-Soxer*] and the famous Cary Grant was being interviewed by Shirley Temple and said he had been taught art at school by a Miss Hallett. I thought he should have asked me first!

Another pupil at Fairfield was a man who calls himself Ted Morley. He says:

Archie never had anything to do with any of the girls at the school. His best sport was "fives," a form of squash played with gloves. He played the school piano quite well, specializing in music hall songs. He had very strong teeth and would perform a trick in which he would place a heavy object in his handkerchief and then pick it up by biting the two ends of the hankie in his molars. He was always scruffily dressed, but his hair was neat and plastered down with brilliantine. In those days, his nose was so upturned that when you looked straight at him you could see all the way up his nostrils.

It would seem that at some stage in his career, Cary Grant had his nose reproportioned.

In the evenings, Archie would work backstage in the various Bristol theaters, eager to meet the performers. He was a callboy, yelling out when an actor or actress was due on stage, running errands, carrying cups of tea into dressing rooms, and helping to fend off the stage-door Johnnies. There was great excitement for him in the week of July 16–21, 1917, when "Bob Pender's Nippy Nine Burlesque Rehearsal," as the act was now called, turned up for two performances a night at the newly built Bristol Hippodrome.* It takes no feat of the imagination to envision the reunion. From November 19–24 of the same year, the great magician David Devant returned to Bristol, where Archie had seen him perform, to do his famous tricks at the Hippodrome, including the Feather Necklet, the Magic Mirror, the German Soldier, David Devant's Disembodied Spirit,

---

* *Replacing the aforementioned Empire-and-Hippodrome, which was pulled down.*

and the Artist's Dream. All of these acts were exquisitely done. The Penders were on the same bill, and it is probable that Bob Pender secured Archie the job of assisting Devant's lighting experts to create the illusions.

Then almost fifty, Devant was at the height of his career. His brooding, attractively ugly face was strong and forceful; he exuded self-confidence and masculine good cheer. But he suffered from recurrent nervous disturbances and periods of actual madness.

Archie watched fascinated from the flies above the stage as he trained the lights on the great magician. Devant tied an assistant with a sixteen-foot ribbon, sealed the knots with wax, and threw the ends to the audience. Then he placed the assistant in a cabinet and drew the curtains. The audience members never left hold of the ribbon. Suddenly, he told them to pull the ribbon, the curtains opened, and a woman was standing there, tied up identically. He showed a beautiful girl, dressed as a moth, drawn to a candle flame, appear to vanish into thin air. He produced two dozen eggs from a seemingly empty derby hat, reduced a six-foot soldier with a flick of the wrist to a two-foot-sized wooden doll, cracked a two-foot egg with a spoon, found another egg inside it, and another and another, finally producing a full-sized girl from the smallest egg of all. The highlight of the evening was the Magic Mirror act in which Archie assisted.

To a dramatic roll of drums, David Devant put on heavy black robes. An audience member in identical robes stood next to him. The two men gazed into an enormous mirror. Archie was supposed to train a spotlight on the mirror, creating an illusion of a flame like a red rose. The figure of Satan would emerge from it, luring the two men in to meet a beautiful, semi-nude girl who lurked in the depths of the colored glass. But Archie trained the spotlight too low, exposing where the girl was hidden. The curtain was rung down, Devant was furious, and Archie was fired on the spot.

In March 1918, Archie was suddenly expelled from Fairfield. There are three versions of what happened. His own explanation, given in interviews over the years, was that he had been found in the girls' lavatory, but this was clearly intended to build up his masculine image. According to Lillian Pearce, he was in the girls' playground with two other boys, reason enough for immediate dismissal. She asked him, years later, why he wouldn't mention the name of the boys who were expelled with him, and he only said, "I don't give names away." Mrs. Pearce adds: "His expulsion was so unfair. Several of us girls were in tears over it, because we didn't like to lose him."

Ted Morley gives a different version. He says:

The reason for Archie Leach being sent away is clear. He was involved in an act of theft with two other boys in the same class in a town named Almondsbury, near Bristol.

Mr. Morley refuses to say what was stolen. But again a clue may be found in *The Bachelor and the Bobby-Soxer,* in which the Cary Grant character tells Shirley Temple that he was thrown out of school for stealing "a valise containing paints." Archie was known to have been keenly interested in painting at the time. Since even in those days a store would have been equipped with a burglar alarm, it is more probable that he stole the valise from a private home.

There are also different versions of the expulsion scene. According to Mr. Morley, Archie, told the dread news by the head teacher, walked down the aisle through the students, who had assembled to hear the verdict. He took a cigarette from a case, put it in his mouth without lighting it, and left.

Lillian Pearce says:

We all assembled in straight rows, girls on the left, boys on the right. We were standing. Archie was called to the platform. He stood to take the quiet but firm punishment in words, but he was not upset in any way. He was told to go home. He walked down the hall halfway, then he suddenly turned to face headmaster Augustus Smith and said, "Please, sir, may I take my schoolbooks home with me?" . . . Mr. Smith said, "Go home and I will promise to send your books after you." And this was done.

Now that Archie was free (we do not know Elias Leach's response to his disgrace) he rejoined the Pender Troupe. Although he tried to color the picture in later years by saying that he ran away from home, there is no evidence of this. It was natural for him to go back to the world of the stage.

His next appearance with the Lomases was at the Norwich Hippodrome in Norfolk, from May 13 to May 18, in nightly performances at six-thirty and eight-thirty. This company moved on to the Ipswich Hippodrome two days later, performing until May 25.

The tour continued, through the south and west of England; records of the period are scattered, but the *Era,* the weekly magazine of show business, recorded the troupe as being present at the Hippodrome, Devonport, back in Bristol at the Empire, at the Aldershot Hippodrome and the Aberdeen Palace in July and August. The Christmas season of 1918 was spent at the Prince's Theatre, Edinburgh, where the Lomases, with Archie, performed in *Cinderella.* The following year, they could be placed at Rotherham, Dewsbury, York, Doncaster, Liverpool, Dundee, Morecambe, Eccles, and back in Bristol in September. They spent another Christmas at the Prince's in Edinburgh, this time starring in *Babes in the Wood.* In many performances, they featured a popular dancing cow, the rear end of which was Archie Leach. Under his heavy canvas cow costume, he appeared to be having a marvelous time. He formed a close friendship with a midget of the troupe, Sammy Curtis, who, over forty years later, was to meet him in memorable circumstances in London.

While on tour, the company was informed that it had been engaged to appear in Manhattan in the energetic revue *Tip-Top,* starring the comedian Fred Stone, which would be presented at the Globe Theater in the late summer of 1920 by the impresario Charles Dillingham. By now, Archie Leach was as much a member of the family as Robert's brothers Tom and Bill Lomas, Bob's wife Maggie, his widowed sister-in-law, another Maggie, and her son, also called Bob. Contemporaries recall that only Doris Pender, who was now nineteen, greatly resented Archie Leach—as a result of her father's favoritism—hating him till the end of her life.

In fact, Robert Lomas did choose Archie to sail with him to New York; the others followed separately, according to Lomas custom. Archie surpassed all the others—except for Bob Lomas himself—

as an acrobat and a stilt walker. Though the Harlequinade had been discontinued many years before, Archie was still indispensable as a knockabout policeman, clown, and general assistant behind the scenes. When, on July 21, 1920, he set sail with Lomas on the *Olympic* from Southampton, scene of so many Elias Leach's peccadilloes, Archie was still, at sixteen, not grown to his full height. The passenger manifest listed him as five feet nine, with sallow complexion. His black hair was parted in the middle, and his eyes were so nearly black that they were described as "dark brown" in contrast to the eyes of the other passengers, which were merely described as "brown." Oddly, he gave his next of kin as "C. Leach"; since nobody with that initial can be found in his family, it is possible that the C was a mistake for an E. Soon after he left, his father, still living out of wedlock with Mabel Bass, would father a child by her, Eric Leslie.

The *Olympic* steamed into New York Harbor on July 28. Among the passengers were Douglas Fairbanks and Mary Pickford, who had just returned from a six-week honeymoon in Europe, conducted in the glare of publicity. Accompanied by fireworks, streamers, and a brass band, an enormous crowd was gathered on the wharf to welcome the most famous couple in the world. Archie had formed a superficial acquaintance with Fairbanks, since they both had worked out with weights in the ship's gymnasium. They would keep in touch on and off through the years.

Archie Leach would recall many years later—as Cary Grant— his new sighting of New York:

> The most prominent spire, in the year of 1920, was the Woolworth Building. If any happy medium, any fortune-telling gypsy, had prophesied I would marry the heiress granddaughter of its founder, no palm would have been crossed with *my* silver.

He was of course referring to his marriage, twenty-two years later, to Barbara Hutton.

The troupe obtained a long, narrow apartment on Fifty-eighth Street, west of Eighth Avenue. The weather was unseasonably mild for July, with temperatures in the lower sixties. The troupe reported for work at the Globe Theater, where rehearsals for *Tip-Top* had begun. They were scheduled to act as crazy cops in an episode involving Fred Stone in a farcical trial. But apparently the combination of constant rewrites and the problem of a low proscenium arch, which made stilt walking difficult, resulted in Charles Dillingham informing Robert Lomas of a change of plan. The Pender Troupe of Giants would instead be cast in the colossal revue *Good Times*, to open imminently at the Hippodrome, one of the largest theaters in the United States. Lomas and Archie Leach were not disappointed. Their only problem was the lack of time to rehearse an entirely different routine for the first night, August 9. The other members of the troupe had barely arrived in New York, and *Good Times* called for a somewhat different approach than *Tip-Top*. Nevertheless, by frantically working day and night, the troupe managed to fit into the elaborate chiaroscuro of the larger musical event.

Charles Dillingham was a genial and charming producer, who instantly electrified Lomas, Archie Leach, and the others. With his white hair, ruddy face, white mustache, and handsome figure dressed in the height of fashion, he was a suave man of the world, far removed from his chief rival, the shrill, vulgar genius Florenz Ziegfeld. To the Lomases' delight, R. H. Burnside, their talented director from 1911, was also the director of this new extravaganza.

The Hippodrome presented a remarkable spectacle to the energetic band of players. The theater could accommodate several hundred people on the stage at once, and about a thousand in the audience. It had a huge revolving stage, and the most elaborate theatrical machinery available. There was a tank that contained almost a million gallons of water, a waterfall that could be produced in an instant, a complicated battery of multi-colored lights, vast prop rooms and wardrobe departments, and cages for a variety of animals ranging from monkeys to leopards and elephants. The Ziegfeld Follies, for all its razzle-dazzle, was somewhat more intimate in mood, tasteful, with exquisitely choreographed dancers whom Ziegfeld always refused to place in straight lines, and magical illusions, and transformation effects. *Good Times* was closer to a circus than anything else.

The music was by Max Steiner, later a reigning composer at Warner Bros. The show, written by a number of people, starred such popular figures as Poodles Hannaford, the most nimble of bare-back riders, and Jack Johnstone, famous for his frantic bicycling routine. Like the *Folies Bergère, Good Times* was divided into three scenes, or pieces, which were entitled "The Valley of Dreams," "A Toy Store," and "The Magic Grotto." Among the fanciful and exotic effects the evening offered were chorines blowing multi-colored bubbles through straws, followed by an enormous bubble bursting over their heads, Elizabeth Coyle as the Statue of Light posing before a sequined backdrop behind which the Shadows of Long Ago danced in silhouette, and Colorland, a marching procession which went up and down an illuminated staircase. At the climax, set in the Land of Happiness, the stage was turned into a lake, and then, in turn, into a series of Venetian canals, into which, carrying the flags of all nations, scantily clad girls dived from 30-foot-high boards or slid down chutes. It was a precursor of the spectacles which Busby Berkeley would introduce to motion pictures just over a decade later.

The Pender Troupe of Giants appeared only once, in the "Toy Store" sequence, which featured dolls from every part of the world coming to life and executing acrobatic routines. They were followed by Abdullah's Arabs, from whom Archie learned a specialty tumbling dance, similar to break dancing in our time, in which the fall was taken on the neck and shoulders and the dancers spun around on their upper backs, leaping with great agility to their feet, somersaulting and spinning around on their backs again. *Variety* said of the Lomases:

> In marches and formations, starting with a midget and winding up with a stilted figure twelve feet tall, they . . . lined up abreast in "pair of stairs" formation for comedy business. . . . The troupe is distinctly European in comedy appeal, but got over as sight asset at the Hip.

Good Times was an instantaneous hit and earned everyone rave reviews, even from the staid *New York Times*. But life in the apartment just off Eighth Avenue was not comfortable. There was the contrast between the thrill of performance and the drabness of temporary digs with, for example, a long line for the one bathroom every morning. The Penders, for all Bob's fondness for Archie, were severe taskmasters. Archie became housemother, assisting Maggie Lomas in washing dishes, making beds, cooking (mostly heavy stews), and sweeping the floors. The favorite of his foster father in the theater, he was the maid offstage. The one thing he was not responsible for was the laundry. At night, after the show, the whole family would line up at the kitchen sink to wash their socks and handkerchiefs, towels and shirts, then they would proceed one by one to the ironing board. The ritual continued until the small hours. The only member of the family other than Mrs. Lomas capable of sewing on buttons or knitting was Archie Leach.

Archie fell in love with Manhattan. He was dazzled by the great stars who were appearing on Broadway and occasionally managed to get a matinee off to see them. He very much liked Poodles Hannaford, who stood, on two horses, bareback one foot on each, as they galloped around a sawdust ring at the Hippodrome. He was horrified when, one afternoon, Hannaford slipped off and was badly injured. Archie never forgot the great equestrian. He formed a friendship with Francis Renault, one of the best female impersonators in the city. A rival of the great Julian Eltinge, Renault was very successful; he wore exquisite costumes and a fantastic variety of wigs, and specialized in impersonating Lillian Russell. Despite the fact that he was virile and muscular, Renault, billed as the Last of the Red-Hot Papas, was unabashedly gay and enjoyed, because of his performance, the attentions of many stage-struck young men. Renault is believed to have become Archie's lover and patron, helping him financially over the years.

More important, George Orry-Kelly became the young Leach's best friend and, it was generally believed, his lover. Jack Kelly, as he was known to all friends, was Australian. He was born in the country town of Kiama, New South Wales, to William Kelly, a tailor, who hailed from the Isle of Man, and Florence Purdue Kelly, on December 31, 1897. He was of slightly less than medium height, well-knit and stocky, a handsome, effeminate young man, with large, dreamy blue eyes, brown hair, and a sparkling, energetic, if at times hot-tempered nature. Fiercely ambitious, he had been named Orry

after an Isle of Man king, as well as the Orry carnation that flour-
ished in his mother's garden. He began his life as actor, clothing
designer, and scenic artist, the protégé of the gifted Eleanor Weston, who ran the local theater. He is still remembered by elderly
people in Kiama, who own his oil landscapes of the bush, and the
ties, silk shawls, and cushions which he designed and painted for
them long ago.

After a brief and unsatisfactory period in London and a short-
lived stint on the New York stage as a chorus boy, Jack Kelly, at
the time he met Archie, was a struggling tailor's assistant in the
garment district. The two men were strongly attracted. Kelly was
barely twenty-four, full of gossip and breezy repartee. His Australian accent had been sandpapered down to an acceptable mid-Atlan-
tic sound. The young men (Archie was seventeen in the early months
of 1921) decided to live together. They settled on a loft in a Greenwich Village house, just behind the present site of the Cherry Lane
Theater. They acquired a third roommate in order to meet the rent,
which was in the region of fifteen dollars a month. The man they
selected as their companion was also gay: Charlie Phelps, known as
Charlie Spangles. He was Australian, and had known Jack Kelly in
Sydney, when he had worked a concession on Bondi Beach. A stew-
ard aboard the *Olympia,* he had jumped ship to join the household of
his new friends. He recalled later:

> The three of us lived in what was a kind of massive loft. I re-
> member that Archie loved fish, particularly English fish, and used
> to go and buy Dover sole, and plaice, at the market. He would
> cook for us.

The three men began to entertain. While Archie continued in
Good Times, Charlie Spangles appeared at the Metropole Club in
Greenwich Village, in an act entitled *Josephine and Joseph:* half of
his costume was male and the other half female; one side of his face
offered a beard and mustache, the other lipstick, rouge, and mas-
caraed eyelashes. Jack Kelly earned a living painting murals and
drawing subtitles for silent films.

The run of *Good Times* ended on April 30, 1921. To his delight,

Archie was told that the troupe would now appear with the Ringling Bros. and Barnum & Bailey Circus, touring the eastern states for a period of three months, starting with a special gala opening at a fairground in Brooklyn. The sweet scent of sawdust would remain a memory for the rest of Archie's life. The Pender Troupe of Giants was ideally suited to Ringling Bros., and the succession of clowns, tumblers, lion acts, bicyclists, girls climbing ladders of swords, trapeze artists, and brass bands leading processions of giants and midgets intoxicated the seventeen-year-old, star-struck youth. Charlie Phelps kept house with Jack Kelly while Archie was on tour. He said later that he enjoyed his role as housekeeper, but there is no indication that he was having an affair with Kelly. According to John Marvin, who knew Phelps well, "Charlie told me it was only Orry-Kelly who was in love with Cary Grant."

At the end of the tour of the Ringling Bros. Circus that summer, Archie returned to New York for a few days before embarking on a series of appearances for Poli's vaudeville circuit, starting September 5, traveling from Worcester, Massachusetts, to Hartford and Bridgeport, Connecticut, with the Lomases. They closed the first half of the bill. After the Bridgeport engagement, they were signed by the United Booking Office for the Keith Circuit, headed by B. F. Keith. This was a step up in the world. The troupe started a grueling schedule. They began in Washington, D.C., on a steamy September 26, proceeding to Brooklyn, at the Bushwick Theater, and then, glory of glories, to the Palace in New York, the most coveted venue in the nation. They were well received there, warmly mentioned in several reviews; leaving the city on a tide of excitement, they proceeded to brief stands in Baltimore, Philadelphia, Buffalo, and then across the Canadian border to Toronto and Montreal. After Boston, Hamilton, Ontario, and Detroit, the tour continued to Rochester, where the Lomases played at the Temple Theater in the dead of winter, January 1922.

It had been an exciting few months. They had met such adored entertainers as Trixie Friganza, Harry Langdon, who was also a screen success, Jean Adair, and Eddie Foy and the Seven Little Foys. All of these headliners warmly befriended the troupe. Archie was particularly fond of Jean Adair. He had first run into her in

Detroit, and was taken with her comedic skill and lively Scottish charm. They met up again when they were billed together in Rochester. It was there that, worn down by the constant shifts of locale and the strenuous work and the second-rate food, Archie Leach's constitution finally gave out and he was stricken with rheumatic fever. He lost weight, was unable to sleep, and tossed and turned with fever. Miss Adair nursed him through his sickness, and he never forgot her kindness. He did not sufficiently recover his strength and the tour was broken off for several weeks while he convalesced.

Forced to drop out of the Keith Circuit, the Penders were rescued by an individual who would one day become one of Archie's closest friends and business partner. Frank Vincent was the sleek, dapper, young and able joint manager of the booking department of the Orpheum Circuit, under President Martin Beck. In his offices at the Palace Theater in New York City, Vincent was a perpetually warm and charming presence, dressed in the height of fashion, sporting elegant spats, and radiating good cheer from his prematurely graying head to his well-shod feet. He took an intense liking to Archie; through the Central Booking Office, the troupe was accorded the great honor of appearing in the Orpheum chain of theaters.

On March 27, 1922, the Pender Troupe of Giants was in St. Louis, at the Orpheum; a few years later, Archie would make a splash in that city's Municipal Opera. There were three further appearances, at the Majestic in Milwaukee, the State-Lake in Chicago, and the 105th Street Theater in Cleveland; then, apparently, some crisis in the family sent Robert Lomas, his wife, all but one of his brothers, and other family members back to England. Archie elected to stay behind. He was probably mindful of the London strike of May 1921, which had thrown many performers out of work. But his decision to take his chances in New York was a dangerous one. He and Robert Lomas's brother Tom hoped to form an act. Unfortunately, even the keen support of Frank Vincent didn't help, and it proved impossible to secure any bookings that summer. Archie returned to the loft in Greenwich Village and Jack Kelly. According to George Burns, he sold Kelly's painted neckties in the street to make a living. Somehow, he and Jack and Charlie Phelps managed to pay the rent.

A job became available. It was humiliating, but at least it was a way to earn a living. A figure of Times Square was the popular stilt walker Fred Wilson. He was a cheerful Bostonian who liked to appear in a policeman's uniform, holding children high above the crowd as he comically misdirected traffic. He advertised various theatrical attractions with a sandwich board.

Wilson fell ill, and Archie was approached by the Chamber of Commerce to take over. He was forced to accept. He was now an even taller figure than he had been on the stage. His 10-foot supports would raise him 16 feet in the air—the stilts, with size fourteen shoes at the ends and flapping goliath trousers, would make up a weight of fifty-six pounds, and his elaborate costume would add twelve pounds more. It was one thing to perform on stage with proper rehearsal and preparation. It was quite something else to force a passage through the dense crowds thronging the theater district without bumping into anyone, stepping on children, or being thrown off the stilts by the determined efforts of hoodlums. The summer heat, and the white New York sun beating through a haze of automobile fumes, were well-nigh insupportable under these conditions. Children mocked him, tugged at his trousers, and tried to dislodge him. He would have lost his job if he had kicked them or hit them with his hat. He must smile at all times, and announce, through a megaphone, what was going on at the various movie and legitimate theaters.

The author Samuel Marx, who became the head of the story department at M-G-M, never forgot Archie. He says:

I recall this handsome young man, whom I would recognize as soon as I saw him on the screen, walking on stilts outside the Capitol Theater, which was run by Major Bowes, later of radio fame, indicating to the crowds through announcements or sandwich boards—and the crowds were fascinated and curious—that there were all kinds of exciting stage activities to be found at the Capitol, including various live acts. My offices were at 1600 Broadway, and whenever I would come out of there, even on Sundays, I would see him and talk to him. . . . He was always smiling.

Brooks Atkinson mentioned Archie, but not by name, in his classic history *Broadway* ("A man with advertising boards over his shoulders walked through the Times Square throngs on stilts"). Sometimes Archie would have a starched shirt studded with electric light bulbs which would flash signals on and off.

When Fred Wilson returned to Times Square, Archie was hired by Thomas McGowan, general manager of Steeplechase Park, in Coney Island. (He remembered that he was engaged by George Tilyou, who created the amusement park, but Tilyou had been dead for some years.) He was supposed to parade up and down the "Bowery," a boardwalk of wooden planks that ran from Feldman's Astroland all the way to Steeplechase Park, but on Sundays, he would sometimes be allowed to sell hot dogs from a stall. He wore a sandwich board (he denied it in later years) which announced STEEPLECHASE THE FUNNY PLACE on the front and 50 ATTRACTIONS FOR 50 CENTS on the back. He remembered that he wore a doorman's uniform of green coat with red braid, green jockey cap with red peak, and long, tubelike black trousers. But eyewitnesses confirm that Jack Kelly designed for him a fantastic suit of pink and white linen that would be of minimum weight in the heat. A bright pink cutaway jacket was worn with three-quarter-inch shirt stripes, and the pants billowed out in enormous bell bottoms. A pink-and-white-striped top hat completed the ensemble.

Matthew Kennedy, today the Executive Secretary of the Coney Island chamber of commerce, has never forgotten Archie Leach as he strolled up and down the Bowery on his stilts:

The kids liked to follow him like the Pied Piper. I was one of them. I was ten years old in 1922 and sold ice creams. Archie felt his job was beneath him, and instead of laughing with us when we teased him, he would look snootily down his nose at us and try to ignore us. I used to shout up at him and he would barely respond. We used to rag him and pull at the stilts. His head was over sixteen feet in the air. And he certainly *had* his head in the air in every sense. Sometimes he would vary his route and go down to Surf Avenue. There was another guy that used to act as a barker and walk with him. That guy wore a dress. The only name we knew him by was Maggie Murphy.

Coney Island was at its apogee in 1922. The subway was bringing crowds by the thousands from the city on sweltering summer weekends, and the marvelous variety of rides, the garish pavilions, the whirling ferris wheels, the merry-go-rounds, the simulated mechanical horse ride with the horses pulled on chains, and the razzle-dazzle of fireworks, freaks, and dancing animals created a magic kingdom long before Disneyland was dreamed of.

THREE

For all of its tinsely glamour, Archie Leach hated Coney Island. He made everyone feel his contempt for the job, and they, as well as he, were greatly relieved when he was made redundant on Labor Day. He was engaged for *Better Times*, the sequel to *Good Times*, and Bob Lomas returned from England to reform the troupe, which was to be headed by Doris, now twenty-two, and her husband, the accomplished acrobatic dancer Jack Hartman. Archie appeared with four other performers as one of the Meistersingers in "At the Grand Opera Ball," dressed appropriately as Wagner's characters. He also appeared in drag in a number with Tom Lomas. Well received by critics and public alike, *Better Times* ran from August 31, 1922, to April 28, 1923. Immediately after the closing night, Bob Lomas returned to England for the last time; he was to retire eighteen months later and open a balloon, novelty, and toy shop at Southend, near London.

Jack and Doris Hartman, Tom and Jim Lomas, and Archie Leach formed, with a few American recruits, what was now known as the Lomas Troupe. It played on the Pantages Circuit, starting in Spokane, Washington, on September 3, 1923. What happened to Archie during the six-month period in between the closing of the Hippodrome show and the beginning of the tour is unknown, except for two brief appearances he made, at the beginning of May, at

Proctor's Theatre in Elizabeth, New Jersey, and in a one-night special revival of *Better Times* for a U.S. Chamber of Commerce 11th Annual Meeting at the Hippodrome. According to the theater historian Milton Goldman, it was widely rumored that Archie was a gigolo in New York, servicing a wealthy woman. However, there is no evidence to support this.

The Pantages tour took the Lomas Troupe from Spokane and Seattle to Vancouver and Tacoma; Portland and San Francisco followed, and the first leg of the tour wound up in Los Angeles on October 29, 1923. They were now top of the bill, along with the William Weston Company, Poppy Chadwick, and "The Musical Attorneys." It was Archie's first visit to Hollywood. He was fortunate in being able to contact Douglas Fairbanks, Sr., who invited him to visit the set of his new movie, *The Thief of Bagdad*, in which he saw the great star and athlete climbing up a trellis, a flying carpet on wires, a genie, a flying horse, and other marvels.

Archie fell in love with the strange and exotic settlement that lay between the desert and the ocean. The hard, white, glittering light, the unblemished blue sky, the low-lying, sand-colored buildings and tall, nodding desert palms created an atmosphere not unlike that of Egypt as seen in the travelogues. Unfortunately, the troupe's appearance was brief, only four days in extent, and soon they were traveling on to San Diego; Long Beach; Salt Lake City; Ogden, Utah; Denver; Omaha; Des Moines, Iowa; Kansas City and Memphis. They continued through Ohio, Michigan, Missouri, Tennessee, and several other states before they wound up in Wilmington, Delaware, in November 1924.

After a brief hiatus, the troupe reunited early in the new year for yet another series of engagements, which took them as far as Saskatchewan and Alberta. They were back in Los Angeles in May 1925, repeating the same circuit and again earning excellent reviews. The monotony of the tours was almost indescribable. For two years or more, in almost every part of America and in Canada, Archie and his seven companions had to repeat, night after night, and twice on matinee days, an unchanging stilt walking and dancing routine, unrelieved by the Harlequinade that had lent the performance color and character in earlier years. At last the tour came to an end and the troupe broke up. Exhausted, several members including Jack and Doris Hartman elected to return to England. Archie returned to Greenwich Village and Jack Kelly. There, he formed a strong new friendship.

Don Barclay was an inspired clown and wit with an attractively ugly face and a tiny, well-knit, athletic physique. He began his career in San Francisco at the beginning of the century, where he sang and danced and sold newspapers to homeless survivors of the 1906 earthquake. He combined his talents as an entertainer with considerable skill as a cartoonist for the San Francisco *Examiner*. Working in medicine shows, carnivals, traveling Shakespeare presentations and burlesque shows, he scored a triumph in the *Ziegfeld Follies* of 1917 and 1918. Although it is claimed that he met Archie Leach in England in music halls, there is no evidence of this. It seems to have been a publicist's idea, to help both their careers by linking them fictitiously together. By 1925 Barclay had become well known in New York. His inspired playing was a much-admired feature of such shows as the *Greenwich Village Follies* and *Go-Go*. He encouraged Archie to break free of the drudgery of stilt performance and make his way into legitimate musical theatre. Meanwhile, Archie found encouragement from Jack Kelly, who was beginning to advance his own career. Kelly was starting to work in theater design, and soon he would become the chief costumer for Ethel Barrymore. Phil Charig was also making headway; he spent long periods of time in London, where he was beginning to establish a major name. One moment he was rehearsal pianist, the next he was composing songs for musicals. Archie Leach's first opportunity to cross the divide between vaudeville stilt walking and working as a featured performer came through the determined and very talented young Jean Dalrymple, who was then on the threshold of what would be one of the most illustrious careers in Broadway's history. Strong, good-natured, optimistic and forceful, this brilliant young woman had set up a partnership with Max Tishman and Dan Jarrott, her lover at the time, to put together comedy sketches which would be toured across the country. They did not involve singing and dancing, but only farcical situations.

Jean Dalrymple never forgot Archie Leach coming in to see her for a role in one of her playlets:

The particular skit that I had put together with my partners was about the handsomest man in New York. The comedy developed from arguments over him by two women. Don't ask me to remember the rest of the plot!

The agents kept sending us Rudolph Valentino types because Latin lovers were all the rage then. Archie walked in with his olive skin and slicked-down hair, and he obviously wasn't a Valentino type. But he was adorable looking, and as soon as I saw him I said to my partners, "That's the one!"

Dan Jarrott, who was very handsome himself, was apparently irritated and jealous of Jean's interest in the young man and said he was quite impossible. He told her that since Archie had a cockney accent and walked oddly, with the bowlegged gait of someone who had spent years on stilts, there could be no question of casting him. But Miss Dalrymple was adamant. Max Tishman recalls:

You should have seen the way Jean worked on Archie to get over that rubber-legged walk! You see, he would put one leg in front of the other as though he were balancing, and it looked peg-legged. His knees were so stiff he had completely forgotten how to cross a stage. If he ever knew! We put him together with a popular young actor, Jack Janis, who was blond to contrast with Archie's dark hair. Jack would show jealousy of the handsomest man in New York. Constance Robinson played one of the two girls. She was quite a name then.

Jean Dalrymple adds:

Archie was extremely nice and gentlemanly. Dan was always accusing me of falling in love with him. But he was living with another young man. We used to have coffee together in tiny little coffee houses, anyplace we could get a cup for ten cents. I didn't love Archie in a way a woman loves a man but as a sister. He had terrific charisma. Constance Robinson and the other girl, whose name no one can remember, were crazy about him. But nothing happened between them. He wasn't dapper in those days. His suits were a little worn, a little shiny, but he did his best with what he had. His shoes were well polished and his hair was always groomed with brilliantine.

Archie grew fond of Jean Dalrymple. The rehearsals were prolonged and difficult. It was hard for him to adapt to techniques of comedy. But there were pleasant evenings when Dan Jarrott and Jean invited him to Jarrott's rooms at the National Vaudeville Artists' Club, on Forty-sixth Street or to her apartment. Dan would sing in a lilting baritone voice as all the others harmonized. Everyone was young, happy, and delighted to be alive in New York.

The Jack Janis Company, as it was known, began touring in May 1926, at the Strand in Atlanta, Georgia, then traveled through the southern states and north to Wisconsin, Illinois, Ohio, and Canada, thence to appearances at the National, Orpheum, and Loew's houses in New York City and Brooklyn. The trio was well received, and Tishman remembers that they enjoyed full houses everywhere.

Back in Manhattan, two other members were introduced to the warm and cheerful circle of friends that centered on the Greenwich Village apartment. These were George Burns and Gracie Allen. Burns's deadpan, sombre calm in the face of Gracie's manic stupidity and dizzy, ceaseless line of chatter enchanted audiences and earned the pair enormous fame. Burns, at ninety-two, still has vivid memories of Archie. He first met him in 1923, during the run of *Better Times,* when Archie's best friend was Fatty Arbuckle's wife Minta. Fatty, who had been ruined by a San Francisco scandal in which he had been charged with sexually attacking a young woman with a Coca-Cola bottle, was living in obscurity in Manhattan at the time. Minta loved to gossip, and so did Gracie, and Jack Kelly was also a great source of news about public and private scandals. Burns says:

I remember a party at Archie's and Jack's in Greenwich Village. I was there with Gracie and Mary and Jack Benny. There were maybe about twenty people and a pianist, and I got up and sang. Minta Arbuckle hated my singing; I could see it in her face. That's all I needed, because then I wouldn't sing to anybody but her. I stood in front of her and kept singing and singing, and Jack Benny fell on the floor laughing. It was a funny thing, standing in front of this woman who despised me, singing love songs right to her. It didn't amuse Archie. He glared at me. He was fond of Minta.

Archie was fascinated by Burns. Always capable of learning from other entertainers, he observed his timing with the utmost care. Told of this in 1988, Burns said he was flattered, and then re-marked:

What the hell is timing? Timing is Gracie finishes a joke and I don't laugh, and I just stare at the audience and smoke my cigar. And the audience laughs and laughs. And when the audience stops laughing at last, I stop smoking and turn to Gracie and talk to her as though nothing has happened. That's timing. Can you imagine me talking while the audience is laughing? It would spoil everything. Maybe Cary liked the way my expression was flat while I was listening. The more disinterested I was, the more the peo-ple screamed. Maybe he took more from Gracie. He would have been better off. She was the talent. She never did anything twice. Nor did he.

Aware of the relationship between Archie and Jack Kelly, George Burns mentions that they had a big quarrel one night after a party. "Gracie loved scandal," he says, "I didn't. Those things didn't in-terest me. I'm not interested in anything that happened yesterday. And how can you deal with Cary's homosexuality?"

With Phil Charig composing for Jack Buchanan, the great British star in London, and Jack Kelly beginning to work with Ethel Bar-rymore, Archie's circle was doing well. He began meeting the young and promising Moss Hart, who shared his sexual ambiguity. Tall, quietly genteel, well-bred and discreet, with a quick, nimble wit, always dressed beyond his means, Hart was a delight, and would soon use elements of Archie in characters in his first stage success, *Once In a Lifetime,* co-authored by George Kaufman. Lester Sweyd, an odd, diminutive, high-powered character with a consuming in-terest in every aspect of theatrical history, was yet another in the rapidly expanding clique. Sweyd became a sort of chairman of the unofficial club, attacking anyone who dared question his judgments as he reigned supreme at the popular Rudley's Restaurant at 41st and Broadway, where 4:00 P.M. coffee clatches of manic intensity were common. Edward Chodorov, on his way to a career as a prominent playwright, Edward Eliscu, who would write the lyrics of such popular songs as "Orchids in the Moonlight," "Flying Down to Rio," and "Great Day," Preston Sturges, destined for a meteoric career in the movies, and the energetic would-be producer Oscar Serlin argued, laughed, flirted with ideas, attacked the reigning critics Alexander Wollcott and Percy Hammond, decided on the fate of the world and plotted tremendous dream careers. Soon their castles in the air would become real life palaces. Not one of them except Lester Sweyd would fail to become famous.

Archie in many ways was a mascot of the group, seemingly the least gifted in terms of burning genius, but, in his alternate moods of great gloom and mischievous darting humor, vividly appealing to the others. He was the outsider, the underdog, the working-class Britisher among smart Manhattan sophisticates. They decided uniformly that he must be given a break. He was known familiarly to his friends as "Digger" or "Kangaroo," because, knowing the antipathy that existed between Englishmen of his class and raw, brash Australians, they liked to tease him by saying that they were sure he was posing as a Bristol man and actually hailed from the outback. And when they heard that the weak but ambitious young Reginald Hammerstein, nephew of the great Oscar and Arthur Hammerstein, was looking for an Australian type for the second male lead in the musical, *Golden Dawn,* they and Jack Kelly, who could of course lie that Archie was Australian, pushed him very hard for the part. But it involved at least a modicum of singing ability, and Archie could barely carry a tune. However, as soon as Reginald Hammerstein saw him walk into his office he knew that he was looking at a star in the making. By 1927, Archie had shed his callow, awkward manner, his strutting, bowlegged, cockney walk and his excessive mugging; he looked like a man-about-town and at the same time he displayed the necessary roughness of an Australian type. He had only to make a slight change in his vocal tones, abetted by Jack Kelly, to be convincingly Aussie. And of course he had all the superb physical characteristics that had become famous when journalists described the Anzac soldiers of World War I.

Golden Dawn was an absurd contrivance about the white goddess of an African tribe, an excuse for a good deal of semi-nudity as the copper-skinned cast whirled about in ludicruously extravagant dance routines; there were sumptuous jungle sets and a variety of fake native masks and costumes to enliven this preposterous entertainment. The implied racism in portraying all of the blacks on stage as mindless savages was unhappily typical of the era. The music was undistinguished, but the show featured the Metropolitan Opera Company star Louise Hunter in the leading role, and, as a witch dancer, Jack Carter created a sensation. He was described by the *New York Times*'s Brooks Atkinson: "Flooded by an irridescent purple light, he leads a heathenish incantation before a pagan, African god, at the head of a chorus garbed in strange patterns and ceremonial masks."

Atkinson went on to describe *Golden Dawn* as "ponderous and mannered." It was an example of the showcase being more interesting than the show: Hammerstein's theater was opened for the occasion, a gothic cathedral with an organ console and an orchestra which rose and fell on a type of lift; stained glass windows shone down on the audience with designs representing the figures of opera.

Golden Dawn cannot be described as a success, but it gave Archie the break he desperately needed: Reginald Hammerstein announced that he was pleased with him and would keep him under contract. Archie joined the prestigious William Morris Agency, and had as his particular agent Billy Grady, who also represented W. C. Fields, one of Archie's idols. Archie was pleased when he was cast in the show *Polly,* which was composed by Phil Charig. *Polly* opened in Wilmington, in November 1928; it was partly backed by the duPonts (William duPont's daughter Marion would later figure in the life of Cary Grant). The reviews were devastating. Although Archie received praise for his spectacular good looks, more than one reviewer pointed out the shortcomings in his musical and theatrical technique.

After an equally disastrous appearance in Philadelphia, Arthur

Hammerstein closed the show following the November 17 performance and brought it back to New York for rewrites, restaging, and recasting: Archie was dropped. When Marilyn Miller, the blonde, pretty, self-indulgent Ziegfeld star, wanted him to appear with her in the hit musical *Rosalie,* the Hammersteins refused to loan him out to Ziegfeld. Instead, they arranged, rather brutally, to sell his contract to the Shuberts.

J. J. Shubert, who had noticed Archie in performance, decided to put him into the cast of the Jeanette MacDonald vehicle, *Boom-Boom,* which was presented at the Casino Theatre, on January 28, 1929. Archie's was a small role in this French musical comedy farce, set on fashionable Park Avenue, with a degree of risqué bedroom humor. Jeanette MacDonald, soon to become internationally famous as Nelson Eddy's co-star in a series of gloriously absurd movie operettas, turned out to be a friend. Although there was some artificially stimulated press gossip about rivalries between them, it was patently groundless because Miss MacDonald was the star of the show, playing with great charm and expertise the various naughtinesses the playwright had created, and Archie was no more than a supporting actor, whose singing was just barely adequate. However, his looks and figure earned him respectable reviews. On the first night, there was a tremendous stir as, halfway through her first song, Miss MacDonald was interrupted by the arrival of the Naval hero Captain Fried, who turned up with his crew in uniform and was shown into a box. The orchestra conductor abandoned the love duet and struck up "The Star-Spangled Banner."

Jack Kelly designed Jeanette MacDonald's costumes for the show brilliantly. After a weakish two months in New York *Boom-Boom* toured in Detroit, Chicago and points west. Archie broke off the tour to make a quick trip to England in the latter part of the year, visiting his half-brother, Eric, who still kept Elsie's existence in the asylum a secret. Returning to New York late in the year he took on the role of Max in *A Wonderful Night,* which was again costumed by Jack Kelly; it was based on Johann Strauss's operetta *Die Fledermaus.* On this occasion, the part called for an ability to sing. J. J. Shubert was so enamored of Archie that he did the unthinkable: he placed him in front of a curtain and stood a practiced singer behind it, who delivered the numbers with great expertise while Archie opened and closed his mouth. No critic suspected that this was taking place and he received some complimentary reviews which noted his improved vocal ability. He was on his way: he even started to get some fan mail. Girls in the company made themselves available to him, but he seemed to be caught up in himself and in the specialized, predominantly homosexual group that surrounded him. There is no record of his having any love affairs with women at the time.

Jack Kelly traveled to St. Louis to design for the St. Louis Municipal Opera Company. He had a violent quarrel about his salary with the Shuberts, especially Milton Shubert, who staged the shows in St. Louis, and returned to New York. Meanwhile, Archie toured in a show called *The Street Singer* in September 1930, only to be humiliatingly demoted from the important role of George to the less important role of Jean-Baptiste when John Price-Jones, who had been in the show on Broadway, rejoined the production on tour. *The Street Singer* was a musical comedy of Americans in Paris, which included, ironically in view of Archie's earlier career as a child performer, scenes set in the Folies Bergère. The tour ended in January 1930. Soon afterwards, Archie signed for the summer season in St. Louis. Jack Kelly had made his peace with the Shuberts and returned there for a second season. They traveled together in Kelly's vivid yellow Packard. Arriving in St. Louis, Archie was pleased to find that his old friend and mentor Don Barclay had been hired to appear in several productions which were staged at the Forest Park Theatre, an amphitheater set among flourishing trees and flanked by verdant hills. The open auditorium seated as many as 8,000 people. Amplifiers were used to carry the performers' voices to the most distant reaches on the edge of the hills, and there was little or no protection, except for the players, in the event of rain. The St. Louis theater-goers favored extravagant, even absurd plots, lavish production values, and rich, iridescent lighting effects. All of these were supplied in amplitude by the young and ambitious Milton Shubert, who, three seasons before, had introduced a revolving stage which provided a great spectacle. As Brooks Atkinson reported in the *New York Times* on May 30, 1930, there was no point in applying the normal conditions of criticism which would be appropriate to hermetically sealed theaters. It was simply a question of 8,000 people having a good time in a densely wooded park under the shimmering light of a brand new moon.

While in rehearsal, as Jack Kelly fought in his customary manner with virtually everyone, particularly the embattled Milton Shubert, Archie proved to be a relaxed and easy-going member of the company. Photographs of the time show a softer, rounder, less ruggedly masculine face than the one millions of women would soon respond to in motion pictures. In some costumes, he even looked positively effeminate, as though he were aching to appear in drag. Yet, already, at the age of twenty-six, he was in the full bloom of his handsomeness. No one could doubt that he would merely have to appear before an audience to captivate virtually every woman in it.

It is doubtful whether he did more than appear in this succession of shows, displaying his handsome face and figure in a variety of period and modern costumes, his barely adequate singing voice swallowed up in choruses or rendered tolerable because of the sheer size of the physical environment in which he worked, and the numbers of expert and graceful performers who surrounded him.

In *The Street Singer,* starring Queenie Smith, he repeated his performance as George, an American Pygmalion figure in Paris, who plans to turn a flower girl into a lady within three months. During the preparations for the show, Archie became a close friend of a small, plump Humpty-Dumpty of a performer, Frank Horn, who would one day be his secretary in Hollywood. Horn became part of his circle. He and Archie and Jack Kelly and Don Barclay would enjoy all the random gossip of the Rialto.

Archie also appeared in *Music in May, Countess Maritza, A Wonderful Night, Irene,* and *Rio Rita.* On June 5, the St. Louis *Post-Dispatch* published a cast picture in its photogravure section, headed, "An afternoon on the stage of the Municipal Theatre in Forest Park." Archie was fourth from the left, the next but tallest, and certainly the best-looking of the company. Crisply dressed in a tweed jacket, well-cut slacks and an open-neck shirt, he looked relaxed and content. He was glowing from the good reviews and the loud, uncritical applause of eight thousand people a night. Milton Shubert and his wife, Jean, were encouraging, warm presences, despite the differences between them that would lead to a painful divorce. While in St. Louis, Archie published an article in the *Post Dispatch,* his first essay into print. He provided a characteristic actor's fiction, describing an early career as a pugilist and falsifying virtually every fact to do with his upbringing. He also pretended that he had returned to England in the late 1920s to perform in repertory theater, an error picked up by several of his biographers. The article's chirpy, buoyant tone was typical of the public Archie Leach, and the boldness of placing the piece in a local newspaper in defiance of all the facts was certainly typical of him. He must have rejoiced in the many favorable comments he received as the first performer in the twelve-year history of the Muni who had broken into print in this manner.

The season ended to general acclaim in August. Archie and Jack Kelly returned to New York in the Packard. There, according to Kelly's friend Vincent Sherman—a young actor who would one day turn director and use Kelly's skills in the film *Mr. Skeffington*—Archie and Jack opened a speakeasy on the west side of Manhattan. As prohibition continued, speakeasies were focuses of social life. New patrons would give a sign, or knock in a particular manner, a small peephole would open in the door, and they would be admitted. Police raids were frequent, and such bars operated under conditions of considerable danger, sometimes sustaining themselves through payoffs to officials. Despite numerous obstacles, the two men managed to succeed in their underground activity for several months. At the same time, they began to cool toward each other. Archie started to have affairs with other men on the side. According to Vincent Sherman:

> They had a code. If Orry-Kelly came home and could hear classical music issuing through the door, it was a signal that Archie was involved in an amorous occasion with a young man. If there was no classical music, it was all right to come in.

After some months of this, Kelly apparently had had enough and accepted an offer from Jack Warner in Hollywood, via John and Ethel Barrymore, to go to the West Coast as a contractee of Warner Bros., designing for the stars. He took the train west, and Archie promised to follow him soon. Their parting was apparently without jealousy, bitterness or regret. They were part of the casual, freewheeling life of the time, and they didn't believe in heavy displays of emotion. They were young, attractive, and healthy, and despite the Depression, the world was at their feet.

Archie became involved with Phil Charig, whom he continued to see even during the period with Kelly. Charig had written the music for *Nikki,* a show based upon *The Last Flight,* by John Monk Saunders, a World War I aviator of moody and unstable temperament who was married to the actress Fay Wray. William Dieterle had made an excellent movie from the material the year before. The touching story disclosed the tortured lives of former heroes, who were unable to adjust to the boredom and monotony of ordinary life after the war and had embarked upon a life of heavy drinking and suicidal, devil-may-care adventure. Their mascot was the pretty, sensitive, and very feminine young Nikki, exquisitely played in the movie by Helen Chandler.

Unfortunately, the script did not lend itself to musical treatment, and Phil Charig's score was well below his best work. Nor was Miss Wray ideal in the title part; she had had no stage experience, and had only worked in movies, and she was nervous and uncomfortable before a live audience. *Nikki* proved to be an ill-fated attempt to reverse the trend in Hollywood's early talkie days and bring a screen performer to Broadway. Although Archie, as Cary Lockwood, one of the three airmen, was personable and charming, neither he nor the fraily handsome Douglass Montgomery could sustain this shaky vehicle satisfactorily, and the show failed, closing on October 17, 1931, after only 18 days of performance. Moved briefly to the George M. Cohan Theatre, it closed again at Halloween. Immediately after the run, Jesse L. Lasky, who had brought Archie to the United States as a child, decided to try him out in pictures. After the failure of *Folies Bergère* in 1911, Lasky had turned his misfortune into an extraordinary advantage: he had headed west with Cecil B. DeMille and Sam Goldfish (later Goldwyn) and with them, had literally founded the movie industry.* By 1930, he was a high-ranking figure of Paramount Studios, and he and his colleague B. P. Schulberg, both of whom had been following Archie Leach's career very closely, decided to give him the chance he had been waiting for.

---

* *Henry B. Harris was drowned on the* Titanic *in 1912.*

They were presenting a series of movie shorts at the time, many of them designed to introduce new screen performers. The demand for British personalities was strong, because the diction of so many American performers at the time was nasal and unappealing; several silent-screen actors and actresses failed when they were heard as well as seen. Although Archie's diction remained an odd blend of Cockney and West Country—gratingly lower class to English audiences who were accustomed to the dulcet tones of West End actors—to American ears it sounded educated and cultivated. A vehicle was found for him: a ten-minute, one-reel example of forgettable trivia entitled *Singapore Sue*.

Casey Robinson, later the doyen of Warner Bros. writers, scripted and directed the short. He told Charles Higham years later that he never forgot Archie walking in for the audition, handsome, cocky, confident, with shining eyes and perfect posture, a matinee idol to his fingertips. Robinson put him in a sailor's uniform and gave him a run-through on camera. Within minutes, the young director knew that a new screen personality had been born. It wasn't merely a question of ideally photogenic features, the bone structure without which no leading man could possibly succeed on film. Nor was it merely a question of a classically constructed physique, with the broad shoulders, sculptured chest muscles and narrow hips of the athlete. It was the extraordinary combination of aggressive charm and confidence, and underneath it a little boy's vulnerability, unease, and even shyness, that provided the sort of contrast which Robinson knew few women could resist. Archie Leach wasn't overbearing or unduly forceful, he didn't seem to have the airs of someone who automatically expected people to be attracted to him. His self-confidence was a mask; the camera saw through the mask to an insecurity within. Women would not feel threatened or overridden by his personality, and yet at the same time they would warm to his apparently unequivocal masculinity. The result of the test was an immediate contract and an invitation to Hollywood.

With little to lose and much to gain, Archie, remembering his happy times in California in the mid-1920s, decided to go west. He had already sold the furnishings of the second apartment he had shared with Kelly, in the West Fifties behind Madison Square Garden; the lot had been bought by Vincent Sherman, who was getting married that year. He was living now at the Variety Artists' Club, in a room near Phil Charig's. They had formed a friendship with the conductor and arranger Lennie Hayton, who later married Lena Horne. Demetrios Vilan, then a young and talented actor, who later became Huntington Hartford's right-hand man on the West Coast, remembers the Hayton's farewell party for them vividly. It was held at Hayton's apartment on West End Avenue; Archie and Phil Charig arrived together, quite obviously a pair, eager and excited over their new adventure. The next day, they left in Jack Kelly's much-driven yellow Packard for the long journey through winter snows, deserts, and mountains to the promised land of Southern California.

FOUR

The two young men arrived in Los Angeles in the last week of January 1932. The city had been drenched in a severe storm that had caused at least one death; hail stones had fallen, and the streets were flooded. Los Angeles at the time was a city of just under 1.25 million population; its spiderweb of streets spread far into the desert and along the coast, the badly paved thoroughfares lined by temporary-looking wooden or stucco-and-spit bungalows, the wide sidewalks punctuated by enormous black telephone poles.

Outside the city were the desolate Hoovervilles, camps of prefabricated shacks housing the army of the unemployed. By contrast, Hollywood and Beverly Hills sparkled with bright flowers, tropical palm trees, handsome Spanish-style villas and mansions in a riot of architectural modes, with swimming pools in the backyards. Houses in the most expensive parts of town could be bought for $25,000, including the use of live-in domestic servants, who were sold along with the property. A fine apartment with two bedrooms and a large living room could be had for $75 a month. The week Archie and Phil arrived, the newspapers were filled with pictures and stories about the movie folk. M-G-M and Paramount publicists had combined to whip up a mythical "Battle of the Exotics" in which Garbo, Bankhead, and Dietrich—whose enormous, sultry faces glowered from the *Times*'s Sunday Supplement pages—were supposed to be vying for men, fame and public acclaim.

The dominant figure of Hollywood social life was William R. Wilkerson, owner of the magazine *Hollywood Reporter* whose wife, Edith, ran a social column that was filled with inside information about industry figures. He owned the Vendôme, a favorite restaurant of the stars, and soon he would buy nightclubs, and become a special investigative agent for the FBI, using his fame and influence as a cover. Among the leaders of Hollywood society was Countess Dorothy di Frasso, the sister of Bertram Taylor, head of the New York Stock Exchange. Though still married to Mussolini's friend Count Dentice di Frasso, she was carrying on a widely discussed affair with Gary Cooper, who had only just emerged as a star. They were mentioned in every gossip column, seen in every night spot: he rangy and lean, with fierce blue eyes and a crinkly smile; she dumpy, unbeautiful, but possessed of irresistible vitality, charisma, and charm. Her jewels were legendary, her international circle of friends glittering. To know di Frasso and to be liked by her was a sure passport to social acceptance anywhere.

That week, the wedding in Phoenix, Arizona, of Paramount executive Benjamin (Barney) Glazer and the actress-singer Sharon Lynn was the buzz of Hollywood; among the guests were John Gilbert and Dolores del Rio. Todd Browning's lurid horror movie *Freaks,* with Prince Ranlof, the Living Torso, Pete Robinson, the Living Skeleton, and the Hilton Sisters, actual Siamese twins, was the most discussed picture in town. Howard Hughes's exciting *Sky Devils,* with Spencer Tracy and William Boyd, was the action picture of the hour. In a matter of days, Garbo's sensational *Mata Hari,* about the exotic World War I spy, would open with a splashy premiere at Grauman's Chinese Theater, where stars immortalized their feet in wet cement.

Archie and Phil found an apartment at 1129½ North Sweetzer Avenue, in West Hollywood; since the flat was not advertised, it seems clear that Paramount had reserved it. The building still stands. A brown stucco-and-brick structure, it was set back from the street in a series of courtyards flanked by tropical plants; in those days imitation black Tudor beams gave it a pseudo-British look. The apartment itself was tucked into a corner, overlooking a flourish of trees. Sweetzer was just a short drive from the Paramount studios on Melrose Avenue.

During the first two or three days, after doubtless contacting Kelly, whose offices were at the Warner Bros. studios, northeast over the Cahuenga Pass and Barham Boulevard, in beautiful downtown Burbank, Archie went over to Paramount to see the production manager, Sam Jaffe, and checked in with the casting department. Once past the almost royal wrought-iron gate, he saw a surrealist spectacle. The enormous parking lot was dominated by a replica of the forward half of a large oceangoing liner, while the executive offices were built in the form of a Mexican palace that had a British oak-timbered facade; they were flanked with a "French" garden and box hedges. In this parched, beige world there stood squat concrete buildings with no roofs, staircases that led up to the sky, half of a Renaissance dining room, ladders leaning against a backcloth of storm clouds, and the ground floor of an Austrian castle, next to a cell of a Moorish prison.

For years afterward, ignoring his previous engagement in New York, Archie would say that he had been hired after introductions and a screen test. Nevertheless, he would always give credit to the studio boss B. P. Schulberg for seeing his merits from the beginning.

Schulberg saw to it that he was cast immediately as the second romantic lead in *This Is the Night,* an imitation of the current success *One Hour with You.* He was to play Steven, a former javelin thrower and new actor at Paramount, whose wife is unfaithful to him during a complicated game of adultery and double-cross. Schulberg cast him simultaneously in the part of a man-about-town in *Sinners in the Sun,* directed by Cecil B. DeMille's brother William; he could walk from one set to the other without changing his white tie and tails, talking his way through two entirely different scripts.

In the pressure-cooker atmosphere of Hollywood in 1932, there was no room for rehearsal. And there were only a few days before Archie would have to start work. Days to catch up with old friends: Douglas Fairbanks, Sr., who had returned from skiing with Charlie Chaplin in St. Moritz and was about to leave on a romantic expedition to the South Seas with movie star William F. Farnum to make a movie about Robinson Crusoe; and Frank Horn, the amiable humpty-dumpty of New York City and St. Louis, who was finding it impossible to get work. The weather suddenly cleared as February began, and the sun shone like an enormous white bulb in the hard, cloudless blue sky, over the seemingly interminable avenues that led from downtown all the way to the beach, haunted by the clanging, swaying red car tram, shadowed at evening by the frowning blue sierra foothills haunted by coyotes.

It was necessary for Archie to change his name. He was rechristened by his old friends John Monk Saunders and Fay Wray, who selected "Cary," in part from the character he had played in *Nikki;* the Paramount publicists chose "Grant." Soon, Fay Wray would be internationally famous as the girl King Kong held in his paw on the top of the Empire State Building.

Cary Grant began work. The schedule was relentless; he had to act two quite different roles with equal conviction, switching sets at all hours of the day and night, toiling well into the early morning hours every Sunday. He had to adjust himself to the contrasting temperaments of Frank Tuttle, a sophisticated Easterner, and William DeMille, a distinguished gentleman in poor health who had once worked with David Belasco. To add to the pressure, Schulberg was not satisfied with DeMille's rushes and replaced him brutally with the smart young Alexander Hall.

In *This Is the Night,* Cary was co-starred with Lili Damita, a tempestuous French girl who at the time was emotionally involved with Prince Louis Ferdinand, son-in-law of the Kaiser, and would soon marry Errol Flynn. One of the supporting cast was Thelma Todd, who became the victim of a much-discussed case of suspected murder. In *Sinners in the Sun,* Cary appeared with Carole Lombard, who swore like a marine in accents that belied her fragile and wistful appearance. Despite his generous salary, the equivalent of seven thousand dollars a week in today's money, Cary, always obsessed with cash profits, began looking, during the early spring of 1932, into areas of possible investment. He met a young man named L. Wright Neale, who had dabbled in the men's clothing business, and together with him and the Glendale interior decorator Bob Lampe, decided to cash in on the booming new Wilshire district, and open a clothing store at 6161 Wilshire Boulevard, slightly to the east of Vermont Avenue. It was, on the face of it, a good time to start such a venture. Bullock's and Magnin's department stores had recently been opened down the street, elevating a once shabby neighborhood into a fashionable shopping area much liked by the well-to-do citizens of the Hancock Park and Rossmore districts, and by the lawyers and doctors and oilmen downtown.

The store opened on May 20, and was named, in a large, glittering electric sign outside, NEALE'S SMART MEN'S APPAREL. The capital was $5,268.72; the monthly rental was $100; the fixtures and fittings were expensive mahogany, even down to the paneling in the changing rooms and the frames of the triple mirrors. In an untypical act of extravagance, Cary ordered twenty-five thousand green-and-gold matchbooks with NEALE'S printed on them, far more than he would need for the immediate future.

Arthur Lubin, a newly arrived Paramount assistant producer, who would achieve fame as the director of a talkie version of *Phantom of the Opera*, recalls an episode during the third week of May. Mr. Lubin had bought a new car, and it suddenly broke down on the corner of Wilshire and Vermont. Looking around for a public telephone to call the auto club, and not finding one, decided to go into Neale's. Cary Grant was standing inside, and he said, "While you're here, you might as well buy a suit and be our first customer!" Lubin bought a zip-up jacket.

Wright Neale was known to Cary as "Sister." He signed all his notes to Cary over that name. Cary was never mentioned on Neale's stationery or as co-owner, in the press. He remained strictly a silent partner, but he didn't hesitate to use his looks and charm to lure people off the street into the store on the rare days in which he wasn't working.

At the same time Cary was making *This Is the Night* and *Sinners in the Sun*, he had to pose with pretty girls for photographs at the beach or in a park, or be seen lobbing a tennis ball over a net (although he didn't play tennis), or tossing a beach ball to a partner at Santa Monica. The studio was promoting him as an athlete, and to improve his physique, he installed weights in his apartment and began working out. He could still do handstands and tumbles with expertise. His easy manner and flashing smile charmed everyone; he was meticulously punctual and never behaved temperamentally. Delighted with Hollywood, loving the sun, he shook off, for a time at least, the darker side of his nature.

During a lunch break one day, he met Randolph Scott, who was to play an important role in his life. Scott was appearing in *Sky Bride* on an adjoining sound stage. Two years earlier he had arrived from Virginia with an introduction to Howard Hughes by his father. Hughes had taken the handsome University of North Carolina footballer and engineering student under his wing; it was common gossip in Hollywood that they had been lovers. Hughes, whose macho reputation was exaggerated, and whose countless affairs with women were largely the invention of his press agents, secured work for Scott as an extra, then as a contract player at Paramount. *Sky Bride* was his first important movie for the studio.

Scott was well over six feet tall and weighed 195 pounds of well-defined brawn. He had a long, humorous, horsy face, a lazy swinging walk, shrewd eyes, and an air of calculating laziness. Self-assured and self-contained, he disliked emotional commitments, indulging the attentions of both men and women while possessing the soul of a cash register. Since he could not act, filmmaking was just an easy path to acquiring a personal fortune. The moment he had completed a sequence and was no longer needed, he would stroll over to his canvas chair, sit down, stretch out his long legs, and pick up the *Wall Street Journal*.

Scott and Cary were instantly drawn to each other and decided on the spot to live together. Phil Charig, who had no liking for Hollywood, moved back to New York without composing a single song for a film, and Randy, as he was called by everyone, moved in with Cary. It was, for obvious reasons, not customary for handsome young movie stars to share accommodations; in the local beehive of gossip, there would be loud buzzing about such an arrangement. The implications were all too clear; the studio publicists had to cover by issuing releases that their two new contract stars were cutting expenses by dividing the rent. The unsuspecting public didn't realize that, at a four-hundred-dollar weekly salary, each man could easily afford to pay what could not have been more than seventy-five dollars a month.

As if determined to create more untoward comment, the two men at first declined even to be seen dating women in public, and instead, with almost incredible audacity, turned up at film premieres as a pair. It is possible that they were banking on the sheer overtness of this to allay suspicion, on the theory that, if theirs were a real liaison, they would be guiltily hiding it. Whatever the motive, their behavior did not go unnoticed, and there were frequent squibs in the columns that were surprisingly daring for the time.

Apparently, this situation prompted the studio to put pressure on the two men to find dates with whom they could be photographed in various exotic parts of Los Angeles. The ideal pair of women was quickly found. Cary and Randy had as near neighbors two gorgeous girls who had just arrived in Hollywood together, thus giving rise to a great deal of scandalous comment, which amused them very much and was quite unfounded but never actually discouraged.

Sari Maritza and Vivian Gaye quickly became as much the talk of the town as their two escorts. Sari Maritza's real name was Patricia Detering Nathan; born in Tientsin, China, she was the twenty-year-old daughter of the influential Major Walter Nathan, a prominent figure in the social whirl of Peking and Shanghai in the first three decades of the century. She met, in Berlin, another colorful young beauty, Sanya Bezencenet, who had Swiss and Russian antecedents and was an up-and-coming London literary agent. They formed a team: Sari was named after two operettas by Emmerich Kalmann. Sanya Bezencenet became Vivian Gaye. Sari made a splash in a German movie, *Monte Carlo Madness*, and she was hired by Paramount on the strength of this success. But, like Cary and Randolph Scott, she put out the story that she had arrived in Hollywood on a chance of getting work, and had been hired on the spot for her beauty.

The two young women were opposites. Sari was a bubbling extrovert, always talking, filled with delightful risqué gossip and alive with extraordinary energy; Vivian was reserved, cautious, moody, and somewhat introspective. Whereas Sari was not strongly attracted to Cary, Vivian fell in love with Scott. But, as Vivian makes clear today, the relationship among the four was innocent and sex-less, consisting largely of spinning around in fast cars to the beach or mountains, dancing to the latest hits in modest night spots, and playing tennis, swimming, or just running around in the sun.

Cary bloomed in this far paradise of the common man. With the Depression going on all around, everyone he knew was bursting with health, suntanned, vigorous; the air in those blessed days was pure and free of smog; occasional bursts of rain only made the atmosphere more sparkling than ever. The accessibility of every kind of sport and the proximity of the mountains and the desert made Los Angeles possibly the most desirable place on earth, for all of the faceless, sprawling ugliness of the city itself.

The summer came, burningly dry and unvisited by wind. Cary continued working without a break. But instead of advancing his position as an up-and-coming actor, the studio capriciously rushed him into a dreary subsidiary role as an actor in a play within the film *Merrily We Go to Hell*. Wearing a powdered wig, white silk coat, britches, and buckle shoes, he spoke rather foolish lines to Adrianne Allen.

Fredric March and Sylvia Sidney were the stars in this story of a newspaperman-turned-playwright who was having an affair with an heiress. Cary observed March's impeccable technique, his polished movements and suave delivery, all the result of years of honing and refining his art on the stage. Sylvia Sidney was the talk of the studio. Born Sophie Kosow in the Bronx in 1910, the tough, ambitious daughter of Russian-Jewish immigrants, Sylvia was a hard hitter whose personality contrasted utterly with the fragile, dewy-eyed waifs she portrayed on screen. B. P. Schulberg had brought her to Hollywood after his wife, Ad, admired her in the Broadway hit *Bad Girl*. Schulberg soon abandoned his wife and son for Miss Sidney, with whom he conducted a flagrant love affair, presenting her with one astonishing gift after another. He also paved the way for the lusciously sensual girl's vivid career at Paramount, casting her with great success in such classics as *City Streets*. To cast an eye on Miss Sidney in the commissary or studio corridor could result in instant dismissal for a male performer or crew member; Schulberg was even suspicious of the harmless director Marion Gering, whom he had imported with Miss Sidney to direct *Bad Girl*. At least his choice of director for *Merrily We Go to Hell* was safe: Dorothy Arzner, who sported cropped hair, a monocle, a cigar, and white tailored suits with sensible shoes.

That summer, the studio was in the grip of bitter boardroom fights, both in Los Angeles and in New York. The formidable executive Sam Katz was struggling against Schulberg, sometimes winning, sometimes losing. By February 1932, he had moved ahead in the race for power, appearing with a theatrical flourish before a meeting of executives and department heads in the Paramount Building in Manhattan to plead for loyalty in the company. In the judiciously silent presence of bosses Adolf Zukor and Jesse L. Lasky, who had nursed the company along from the beginning, Katz slashed production by twelve pictures and many millions of dollars, hoping to salvage the wreckage of bad administration and overproduction. In another reshuffle, Katz was set up at the head of the theater chain, while Zukor continued as president and Lasky as production head. Constantly nagged by Katz to improve the standards, Schulberg was made a member of the Paramount board of directors in March. Whether in the Fredric Marches' Laguna beach house or Sylvia Sidney's luxurious Beverly Hills ménage or Cary Grant and Randolph Scott's North Sweetzer home, the discussions of what the future of the studio would be raged fiercely.

Sometime later that summer, with the excellent *Merrily We Go to Hell* completed, Cary and Scott decided to move to a more substantial residence. With a new friend, Mitchell Foster, a gifted interior decorator from New York, who had formed a partnership with the movie star William Haines, they obtained a lease on a comfortable dwelling in the Los Feliz district, at 2177 West Live Oak Drive. It still stands just north of Western, above the beginning of Los Feliz Boulevard before that street turns east towards Griffith Park. Griffith Park was, and would remain, the haunt of homosexuals and was considered to be a major pickup area.

In July, Cary began work on two more films at once—movies that, after the commercial disappointment of *Merrily We Go to Hell*, were designed to improve his career. He had by now earned the confidence of B. P. Schulberg and had befriended Schulberg's son,

Budd, now sixteen, to whom he gave small but welcome gifts. The problem was that Cary preferred the warm-hearted Ad Schulberg to Sylvia Sidney, but he skillfully played the game of alliances and did not offend his powerful boss.

The two movies he made now were *Blonde Venus* and *The Devil and the Deep*. In *Blonde Venus* he acted the role of a superficial, wealthy playboy who supports a married woman, an exotic nightclub singer played by Marlene Dietrich. Clad in white tie and tails, he would walk from the set of *Blonde Venus* to his dressing room and change into uniform to portray a submarine lieutenant at an African naval base in *The Devil and the Deep*. In this story of a tormented commander (Charles Laughton) insanely jealous of his moody wife (Tallulah Bankhead), Gary Cooper played another lieutenant in love with Bankhead.

The director of *Blonde Venus* was the proud, haughty and stubborn Josef von Sternberg. He had added the "von" himself. Cary was fascinated by him. Pale-skinned, he had a shock of unruly dark brown hair, brooding eyes, and a carefully cultivated black mustache. He affected an ivory-topped cane and poison green coats. He stared at his actors from under theatrical black hats. When von Sternberg went to a restaurant, there had to be six large black grapes on the table, or he would not sit down. He was frequently seen holding a volume of the poems of Hāfez in the original Persian, a language with which he was not familiar. He would stand in the Hollywood Hills, looking at the lights below and crying, "My Hollywood!"

Sternberg was deeply involved with Miss Dietrich, whom he had propelled into international fame as the vicious slut Lola Lola in *The Blue Angel*. He was responsible for the Dietrich the world knows. She became famous for her blank, mysterious stares into the camera, achieved by silently counting backward from one hundred. Obsessed with her daughter, Marlene had decided she wanted to make a picture in which she would have a child; hence the creation of *Blonde Venus*.

Schulberg decided he would separate Marlene and Sternberg, and she was fired for refusing to work without him. While she was temporarily out of work, a kidnap attempt was made on her daughter. Schulberg relented, and *Blonde Venus* began, with Sternberg directing.

Cary was fascinated by Marlene. But when Charles Higham asked her in 1966 about her feelings for Grant during the making of the picture, she replied, "I had no feelings. He was a homosexual." Cary watched her in scenes in which he did not appear; in one Penderish sequence, she was dressed as a gorilla, pulling off her monkey arms to disclose braceleted wrists as she sang "Hot Voodoo." Sternberg had the scene done 125 times. Then the "gorilla" slumped over: Marlene, stifled inside the costume, had fainted. B. P. Schulberg walked onto the set and said, "Get the ape back in action. We're over budget!"

Sternberg had put up a huge sign on the set reading ABSOLUTE SILENCE. When production manager Sam Jaffe walked on and said something, he was asked whether he had read the sign. Sputtering that he was the production manager, he was removed from the sound stage. Furious, he left the studio soon afterward.

Marlene and Sternberg fought continuously, much of the time in German. In one scene, Marlene was supposed to walk into a room and throw her hat on the bed. She refused to do so, saying it was bad luck, like wearing green socks, whistling in a dressing room, or quoting from *Macbeth*. Finally, she won. Someone wheeled in a couch, and she threw her hat on it instead.

Making *The Devil and the Deep* was equally problematical. Tallulah Bankhead made token passes at Cary, which he summarily rejected. Annoyed, she began to set off a train of gossip about Cary's lack of virility. In fact, she wasn't his type and was too old for him. Bankhead misbehaved constantly, deliberately flubbing lines, arguing with director Marion Gering, and laughing at the dialogue given her. In one submarine scene, she asked a radio operator, "Have you tried the radio?" When he replied, "The oscillator isn't working," she threw back her head and roared. The actor playing the operator was so upset he tripped against a water cooler and shook the lights, and a camera fell on his head, knocking him out.

Cary hated Bankhead and her heavy drinking. Charles Laughton was deeply attracted to Cooper and envied his style, wishing he could look like the rangy, fashionable actor. The players had to struggle with tiny, carefully scaled-down sets of the submarine. They were flooded with water in several sequences, working through the night until as late as four in the morning. Laughton took a brotherly interest in Cary, who was depressed by the somewhat meaningless part he was playing in the exhausting summer heat in those days before air-conditioning, as well as by his having to switch from role to role without sufficient preparation. Laughton made him look at everything in perspective, indicating that Laughton's own suffering as a physically unattractive man made Cary's discomfort seem trival by comparison.

On September 23, Cary and Randolph Scott attended the premiere of *Blonde Venus* at the Paramount Theater in Hollywood. Afterward, they went to the Brown Derby restaurant on Wilshire Boulevard. As they left, well after midnight, the stars clustered on the sidewalk waiting for the traffic light to change, so they could cross the street to the parking lot. Cary glanced over and noticed a pair of acquaintances, the lawyer Milton Bren and Bren's wife, Marian. A couple was standing with the Brens. The actor was a well-known, handsome young homosexual actor; with him as a "beard" was the blonde and beautiful star Virginia Cherrill. Cary knew Virginia by name: the year before, she had appeared with great success in Charlie Chaplin's *City Lights*. Chaplin had discovered her at a boxing match and cast her as the blind flower girl in the picture. Furious when she rejected his advances, he had tried to scrap all the footage she was in after months of work, only to be told by his financiers that he must continue with her. The story was the talk of Hollywood.

Milton Bren made the introductions. Cary was fascinated with Virginia. It is illustrative of the superficial nature of his relationship with Randolph Scott that he thought nothing of calling her three days later from Paramount, to ask her out to dinner. She was living with her mother in an apartment in West Hollywood, just a couple of blocks below Sunset Boulevard. Virginia had liked Cary's performance in *Blonde Venus* and was attracted to his dark good looks. After some hesitation, she agreed to date him.

Virginia was a carefully sheltered, well-brought-up young woman— she was twenty-four at the time—the daughter of a bank president in Carthage, a small town in Illinois. Very much the apple of her family's eye, she had never wanted for anything and she was widely adored at Northwestern University as a soft, sweet-natured, gentle, and ravishingly attractive girl. On an impulse, she had decided to come to Hollywood. Her mother, who was no show-biz parent, joined her as a chaperone. Far from pushing Virginia into a career, her mother had very mixed feelings about Hollywood. Virginia's suffering at the hands of Chaplin, whose contract with her put her virtually under lock and key, unable to see men or even appear in public for well over a year, disturbed that good woman.

Cary, with his more than twenty years in show business, his easygoing sophistication, and his British background, fascinated the sheltered and sensitive Virginia, but his moodiness proved unsettling to her. Before long, she found herself out of her depth, swimming in dark waters.

They had dated a few times, going to parties in Beverly Hills and to informal gatherings at Vivian Gaye and Sari Maritza's, when Virginia received an unpleasant shock. Jack Kelly came to see her and issued a serious warning. She knew him well enough to listen to him carefully. "He told me that I should be very cautious indeed before entering into a committed affair with Cary; he added that Cary was the lover of Randolph Scott and that he [Kelly] was in a position to know it. I was so young and innocent I didn't give the matter a second's thought," Virginia says.*

Cary's evenings with Virginia consisted largely of candlelit dinners in medium-priced restaurants or weekend trips to the beach with Cary's gang. Even the fact that Cary now engaged a male secretary, a former actor named Larry Starbuck, and installed him in the house on West Live Oak Drive, didn't seem to ruffle her. She found herself spending a good deal of time in what was fairly obviously a homosexual household, blissfully unaware of much that went on around her.

That fall, the studio boldly decided to cast Cary and Randy together in a picture entitled *Hot Saturday;* this was perhaps to help

---

* *After she divorced Cary, Jack Kelly came to her and said, "We both loved him and lost him, didn't we?"*

allay any possible rumors surrounding their cohabitation by explaining that they were working in a film together. *Hot Saturday* starred the fiery Nancy Carroll; Cary played a relaxed, cheerful libertine, and Scott the decent, upright boyhood sweetheart of the heroine. Both actors walked genially through their parts, giving little evidence of commitment or even interest in the work. During the shooting, a journalist, Ben Maddox, dropped by their home, and afterward, in racist terms fairly typical of the time, and hiding a good deal more than he undoubtedly knew, wrote in *Modern Screen:*

A late supper was served by an old-fashioned negro mammy cook who came with the house and referred to her new employers as "the young gentlemen." Cary and Randy are really opposite types, and that's why they get along so well. Cary is the gay, impetuous one. Randy is serious, cautious. Cary is temperamental in the sense of being very intense. Randy is calm and quiet. . . . Cary tears around in a new Packard Roadster, and Randy flashes by in a new Cadillac. Oh-oh-oh how the girls want to take a ride!

There was no mention of Virginia Cherrill in the article. Soon afterward, observing a published photograph of Grant and Scott in aprons, washing dishes, the venomous columnist Jimmie Fidler announced that the two men were "carrying the buddy business a bit too far." Carole Lombard, in an interview for the Los Angeles *Times*, asked the question, "I wonder which one of those two guys pays the bills?"

Cary began shooting a nonmusical version of Puccini's opera *Madame Butterfly*, with Sylvia Sidney in the title role. He hadn't finished the picture when he was suddenly cast in Mae West's *She Done Him Wrong* as Captain Cummings, a police agent who disguises himself as a missionary to investigate the activities of the voluptuous Lady Lou. Cary's casting in the picture was a step up in his career. Miss West always claimed that she saw him as an extra around the studio and cast him on the spot; the truth of the matter is that B. P. Schulberg had decided that the combination of the new and impressive leading man and the aggressively sexual Miss West would excite audiences in those ribald days before the Motion Picture Code effectively emasculated the industry. Miss West's songs were calculatedly daring in their overtness, including "My Easy Rider's Gone" and "I Like a Guy What Takes His Time." Asked many years later how she had enjoyed working with Cary, Miss West said shrewdly, "That part kinda built him up with the ladies." She had always been fascinated by men of ambiguous sexuality; she had even had the nerve to present in 1927 a play entitled "Drag," about homosexuality, at a time when the subject was entirely taboo in the theater. Cary was irritated by Miss West's childishly egocentric nature. Yet he acted as an admirable foil for her almost brutal approach to sex in the picture; looking him up and down in one sequence, she called him, "warm, dark, and handsome," and in another scene she addressed him in a much-misquoted line: "Why don't you come up sometime . . . see me?" As soon as this racy dialogue became common coin, Cary was actually for the first time famous. There was no question of any attraction between the two performers. Miss West's personal life was somewhat austere, far removed from the sexual freedom she personified on screen. And Cary's life was already filled with the complexities of his household relationship with Randolph Scott and his tender but quite unphysical romantic friendship with Virginia.

On Christmas Day, 1932, Cary and Virginia attended a party given by Gary Cooper and Countess Dorothy di Frasso to welcome Douglas Fairbanks home from the South Pacific, where he had been filming *Mr. Robinson Crusoe*. In the handsome ballroom at Cooper's house in West Los Angeles could be found many of the great figures of the screen, among them Norma Shearer and her husband, Irving Thalberg, head of M-G-M, Samuel and Frances Goldwyn, Fredric and Florence March, the Charles Farrells, the Clark Gables, and the Lionel Barrymores, as well as Cary's old friends from the *Nikki* days, John Monk Saunders and Fay Wray. Cary arrived not only with Virginia but with Randy, Vivian Gaye, and Sari Maritza, a bizarre group that prompted comment in the columns. Seemingly unexhausted by shooting the first part of *She Done Him Wrong* simultaneously with the last part of *Madame Butterfly*, Cary looked magnificent in white tie and tails; Virginia was spectacular in a backless black evening gown, with jewels at her neck and wrists. A twenty-piece orchestra played tangos, two-steps, and fox-trots. The party helped Virginia professionally: M-G-M had been doing nothing with her for almost a year, and she was acting at the time in *Fast Workers*, a second-rate vehicle of the now failing former superstar John Gilbert. After the much-discussed evening, the studio put her into a better movie, *The Nuisance*, a fast-moving comedy-melodrama about a pushy shyster lawyer, played by Lee Tracy.

The new year brought a crushing work load for Cary. He was in *Woman Accused* with Nancy Carroll, based on a *Liberty* magazine serial written as a gimmick by ten well-known writers, including a new acquaintance of Cary's, Howard Hughes's uncle Rupert Hughes. He went on to shoot *The Eagle and the Hawk*, with Fredric March; he was cast, in an inside studio joke, as Henry Crocker, name of a well-known local man-about-town and scion of a banking dynasty. Cary and Fredric March played airmen in constant conflict; the author of the story was John Monk Saunders. In one sequence, during an explosion, Cary flung himself across Fredric March to protect the actor from the glass—or so the studio publicity department claimed.

Perhaps because of the pressure of work, perhaps because of the strain of sustaining two relationships at once, Cary became exceptionally moody, testy, and difficult in the first months of 1933. He was not appeased by the collapse of his men's shop; Wright Neale had done everything possible to save it, but it had gone bankrupt, beaten by the fierce competition from the big stores on Wilshire Boulevard. Most of Cary's and Neale's investment went down the drain, and there was a series of creditors' meetings at lawyers' offices. Cary ended up buying the firm outright, including goodwill and stock, from his distraught partner, for a little over three hundred dollars. After he had paid off as many debts as he could, Cary sold the store at a loss.

Virginia Cherrill remembers that he often had outbursts of temper at the time; but increasingly involved with him psychologically and still blinded by her innocence, she ignored the warning signals and began to long for him to propose to her. His jealousy and possessiveness were disturbing, contrary to the picture she had of him as an easy-going character, but again she failed to heed the dangerous indications. Appearing on the set of *The Nuisance*, he would glare as she enacted the love scenes; he was suspicious of the attentions of Lee Tracy, a gifted actor with an electric, driving personality, though he was by no means handsome or even attractive. These incursions into her daily work made Virginia increasingly nervous. She asked Cary to stop driving over to M-G-M to spy on her. The result was a series of violent quarrels; Virginia might have been unworldly, but she was certainly neither weak nor submissive. Painful though it was to her, she had to hold her own.

Despite his unacceptable behavior, Virginia was in love with Cary by the summer. They continued to be seen together everywhere. In June, they ran into the famous comedian and acrobat Jack Durant at a party at the Santa Monica Beach Club. Durant told Virginia that when the occasion arose, she should ask Cary to show her his extraordinary skill at tumbling. The opportunity came soon afterward, at a ball at the Beverly Hills Hotel. Everyone was in white tie and tails. Suddenly Durant said to Cary, "I bet you fifty dollars you can't do a *temsuka.*" It was an Arab word, as Virginia later learned. Cary said, "You're on." He hitched up his trousers and walked to the orchestra leader and asked for a drum roll.

The conductor signaled the drummer, and as the roll began, Cary performed a double forward somersault involving a full roll of the body, the head seeming to hit the floor, the full impact of the fall actually taken on the neck. Everyone applauded loudly. Virginia recalls, "Cary got up and walked back to our table and said to Jack, 'Give me the fifty dollars!' and Jack peeled off the bills and gave them to him, and everyone clapped again."

Virginia became convinced Cary was of Arabic origin; to this day, she insists he was an Arab. His deep tan never left him, and his facial features made her think of the Levantine immigrants to Bristol in the sixteenth century.

The work at Paramount was still not much better than road mending. In a desperate effort to save the studio from ruin, Adolph Zukor and his executives continued to overwork their stars, forcing Cary into *Gambling Ship* and into *I'm No Angel*, opposite Mae West.

That summer of 1933, Virginia was on loan to another studio and proceeded to Hawaii to make a movie entitled *White Heat*. She was reluctant to leave Cary, but the role was a good one and, for the first time since *City Lights,* she would actually be starred. The veteran director Lois Weber, at one time among the highest-paid figures of the silent screen, would make the picture for a small independent company named Seven Seas/Pinnacle. Virginia would play a San Francisco socialite married to a sugar planter in Kauai; frustrated and bored by the alternating rain and wind-driven dust of her environment, the restless Lucille Cheney almost succumbs to the charms of a good-looking Hawaiian boy. When her husband violently assaults the youth, the heroine's mind is disturbed, and in a dramatic sequence she sets fire to the cane fields.

Cary's parting from Virginia was painful. He hated the fact that he couldn't keep an eye on her during the many weeks of shooting. He would telephone her in Kauai, or try to check up on her with the switchboard at her Japanese boardinghouse, a difficult task in those days of comparatively primitive telephone services. He was maddened by an unfounded belief that she was having an affair with William Lindsay Fiske, one of the producers.

Virginia remembers both the unpleasantness of the filmmaking and the intensity of Cary's jealousy. She had to work day after day on a sugar plantation, covered with red dust blown by a savage wind. At night, she would return to the boardinghouse to be scrubbed by the housemaid in an effort to remove the dust from her hair, pores, and nails. Fiske, accompanied by his coproducer, would disappear to a local brothel; the director went to her room; and Virginia was left completely alone.

In September 1933, Cary made an appearance as the Mock Turtle in a grotesque version of *Alice in Wonderland.* Encased in a suffocatingly hot costume, with a papier-mâché shell and a large head with false eyes, through which his own could only dimly peer, he could not have been more uncomfortable. The weird parody of an English classic he had liked as a child can scarcely have improved his spirits. He was moodier than ever when Virginia returned from Hawaii. William Lindsay Fiske checked into the Beverly Hills Hotel, and Cary tipped the operators to listen in to his calls to Virginia. Despite the fact that the calls were strictly business, Cary remained angrily suspicious.

FIVE

Virginia took the train to San Francisco to shoot a couple of additional scenes of *White Heat*. Cary had her followed by detectives and seemed to be more irritable than ever when he found that nothing she was doing in that city gave him the slightest grounds for suspicion. She discovered she was being followed, but she was forgiving and understanding, perhaps even touched by the extent of Cary's possessiveness. When she returned to Los Angeles, Cary was resting between pictures. He decided that as soon as Scott finished shooting a movie named *Broken Dreams* at Monogram, his circle of friends, including Scott and Virginia, would go to London. He wanted to introduce them to his old friends in show business. Newspapers reported an unseemly quarrel between Cary and Virginia on the Monogram set where Randy was working; more than one columnist hinted that the argument was over Scott. But it was probably just a trivial difference of opinion.

They would leave in late November. But meanwhile, Cary and Virginia began an elopement that did not end in a marriage. Going off to Arizona together, they stayed at the Biltmore Hotel in Phoenix, then traveled on to Juárez and Tucson, taking in the local sights. They had several arguments during the trip.

After ten days, they returned to Hollywood, on November 5, 1933. That same day, it was announced that Randolph Scott and Vivian

Gaye would be married before Christmas. Simultaneously, Virginia had a furious argument with Cary, their worst to date; she took off to New York without warning, finding refuge there with her friends Laurence Olivier and his wife, the actress Jill Esmond. Angry and frustrated, Cary flew to the city in a drunken and unshaven condition, bursting into the Oliviers' apartment and demanding that Virginia return to Hollywood. He said the trip to England was off and that she must forget all idea of it. She said she was going ahead anyway; he explained that he had problems with his immigration documents and didn't dare accompany her in case he would be unable to re-enter the United States. Distraught, in tears, she sailed without him.

Cary impulsively flew back to Hollywood, picked up Randy, and returned to New York, to sail for Southampton on the French liner *Paris*, departing November 23. The two men callously left Vivian Gaye behind. On board the ship, they risked untoward gossip, sharing an elaborate first-class suite supplied by Paramount. The British actor David Manners was on the same vessel. He recalls today that the studio had installed a grand piano in the suite for Cary. The three men joined in lusty baritone choruses, remaining closeted for almost the entire crossing. The studio had also reserved a suite at the Savoy in London. Virginia stayed at another hotel, but apparently even the insensitive Randolph Scott found the situation a little strained; he returned to New York after only a week.

Cary took Virginia to Bristol to show her Fairfield Grade and Secondary School and to introduce her to his father and to his half-brother, Eric. Genial, good-natured Elias sat on his tailor's table in his workroom to talk to the couple. Elias's mistress, Mabel, was present during the meetings; Virginia noted that Cary seemed to behave respectfully toward her. He still thought his mother was dead, and she was never mentioned during the brief but, for Virginia, touching visit. There were several family reunions that week. Everyone wanted to meet the local boy who had become a major Hollywood star. There was a party at the Grand Hotel, where Cary and Virginia occupied separate suites, and another at Elias's Picton Street house; Elsie's brother David and nephew Ernest were present. During a walk with some of his cousins, Cary felt an impulse to go into a fish-and-chips shop; he probably enjoyed the newspaper-wrapped repast more than any elaborate meal in Beverly Hills. Still quarreling and making up, Cary and Virginia went to Paris at the beginning of December. Edith Gwynn wrote in her *Hollywood Reporter* column, "Cary, poor fellow, has to [put up with] all those 'Come up and see me sometime' invitations. If only he were free to follow. . . . But he isn't, poor lover." On their return to London, the couple were talking about getting married on Christmas Day.

Cary was proving more difficult than ever: he refused to attend the London premiere of *I'm No Angel* because Paramount wouldn't pay him a big fee for his appearance at the theater. And his once perfect health had begun to decline; he began suffering from alarming symptoms of rectal bleeding. He also had a severe gum infection and an inflamed tooth that caused him a great deal of pain. It was a horrible Christmas week; after an excruciating dental treatment, which at least temporarily solved his problem, Virginia persuaded him to see a Harley Street specialist, who gave him a proctoscopic examination. Cary was horrified to discover that he had a precancerous condition of the rectum. An immediate operation was called for which would involve delicate surgery. Cary was admitted to a clinic in the Fulham Road. The surgery and its aftermath were very unpleasant. Virginia was constantly at the hospital, where Cary, in great distress, recovered from the operation. He was shocked to be stricken at such an early age, nervous that there might be some leak of information about his illness to the papers. Virginia herself was exhausted, suffering from severe laryngitis.

Perhaps because they felt that if they didn't now they never would, the couple decided to marry as soon as possible. Doctors had told Cary he must stay in bed for at least four more weeks. The couple at last set the wedding day for February 9. The nuptials took place at the Caxton Hall Registry Office in London. A large crowd gathered. Weak, still in pain, Cary arrived on his own, only to find that Virginia was missing. She had been delayed by some last-minute problem with her clothing; he himself was unsuitably attired, hatless, tieless, with a dark-brown ascot tucked into his beige tweed overcoat. He appeared to have dressed in haste, and he needed a shave. Virginia looked pale and slightly disheveled in a yellow-and-

black-checked suit and a sable coat. Asked by reporters how he felt
to be married, Cary said: "We are both very happy. Now we are
going straight to Hollywood. We have got to get back to work. We
intended to get married quite a while ago, but my illness prevented
that.* I am getting better now." A moment later, the crowd closed
in, shoving so violently that Virginia's glasses were knocked off. The
couple were separated and for an unpleasant moment feared that
they might miss the boat train to Southampton. But they managed
to climb into a taxi and arrived at the station just as the train was
about to depart.

The S.S. *Paris* was preparing to weigh anchor for New York, at
midnight, when Virginia received offers from two studios, Gaumont
and V.I.P., for parts in new films. She hesitated, wanting to go back
to London, but Cary insisted that they proceed. They arrived in
Manhattan on February 15, 1934, and spent the evening seeing the
play *The Pursuit of Happiness*, which Paramount was considering as
a vehicle for both of them. Cary was still somewhat weakened by
his operation and suffering from radium treatments when they took
the train to Hollywood. They stopped off briefly to visit with Virginia's family in Dallas City, Illinois, a pleasant small town on the
Mississippi River, just sixteen miles from her birthplace, Carthage.
They saw her aunt and grandmother and her brothers and sisters,
most of whom lived and farmed around La Harpe. "Cary was fascinated by my folks and by that part of the country," Virginia says.
"Of course, almost everyone was fascinated with him. But Mother
was very jealous of Cary, and there was much tension between them."

Surprisingly, Virginia moved into the Los Feliz house, thus creating a bizarre ménage. After three weeks, they all suddenly moved
to the quasi-Spanish La Ronda apartments on Havenhurst, Randy
taking apartment 11, on the ground floor, next to the Grants. "The
Grants and Randolph Scott have moved, all three, but not apart,"
wrote the knowing Edith Gwynn.

From the moment they moved to La Ronda, with its tropical flowers and fountains in courtyards, Cary and Virginia were miserable.

---

* His illness was described as influenza in all newspapers and in subsequent articles and
biographies.

They argued day and night. Cary's jealousy reached maniacal proportions; he was jealous of everyone and everything Virginia showed
an interest in—jealous, even, of her charming and quite unposses-
sive mother. Virginia says she continued to hope for a miracle that
would save their marriage: "I knew if we went on together, we
would both be destroyed."

One late afternoon, she and Cary were returning from the beach.
On Sunset Boulevard, with its winding curves, a man passed them
in a car and waved. Without her glasses, Virginia couldn't see who
the man was, but, relaxed from the sand and the sun, always outgoing and free-spirited, she waved back. Cary flew into a violent
temper and hit her with the back of his hand. She recalls that the
blow was so severe it split open the inside of her mouth.

Bleeding all over her dress, she insisted that Cary drive her home;
he refused. Her mother, she knew, would only scold her, disliking
Cary as she did, so, sorely pressed, Virginia went to stay with a
girlfriend. The next day, Cary somehow located her there and called
her up as though nothing had happened and asked what she was
doing there. Virginia said, "Don't you remember?" He replied, "I
don't know what you're talking about." And Virginia says she honestly doesn't believe that he did.

In desperation, Virginia went to San Francisco to consult with a
psychiatrist friend of hers, Dr. Margaret Chung. Dr. Chung attributed Cary's violence to his deep emotional insecurity. Returning
to Hollywood, Virginia decided to give Cary another chance; she
moved back in with him at La Ronda, responding to his endless
telephone pleas, in which he called her a silly, hysterical girl and
begged her to forget all about what she claimed had taken place.

Cary didn't change. While shooting yet another insignificant movie,
Thirty-Day Princess, he was on the verge of a nervous breakdown,
screaming hysterically night after night at his unhappy wife. One
evening, they were to go to a party given by the distinguished Danish actor and former middleweight boxing champion Carl Brisson
and his wife, in whose twenty-two-year-old son, Frederick, Cary
had a romantic interest. Virginia was putting on a pale blue evening
gown and doing her hair in front of the mirror, when Cary walked
in and said, "You're always so goddamned late!" She replied calmly

that she was ready to leave. He threw her to the floor so that she fell on the iron fender in front of the fireplace. Her face was cut, and again blood drenched her dress. He walked out and drove to the party alone.

The Brissons and other friends kept calling Virginia all evening, wondering what was wrong with her and why she hadn't come to the party. All she could say was, "Ask Cary." When he returned late that night, to find her bandaged and sobbing, he asked her what had happened to her. Had she had an accident? She realized now that he was suffering from dangerous schizophrenic symptoms.

Their tormenting relationship continued all that summer. Whenever Virginia would complain about Cary's behavior the day before, he would say, "You imagined it. Nothing like that ever took place." Virginia walked out on Cary and returned to her mother on several occasions, most firmly of all on September 15, following an especially savage argument. Friends like Vivian Gaye and Sari Maritza did their utmost to cement the rift, but it was useless. Cary began drinking heavily; on the set, he took alcohol from coffee cups, but he fooled few at the studio. Virginia made plans to move to England, where she would make, the following year, an early vehicle for the very young James Mason, *Late Extra*, also known as *What Price Crime?* The script was worthless, but at least she would escape Cary for a while.

On September 28, Virginia yielded to Cary's pleas to join him at a dinner party, but he became drunk during the meal, and when they returned to his apartment at La Ronda, he accused her of ignoring him all evening. He walked toward her, raising his hand as though to strike, and she ran out and returned home to her mother, calling the ever-vigilant columnist Louella Parsons to say that she was in consultation with lawyers. Virtually incomprehensible, stumbling over his words, Cary telephoned Virginia on October 4 and blurted out his longing for her to return. When she refused, he snapped, "This will ruin me!" and hung up. There was something about his voice Virginia didn't like. She telephoned back and got the Filipino houseboy, Pedro; Pedro ran upstairs to the bedroom. Cary was stretched out on the bed, dressed only in undershorts, a large bottle of sleeping tablets almost empty beside him. Pedro called for an ambulance, and Cary was rushed to the hospital, where his stomach was pumped.

Because there was some question of foul play, police surgeon Dr. C. E. Cornell was summoned to the hospital. Virginia is sure that, in his drunken stupor, Cary faked a suicide attempt to frighten her into returning to him. She was too strong to yield to this theatrical device. Cary screamed at anyone who would listen that she had betrayed him. He was barely able to finish his latest, dreary film, *Ladies Should Listen.* In December, Virginia sued for divorce on the grounds of cruelty, insisting that he give her a full share of their joint property, valued at $50,000, and $167.50 a week; and that he not contest the divorce. He refused to respond to her settlement request, and even succeeded in withdrawing all the money from their joint bank account, forcing her to pawn her engagement ring and other jewelry and to borrow money, using her automobile as collateral.

Cary's divorce from Virginia became final on March 26, 1935. Pale, her red-rimmed eyes concealed behind dark glasses, she sat in a courtroom in downtown Los Angeles and, in response to a question by her lawyer, Milton Cohen, described her marriage. She said, so quietly that she was barely audible, "He was very solemn and disagreeable. He refused to pay my bills. He told me to go out and work myself, and then discouraged me every time I had an opportunity. He was like this almost from the first. . . . He told me he didn't care to live with me anymore, a number of times. . . . He was sullen, morose, and quarrelsome in front of guests. He falsely accused me of not appreciating him or his efforts. He was inclined to drink quite a bit all during our marriage." Her mother, Blanche, confirmed the many examples of Cary's insults to Virginia. Cary did not appear in court, and within fifty minutes she was free.

Virginia decided to proceed to England on April 27. Cary had been walking through another role, in *Enter Madame,* with Elissa Landi, and felt embittered, not only by his private life but by his career. Getting wind of Virginia's departure by train, Cary flew to New York, convinced she was having an affair with someone. But she had had more than enough of personal stress. All she wanted to do was live in a different environment and to work. Cary's justification for being in New York was his scheduled appearance in "Adam and Eve" on the *Lux Radio Theatre*, opposite Constance Cummings. He received $1,750 for thirty minutes on the air. Unable to reach Virginia, he lingered on in Manhattan, deciding to make the best of a bad situation. He began dating an international playgirl named Sandra Rambeau.

Shortly afterward, Cary dropped Miss Rambeau for the equally attractive Betty Furness. The daughter of the radio pioneer George Furness, Miss Furness had been raised on Park Avenue and begun appearing in movies at the age of sixteen. Like Cary, she was between pictures, and when he returned to Hollywood at the end of May to begin *The Last Outpost*, she returned with him, to make *McFadden's Flats*. She was seen everywhere with him in Hollywood. It is almost certain theirs was a platonic relationship; she says it was. They were seen dancing at the Trocadero on June 8, at a party that included Dorothy di Frasso and the newly arrived mobster Benjamin (Bugsy) Siegel. On June 18, Carole Lombard invited them to a gala in the funhouse at the Venice Pier. Some three hundred guests rode the carousel, enjoyed the peep shows, hurtled down slides, and plunged into a whirling steel bucket thirty feet wide, known as a social mixer, with Cary, Marlene Dietrich, Claudette Colbert, Cesar Romero, Frances Drake, Randolph Scott, and Vivian Gaye (who would soon break off her engagement to Scott and marry the director Ernst Lubitsch) tumbling in a heap as the machinery stopped dead. George Cukor remarked at the end of the party that it was great to see so many "star fannies" close up; Miss Dietrich wound up with her legs around Miss Colbert's neck; agent Phil Berg had a broken foot; and Richard Barthelmess was black and blue from head to foot.

In her column, Edith Gwynn commented upon Cary's widely known and discussed bisexuality. Since she couldn't state it directly, she disguised the barb in an account of an imaginary party game in which the guests would come as famous movie titles. Marlene Dietrich came as *Male and Female*, Garbo as *The Son-Daughter*, and Cary, audaciously, was represented as *One-Way Passage*, a sly reference to his sexual inclinations.

Despite such barbs, Cary was at last beginning to relax. It was easier for him to enjoy a lighthearted, much-publicized "romance" with Miss Furness than to experience the tensions of a real-life marriage. To help promote *The Last Outpost* and their own careers, he and Miss Furness appeared at one social event after another, he in custom-made tuxedos, she in enormous skyscraper hats. The ever-knowing Edith Gwynn told her readers: "Betty is still wearing a high hat. . . . Be sure to ask Cary what is the height of indifference."

That summer, the gossips were concentrating upon another of Cary's friendships—one that, according to witnesses, was a more personal one. Howard Hughes, then twenty-nine years old, had inherited the Hughes Tool Company at eighteen and had used his oil-drill fortune to indulge his passions for moviemaking and flying. Tall, bony, with carved features and a thatch of dark, unruly hair, the taciturn Hughes had an odd, high-pitched voice. He wore baggy suits and poorly polished shoes, drove an assortment of shabby, second-rate cars, and lived not in Beverly Hills or the still-fashionable Hollywood Hills, but in an unpretentious house among the old money in Hancock Park. According to his late aides Noah Dietrich and Johnny Meyer, and to his publicist of the 1940s, Guido Orlando, Hughes was bisexual, but, intensely guilty about his hunger and his divided nature, he sought to hide his more secret activities under a cover of promiscuity. This determined attempt to play Don Juan for the public sabotaged his relationships with both sexes. A brief marriage ended in disaster; all attempts to maintain a household of any sort failed. His love affair with the beautiful screen actress Billie Dove collapsed when her former husband, the tough director Irvin Willat, threatened Hughes's life if he continued to see her. Willat told Dietrich he knew that Hughes was "a faggot" and didn't want Miss Dove's life to be destroyed by a marriage to him.

Hughes's discovery of Randolph Scott had led to what appeared to be a brief relationship; now he was interested in Cary. Hughes had returned to Hollywood in summer 1935 after working incognito with American Airways (as it was then known) as a luggage handler, in order to learn the business from the ground up. He had emerged rapidly as a brilliant aviator, achieving 225 miles an hour, an extraordinary speed for the period, in his 580-horsepower Waspengine plane; he won his first major aviation prize at the All-American Air Meet in Miami on January 14, 1934.

Hughes paid Cary the great compliment of taking him to his secret hangar at Grand Central Airport in Glendale. Closed to all but a handful of visitors, the hangar was the construction site of its creator's beloved H-1 airplane. All that Hughes could think about, other than Cary, was his desire to fly the H-1. Noah Dietrich was with him constantly, acting as his financial adviser, attempting to restrict his expenditures on the plane, trying to make him rest, as he would work all night, the following day, and the next night without sleep, finally collapsing at his drawing board.

It was in the midst of this intense period of Hughes's life that he managed to break free from his obsession long enough to take Cary on a yachting voyage down the coast as far as Ensenada and then up north to San Francisco. Paramount began to panic, and the publicists called Edith Gwynn repeatedly to say that Cary's real interest was in a probably fictitious girl described as "Little Miss Moffett." Exactly what took place on the yacht will probably never be known, but the near-certainty is that Cary and Hughes formed, in those days at sea, a profound romantic friendship that would remain unbroken until the day of Hughes's death, almost half a century later.

At the same time, Cary remained very close to Randolph Scott, and Randy continued to live at La Ronda. Soon they would resume living together. On July 30, Vivian Gaye married Ernst Lubitsch, after many delays. The next day, having made no less than eighteen movies in twenty-four months, Randy flew to his home in Orange, Virginia. There, he ran into the richest local citizen, the forceful, tweedy Marion duPont, heiress to the vast fortune, almost certainly over $100 million, of her late father, William duPont. The invention of nylon and rayon had made the duPonts wealthy beyond calculation. Like her father, Marion was obsessed with horses, which in fact were almost her entire life. In 1932 she had bought, for an undisclosed sum, the five-year-old Battleship, son of the internationally famous racehorse Man O' War. In 1934, Battleship had won the Grand National at Belmont Park, America's greatest jumping event, and again he triumphed at the National Hunt Club at Brookline. In 1935, when Randolph Scott was in Virginia, Marion had temporarily retired Battleship to stud, placing him for one year on her breeding farm before she would take the supreme gamble and enter him for the world's greatest steeplechase, the British Grand National at Aintree.

With her vigorous stride, square shoulders, close-cropped black hair, and plain, mannish face, Marion duPont was scarcely a beauty. Yet her seeming lack of femininity, which led many to believe she was a lesbian, was quite deceptive. According to her close friend Seth Green, former publisher of the Orange *Record*, she had an insatiable desire for men and was prepared to pay any amount of money to obtain them. She had married a former jockey and trainer named Tom Summerville and, after tiring of him, acquired other men, running her private life very much as she ran her stud farm. Randolph Scott, who looked rather like a horse, was the next on her list. His relentless financial ambitions were not satisfied by the succession of increasingly mediocre films to which he was assigned, and Marion duPont offered to invest in him. There were rumors that she bought a substantial shareholding in Paramount to improve the level of his roles, but that is scarcely borne out by the record, since soon afterward he drifted away to 20th Century–Fox and RKO. Whatever the truth, he was suddenly a far richer man than he had been. Marion duPont, never bothering with social niceties, settled him in her mansion, Montpelier, once the residence of President James Madison and his celebrated wife, Dolley; she installed a sauna—a novelty in the United States at the time—and a private gymnasium for her lover's use.

Cary met Marion during one of her brief visits to Hollywood that year. Perhaps because of her enthusiasm for racing, he acquired a sudden interest in the sport, and frequented Hollywood Park and Santa Anita racetracks.

That August, whether to have access to Cary or out of a genuine romantic interest in Katharine Hepburn, the ever-mysterious Howard Hughes kept turning up on location at Malibu, California, where Cary was shooting *Sylvia Scarlett* with Miss Hepburn. Cary was on loan-out to RKO; the movie, a story of traveling players, was an example of self-indulgence by the homosexual director George Cukor. There were all manner of sly and outrageously risqué references in the script to Cary's bisexuality, presumably included in the well-founded belief that the public would remain oblivious of his predilections. Miss Hepburn was disguised as a boy through much of the action, and Cary was shown fondling her while she was dressed in male clothing. (He says to her at one stage, while in her male guise, "It's nippy out tonight. You'll make a proper hot water bottle," and, at another, "There's something that gives me a queer feeling every time I look at you.") The actress regarded the matter of making movies as an extended vacation and always brought a cook on location to prepare lunch. Cukor brought his own chef, and they vied with each other to prepare the best meal. Long breaks were taken for afternoon tea, while the cast, including Cary, sat on long wooden benches at tables laid with linen cloths, on the cliffs above the sea. The actor Brian Aherne recalled:

> One day, we were sitting down to eat when a biplane roared up and settled on the landing strip. Out stepped Howard Hughes. He was supposed to be having an affair with Kate, but I think he was more interested in Cary. He came over and sat with us, using that odd, high-pitched voice of his. Kate and Cary would tease him by whispering such words as, "Pass the bread, please," right in front of him, and he'd wonder what was going on. He'd suspect them of romancing each other and would start to shout, and then they'd scream with laughter at his discomfiture.

Aherne said that Cary was relaxed and charming during the work, very much at ease with everyone. But there was one sequence in the film at which he balked. The actress Natalie Paley was swimming and had gotten out of her depth. She began waving and calling for help. Cukor said, "Go on in, Cary. Natalie's drowning," and Cary replied, "I won't. It's too goddamned cold!" As everyone stared at him, Hepburn laughed and dove into the sea. She pulled Natalie Paley out, and the first thing Natalie said to her was, "Why did *you* have to do this! I was hoping to be carried out in Cary Grant's arms!"

The picture was a freakish failure, notable more for its extravagant hints at the sexual peculiarities of some members of its cast than for its intrinsic merits. The producer, Pandro S. Berman, still groans and holds his head at the mention of the movie. He says he called Miss Hepburn and Cukor to his house and told them he never wanted to work with them again. How the movie got past the vigilant Motion Picture Code Board remains an unsolved mystery of Hollywood.

By now, Edith Gwynn was beginning to make more overt innuendos in her column. She talked of "a long-haired town for males," including on her short and deadly list Gary Cooper, James Cagney, Cary, and Randy, with special mention for Scott's newly acquired curls. Cary responded by appearing at the Trocadero on September 30 with Scott as his date. Apparently, RKO objected, because Cary's next appearance, at the same night spot, was with Betty Furness, and on October 20, Miss Furness accompanied him to a party at Cukor's house to celebrate the wrap-up of shooting.

On a Sunday in the final days of filming *Sylvia Scarlett*, Howard Hughes again paid Cary a supreme compliment: he took him (the only person so honored) for a joyride in the H-1 over Los Angeles, achieving a speed of about 300 miles per hour. On September 12, 1935, Hughes decided to aim for the world speed record for a plane flying over land; the site chosen for the test was Martin Field, near Santa Ana, California. The judges were air ace Amelia Earhart, Hollywood stunt pilot Paul Mantz, and National Aeronautic Association official Lawrence Therkelson. After an initial failure, Hughes, to Cary's excitement, posted world record speeds, reaching a maximum of 354 miles per hour. But in his passionate pursuit of victory, Hughes forgot that his gas was low, and his engine failed before he could access the auxiliary tank. He made a forced landing but, to Cary's relief and surprise, was uninjured.

Immediately after *Sylvia Scarlett* was completed, Cary signed a contract to make a picture in England. *The Amazing Quest of Ernest Bliss* was an uninspiring script, but he wanted to return home. His father was suffering from stomach disease that was sufficiently serious to cause alarm. Cary also wanted to see Eric, his half-brother. Randy caused a new flurry of comment by seeing Cary off when he flew to New York in November to board the *Aquitania*.

Before filming started, he saw a good deal of Virginia Cherrill in

London. She had partially forgiven him, and her sympathy when he told her of his father's sickness appeased him, though with his amazing capacity to deny the inconvenient past, he indicated no remorse for what he had done to her. He traveled to Bristol, where he found Elias in desperate health. Septicemia of the bowel had set in, along with gangrene, following a radical operation for cancer. Though not much over sixty, Elias was shockingly aged.

Cary returned with a heavy heart to London, to begin work on *Ernest Bliss* for Grand National Pictures under the direction of Alfred Zeisler. He was consoled partly by the presence as leading lady of the gentle, subdued Mary Brian. Born Louise Byrdie Dantzler, the twenty-six-year-old Texan had won a beauty contest and at the age of sixteen had made a vivid debut as a winsome and touching Wendy in *Peter Pan*. She had gone on to appear effectively in such celebrated movies as *Beau Geste*, *Forgotten Faces*, *The Virginian*, *The Royal Family of Broadway*, and *The Front Page*. But she lacked the weight and presence to survive at the top in the harshly competitive world of talkies. By 1935, she was adrift, and the starring role in *Ernest Bliss* was her last chance for success. But by now, she was past caring about a career; her main reason for making the movie was Cary Grant.

On December 2, Cary received a phone call from Bristol to say that his father had passed away after a second operation. Cary, the quintessential professional, told his director, and Garrett Klement, the head of the production company, that he would not break the shooting schedule to take care of the funeral arrangements. But Klement insisted he leave for Bristol immediately after the morning shooting on the fourth. He played his scenes perfectly, giving no inkling of his distress, then he drove down to join the Leaches at the Church of England rites. Some historians have stated that he learned of his mother's (or his foster mother's) existence at the time, but this is contradicted by the available evidence. In fact, it was to be three more years before he learned the truth.

Returning to his apartment in Park Lane, Cary found a beautiful note from Virginia Cherrill. He wrote to thank her, saying how fond his father had been of her; he wished he had invited her to the funeral—"In fact, I seem to have some peculiar idea you were there this morning." He added that Elias would have liked Virginia to attend and had even expressed that wish.

Cary went on to say:

But somehow I didn't quite know how to ask you. . . . I was afraid the invitation might seem wrongly motivated. Everyone in Bristol thanks you for your kindness. They've been so sorry about us, and now are so kind and helpful in their little manner. But oh, so pityingly sad without Dad. . . . Forgive me if I haven't made much sense. All I know is you've been kind, Baby. Cary.

He continued working with a heavy heart, but consoled by the thoughtfulness of Mary Brian. However, seen today, *The Amazing Quest of Ernest Bliss* only too clearly reveals the lack of even a hint of genuine romantic warmth between them. Their "romance" consisted of nothing more than the inventions of a skillful studio publicity department and Miss Brian's tender hopes; soon the situation would change. She says: "When Cary came back to London after his father's funeral, it was as if he shut that period of his life away. I'm sure he was grieving, but he didn't talk about it."

She remembers that they would spend Sundays together, walking out into the London streets, looking at the announcements of destinations on the front of the red double-decker buses and flipping coins to see which one they would take. They would sit at the top of the bus at the front and travel as far as the bus went, to obscure suburbs of London that for Cary had always been mysterious, romantic and unknown. To help get rid of his grief, Cary would take Mary to his beloved pantomimes; she herself had almost been cast in a new production of the same *Jack and the Beanstalk* in which Cary had appeared in London at the age of seven. When he told her of his exciting experiences in pantomime, she was very regretful she had not accepted the part of Jack, the principal boy. They also went to music halls together after a day's work; Cary would discuss with her the histories and personalities of the performers, with whose talents and backgrounds he was so intimately familiar. He talked to her of his years in stilt walking, and said that the music hall was still the chief passion of his life.

The high spot of that London winter season was Noël Coward's striking collection of playlets, *Tonight at 8:30*. Cary and Mary tried to get tickets, but even Cary's considerable name failed to prove influential; Coward, who had visited Cary and Virginia in Hollywood the year before, answered Cary's pleas and arranged for him and Mary to see the performance from the wings. Later, Laurence Olivier and his wife, Jill Esmond, joined the couple at an after-show party. That same season, still fighting against his grief, Cary was seen with Mary at several other major social events. Ad Schulberg, who was in town, hosted a soiree for the couple. Virginia Cherrill arrived with the enormously wealthy Maharaja of Jaipur; Fay Wray and John Monk Saunders came, and so did the junior Douglas Fairbanks, now Cary's great friend. On December 13, the actress Kitty Kelly gave a party for Cary and Mary; the Duke of Kent, Lord Milford Haven, and the actress Betty Balfour were among the guests. Cary again became close to Fay Wray and her husband, who was writing a script for Alexander Korda based on the life of Lawrence of Arabia. He wanted Cary to play the role; unfortunately, this idea never came to fruition, and the picture wasn't made until decades later by Sam Spiegel, starring Peter O'Toole.

Fond as Cary was of Mary, tension and stress made him flare up at times. She says:

> I think he had a few emotional scars from his divorce from Virginia. He had a terrible temper, and then he'd come running back saying how sorry he was. He would be angry at someone and take it out on someone else. He never hit me. His anger was short-lived.

Cary returned to New York on the *Bremen* on February 5, 1936. According to Mary Brian, his feelings for her now deepened, and they soon began what she now describes as a platonic love affair. Mary was still in London, appearing in *The Charlot Revue;* Cary had gone home to make *Big Brown Eyes*, a comedy co-starring Joan Bennett, to be followed by *Suzy*, with Jean Harlow.

He found Randolph Scott depressed: Scott's father was dying of cancer. He passed away on March 5 in Virginia; only a few days later, Scott traveled on to Charlotte, North Carolina, to marry Marion duPont in a ceremony that neither Cary nor any of their Hollywood friends attended. On the day of the wedding, Mary arrived in Los Angeles and was met at the train by Cary; the following night they were seen dancing at the Trocadero. They became very friendly with Gene Markey and his wife, Joan Bennett, with whom Cary enjoyed working in *Big Brown Eyes*. Mary Brian says of her relationship with Cary in the spring and summer of 1936:

> He had even called me on the ship as I came back from England to New York. Romance would be my word for our relationship. It was flowers and attention and two people completely enjoying each other and doing the same things. It was a very exciting, lovely part of my life. In a very innocent way, I loved him and he loved me. And we would always be friends. It was a great capacity Cary had, keeping friends, even girls that he had gone with, seeing them again with no embarrassment on either side. He met my mother, and they got along well. Everything seemed fine.

This was probably one of the happiest times for Cary. He had no passionate entanglements, Mary was a sweet and undemanding lover, and Hollywood was at the height of its glamour and luxury. *Big Brown Eyes* and *Suzy* were conventional movies, which made few demands on his resources of energy. The Trocadero was aglitter night after night, with the stars dancing fox-trots and quicksteps and waltzes to an orchestra led by the irresistible Spaniard Xavier Cugat; everyone table-hopped and gossiped and made sure they were mentioned in Louella Parsons's column in the morning. Those were carefree days, far from the thunderclouds of the increasingly dangerous and threatening European scene. But then Cary heard shocking news.

S I X

On the night of July 11, 1936, Howard Hughes was driving to his house in Hancock Park from downtown Los Angeles. Passing a streetcar safety zone at Third Street and Lorraine Boulevard, he drew out behind the tram, impatient as always, and struck and killed a pedestrian, fifty-nine-year-old salesman Gabe S. Meylan. Hughes called Cary and other friends in desperation; he was charged with negligent homicide, but so great was his wealth and influence that he got away with saying he had made a sharp turn to avoid an approaching car. He was acquitted at the preliminary hearing. Hughes was badly shaken by this episode and became more reclusive, depending increasingly on Cary for his friendship and support. And in fact Cary was virtually his only intimate male friend during this time. Hughes's romancing of Katharine Hepburn was not going well and Cary proved consolation to him in his severe bouts of depression.

That summer, Cary continually ran into the agent Walter Kane and the stunning blonde Phyllis Brooks. Born Phyllis Steiller in Boise, Idaho, the twenty-two-year-old actress was not well known at the time. She had a radiant, freewheeling, extroverted quality, a deep, throaty laugh, and a habit of tossing back her magnificent hair and pushing it down with her hand as she cracked risqué, charming jokes. She was the opposite of the reserved Mary Brian. She made no great impression on Cary, and she only recalls meeting him much later. But he noticed her, no doubt of it. Everyone who met her immediately loved Brooksie, as she was known in Hollywood. Even in the company of so many dazzling young women, she stood out. She was the toast of the Vendôme and the Trocadero, and Edith Gwynn and Louella Parsons constantly mentioned her in their columns, pushing her career along. Hollywood was not a place in which people often gave a helping hand, but just about everyone wanted to assist Brooksie. They all felt she deserved to be a major star.

In August, Cary at last proposed marriage to Mary Brian. But she hesitated; although she decisively rejects any suggestion that she knew about his ambiguous personal life, she undoubtedly sensed that he was first and foremost consumed with himself and his career. And even after he proposed, Cary himself seemed shaky about his intentions. He had no sooner indicated his desire to marry Mary than he wondered if it was the right time for him to get married. Mary Brian says, "I wasn't pressing for it. I went to New York. I felt that if there was any indecision on Cary's part, it was certainly not the time for us to get together."

She wasn't aware of another complication: while Cary had been dating Mary in England, he had seen a good deal of Frederick Brisson. Brisson, who was then twenty-four years old, still fascinated him.

Phyllis Brooks went to New York to appear in the play *Stage Door*. She was a name to watch; but the play closed quickly when its temperamental star, Margaret Sullavan, became pregnant with the child who is today famous as the author Brooke Hayward, author of *Haywire*. Phyllis returned to Los Angeles. Cary had just finished shooting *Wedding Present* with Joan Bennett; his friend and mentor B. P. Schulberg was the producer. Cary called Mary Brian only sporadically, his interest in her now rapidly fading. One night at the Trocadero, Phyllis was entertaining a friend from New York, Eleanor French, a society nightclub singer who was popular at the Stork Club. Eleanor had always wanted to meet Cary Grant; when Cary stopped by the table to remind Phyllis of their previous meetings, Eleanor was enchanted. The Earl of Warwick, an old friend of Phyllis's who was in Hollywood to pursue an acting career, wanted to entertain Eleanor French and asked her advice. Phyllis replied that he could give a party and invite Cary, in the hope that he would be attracted to Eleanor.

That same week, Randolph Scott returned from Virginia to make *The Last of the Mohicans*. His wife had settled several million dollars on him, and he had taken a beach house at 1019 Ocean Front,* Santa Monica. Cary soon moved in. It was an intriguing house, a typically odd California mixture of styles. The front patio and entrance corridor and walled garden suggested a Spanish hacienda. But, inside, there was an imitation Regency staircase that twisted up to the left in a semi-circle; there was a circular Regency hallway on the second floor, with bedrooms off to right and left. The rest of the lower part of the house was a cross between Cape Cod and British Stockbrokers' Tudor in equal parts. The front of the house, leading on to a swimming pool, tennis court and the beach, featured Cape Cod eaves and a heavy gray slate roof. Somehow the architectural jumble was appealing; it was at this house that the Earl of Warwick arranged a housewarming, to which Phyllis and Eleanor French came, both unescorted.

Phyllis was apparently quite unaware that this was the home of two men of ambiguous sexuality. The only surprise she experienced was that Cary was attracted to her. Cheerful and detached as ever, Randolph Scott seems to have cared no more about Cary's interest in Phyllis than he did for his own wife, who seldom came to visit him from Virginia. He went on to make *Go West, Young Man* with Mae West, acting out the comic quasi-sexual scenes with what seemed to be total conviction.

Not since the heyday of his marriage to Virginia Cherrill had Cary felt so warm an interest in any woman. All thoughts of Mary Brian were forgotten as he and Phyllis began dancing up a storm at nightclub after nightclub, rapidly becoming the most talked-about couple in Hollywood. The obstacle to this burgeoning relationship was Phyllis's mother, who, unlike Virginia Cherrill's parent, was a frustrated actress whose career had never taken off. Mrs. Steiller was a neo-Victorian, correct and moralistic, and she was not at all

---

* *Renumbered 1039, it is standing today.*

happy with the idea of Phyllis's conducting an affair, no matter how innocent, with a divorced movie star in whom countless women were interested. There is no indication that either Cary or Phyllis was concerned about Mrs. Steiller's attitude. With breezy charm, Phyllis simply waved away her mother's objections when she returned home late at night after exciting evenings with Cary at the Trocadero.

At this time, Cary renewed an old friendship from his vaudeville days. He had never forgotten the theatrical and movie manager Frank W. Vincent, who had booked him and the rest of the Pender Troupe into the Orpheum Circuit after Cary's illness in Rochester in 1922. A gentleman of the old school, Vincent had not ceased to keep a firm eye on Cary's career. He had formed a partnership with the powerful agent Harry E. Edington, whose clientele included the mysterious Greta Garbo. Cary, always shrewd where money was concerned, secretly entered into a partnership with these two important agents, investing much of his savings in the business. The situation was unique and of questionable legality, since in effect Cary became his own agent, receiving a split of the ten percent that went automatically to Vincent and Edington. Moreover, and still more surprisingly, he was now the agent for several major stars; the Edington-Vincent list was spectacular and included such figures as Marlene Dietrich, Douglas Fairbanks, Jr., Leopold Stokowski, the up-and-coming Rita Hayworth, and Joel McCrea. Being secretly the agent of Garbo and Dietrich was intoxicating. Cary would soon make far more money from his under-the-table agenting and managing than from his work as a screen actor. And almost no one in Hollywood knew the truth. Had they known, several of the stars would undoubtedly have been furious.

In the early months of 1937, Cary continued to see Howard Hughes whenever possible. On January 18, Hughes flew the H-1, renamed the "Winged Bullet," from Burbank Airport, where he had built special hangars, over the Midwest and the Appalachian Mountains in Pennsylvania, all the way to Newark, in 7 hours, 28 minutes, and 25 seconds. Several years would go by before this transcontinental record would be broken. President Franklin D. Roosevelt received Hughes at the White House and presented him with the

Harmon International Trophy. The elated Hughes returned joyfully to Hollywood, and Cary gave him an elaborate party at the Trocadero. Hughes immediately began plans for an around-the-world flight; that summer, he applied for permission from the Bureau of Air Commerce, but to his intense fury, he was turned down. Such a journey was considered too dangerous at the time, despite the fact that Charles Lindbergh and others had successfully flown the Atlantic and that zeppelins were making regular crossings.

In the spring, Cary was working on *Topper*, adapted from the popular novel by Thorne Smith about a couple killed in a car crash who return in whimsical good spirits to haunt their friends. The film provided an agreeable opportunity for Cary to renew his acquaintance with the charmingly flustered Roland Young, who played the title role with effortless artistry; Constance Bennett was Cary's antic co-star. More flamboyant, reckless, and extroverted than her staid sister, Joan, she was engaged to be married to the Latin lover Gilbert Roland. Constance was on edge and extremely temperamental during much of the shooting, affected by the alcoholism and hysterical crying fits of her sister Barbara.*

His co-star's behavior proved unsettling to Cary, who liked above all an atmosphere of calm on a set; her frequent lateness grated on him.

Cary, who was drastically opposed to Hitler and Mussolini, disapproved of Britain's appeasement policy, and was concerned about the advance of Fascism in Europe, began to take steps toward the commitment that would lead him to become a British Intelligence agent in World War II. He was, interestingly, a staunch Republican, who, had he been a citizen, would undoubtedly have supported Alf Landon in the 1936 election. He knew, friends confirm, of the pro-Nazi stance of certain prominent Hollywood figures, including the producer Winfield Sheehan, who had recently left his post as head of 20th Century–Fox and would soon form a questionable association with the Nazi consul general in Los Angeles, George Gyssling.

---

* *Mother of the controversial TV talk show host Morton Downey, Jr.*

Cary was also aware of the dangerous activities of Victor Mc-Laglen, who had won an Academy Award for his performance in *The Informer*. McLaglen was frequently seen riding through Hollywood on horseback or appeared at meetings in various parks as commandant of the Hollywood Czars, a radically anti-Semitic, pro-Nazi group that was discovered more than once beating up Jews. And it was known to most people, including Cary, on the Hollywood grapevine fed by William R. Wilkerson and his wife, Edith Gwynn, that Walt Disney, whose outright defiance of the Hollywood unions was already earning him notoriety, had an admiration for Hitler that was reciprocated (he would soon entertain Leni Riefenstahl, a female favorite of Hitler's, who had made the outrageous German propaganda movies *Berlin Olympiad* and *Triumph of the Will*). Nor was Cary unaware of the political leanings of Gary Cooper, who in 1938 would go to Berlin and be entertained by Hitler. Yet for some incomprehensible reason, Grant was blind to Dorothy di Frasso's role as Mussolini's agent and collaborator. He was taken in, apparently, by her repeated statements that she was an enemy of the Italian dictator, at the same time that she was entertaining Mussolini and Field Marshal Göring at her Villa Madama near Rome.

Even as he appeared in scene after scene of lighthearted, emptyheaded farce in *Topper*, Cary continued his careful surveillance of the Hollywood anti-Semitic scene. Simultaneously, he was behaving in a manner that shocked several of his friends. Even the columnist Hedda Hopper, a homophobe who hated Cary, could not bring herself to speak of how he and Randolph Scott turned up at the Santa Monica costume party Marion Davies gave in honor of her lover, William Randolph Hearst, on April 29, 1937: they were dressed as identical circus acrobats, and neither Mrs. Scott nor Phyllis Brooks accompanied them.

Life continued at the beach house Cary shared with Scott. Marion duPont was uneasy when she visited, unhappy, out of place in Hollywood, probably only too keenly aware of what was going on between her husband and his housemate, who, for appearance sake, moved temporarily into the house next door. She spent most of her days at the racetrack, trying to suppress her disappointment. But it didn't work: she returned to her home in Virginia that spring and never came back. She didn't even mention Randolph Scott in her memoirs. Cary moved in again, and he and Scott seemed quite content to be photographed for fan magazines in and around the swimming pool, playing beach ball, cooking in matching aprons in the kitchen, washing the dishes together, and fooling around on the patio in a manner that left little to the imagination. They continued to be confident that the public would never suspect anything and (presumably) that the more they flaunted their relationship, the more everyone would think that if they had anything to hide they would not allow themselves to be pictured or written about in their habitat. During Scott's prolonged absence on location that summer, shooting *High, Wide and Handsome*, Cary continued to see Phyllis, who often motored down to the beach house. It is probably indicative of the uncommitted nature of their relationship that during the shooting of the movie *Toast of New York*, Cary was seen from time to time with the voluptuous Jean Rogers, whose main claim to fame was playing opposite Buster Crabbe in the *Flash Gordon* serial.

Cary was introduced to Jean during a brief trip to New York, where he was among the many expatriate Britishers who welcomed Alfred Hitchcock and his wife. The great English director, who had never been to Manhattan before, was conferring with David O. Selznick about possible future projects, following the great success of his British movies, *The Lady Vanishes* and *The Thirty-Nine Steps*. Cary was fascinated with Hitch; the rotund filmmaker was shrewd, hard-bitten, bright, and sharp-witted, with a wicked, enjoyable sense of humor. Knowing that Cary was very tight with money, he delighted in deliberately passing him the checks at the end of meals in expensive restaurants. For once, Cary didn't mind: he was captivated by Hitchcock's talent and wanted to work with him someday.

That fall of 1937, Phyllis Brooks was enjoying good reviews for her acting as a radio band singer in a Shirley Temple vehicle, *Rebecca of Sunnybrook Farm*, with Randolph Scott. Cary starred in *The Awful Truth* and *Bringing Up Baby*. *The Awful Truth* turned out to be his first major success, the picture that would launch him at last as a major international star. Yet the conditions under which he made this antic comedy at Columbia—on special loan-out from Paramount—could not have been less promising. The director, Leo

McCarey, was an alcoholic of unstable temperament, whose Irish-American charm secured him one job after another, but whose way-ward approach to picturemaking exasperated even his warmest ad-mirers among the studio executives. Ralph Bellamy, the accomplished, thirty-three-year-old former Broadway actor who had made his name in the Ellery Queen series of B pictures and in *Hands Across the Table*, with Carole Lombard, appeared with Cary and Irene Dunne in the movie. He recalls the chaos from which *The Awful Truth* was born. The script was rewritten three times at least; among its suc-cessive authors were Dorothy Parker and her husband, Alan Camp-bell. The final draft was cobbled together from the existing ones by a hack writer named Viña Delmar, who fortunately retained suffi-cient of Dorothy Parker's witty lines to make the whole movie work. But there was still no structure or proper progression of scenes, and McCarey, smiling incessantly in his crinkly Irish manner, seemed cavalier in his attitude and unconcerned whether the picture would work or not.

Cary, who liked thorough professionalism, prepreparation, and pinpoint precision in every detail of moviemaking, was exasperated from the very beginning of the filming. When he walked onto the set for the first time, Irene Dunne was pounding away at the grand piano in a desperate attempt to play "Home on the Range," which Ralph Bellamy was bawling out in a bathroom baritone. McCarey was lying under the camera, laughing at this grotesque display of amateurishness; the perfectionist Miss Dunne, on the verge of tears because she couldn't read sheet music, was appalled by her own clumsy vamping of the song. Delighted, McCarey yelled, "Cut! Print it!" Irene Dunne began to cry. Ralph Bellamy, red in the face, walked over to shake hands with Cary for the first time. He recalls saying, "There's no script!" And Cary replied, "Then what are we doing here?" "I haven't any idea!" Bellamy exclaimed.

The random process of shooting continued well into the night. Cary was beyond fury, beyond embarrassment. He apparently didn't know that McCarey had method in his madness: he had spent much of his early career making slapstick comedies for Hal Roach—Char-lie Chase farcical shorts and later Laurel and Hardy pictures, in which much of the comic business was made up as he went along.

Cary offered several thousand dollars and a free picture to studio boss Harry Cohn if he could be excused from the movie immediately. But Cohn held him to his contract. Day after day, McCarey would walk on the set with a few scraps of paper scrawled with notes, and would insist the actors memorize lines that he had cooked up on a drunk a few hours before. There would be a quick run-through, or sometimes not even that, and then the actors would plunge into their roles. It was nerve-racking for everyone, but as the shooting continued, Cary began to realize that this freewheeling approach, which would one day become standard in Hollywood, had its advantages. The fixed, claustrophobic, airless atmosphere of Hollywood picturemaking was being broken apart; McCarey was bringing back the freshness, attractiveness, and charm of his silent movies and of the glorious Marx Brothers picture *Duck Soup*, a classic of comedy. Harry Cohn was delighted with the rushes and, monster though he was, actually was heard to laugh at some of the gag lines.

There were problems. Cary did not appreciate McCarey's anti-Semitism, crypto-Fascism, and extreme racism, but despite the fact that McCarey's attitudes grated on his nerves, he appreciated the man's extraordinary abilities.

Alexander d'Arcy, who played an exotic gigolo with whom Irene Dunne has a brief but provocative liaison, has vivid recollections of making the film. He recalls that Cary sometimes would step in and try to direct his performance:

> There was one particular time that I remember, when he took over. He tried to move me around and tell me where to stand. I had a very tough reaction: I didn't let anybody push me around, and to this day I don't. So I said, "Cary, you're not the director. If there's something to be changed, ask Leo McCarey and he will tell me, and then I will follow. I follow directors, I don't follow other actors." Cary didn't say anything. The matter never came between us again.

During the shooting, d'Arcy became aware of the widespread rumors about Cary's bisexuality. Somebody told him that Cary was having an affair with a male pianist. D'Arcy says: "Everybody knew that Cary was homosexual. It was an established thing. I knew Cary and Randolph lived together as a gay couple. Cary was not obnoxious. His mannerisms were not feminine at all; he was a regular guy. I think Cary knew that people were saying things about him; I don't think he tried to hide it."

The Awful Truth turned out to be a joy. The story, of a divorcing couple who really love each other and find excuse after excuse to get together again, had a relaxed, carefree, open quality that makes it quite undated today. The dialogue McCarey concocted had a marvelous naturalism, effortlessly delivered by the stars, and Irene Dunne, who seemed inhumanly noble in most movies, let her hair down charmingly under McCarey's careful coaxing. Only the ending, when the couple finally unite in a vacation lodge, seems strained; nobody could think of how to conclude the movie, and a stagehand was responsible for the somewhat protracted denouement.

It was during 1937 that Cary began a major career in radio, then a superb dramatic medium, whose standards were far higher than those to be found in television some thirteen years later. Apart from his appearance in CBS's "Adam and Eve" in 1935, with Constance Cummings, and occasional interviews with Louella Parsons on her gossipy *Hollywood Hotel* program, Cary had done little in the medium in the preceding years. But now he began to enjoy the freedom of radio, the easy money it brought, and the fact that he did not have to deal with tedious rehearsals, numerous takes, hot lights, and quirky directors. In March, he starred with his former colleague Jeanette MacDonald in "Madame Butterfly" on Cecil B. DeMille's famous *Lux Radio Theatre*, happily renewing his acquaintance with the actress six years after the harrowing days of *Boom-Boom*. On October 15, he appeared in the audio version of *The Awful Truth*, and on November 21, in "Medicine Girl," from a story by P. G. Wodehouse, with the troublesome Constance Bennett. It was the start of a forty-year, very happy association with CBS, whose boss, William Paley, was among Cary's warmest admirers.

The Awful Truth opened in the fall of 1937. In a matter of weeks, it netted half a million dollars, the equivalent of twenty times that sum today; it proved to be one of the biggest box-office successes Columbia had ever known. As his own agent, Cary kept the whole of his $150,000 fee, as well as retaining ten percent of the picture by special arrangement. At the same time, Randolph Scott had followed suit in leaving Paramount and was now under contract to 20th Century–Fox, his career at that studio assisted by the substantial number of shares in it bought by Marion duPont before her disillusionment set in. It became common currency in her hometown that she had, in the words of her friend Seth Green, "bought the studio." This was, of course, an exaggeration.

The reviews for Cary in *The Awful Truth* were ecstatic; almost overnight, by the mere device of leaving Paramount, he had entered the big time. A friend of his, who wishes to remain anonymous, says:

> The biggest mistake Paramount ever made was not building Cary's career. Why did they throw him away? Why did they never let him be a star but only a minor leading man? Because certain of the executives were homophobes. They hated it when they found out he was bisexual. Even B. P. Schulberg, his mentor, gave up on him in disgust when it was discovered. Cary was crying all the way to the bank.

At the end of 1937 and beginning of 1938, Randolph Scott was troubled by a matter which was never made public. His sister, Catherine Strother Scott, who lived in Ireland, was in trouble. She had been experiencing emotional distress. Brought in by consular officials in Hamburg and in Southampton, England, she announced herself as destitute. Every effort was made to persuade her to return to the United States, and Randolph paid for her passage, but she declined until Scott had informed her by telegram that he would give her no money unless she came back to the family in Virginia. The division of Foreign Service Administration authorized two FBI officers, one of whom was a woman, to escort her from the Parkside Hotel in Dublin to the ship *Antonia* at Cobh.

This agonizing matter caused the normally unflurried Scott considerable concern. Catherine docked on January 10, 1938, and Randolph took care of her from then on. During the extreme stress of this affair, Cary had as usual to act as though nothing in his life was untoward. He was appearing in Howard Hawks's farce *Bringing Up Baby*, once again co-starring with the inexhaustible Katharine Hepburn.

Hawks proved to be fascinating. Tough, flinty, lean, with a face like a meat hatchet, he was a perfectionist. At first, Cary had not liked Hawks or his role of a paleontologist in glasses who gets into a series of uncomfortable scrapes. He had told the director that he didn't know how to tackle such a part; he certainly wasn't an intellectual. Hawks told him, "You've seen Harold Lloyd, haven't you?" Cary nodded enthusiastically. The question gave him a clue: he would be playing an innocent abroad, a bespectacled brainy man in a world full of tragicomic menace.

As work began on this story of a scientist, David Huxley (a deliberate reference to the famous family of that name), and his bizarre affair with Susan, an eccentric Connecticut heiress, Miss Hepburn made a serious mistake. Hawks said:

She kept laughing. And she took the comic situations *too* comically. I tried to explain to her that the great clowns, Keaton, Chaplin, Lloyd, simply weren't out there making funny faces, they were serious, sad, solemn, and the humor sprang from what happened to them. They do funny things in a completely quiet, somber, deadpan way. Cary understood this at once. Katie didn't.

Miss Hepburn says:

It's true. I did keep laughing at my own lines. Cary Grant taught me that the more depressed I looked when I went into a pratfall, the more the audience would laugh.

Cary and Hawks conspired to teach Katharine Hepburn the delicate art of farce. In a scene in a museum involving the skeleton of a prehistoric animal, the veteran comedian Walter Catlett, a big, overweight, moon-faced man in thick horn-rimmed glasses, suddenly began to tease Cary, even at one stage kissing him, off camera, to the enormous amusement of Miss Hepburn. Hawks remembered:

Walter used every mannerism of Kate's, but with a deadly seriousness, and she was entranced. After that, she played perfectly, being herself.

As in other movies, Cary appeared in drag in one scene. Dressed in a fluffy nightgown, he is asked by an angry old lady, "Do you dress like that all the time?" He replies, "No, I've gone gay all of a sudden!"

Fritz Feld, who played a comic psychiatrist in the movie, remembers the pleasure of working with Cary, observing his effortless timing. He says:

Life in Hollywood in those days was easy. Howard Hawks would come in in the morning and say, "It's a nice day today. Let's go to the races." And Cary, who loved the horses, was especially delighted when we would pack up and *go* to the races. Kate Hepburn also amused Cary by serving tea, as was her custom, every afternoon on the set at four o'clock. After one scene Hawks had especially liked, he delivered the cast two cases of the best champagne. Those were the days!

Cary and Hepburn had as their co-star a leopard, which constantly threatened to scratch them to pieces. Cary hated it. Miss Hepburn had a tendency to spin around while talking, flaring out her skirts; the leopard would paw at her, frightened by the movement. Once it lunged so violently that Hepburn broke the heel off her shoe. She looked around, wondering what to say next to cover this unscripted mishap. Cary whispered in her ear. Suddenly she said, referring to her heelless shoe and her hastily improvised heavy limp, "I was born on the side of a hill!" The leopard's trainer, Madame Olga Celeste of the Ringling Bros. Circus, said:

Neither Cary Grant nor Miss Hepburn were the slightest bit afraid of Nissa, my wonderful leopard. They both put resin on their shoe soles so they wouldn't skid at all and startle Nissa. By moving normally around her, they didn't disturb her. All three became friends by the end of the picture.

Cary, perfectly Harold Lloydish in his round, scholarly black horn-rims, played the part of an overgrown schoolboy to perfection; the result was a masterpiece of screen comedy, in which Miss Hepburn also provided a performance of pure gold. The reviews were extraordinary, headed by *Time* magazine's rave (*"Bringing Up Baby* comes in second only to last year's whimsical high spot, *The Awful Truth"*).

Phyllis Brooks often dropped by during the shooting to watch the antics of the stars; as she watched Cary work, her love for him was enhanced by an intense professional admiration. She longed to marry him. Yet he was still skittish and uncommitted; she kept ignoring the rumors about his relationship with Scott. However, she did experience a jolt when Marion Davies, apparently on instructions from William Randolph Hearst, who must have had considerable detective work done on Cary in England, told her that Cary was Jewish on his mother's side and that she should think seriously before marrying a Jew. Phyllis, completely devoid of racism, swept aside this warning, blaming not Marion but rather the notoriously pro-Fascist Hearst.

The platonic romance continued, conducted largely in public, unruffled by the quarrels that had marred Cary's earlier relationships. On January 11, 1938, while *Bringing Up Baby* was shooting, Phyllis appeared with Cary at a tennis party attended by Mr. and Mrs. Douglas Fairbanks, Jr., the Fred Astaires, Cedric Gibbons and Dolores Del Rio, Gilbert Roland and Constance Bennett, Marlene Dietrich with three men, the Charles Boyers, Rudy Vallee, and the William Powells. A few days later on January 14, most of the guests and dozens more turned up for one of the biggest premieres in the history of Hollywood, the opening of *In Old Chicago*. Afterward, they attended a double celebration (it was studio boss Joe Schenck's wedding anniversary) at the Schenck house, decorated for the occasion by the expert interior designer, Jack Harkrider. Three nights after that, the eve of Cary's thirty-fourth birthday, there was the almost equally spectacular Hollywood Hotel party, at which the guests arrived in blackface and danced to music by Louis Armstrong and his band. The rumba, the conga, and the Big Apple were the dances of the hour.

Phyllis began work on *Little Miss Broadway* with Shirley Temple, enjoying the work and disappointed only that Cary was forbidden by studio chief Darryl F. Zanuck to watch her. Zanuck was afraid Cary's presence might distract her and the ten-year-old Miss Temple, who had a hopeless crush on him. Another party launched the dazzling new La Conga nightclub, at which Cary and Randolph Scott yet again appeared boldly as a pair, Phyllis trailing along behind in a group that included Bing Crosby, Liz Whitney, and Marlene Dietrich. Still more parties were given by the Chinese Princess Tai Lachman, whose husband, Harry, had directed Cary in *When You're in Love*. The partying went on and on in that year before the curtain rang down on a gilded era. As Cary started shooting Philip Barry's *Holiday* under the direction of George Cukor on February 28, he and Phyllis still managed to find time and energy at the end of the day's work to go dancing two or three nights a week at the Trocadero.

Holiday had been made before; it lacked much of the sparkle of *The Awful Truth* and *Bringing Up Baby*. The complications of interlocking relationships in high society seem tedious today, despite the expert playing of Grant and (again) Katharine Hepburn. What had seemed spontaneous and relaxed in the earlier movies now was strident and shrill. Cukor, always uneven in temperament and prone to sudden tantrums, was not at his most inspired, and Harry Cohn, who said that he judged films by the movements of his fanny, squirmed continuously through the day's rushes and complained in words of one syllable to anyone paid to listen to him. On March 26, Cary heard the pleasing news that Marion duPont's stallion Battleship, watched by its owner, who had made a last-minute dash by zeppelin across the Atlantic, triumphantly galloped in by half a head to win the Grand National at Britain's Aintree, the first horse from an American stable to triumph in that classic event. Randolph Scott failed to share Cary's enthusiasm; that coldhearted man didn't even bother to send his wife a telegram of congratulation.

The reviews for *Holiday* were surprisingly good, the *New York Times* remarking that "Mr. Grant's Mr. Case is really the best role, although it is quite possible that neither Mr. Barry nor Columbia saw it that way." Unfortunately, neither *Bringing Up Baby* nor *Holiday* succeeded at the box office. But Cary's reputation was enhanced by each. By mid-1938, he was being deluged with fan mail, Cary Grant fan clubs were being formed all over the country, and efforts, unsuccessful as it turned out, were being made to have him address women's clubs, present prizes at high school athletic meets, and attend the Academy Awards.

Despite all this visibility, he continued his dangerous relationship with Scott. Mrs. Reginald Gardiner describes an episode which took place at the time Gardner was dating the actress Margot Grahame:

> One night, Margot was leaving the Mocambo nightclub very late. [She] saw two figures pressed close in the parking lot. With a shock, she suddenly realized that two men were kissing. The two men were Cary Grant and Randolph Scott.

In May, Phyllis was shooting the comedy *Straight Place and Show* with the manic Ritz Brothers, while Cary mysteriously turned up at certain social events with Dorothy Lamour. But this was only because Phyllis was working at night, and he could never resist going out. In her memoirs, Miss Lamour took great pains to make it clear that Cary never made the slightest attempt to seduce her. As it happened, Cary was already thinking seriously of marrying Phyllis. He told his friends the Hoagy Carmichaels, "I'm going to marry Brooksie and have all the children we can. That's what life's all about."

Murmurs of Fascism continued in Hollywood. On June 13, 1938, Edith Gwynn asked her readers: "Will that big M-G-M star explain why he posed with a swastika armband around his coat sleeve in Germany? The local [German-American] bund boasts of it!" She was probably referring to Wallace Beery, who had long been a suspected Nazi sympathizer. If, as seems possible, Cary was beginning his investigative work for British Intelligence, he cannot have failed to note this item and follow it up.

At the same time, Cary was preparing to shoot an adventure film, the classic *Gunga Din*, under the direction of the subdued, slow-speaking, part American Indian George Stevens. *Gunga Din* was, according to Cary's co-star Douglas Fairbanks, Jr., a thinly disguised attack on the Hitler regime, represented in the screenplay by the evil Indian guru played by Eduardo Ciannelli, and his cohorts. The plot, a mixture of *The Three Musketeers*, *The Front Page*, and Kipling's *Soldiers Three*, involved three tough sergeants of the Royal Engineers getting involved in Rover Boy heroics and adventurous antics on the North-West Frontier.

The movie started shooting on June 27 and finished on October 19. The final scenes were done in a desolate, windswept landscape at Lone Pine, where a fort had been laboriously constructed. The dusty conditions were unpleasant, and a ceaseless wind howled across the rocks, getting on everybody's nerves. Phyllis Brooks drove out to the location, pleasing Cary by her presence but greatly irritating Joan Fontaine, who was in turn frustrated by Cary's lack of romantic interest in her. Deliberate, precise, perfectionist, Stevens began to go seriously over budget and schedule, and the studio bosses were panic-stricken. Pandro S. Berman, who produced the film, recalls that he was especially irritated with Stevens because he had replaced Howard Hawks on the ground that Hawks had been very much behind on *Bringing Up Baby*. Now Stevens was proving just as bad. Yet Berman, suppressing his extreme nervousness and hypertensiveness, allowed Stevens to have his head. The result was a movie that was destined to be a colossal box-office success.

While *Gunga Din* was in progress, Cary, like the rest of the world, hung upon radio announcements of Howard Hughes's spectacular around-the-world flight which he began on July 10, 1938, in suffocating heat at Floyd Bennett Field in Brooklyn. Hughes stopped in Paris and then continued to Moscow, his progress delayed by a damaged rear landing strut. After flying over Siberia, skimming across terrifying mountain ranges, he at last reached Fairbanks, Alaska, returning over Pennsylvania to his final touchdown on July 14. He had achieved a world record in less than four days. He was welcomed in a ticker-tape parade through Manhattan; more than a million people yelled their greeting as he drove by with Mayor La Guardia. Cary, breaking off filming, was among the first to call him with urgent congratulations. Everyone on the set celebrated with champagne.

During the shooting, Phyllis Brooks remembers, Cary received an astonishing telegram: "It told him his mother was alive and had been released from the asylum. He was stunned but could not break off shooting to go see her." Is it possible that at the same time he was informed of the existence of his real mother: the Jewish woman who had given birth to him?* Circumstantial evidence to this effect may be deduced from the fact that at almost that exact time, Cary called Sam Jaffe aside and handed him a check for ten thousand dollars for the Jewish Refugee Fund, to assist Jews in escaping Hitler. He specifically told Jaffe that he did not want any mention made of his Jewish origins but that the gift was made in honor of his family. Jaffe was astonished but happily accepted the gift. There is a certain irony in the fact that when this money was handed over, Cary was acting in a scene with the anti-Semitic crypto-Fascist Victor McLaglen.

Gunga Din at last finished shooting after 115 grueling days. Cary, who had been very fretful, longing to leave on his dramatic journey to Britain, at last shook clear of the work and took off by plane to join the *Queen Mary* for Southampton.

---

* *In* Who's Who in America, *until 1962, he listed his mother's name not as Elsie but as Lillian Leach.*

SEVEN

What exactly took place during Cary's visit to England in November of 1938 remains a mystery. In view of subsequent events, it is most likely that after meeting Elsie Leach, he located his real mother, Lillian (?), who died soon after. In 1948, he would give money to the new state of Israel in the name of "My Dead Jewish Mother." In an oddly detached, calm, and almost resigned mood, he returned, from Le Havre, France, to New York on the *Normandie* on November 24, 1938. Phyllis Brooks, who had just finished making *Charlie Chan in Honolulu*, was in New York, staying with Dorothy di Frasso's brother, Bertram Taylor, and his wife, Olive. All three went to meet Cary off the ship. It was a joyful reunion, but Phyllis suddenly began to exhibit symptoms of influenza, which developed rapidly, until she was diagnosed as having double pneumonia. She had struggled out of bed to accompany Cary and the Taylors to the surrealist farce *Hellzapoppin*, and when she returned, her temperature was 105. She collapsed; she was given an injection of sulfanilamide. She was only the second person, she says, to have taken the drug; the first was Franklin D. Roosevelt, Jr. Fortunately, unlike Merle Oberon, who took the same drug shortly afterward and broke out into a devastating rash that threatened to destroy her beauty, Phyllis had no allergy; but her condition was still serious, and the drug did not work on her as well as she would have wished.

Cary was required to return to Hollywood immediately, for work on Howard Hawks's new picture *Pilot Number 4* (later retitled *Only Angels Have Wings*), in which he would play an intrepid flier not dissimilar to the character he had portrayed in *The Eagle and the Hawk*. With an extraordinary lack of consideration that was reminiscent of his behavior toward Virginia Cherrill, he insisted that Phyllis accompany him, though she was in no condition to do so, and in fact her doctors forbade the journey.

Extremely weak, and barely off the critical list, Phyllis was taken by train in an ambulance, lying on a stretcher. She was accompanied by a nurse. Her condition did not improve aboard the train, since the constant jolting of the carriage on the uneven roadbed made sleep virtually impossible. In those days, telegrams could be sent off a train. At Green River, Wyoming, Phyllis cabled her mother, telling her to be sure to arrange for a wheelchair to be in readiness when the train arrived in Los Angeles at 8:00 A.M. on December 14. Mrs. Steiller was furious with Cary for forcing her daughter to undertake this dangerous journey. Matters were not helped when a rainstorm burst upon the train as Cary lifted Phyllis in his arms to make his way down the steps, protected only by an umbrella carried by the nurse. Still very feverish, and back on the danger list, Phyllis was taken to her mother's home in West Los Angeles. It says much for her devotion to Cary that she didn't hold this episode against him. Her sturdy constitution put her back on her feet by early January.

Work on *Pilot Number 4* began. Cary was cast, for once, as a strong and dominating, Howard Hughes–like figure, and Hawks was at the top of his form as he directed the powerful action picture. He and the art director, Lionel Banks, effortlessly re-created a South American jungle town, Barranca, set at the foot of the Andes, in the confines of the Columbia studios. Rita Hayworth and Jean Arthur were Cary's fellow players. Both were far removed from their screen images: Miss Hayworth was subdued, shy, gentle; she had a sweet intelligence. Jean Arthur was so high-strung that she would sometimes vomit before coming on the set. Hawks's impatience with any form of hypersensitive behavior didn't help, but she proceeded to give one of her best performances. Cary liked her immensely, and she says she regarded working with him as a pleasure.

At the same time he was making *Pilot Number 4*, Cary was seeing a good deal of Dorothy di Frasso again. She gave him details of an astonishing voyage, which he had co-financed, taken by Bugsy Siegel, Marino Bello, Jean Harlow's stepfather, the British man-about-town Richard Gully, Harry (Champ) Segal, former ring manager and Bugsy's personal trainer, and several others, under the German shipmaster Robert Hoffman. Aboard the yacht *Metha Nelson*, they had sailed south along the California coast to Costa Rica, where they searched for buried treasure on legendary Coco Island. They found nothing except some rusty nails, moldy boots, and evidence of former treasure hunts. Annoyed that he had been shanghaied into this absurd expedition, Bugsy flew home from Guatemala; on the way back, Champ Segal clashed with the captain; when mutiny was threatened, Hoffman put two Jewish seamen in irons. Just as the situation seemed to be deteriorating beyond recall, the *Metha Nelson* was struck by a typhoon in the Gulf of Tehuantepec. Cary listened enthralled to this bizarre narrative. He didn't seem concerned that Bugsy Siegel was understood to be a dangerous and murderous gangster.

Martin Dies's House Committee on Un-American Activities was in town. Disgraced in later years for its excessive zeal against Communism which resulted in the infamous blacklist era, it was never given credit for its pursuit of Nazi sympathizers in California. Although many of the records are still classified, it is believed that Cary Grant testified before the committee, indicating where certain Fascist cells had begun to flourish. Simultaneously, he was appearing in a short-lived NBC radio show entitled *The Circle*. It was a lighthearted discussion program in which Cary played the Beadle, a jocular master of ceremonies. Among subsequent masters of ceremonies was Ronald Colman; Carole Lombard was on the panel. A more questionable member was Lawrence Tibbett, the opera star, whose politics leaned in the direction of Mussolini and Hitler. Noël Coward was also on the show; throughout January 1939 he was in Hollywood, staying with Cary at the same time he was working with the Deuxième Bureau, French Secret Intelligence, as a special agent, his activities disguised by the apparent frivolity of his character. From a statement made by telegram to the present authors by Sir William Stephenson, who was head of British Security Coordination (the equivalent of M.I.6, or the Secret Intelligence Service in the United States after mid-1940), Cary was working with Coward for the SIS. Cary presided over two broadcasts as the Beadle, the first on February 12, with Marian Anderson and Basil Rathbone, the second with John Gunther, author of *Inside Europe*, Tibbett, and Rathbone again. Groucho and Chico Marx were on several of the programs, providing comments from the Jewish point of view. *The Circle* was unpopular, and on July 9, 1939, a mere six months after Cary was forced to leave it because of the pressure of work on *Pilot Number 4*, it folded.

That summer, with war rapidly approaching in Europe, Cary and Phyllis were in New York. While there they received word of the excellent Hollywood previews and the advance reviews of *Only Angels Have Wings*. Phyllis sailed to England to make *Flying Squad*, co-starring Jack Hawkins. There was no trace of her illness by now, and she had never looked more beautiful when she set sail in May. Cary stayed on for a series of still-classified meetings in Washington, where he was issued a special diplomatic visa on June 12. He followed Phyllis to London on June 16; on board the *Normandie* he met Barbara Hutton, the Woolworth heiress, a hypersensitive, retiring, neurotic girl with a disastrous capacity to choose the wrong men. After his arrival in London, Cary slipped away to Bristol, where he tried persuading Elsie to come to America for safety. She declined, saying that she would stand with England, whether or not war broke out.

In July, Cary gave Phyllis a handsome diamond ring; they were now unofficially engaged. She didn't dare tell her mother. They took off for the south of France, drove through northern Italy and down to Rome, to stay with Dorothy di Frasso. They were overwhelmed by the Villa Madama, a huge wedding cake of a house, with its vast entrance hall, its display of Raphael paintings and its enormous swimming pool flanked by cypresses. It was supposed to have been built originally during the time of the Borgias. Di Frasso delighted in terrifying Phyllis with stories of hauntings by previous generations of owners, and one night Phyllis was startled when large double doors blew open, seemingly of their own accord. The countess told hilarious stories about Göring wallowing in her famous gold bathtub and Mussolini gobbling all the food at her table. Dorothy's diatribes against the Italian dictator convinced Cary that she was anti-Fascist. The Count di Frasso was around at the time, handsome and bland, unflustered by her apparently seditious remarks. He probably knew all too well what her real politics were.

Cary and Phyllis boarded the *Île de France* in Le Havre on August 7, only twenty-seven days before war broke out. They announced their engagement publicly for the first time in Manhattan. Their train ride to Hollywood was much happier than the previous one.

Cary began making *In Name Only*, again with Carole Lombard, a heavy-weight soap opera about a wealthy socialite who falls in love with an attractive woman when the wife who has married him for money proves increasingly cold. The story, which could have been the basis for an entertaining screwball farce, was turned into a sentimental melodrama, in which only Kay Francis as the unscrupulous wife seemed to be at home. Her somber, tearful presence lent a touch of distinction to an otherwise meaningless movie. Cary was much more comfortable in a (second) radio version of *The Awful Truth*, in which Phyllis Brooks excelled, and in which Claudette Colbert appeared.

That July, a significant partnership was formed in Hollywood. Alexander Korda, the gifted but erratic Hungarian producer, Douglas Fairbanks, Sr., Samuel Goldwyn, and Walter Wanger set up an organization in association with Korda's London Films that would, for the next seven years, be a front for M.I.6. Sir William Stephenson confirms that Cary Grant worked with this partnership to flush out Nazi sympathizers in California; nor can it be doubted that he found another major contact in Cecil B. DeMille, who used his production unit at Paramount and his *Lux Radio Theatre* as similar fronts. One of DeMille's agents, Charles Bennett, a writer for Alfred Hitchcock and others, has attested to this.

In August, Cary was in New York, on behalf of M.I.6. Noël Coward, his chief intelligence contact, had gone to London in July to confer with Sir Robert Vansittart, former undersecretary for foreign affairs and special adviser to the government on intelligence matters. Vansittart, who also used London Films as a cover, writing screenplays (he was among the many authors of the children's fantasy *The Thief of Bagdad*), was Korda's control in London.

War broke out on September 3, 1939. Deeply distressed but not surprised by the news, Cary was back in Hollywood with Phyllis. Twelve days later, he started work on *His Girl Friday*, an adaptation of *The Front Page*, directed by Howard Hawks and co-starring Rosalind Russell. In early October, local FBI agents Richard Hood and Frank Angell were busy investigating, as Edith Gwynn knowingly wrote, "a major studio in regard to the Nazi spy situation which [they] believe has a stronghold in that neck of town." The reference can only have been to Warner Bros., which, paradoxically, had just embarked upon a major anti-Nazi propaganda movie, *Confessions of a Nazi Spy*. Errol Flynn was already embroiled in Nazi activities, protecting his German friend Hermann F. Erben from federal agents' intensive investigations; Hood interrogated him repeatedly at the studio.

Erben had first interested Flynn in the Nazi cause in 1933, when, as a German Naval Intelligence agent in the South Pacific, he had indoctrinated the Australian actor aboard the North German Lloyd steamer *Friderun*. In England, Flynn had written passionately pro-Hitler letters, including one in which he stated that he would like to see the Führer in Britain to take care of the Jews. In 1937, Flynn had accompanied Erben to Spain during the civil war. Pretending to be bringing a large sum of money to the Loyalists in Barcelona, they in fact were seeking to undermine the Loyalist cause, and they obtained hundreds of photographs of Loyalist installations, trucks, and troop movements, delivering them to the German agent Bradish Johnson in Paris. When Erben delivered the pictures—some showing Flynn standing next to Loyalist gun emplacements—to German intelligence headquarters in Berlin, he was observed by Count Vejarano y Cassina, subsequently an alleged Nazi agent who would dupe Cary Grant.

On November 12, 1939, Alexander Korda arrived in Hollywood to continue work on *The Thief of Bagdad*, while he proceeded to coordinate M.I.6 arrangements in Los Angeles. The situation there was potentially dangerous, not only because of Nazi infiltration into the industry, which could be most effective in the event that England lost the war, but also because Los Angeles was a highly strategic region. At Santa Monica, the Douglas Aircraft Factory was turning out warplanes under the instructions of the Department of

Air in Washington and arming against possible attack from Japan, which at the time had entered into a tripartite agreement with Germany and Italy. Many of the most valuable American warships were docked at the San Diego Naval Base, as well as the San Pedro and Wilmington bases. Mexico was considered a potential danger to American security: Nazism was widespread in that country, and General Maximino Comacho, the president's brother, was known to have strong Fascist leanings. Correspondents of the *New York Times* and the *Washington Post* in Mexico City warned of the existence of a powerful Nazi cell operating inside a converted convent and running a radio station that beamed Hitlerian messages from coast to coast.

Cary Grant was not the only star enlisted in the British cause and issued a "special order" travel document RR, as mentioned in his files in Washington. David Niven was sent to New York to investigate a German agent. The actress Carmel Myers joined Korda's and the FBI's investigative group, along with her husband, the agent Ralph Blum. Samuel Goldwyn used his studios as a front for such figures as Merle Oberon, Mrs. Korda, who was working underground and would soon risk her life carrying messages to Europe in bombers. June Duprez, star of *The Thief of Bagdad*, was used as an informer.

On September 15, 1939, Cary was working on *His Girl Friday*, with Rosalind Russell, who proved to be one of the most adroit performers Cary had ever appeared with. Typically, he introduced into the script gags in which the names Archie Leach and Ralph Bellamy were mentioned. Howard Hawks was so enamored of his stars that he allowed them to ad-lib constantly. Toward the end of shooting, Cary introduced Frederick Brisson—who was working with Frank Vincent and was thus a junior partner of Cary's—to Miss Russell, who fell in love with him.

In the fall of 1939, Cary's relationship with Phyllis Brooks began to cool. He made the mistake of having a lawyer draw up a premarital contract, which provided that in the event of a divorce, he and Phyllis would make no demands on each other; it further stated that Phyllis's mother—called "very disruptive"—must never enter the Grants' home; and implied that it was time Phyllis gave up her career. Mrs. Steiller was furious. "She screamed for four days," Miss Brooks says. "It was a sad and dreadful time." There was no way that she could forbid her own mother to enter her house. Despite her protests, Cary wouldn't withdraw the agreement or relent in his attitude to Mrs. Steiller. Both Cary and Phyllis seemed to realize that they were making a dreadful mistake; there appeared to be no chance of a solution. Miss Brooks says:

I have sympathy for Cary in this matter, and I have sympathy for me as well. The prenuptial agreement undoubtedly did us in. Cary said to me, "I had one great love in my life, Virginia, then I found you. I knew that if anything ever happened to us I would be done. Most people never find one great love. I've had two. You are young enough to find another. I never will. See how all these threads knit together? I do."

Miss Brooks comments:

He was imperfect, as are all we mortals, but he was my love. He was careful, gentle, kind, tender, and fatherly to me. So far as I knew, he was a loving and passionate heterosexual. He had a very strict moral code as to loyalty, fidelity, and like virtues, and lived by them when I knew him.

The long relationship ended; the pain was intense for both. Ironically, Cary's next picture would be *My Favorite Wife*. It was begun, on December 3, by Leo McCarey, but a few days later he drove off in a drunken stupor from his house in Santa Monica, collided with another vehicle, and was badly injured, almost severing his right arm. He was replaced by Garson Kanin.

The sharp, energetic, twenty-seven-year-old Kanin instantly appealed to Cary. He was cynical and loquacious, far removed from the amiable, ambling McCarey. Kanin had been a vaudevillian and he expertly played the clarinet and the saxophone, two further attractions. This prodigious young man expertly took the reins. The movie, a reworking of the old chestnut *Enoch Arden*, was about a woman who, thought to be drowned at sea, returns to find her husband about to remarry. She sets out on an ambitious campaign to destroy the relationship. Leo McCarey, who had written the screenplay with the husband-and-wife team Samuel and Bella Spewack, daringly included more than one sly reference to the Grant-Scott relationship. In a revealing sequence, Nick Arden, played by Grant, goes to a swimming pool to cast eyes on his chief rival for his returned wife's affections, Burkett, played by Scott. Seeing Scott on a diving board, looking rather like Johnny Weissmuller's Tarzan, the character should normally have reacted with dismay at seeing what he was up against. But Cary's eyes lit up at the spectacle; and later, in his office, Nick Arden is shown unable to work, haunted by the vision of Burkett in swimming trunks on what appears to be a kind of trapeze. Bert Granet, who was the script supervisor on the picture, recalls:

We shot the pool sequence at the Huntington Hotel at Pasadena. Cary and Randy Scott arrived as a pair and, to the total astonishment of myself, the director, and the ultra-macho film crew, instead of taking separate suites moved into the same *room* together. Everyone looked at everyone else. It seemed hardly believable.

The staid Irene Dunne seemed oblivious to what was going on around her. She gave one of her best performances; she was especially appealing in a scene in which the wife returns from Southeast Asia to observe her children splashing in the pool; she has left them as babies, and, some seven years later, they no longer recognize her.

Cary took a break from shooting to appear as Romeo opposite Irene Dunne's Juliet on the radio *Silver Theatre*. He also broke off work to attend the funeral of Douglas Fairbanks, on December 10, 1939. The star's death was a great loss to him. Cary had never forgotten his first encounter with Fairbanks and Mary Pickford aboard the *Olympic* in 1920, or their countless meetings since.

With characteristic professionalism, Grant returned to work the following day, playing an antic sequence in a honeymoon hotel, in which he assumed female guise.

During the shooting, Cecil B. DeMille offered Cary one of the

A very young Archie Leach (Culver Pictures, Inc.)

Archie Leach, age six, in theater costume (Roy Moseley collection)

Robert Lomas, Archie Leach's mentor, in clown costume (*Pall Mall Magazine*, January 1910)

Archie Leach in *A Wonderful Night*, 1931

Randolph Scott and Cary Grant at their Griffith Park home, Los Angeles, 1932 (Roy Moseley collection)

Grant and Scott preparing dinner in their Griffith Park home, Los Angeles, 1932 (Roy Moseley collection)

Grant in the mid-1930s (Charles Higham collection)

Cary Grant and Virginia Cherrill at the
Academy Awards dinner, 1934 (AP/Wide
World Photos)

Cary and his first wife, Virginia Cherrill,
returning from their honeymoon (AP/Wide
World Photos)

Grant with Sylvia Sidney in the 1930s
(Charles Higham collection)

Grant with Phyllis Brooks, the love of his life,
1938 (Phyllis Brooks Macdonald collection)

Randolph Scott and Phyllis Brooks with
Grant at a boxing match in the late 1930s
(Phyllis Brooks Macdonald collection)

Grant in Bristol with a group of admirers,
1939 (Keith Blackmore collection)

Ted Donaldson with Grant, 1943 (Ted Donaldson collection)

Mr. and Mrs. Cary Grant (Barbara Hutton) with Randolph Scott at the premiere of *Talk of the Town* (AP/Wide World Photos)

Cary Grant with second wife, Barbara Hutton, at their wedding. With them are Frank Vincent and Madeline Hazeltine (AP/Wide World Photos)

Cary Grant with wife number three, Betsy Drake, hours before the wedding, 1949 (AP/Wide World Photos)

Betsy says goodbye to Cary, as he leaves for Prague (AP/Wide World Photos)

Cary Grant aboard ship with wife Betsy Drake and *To Catch a Thief* co-star, Grace Kelly (AP/Wide World Photos)

Cary Grant and Sophia Loren dance the cha-cha between takes of *The Pride and the Passion*, 1956 (AP/Wide World Photos)

Cary Grant and Betsy Drake just before announcing the first of many separations, 1957 (AP/Wide World Photos)

principal roles in a patriotic epic of Canada, *North West Mounted Police*. But Cary disliked the part as written, and gently declined it.

There was no woman in his life at that time; the relationship with Scott continued, and for the gossips' sake he dated the actress Louise Stanley and Rosalind Russell, as well as Fay Wray. She had divorced John Monk Saunders who would commit suicide soon after, hanging himself with a necktie. Miss Wray cohosted Cary's elaborate party on Christmas Day. Both then and at a New Year's Eve event, he tried vainly to contact Elsie in Bristol (the wartime telephone connections were appalling). On New Year's Eve, Phyllis Brooks turned up unexpectedly and in a restless mood; close to 5:00 A.M., she had a fight with the feisty Australian actress Constance Worth, former wife of George Brent.

In February, Cary was at the housewarming Douglas and Mary Fairbanks gave for Westridge House, the handsome Pacific Palisades home they had just bought from the Italian-born actress Elissa Landi, who had ruined herself financially by excessive party-giving. On January 18, Cary and Constance Moore—a new friend, whose talents as a band vocalist and radio singer matched her gifts as an actress, and who was married to the popular agent Johnny Maschio—celebrated their joint birthday at a shindig at Cary's house. Phyllis Brooks again turned up uninvited. Edith Gwynn wrote: "Cary would not allow his former girlfriend . . . to touch as much as an eyedropperful." That same week, Phyllis was seen dancing with Frederick Brisson in several night spots.

My Favorite Wife ended shooting on February 11; the same night, Cary substituted for William Powell on short notice, giving a much-admired performance on the *Radio Guild Air Show*.

That month, a new visitor in town was causing a sensation, which never leaked into the press. Hilda Krueger, who was allegedly a former girlfriend of Dr. Joseph Goebbels, the Jewish radio executive Donald Flamm, and J. Paul Getty, among other oddly assorted figures of society, was presently enjoying a relationship with Errol Flynn. The FBI had her under surveillance as a suspected Nazi agent or sympathizer, tapping her phone calls, searching her luggage, and tracking her on her visits to German consuls Fritz Wiedemann in San Francisco and George Gyssling in Los Angeles. Whether Cary was among the several Hollywood personalities keeping an eye on Hilda Krueger's behavior is uncertain; in view of his position with M.I.6, he probably was. Among those specifically delegated to watch her was Cary's close friend Reginald Gardiner, the accomplished English comedian. Because of his polished, sophisticated, but not particularly intellectual personality, Gardiner was beyond suspicion. Becoming Krueger's lover, he examined her papers (at one point, he accused her point-blank of Nazi connections). In his reports to the FBI, he stated that she was the most dangerous German agent in the United States. June Duprez, Marlene Dietrich, and Carmel Myers also reported on Krueger, who denies she was a Nazi spy.

On March 16, 1940, Cary took the freighter *Tampa* to Cristobal, Canal Zone, where he switched to the *Santa Elena*, arriving in New York on April 2. The passenger manifest shows he was on "special orders"—i.e., British government secret service—Travel Document RR 98872/178/99. He met Alexander Korda in Manhattan, and they flew to London by bomber, returning the same way. On April 22, Cary began work on *The Howards of Virginia*, shooting in Randolph Scott's home territory and later in northern California and at the Columbia studios in Hollywood. He played Matt Howard, a friend of President Thomas Jefferson. The inconsequential script by Sidney Buchman and the unenterprising direction of Frank Lloyd were notably uninspiring to Cary, who gave one of his worst performances.

In May, back in Hollywood, Cary again conferred with Korda on what must have been secret intelligence matters. At this time, he renewed his acquaintance with Barbara Hutton. Born in New York on November 14, 1912, Barbara was the daughter of Franklyn Laws Hutton and the former Edna Woolworth. Her mother died when Barbara was five, leaving her about sixty million dollars. As a child, she was surrounded by bodyguards; she was pampered, sheltered, fat, and miserable. Her New York debut in 1930 was the social event of the season and cost her father fifty thousand dollars.

Paranoid, fearful, cut apart by surgeons, she was at the same time gentle, sweet-natured, and poetic: she even published a volume of verse, at her own expense. At twenty, she had married "Prince" Alexis Mdivani, one of the "marrying Mdivani" brothers, whose princedom consisted of a pig farm in Georgia, Russia. He received one million dollars as a stud fee at the time of the wedding. Franklyn Hutton commented, "You know the old saying: One can't choose one's relations."

In 1935, announcing that her husband "threw money around like confetti . . . you know these titled foreigners," she divorced Mdivani, announcing that she would never marry again. Next day, she married the Danish Count Court Haugwitz Hardenberg Reventlow. (A year later, Alexis Mdivani was killed in a car crash.) On February 24, 1936, her son Lance was born; in 1937, Miss Hutton renounced her citizenship and became a Dane. The marriage to Reventlow was no better than that to Mdivani. There were constant quarrels over Lance, and the couple separated. When she met Cary again, Miss Hutton had just returned with Dorothy di Frasso from a vacation on Windward Island, Chris R. Holmes's private atoll near Waikiki. Barbara was unhappy; an unsatisfactory relationship with the British golfer Robert Sweeny had recently burned out; she was drifting from one social event to another. Sensitive, deeply insecure, she obtained no happiness from her great wealth. City after city, resort after resort failed to satisfy her. Miserable, she was looking for a new romantic relationship, and Dorothy di Frasso, who delighted in matchmaking, reintroduced her to Cary at a party at her house. Cary and Barbara had seen each other during his long relationship with Phyllis Brooks, but there was no evidence of any attraction between them.

As it happened, there was no attraction now. Nevertheless, they liked each other and began going out to nightclubs and restaurants, including the Trocadero, the Mocambo, and the newly popular Victor Hugo, owned by William R. Wilkerson. Cary was still living at the beach house with Randolph Scott, but this did not seem to bother Miss Hutton, who decided to stay in Hollywood. She sublet Buster Keaton's mansion at 1004 Hartford Way, in Beverly Hills. It was an Italianate villa with thirty rooms, terraces that had been landscaped by a gardener who worked for Pope Pius XII, a thirty-foot Romanesque swimming pool, flanked by classical nude statues, and a brook stocked with trout, which the servants would catch and the cook prepare for dinner. There were three tennis courts and fifteen acres of lawns and flower bushes.

When the columnists began buzzing over them, Cary and Barbara started to restrict themselves to friends' or their own houses. Barbara rejected the advances of a young Frank Sinatra in order to spend most of her time with Cary. He began giving parties at her villa, at which she appeared as a somewhat reluctant hostess. The Kordas, Dietrich, Rosalind Russell and Frederick Brisson, Constance Moore and Johnny Maschio, and Jimmy Stewart were among the frequent guests. These expensive soirees failed to appease Barbara's restless, dark spirit. She brooded constantly, and her temper was not improved when Cary proved reluctant to appear at parties she gave for her own circle of friends. Again, there is no indication that theirs was a sexual relationship; indeed, Miss Hutton, who was covered with internal and external scars from her serious operations, and who suffered from very delicate health, appears to have had little interest in any form of physical liaison. She was concerned at the time about the fate of her close friend, the handsome tennis champion Baron Gottfried von Cramm, who had recently been imprisoned by the German government for homosexuality, and she was also struggling with Count Reventlow for custody of their son. Cary became a surrogate father for Lance, working out his frustrated paternal instinct in a deeply felt relationship with the four-year-old boy. He gave him gifts, played ball and bicycled with him, and joined Barbara in assailing Reventlow, who FBI documents allege was a serious Nazi sympathizer. On May 25, Douglas and Mary Fairbanks entertained Cary and Barbara at another big party at Westridge House. Phyllis Brooks arrived as Randolph Scott's date for the evening, which caused much amused comment in the columns.

The group that included Alexander Korda, Walter Wanger, Samuel Goldwyn, and Cary Grant was continuing to conduct its investigations into untoward political activities in Hollywood. Since William R. Wilkerson was a chief contact for the group and for the FBI, his wife would provide little glimpses of her husband's activities in her column. In view of the secrecy of the operation, this was exceedingly ill-advised but she seemed to have no scruple in pursuing her journalistic activities. On May 25, she reported: "Fifth column investigations going on in the studios will be a secret, with only the producer group behind them, and the FBI getting the responses as they come in." Four days later, the group was reported to have determined that 85 percent of the German servants in the movie colony accepted the direct orders of the German-American bund.

Noël Coward, who was still involved in activities for Free French Secret Intelligence, again moved in as Cary's houseguest on June 9. Apparently, Edith Gwynn's disclosure of this fact blew the spy cover of both of them; a few days later, they staged a quarrel, which they made sure she included in the *Hollywood Reporter*, and Coward moved out. Principal photography on *The Howards of Virginia* was completed on June 24. It had dragged on for an unconscionably long time, and turned out to be a disaster for all concerned.

On June 20, W. S. (later Sir William) Stephenson, who worked directly with Sir Stewart Menzies and Sir Robert Vansittart for British Intelligence in Whitehall, arrived in New York aboard the *Britannic*. He set up as a British passport control officer, with offices at Rockefeller Plaza. During the next few weeks, he began organizing a complex system of spies, calling his organization, for want of a better term, British Security Coordination. BSC was now the center of M.I.6 operations in North and South America. Stephenson has confirmed Grant's precise role as a key figure of BSC: along with Alexander Korda and others, he was a special link with Noël Coward, who would be traveling through Latin America and the South Pacific on BSC business. Like Cary, Coward would be the last person anyone would suspect of espionage. Among those whom Cary specifically investigated was Barbara Hutton, who was in contact with Nazi Germany in the interests of Baron von Cramm. Her mail was intercepted and sent to FBI headquarters for inspection and filing. Since it is doubtful the FBI could successfully have organized a plant in her own household, the most likely person to have forwarded her mail to the authorities was Cary himself.

At the same time, Alexander Korda was in Lisbon, setting up his own M.I.6 organization there; among others, Vivien Leigh, Beatrice Lillie, and Leslie Howard would assist him in that region during the war years.

Cary flew to New York at the time to confer with Stephenson, then continued through a severe thunderstorm to Washington, where he met the British ambassador, Lord Lothian, along with the director and writer Herbert Wilcox, the actors Brian Aherne and Sir

Cedric Hardwicke, and other British exiles. Told to continue his film work rather than enter war service in England, he returned to Hollywood.

There was reason to investigate Nazis in Hollywood that July. Werner Plack, an alleged Nazi agent and member of Dr. Goebbels's staff in Berlin, was in town under the guise of being a champagne salesman, a job originally occupied by German Foreign Minister Joachim von Ribbentrop. Sy Bartlett, a White Russian Hollywood producer, had a fistfight with Plack at the Café la Maze, accusing him point-blank of being a German spy, and forcing Plack to flee the country. At the same time, Errol Flynn was going around town with his Nazi friend Hermann Erben, who had the nerve to appear in German uniform, with a Hitler mustache. And this at a time when for any British citizen or subject to associate with an enemy of Great Britain amounted to treason. So complete was Flynn's power as a film star that nothing seemed to affect his popularity, even in a movie colony dominated by Jews. When Flynn traveled to South America that summer, he was asked by various U.S. ambassadors or consuls to comment on Erben's activities. In every case, he protected him, pretending that Erben was a Jewish refugee and a harmless eccentric. He was supposed to be reporting on Fascism in South America for *Collier's* magazine, a device that enabled him to be in touch with Nazis in Mexico City without exciting suspicion.

Cary at this time was shooting *The Philadelphia Story* with Katharine Hepburn and James Stewart, under the accomplished direction of George Cukor. Howard Hughes had secretly obtained the rights to the Philip Barry play for Miss Hepburn, and she in turn, after appearing triumphantly on the stage in the central role of Tracy Lord, had sold the property to Louis B. Mayer at M-G-M. Cary was cast as C. K. Dexter Haven, a wealthy socialite who sponsors reporter Macaulay Connor (Stewart) and camera assistant Liz Imbrie (Ruth Hussey) as they invade Tracy Lord's Main Line Philadelphia estate. The complicated story of intrigue, double-cross, and romantic misadventure provided Cary with a marvelous opportunity. He proved an admirable match for Miss Hepburn's emotionally repressed, highly theatrical heiress.

The cameraman on the picture, Joseph Ruttenberg recalled:

Everyone had enormous fun on the movie. The days and nights were sweltering that summer of 1940, but nobody cared. Cary got along very well with Kate Hepburn. She enjoyed him pushing her through a doorway in one scene [so she fell over backward], so much that she had him do it to her over and over again. There was a scene in which she had to throw Cary out the door of a house, bag and baggage, and she did it so vigorously he fell over and was bruised. As he stood up, looking rueful, Kate said, "That'll serve you right, Cary, for trying to be your own stuntman!"

Hepburn, Grant, and Stewart were determined to play a practical joke on Cukor. The fussy director preferred a very quiet set. One morning, Cary arranged for every crew member to make as much noise as possible, shouting, hammering, sawing planks of wood. Cukor was furious; he walked off to collect his temper. By prearrangement with Cary, Miss Hepburn put up her hand and the noise stopped. Then she signaled her fellow players, and the entire crew, to follow her up to the flies above the soundstage. When Cukor returned, the stage was deserted. He thought he must have gone mad, or wandered onto the wrong stage. As he turned to leave, severely puzzled, Miss Hepburn and Cary gave a signal, and all seventy people in the flies shouted, very loudly, "*Quiet!*"

During the shooting, Cary was preoccupied by work at the Frank Vincent Agency, which helped to renegotiate a deal for Garbo at M-G-M and a new contract for Rita Hayworth at 20th Century–Fox, beginning with the film *Blood and Sand*, which Cary had been scheduled to make for Paramount in 1933. He advanced the career of Brian Donlevy, greatly improving his Paramount contract. Marlene Dietrich's Warner Bros. contract the following year would owe much to his influence: he helped organize her special loan-out from Universal to Warners for *Manpower*. The stars concerned still did not know that he was meeting with Vincent to assist them professionally. He refurbished the agency's offices on Sunset Boulevard, which became, under his guidance, the most luxurious in Hollywood, with antique furniture, deep carpets, fine oak paneling. A butler would greet important clients or guests, and a waiter in uniform would serve them in the penthouse.

Cary gave his salary for *The Philadelphia Story*, $175,000, to British War Relief and the Red Cross. He was distracted during the making of the film by word of the bombing of England by the German Air Force. He was concerned about Elsie, and he also must have been distressed by the dangerous conditions in which his friend and associate in M.I.6, Alexander Korda, and Mrs. Korda, Merle Oberon, were flying across the North Atlantic to bring information about American appeasement to the headquarters of the organization and Sir Robert Vansittart in London. Virginia Cherrill, now the Countess of Jersey, was in town following a rough voyage across U-boat-infested waters. She was pregnant, and she had been evacuated to the United States by ship with Somerset Maugham's daughter Liza. Landing in Montreal on July 4, she traveled to New York, where she had a miscarriage brought on by her long and difficult journey. She proceeded to Hollywood, where she saw a good deal of Cary. They were friendly now; Virginia had set aside much of her bitterness. She appeared at social event after social event, escorted by a number of eligible bachelors. But she was devoted and faithful to her husband; her chief concern was to get back to London and help with the war effort. It took her some months to obtain permission from the authorities to take the Pan American clipper to Lisbon.

Phyllis Brooks was in Hollywood at the time; she says today that she continued to love Cary and deeply regretted the termination of their relationship. The pain of seeing him so often at different nightclubs, frequently with Barbara Hutton, was too intense for her to bear. By September, she had left Los Angeles for New York, happy to accept a part in Cole Porter's *Panama Hattie* in order to liberate herself from an impossible situation.

That summer, Noël Coward returned to Hollywood and again stayed with Cary, planning trips to South America and to Australia on behalf of M.I.6. Cary would give people the impression that Coward was simply a houseguest who was preparing for his concert tours. Coward in fact used his nightclub and restaurant act, singing his amusing songs, telling his witty stories, as a front for his activities as a secret agent reporting on pro-Nazi activities in the Southern Hemisphere. Coward said in an interview with the author William

Stevenson for *A Man Called Intrepid* (New York: Harcourt Brace Jovanovich, 1979):

> I was fluent in Spanish and could "do" the whole of Latin America, where the Germans were very active preparing their campaigns in the United States. And so that's where I started. . . . I reported directly to Bill Stephenson while I sang my songs and spoke nicely to my hosts. A whole lot of tiny things are the stuff of Intelligence. Smallest details fit into a big picture, and sometimes you repeat things and wonder if it's worth it.

Thus, Coward was in fact spying not only on South Americans but North Americans as well. Cary, in a statement made to Ray Austin, his assistant, chauffeur, and closest friend, some twenty years later, spoke of how he and Coward would mix as much as possible in the Hollywood community, determining who was dangerous and who was not.

To protect Coward in case any German agent should penetrate his activities, Winston Churchill let it be known on the grapevine that the entertainer had been dismissed from M.I.6 because he sought to publicize his activities as an agent; this absurdity was swallowed not only by the Germans but by British journalists, who were encouraged to print it in their columns.

While Noël Coward was in Los Angeles, his collection of playlets, *Tonight at 8:30*, which Cary had enjoyed so much in London six years earlier, opened with an all-star cast that included Joan Fontaine in *Family Album*, Judith Anderson and Isabel Jeans in *Hands Across the Table*, and Roland Young in *Fumed Oak*. Following the premiere, William R. Wilkerson and Edith Gwynn hosted an elaborate party at Ciro's, which they owned. Even Garbo turned up; Frederick Brisson and Rosalind Russell were there, and so were Alexander and Merle Korda, back from one of their perilous missions, and Johnny Maschio and Constance Moore. But there were notable absentees on this supremely patriotic occasion: Errol Flynn was not present, nor, oddly enough, were the Cary Grants. Cary's motive in not appearing might be interpreted as an ingenious method of supporting the widespread belief that he was opposed to the war effort and was failing to help it in any way. It is also possible that Barbara Hutton was having one of her nervous attacks and that he stayed home with her.

That August and September, Cary renewed his earlier warm acquaintance with the mischievous Alfred Hitchcock, who was staying with his diminutive wife Alma at the Korda house while they looked for a suitable residence. Hitchcock started work on September 5 on an uncharacteristic comedy, *Mr. and Mrs. Smith*. Meanwhile, Korda was busy preparing sets for *Lady Hamilton*, called in the United States *That Hamilton Woman*, the story of the ill-fated mistress of Lord Nelson. The legendary story would be used as a thin disguise for a propaganda attack on Hitler, represented in the movie by Napoleon, poised to strike against the British on the other side of the English Channel. Cary was delighted to renew his acquaintance with Vivien Leigh and Laurence Olivier, co-stars of the Korda production.

Clifford Odets, a reigning playwright of the American stage, was in town that season, following a stormy protracted divorce from Luise Rainer and a disastrous relationship with Frances Farmer. Author of a string of highly praised plays written under the aegis of the Group Theatre, he had recently scored a great success with *Golden Boy* (which was filmed in 1940 with the twenty-two-year-old William Holden). Tall, dark, brooding, capable of flashes of wit and charm, but more often morose, difficult, and profoundly introverted, Odets fascinated Cary as few men had ever done. He was the first serious intellectual with whom Cary had come in touch. Odets was well read in a number of different cultures; he had a commanding knowledge of music and painting; he had a fluent, sometimes pretentious, but always stimulating line of speech. Peering through scholarly spectacles, he would rivet people but then exhaust them with his excessive knowledge, which made them feel uncomfortable. He was in every possible way out of place in the movie community. Yet his hunger for the bodies of beautiful young girls was insatiable, as burning and fierce as his talent in its demands upon him. At the age of thirty-four, he was at the height of his physical strength and of his power as a dramatist, and few women could resist his fame, his looks, and his lean, athletic physique.

Odets would remain the one human being who reached into Cary's soul and understood it. Clifford Odet's son Walt comments upon his father's relationship with Cary. In conversation, he told Charles Higham:

Although I do not believe they had a physical relationship, I think I am right in saying that they had an intense love for each other. My father was also bisexual, and I know he and Cary discussed this. Also, it tortured both of them. Yet at the same time, whereas my father was extremely repressed in private, never revealing anything of the other side of his nature, Cary often acted quite overtly effeminate in our home, startling me and my sister. Of course, I'm talking about years later; I wasn't born until the late 1940s.

Some part of my father—that part of himself which came from his very ambitious, immigrant father—clearly aspired to be Cary Grant, so to speak. This is partly what kept him in Los Angeles hanging out with movie people. Cary, on the other hand, must have aspired in some serious way to be like my father. . . . Both men seem to have been quite conflicted and pained about . . . private parts of themselves. This was one of the reasons their friendship was often difficult; each was especially sensitive to the other's expectations, because those expectations also came from within.

Although it would be several years before they would work together, they remained in touch even when Odets was in New York and even though their politics were in opposition. Odets was a creature of the traditional left, Cary still a died-in-the-wool Republican.

Cary continued to associate with Dorothy di Frasso. He seemed unwilling to reveal to anyone that her purpose in coming to Hollywood was to use it as a point of departure for Mexico, where she was engaged upon a highly questionable enterprise—financing an explosive device which she and Bugsy Siegel hoped to sell to the Italian government. Was he only pretending to support the Countess, while in fact really investigating her and her activities?

On October 10, 1940, Cary began work on a new film, *Penny*

Serenade, with Irene Dunne, directed by George Stevens. It was the story of a young couple, a journalist and his sensitive, good-natured wife, who struggle against poverty in the United States and Japan. Following an earthquake in Tokyo, the wife suffers a miscarriage and the couple return to New York. They adopt a child only to lose it in tragic circumstances. The parallels with Cary Grant's life are startling: Elsie's loss of her first baby, Barbara Hutton's long-unsatisfied hunger for a child following postnatal problems after Lance's birth, and Cary's own penurious origins all provided potent echoes of present and past. Stevens's delicate craftsmanship animated what could have been an intolerable soap opera. The story, told in flashback as the unhappy wife plays a series of phonograph records that evoke the past, the circular trademark labels irising out into remembered heartbreaking images, ensured a magical surface of effects. Cary's feckless, unreliable charmer provided an ideal foil for Irene Dunne's exquisitely acted, purehearted wife. Cary's acting was so expert that a few months later he was nominated for his first Academy Award.

On November 18, the Countess di Frasso threw a birthday party for Barbara Hutton, co-hosted by Cary and attended by Douglas and Mary Lee Fairbanks, Ronald and Benita Colman, Jack and Ann Warner, and Darryl and Virginia Zanuck. The party was also a farewell bash for Virginia Cherrill, who left for New York and Lisbon on November 24. Three days later, the Associated Press reported that Mussolini had paid the Countess di Frasso two million dollars for the Villa Madama; at the same time she was complaining loudly that the Italian government had expropriated the residence.

Barbara Hutton flew to Charleston, South Carolina, on November 27 to see her ailing father, Franklyn Hutton. Cary, unable to travel because of additional scenes for *Penny Serenade*, sent sympathetic get-well messages with her. For years an alcoholic, Franklyn Laws Hutton was stricken at sixty-three with cirrhosis of the liver. He died on December 2, and, despite Barbara's last-minute flight to his bedside, he expressed his disapproval of what he thought to be an affair with Cary Grant by cutting her out of his will. She of course had considerable sums, over $200 million, under the terms of her mother's estate, but the decision was still a bitter blow, and she sued trustees for $530,000 plus five percent accrued interest, indicating that she had lent substantial amounts to her father over the years. Irene Hutton, her stepmother, repaid the debt in full.

At the same time, Barbara was involved in complicated arrangements in order to secure her divorce from Count Reventlow in Denmark. As a Danish citizen, she was not morally entitled to make deals with the occupying Nazi government. The Copenhagen courts were, of course, under German jurisdiction. A spokesman for Miss Hutton in New York made the unfortunate and much-quoted remark: "Hitler Blitzkrieg or no Hitler Blitzkrieg, Barbara's divorce will come through according to Hoyle." Neither the U.S. State Department nor the Federal Bureau of Investigation was at all happy about her dealings with America's potential enemy, and a substantial file was opened on Miss Hutton. There was still no serious indication that she and Cary would be married when her divorce became final.

Barbara was depressed that Christmas of 1940, not only by her father's death but by a close friend's fatal injuries in an car accident. She was under a cloud, and Cary went alone to a party at Dorothy di Frasso's where a boxing ring, erected on the lawn, featured a series of brutal fights in which ancient retired boxers beat each other to a pulp while everybody screamed with delight. Occasionally, she would surface from her bleak mood to give a party. She would retreat into her shell when guests stupidly asked her how she felt to be the heiress to her father's fortune; although she never snapped back with the statement that he had left her nothing, Barbara was seriously embarrassed by discussions of money and hated it when people said, "You're quite a nice gal, even with all that cash" or "For all that money, you're quite normal." At times she would display some wit. One night, at a dinner party, with Cary at her side, someone asked her, "How does it feel to have so much money?" She replied, with deadly swiftness, "It's terrific." The smile froze on her inquirer's face.

Barbara began to entertain only very intimate groups; she had to be sure she knew every guest, no one was allowed to bring a stranger. She refused to talk to the press, because she was irritated by constant mentions of her forthcoming nuptials. And of course, since

Cary was involved in secret war work, it was essential that she keep the lowest possible profile and make sure that no strangers entered the house.

After several weeks of reclusiveness, and giving no major parties, Barbara, contradictory as always, spent a fortune on Cary's birthday event in 1941. Constance Moore, also born on January 18, was honored as well. The walls and ceiling of the house were draped with hundreds of yards of white satin, while the pool was surrounded with beautifully set tables displaying flourishes of dark red roses. The waiters were in red and white; the champagne flowed freely; and two bands played dance music until the sun began to gleam on the palm trees and tropical shrubs. Barbara was dazzling in a gold Chinese formal dress and a blaze of emeralds; Cary was resplendent in white tie and tails. It was an evening to remember, but soon after it Barbara slipped back into seclusion.

EIGHT

Cary's winter was brightened by the extraordinary reviews for *The Philadelphia Story*, which had opened just after Christmas at Radio City Music Hall. Bosley Crowther had written in the *New York Times*:

> All those folks who wrote Santa Claus asking him to send them a sleek new custom-built comedy with fast lines and the very finest in Hollywood fittings got their wish just one day late with the opening of *The Philadelphia Story* yesterday. . . . This [movie] has just about everything that a Blue Chip comedy should have . . . and a splendid cast of performers headed by Katharine Hepburn, James Stewart and Cary Grant [who] is warmly congenial as the cast-off but undefeated mate.

Glowing from the public's response to the picture, ideal escapist fare when war threatened, Cary cheerfully said farewell to Noël Coward on January 19, 1941, as Coward set off for Australia, fully briefed by William Stephenson for his dangerous mission under the guise of a concert tour. His messages from the Antipodes were relayed via Cary to Stephenson's British Security Coordination operation at Rockefeller Center.

In the course of his paradoxical career, Cary not only was working in consultation with Stephenson, but at the same time he was in close touch with Bugsy Siegel. In the summer of 1940, Siegel, much to the distress of Dorothy di Frasso, had been indicted for the murder of the gangster "Big Greenie" Greenberg. On August 16, police found Siegel hiding in the attic of his Bel Air estate. He was imprisoned in the county jail in downtown Los Angeles. A Smith & Wesson .38 revolver and a .38 Colt automatic were found in Bugsy's strongbox. On December 11, Assistant District Attorney Vernon Ferguson moved for the dismissal of the indictment, and John Dockweiler, the newly elected D.A., also brought influence to bear. Journalist Florabel Muir disclosed in her column that Siegel had contributed thirty thousand dollars to the Dockweiler campaign. Bugsy was released; within minutes, he was on his way to his friend George Raft's house in Coldwater Canyon. Wielding a gun, he charged Raft with having informed on him because he claimed that Raft was interested in Bugsy's girlfriend, Wendy Barrie.

Almost as though he wanted to give Siegel some respectability, Cary invited him to various parties and encouraged him to strike a new figure in society as a dandy, wearing handsome shirts, suitings, and silk pocket handkerchiefs. Siegel and di Frasso were seen often at Barbara Hutton's mansion or Cary's beach house.

At the same time, Cary began work on *Suspicion* for Alfred Hitchcock. Based upon Francis Iles's novel *Before the Fact*, the movie had been planned for years, firstly with Louis Hayward as the star, and then with Robert Montgomery and Laurence Olivier. It was the story of a disreputable, lying, and treacherous husband whose charming self-indulgences at the racetrack succeed in squandering his new wife's insubstantial savings. Johnny Aysgarth was the sort of superficial, winning scoundrel Cary Grant could play in his sleep. The more difficult role was that of the wife, whose original naïveté had to be seen to be eroded until at last she is convinced that her husband has killed his best friend. The ending was never correctly resolved. In fact, the one finally imposed by RKO, the producing studio, was absurd: Aysgarth turns out to be innocent of any crime, his wife's terror totally unfounded.

The shooting began on February 10, 1941. Cary was again not impressed with Joan Fontaine, who had appeared with him in *Gunga*

Din. Like her character in the film, she was unhappily married. Her husband, Brian Aherne, showed her little affection. Her life resembled the plot of *Rebecca*, in which she had acted with great success; she was troubled by the presence in her home not of an imposing housekeeper but of a menacing butler. And Aherne seemed still to be in love with his former mistress, the actress Claire Eames who had died young. Living the plot of another movie while making this one was extremely distracting to Miss Fontaine, and Hitchcock knew exactly how to use her disquiet.

But he could not foresee her temperamental behavior or her repeated absences from the set on the grounds of illness. Cary was irritated by what he wrongly felt to be her fancied sickness; professional to the core, and impatient of star tantrums and real or imagined ailments, he wanted to get on with the job and finish it with the least number of delays or aggravations. Cary was in a foul temper by the time the picture was finished. He tried to appease himself by going to boxing matches with Barbara, attending a reception given by Dietrich for the newly arrived German author Erich Maria Remarque at her Beverly Hills Hotel bungalow, and going to a farewell party for Dorothy di Frasso, who left for Mexico with Ann Warner and Mrs. Charles Feldman on board the *America* on March 26. In Mexico City, the FBI undertook its most intense surveillance of the countess. Among the houseguests at her apartment was Richard Gully, Anthony Eden's cousin, who was the social secretary to Jack Warner and a well-known Hollywood man-about-town. Gully recalls that he and the countess were watched day and night. One of the intelligence agents in Mexico was the motion picture actor Eddie Albert, while the actress Rochelle Hudson acted as liaison for U.S. Naval Intelligence. When Hilda Krueger moved to Mexico, and when the allegedly dangerous Maximino Camacho, brother of the president, came to stay with Tyrone Power in Hollywood, the surveillance intensified.

After the completion of *Suspicion*, Cary was intent on taking a well-needed rest; but he was called to London on a special mission, flying there by bomber with Alexander Korda. When he returned in May, he turned down a role in the film *Bedtime Story*, opposite Loretta Young, and also a part in *Joan of Paris*, with Michelle Morgan.

He very much wanted the role of the irascible, Alexander Woollcott—like columnist and radio personality Sheridan Whiteside in *The Man Who Came to Dinner,* but the part went to Monty Woolley.

In late May, several admirals representing the navies of the Latin American countries were in Hollywood; they were entertained by various leading figures of the film industry. There was a big party at M-G-M, an evening event at Ciro's, and another at the home of Constance Bennett and her husband, Gilbert Roland. It was at Bennett's party, on May 20, that Joseph Longstreth, a young New York literary agent, met Cary Grant. Sometime during that evening, Grant confided in him; Longstreth kept that confidence until the actor's death. He says:

> Mr. Grant told me in great secrecy that he had discovered that Errol Flynn was a Nazi agent and collaborator. He said to me that he had exposed Flynn to the authorities but the decision was made to do nothing about it. I was amazed and riveted, and promised to say nothing.

How had Cary determined this? It was most probably through Korda and Noël Coward, or possibly through William R. Wilkerson. The previous November, Flynn—in an act of treason, since his country was at war with Germany—had arranged a rental car for Dr. Herman Erben's escape, November 15, 1940, across the border into Mexico, where Erben joined the *Abwehr*, German Military Intelligence. Flynn already had considerable knowledge of this organization and knew whom to contact. His former business manager, C. J. Wood, remembers Flynn's desperate efforts to get Erben's papers to Mexico. By May of 1941, when Cary's conversation with Longstreth took place, Erben was in China, an important member of Bureau Ehrhardt, the Nazi spy ring in the Orient.

Flynn, in breach of the British Trading with the Enemy Act, corresponded with Erben through a mail drop in Istanbul, conveying his desire to join him in Japanese-occupied territory. Korda specialized in intercepts of messages from Japan and China, using experts fluent in Japanese and Chinese. A former crew member on Flynn's yacht has testified under promise of confidentiality that after Flynn's return from Pearl Harbor as the guest of Captain James Robb, Flynn conferred aboard his boat with the German Hans Wilhelm Rohl on the matter of military and naval constructions at Honolulu. The crucial information on the whereabouts of the camouflaged buildings was given to the German agent Ulrich von der Osten, who in turn passed the information on to the Japanese.

Why was nothing done about Flynn despite Grant's reports? Possibly because it was felt he would be of more use as a representative of anti-Nazism on the screen than as the defendant in a lengthy and protracted espionage trial, which could only affect public morale adversely and, given his immense popularity, might even make a martyr of him. There is also the possibility that he could unwittingly lead the authorities to other suspects, who could be rounded up. In addition, Flynn had the powerful protection of Charles Howard Ellis, a Nazi agent who was chief passport officer in New York, as well as of the Nazi collaborators Major Lemuel Schofield, head of the Immigration and Naturalization Service, and Breckinridge Long, chief of the Visa Division of the State Department.

A new and pernicious influence entered the lives of Cary Grant and Barbara Hutton. Count Carlos Vejarano y Cassina, the darkly handsome twenty-six-year-old son of the Spanish vice-consul in Hendaye, France, had been recruited by the intelligence branch of the Gestapo in Biarritz in the summer of 1940 to go to the United States and contact potential or actual Nazi sympathizers. He was also to try to influence prominent socialites through his title and good looks, urging them to call upon their congressmen for a negotiated peace in Europe. Arriving in New York City on November 22, 1940, he had met the British diplomat Sir Charles Mendl, a friend of Barbara Hutton's, who had given him an introduction to Cary and Barbara. Cassina and his wife, Wilma, the daughter of a Hudson River barge captain, arrived in Beverly Hills in April and instantly attached themselves to Cary. He and Barbara sponsored them in obtaining a handsome apartment in West Hollywood. J. Edgar Hoover, always determined to keep his own suspects under cover when possible, failed to report Cassina's whereabouts and intentions to the British authorities, with the unfortunate result that

Cary and Barbara became the unwitting host and hostess of a Nazi agent.

That spring, Howard Hughes was in constant touch with Cary, keeping him informed about the colossal growth of Hughes Aircraft, which, by May 1941, had over five hundred employees. Hughes was consumed with the D-2, originally a bomber but converted, because of technical problems, to a twin-engine fighter plane. According to the late Noah Dietrich, Hughes brought considerable influence to bear on certain figures in Washington, to ensure that Hughes Aircraft received a substantial procurement order (which would grow after the United States entered the war following Pearl Harbor). On May 26, Hughes got a hefty contract to develop the Constellation, a new flying ship that would average 250 miles per hour. In one of his rare public appearances, Hughes turned up at Ciro's, where Cary and Barbara threw a celebration party for him.

In June, it became known that much of the money Cary and Ronald Colman, who was head of the committee for BWR, had raised for British War Relief had been stolen by a publicist trusted with its transmission to England. There is no record of any subsequent trial, so presumably the matter was swept under the table. Also that month, the British Secret Intelligence Service—working with the FBI and Carmel Myers, who had checked into the hotel on the ground that her house was undergoing repairs—determined that the Beverly Hills Hotel was largely staffed with German maids who, unbeknownst to the owners, were in fact Nazi agents. All were rounded up and deported; no word of this appeared in the papers.

That same month, Cary appeared in a *Lux Radio Theatre* show, "I Love You Again," for Cecil B. DeMille; his salary went to the Chinese War Relief Fund. For several weeks, Cary disappeared from the columns, and it seems he made another bomber trip to England, again with Korda. He was back by July 26, when he and Barbara Hutton threw a party for Wendell Willkie. The following night, Grant, Hutton, and their close friend Robert Taplinger, a film publicist, drove at a snail's pace in the long queue of cars heading to the Hollywood Bowl for a Willkie rally; a man screamed at them through the half-opened window, "I wish Hitler would come and mop you guys up!" Taplinger jumped out and struck the man to the ground.

Grant was outspoken in his opposition to current investigations into the film industry by Senator Burton K. Wheeler and his associate, Senator Gerald P. Nye. Wheeler, documents show, was in the direct pay of the German government and was involved in intensive efforts to achieve a negotiated peace in Europe; with support from the German embassy in Washington, he was already bent upon the presidency. Spearheaded by William R. Wilkerson, the industry almost uniformly fought against the Wheeler-Nye committee, which objected to anti-German content in American films. But ironically, at the same time, Louis B. Mayer's M-G-M was continuing to do business with Hitler in Europe, and Winfield Sheehan, former head of 20th Century–Fox, was discussing the possibility of his taking over the film industry when Hitler was victorious.

On August 18, 1941, Cary left for Mexico by car. Rather mysteriously, he traveled alone, Barbara Hutton following two days later. They checked into the Hotel Reforma in Mexico City. Perhaps by coincidence, perhaps not, Errol Flynn was also at the Reforma, at a most sensitive time in Mexican history. In her book *Covering the Mexican Front*, Washington *Post* correspondent Betty Kirk wrote:

> Seven hundred Nazi agents poured into Mexico from the United States, Japan, Central America, and Spain. These agents were preparing for the Axis conquest of Mexico. German was heard on the streets, in cafés, bars, and nightclubs. German drinking songs rang out at the cocktail bars, followed by blustering shouts of "Death to the Jew Roosevelt!" Germany's coming victory was shouted to the sky.

From Mexico, Barbara Hutton made a serious attempt to contact Baron Gottfried von Cramm. Richard Gully recalls that she succeeded in telephoning Mussolini, who promised to help; the Italian dictator called Hitler, and Barbara delightedly informed her guests that she was confident von Cramm would be prevented from being killed in a concentration camp.

Due to her extraordinary influence at the highest levels in Germany, Barbara was permitted to talk directly to Dr. Heinrich Kleinschroth, von Cramm's personal trainer, from her house in Beverly Hills on her return with Cary in late September. Cary was present during all these conversations. On September 30, 1941, J. Edgar Hoover wrote to Assistant Secretary of State Adolf A. Berle:

As a possible interest to you, there is set out hereinafter a copy of a letter from Countess Haugwitz-Reventlow, formerly Barbara Hutton, to Dr. Heinrich Kleinschroth which was received from a strictly confidential source.

"How happy I was to hear your dear voice over the telephone the other day. . . . I did not call you up again as frankly I was frightened to, as nowadays they have a record of all foreign calls, and as I am not a citizen* I dare not do anything that the powers might disapprove of. So please don't ask me to phone you again as I honestly do not dare to, and if ever the newspapers got wind that I have friends in your country, that I not only write to and wire all the time but speak to as well on the telephone, I would hate to think what would happen to me. . . . [The United States] is anything but neutral.

"The night of our phone call I sent you a cable saying . . . I would not call you again for reasons which I would explain later. . . . I sent the cable to the Geneva Hotel, Geneva, where you said you would be until the 31st then two days later I got word from the telegraph company that they had been advised by Switzerland that the Geneva Hotel no longer existed!!!

"I just received a letter from Sylvia [de Castellane]. She says she saw you in Paris. . . . She also tells me that you are very important indeed in Paris nowadays. . . . Luckily lately I've managed to send her [Sylvia] $100 a month. . . ."

The Hoover report continued with the statement that Kleinschroth was in the German diplomatic service and that Sylvia, Countess Castellane, had received letters from Hutton through an intermediary, the Count de Nava de Tajo, father of the Grant-Hutton protégé Count Cassina.

Barbara's pleas failed. Despite every effort made by von Klein-

---

* *Barbara Hutton became a Danish citizen upon her marriage.*

schroth, von Cramm was not excused; he served on the Russian front and in North Africa as a common enlisted man, not as harsh a fate as punishment in a concentration camp but certainly a degrading assignment for a major tennis star and public idol. He remained in disgrace with Hitler.

Who leaked Barbara Hutton's secret correspondence, apparently sent through diplomatic pouches, to J. Edgar Hoover? Was it an FBI plant on her staff, or was it Cary Grant himself? Further FBI reports failed to name the informant.

At the end of September, Cary had a series of meetings over lunch and dinner with Frank Capra, who was preparing the screen version of the popular stage play *Arsenic and Old Lace*. Cary agreed to act the central role of the manic Mortimer Brewster—scion of a crazy family that included two murderous aunts and an uncle who thought he was President Teddy Roosevelt—if it was much enlarged and improved. Cary was pleased to learn that Jean Adair, who had been so kind to him in 1922 in Rochester, New York, when she appeared with him and the Pender Troupe and nursed him through his bout of rheumatic fever, would be playing one of the aunts. On October 6, the day preparations for the picture began, Cary and Barbara entertained Lord and Lady Mountbatten, who were visiting the movie colony. A week later, the couple once more left for Mexico City on urgent business; Barbara was again attempting to reach Germany and knew that her telephone and mail were being intercepted. Meanwhile, in great haste, *Arsenic and Old Lace* was being rewritten to Cary's specifications. Oddly enough, his version, put together with Capra and the writers, was an ironical comment on his own peculiarly unsatisfactory private life. The story took place on Mortimer Brewster's wedding night, in which the fool seems to be thwarted at every turn from getting into bed with his wife, played by Priscilla Lane.

Shooting began on October 20. Capra had decided to make the film in sequence, which put considerable strain on the studio resources. Cary was testy throughout the filming, very unhappy with the set of the Brewster house near Brooklyn Bridge, and complained constantly about it. He changed the lamps, the furniture, the curtains, fussed over the clothes of the entire cast and had a stand-up quarrel with his old friend and former lover Jack Kelly, who had done the costumes. He was annoyed to find Jack Kelly on the picture, because he was busy burying his New York past. He told anyone who would listen that he would have much preferred to appear in a film version of Noël Coward's play *Blithe Spirit* as the newly married husband, who is visited by the spirit of his dead spouse, a story reminiscent of *My Favorite Wife*. He was also talking about appearing in *Saratoga Trunk,* from the novel by Edna Ferber, for Howard Hawks.

Cary divided his salary for *Arsenic and Old Lace* between the United Service Organization, British War Relief and the Red Cross. This arguably generous gesture was interpreted by many as an attempt to save on taxes since Cary's income had already reached astronomical proportions and was being taxed at some 85%. The Treasury took exception to the fact that after he had made the gift he tried to withdraw part of it and give it to the slush fund for British ambulances and other war-associated groups in Hollywood. He was forbidden to make the change, and the Treasury memorandum rather heavily implied that the donation was made to help solve his tax problem.

On December 3, 1941, Cary gave Barbara a large diamond ring. The announcement of their forthcoming marriage was underplayed; the reason may have been that at the last minute, Barbara was compelled to bribe the German government of Denmark to finalize her divorce from Count Reventlow. It cannot have been convenient for her that Reventlow was believed to be guilty of subversive Nazi activities during his marriage to her and that he was under constant surveillance at the St. Regis Hotel in New York, in Vermont, where he was visiting friends, and in Los Angeles.

On Sunday, December 7, the Japanese bombed the American fleet and military and naval installations at Pearl Harbor. The cast of *Arsenic and Old Lace* assembled the following morning in a grim mood, but schedules were schedules, and Jack Warner insisted they proceed with the work. Everyone had to mug under the excessively overdone direction of Capra; it is possible that the strained mood of much of the film is due to the fact that everyone who made it was depressed, concerned, and fretful over the future. Capra had already been drafted into the army and, while production continued, he was informed he must report to Washington as soon as possible. Nevertheless, he ran considerably over schedule—and budget—on the picture, and Jack Warner was not pleased with the results. The stage version was still running in New York, and for this reason, among others, the film was not shown to the public until September 1944. Cary returned to Columbia Studios (which he increasingly disliked) to make *The Talk of the Town* for George Stevens.

The Talk of the Town was the tale of Leopold Dilg, an escaped criminal who hides out in the home of a Harvard law professor, played by Ronald Colman; the comedy sprang from that irony, and from the peculiar and farcical events that surrounded the relationship of the housekeeper (Jean Arthur) with Dilg. Once again, Cary was especially touchy and irritable during the filming. He complained about minutiae of the charming Early American decor of the professor's house, constantly switching chairs around and complaining if the banister rail was not sufficiently polished. Although he had respect for Jean Arthur's comedic gifts, he was also afraid of them; at one point, when Miss Arthur had to follow him down a Supreme Court corridor, he was convinced that the crew's laughter was for her performance only. He sulked like a child.

At Christmas, when shooting was concluded, three weeks late, he provided cast and crew with gift certificates for turkeys, only to realize that he was causing ripples of laughter because it was assumed he was referring to the quality of *The Talk of the Town* itself. No turkey, the movie became a critical and commercial success.

That same week, Cary attended a party for King Carol of Rumania and King Carol's mistress Magda Lupescu given by Dorothy di Frasso. In a Foreign Activities Correlation report dated December 13, 1941, she was described as "very anti-American, being both pro-Nazi and pro-Fascist." The report continued, "In September 1941, she was in close contact with the Italian minister Marchetti, and the German minister von Collenberg." A naval information file was also sent to the various authorities stating that the Countess "had made about fifteen trips to Italy within the last five years, recently traveling by clipper. She is well acquainted with Mussolini, Ciano and Edda Mussolini." The report continued, "(The Count-

ess) is an aunt of Alesandro di Bugnano, Italian Consul at Pitts-
burgh until the closing of the Axis consulates in June 1941. . . .
(She) is further reported to be an intimate friend of Prince Boncom-
pagni, Italian alien now in custodial detention at Ellis Island, New
York, also of Vladimir Behr, suspected Axis agent."

It should be noted that, unlike the FBI, both Foreign Activities
Correlation and the Office of Naval Intelligence were careful and
meticulous in such reports and did not base their findings upon
random statements by scurrilous gossips. The unsolved mystery is
whether Grant was informed of these memoranda so that he could
be wary of what he said to di Frasso and also keep an eye on her.

The new year of 1942 opened with Barbara Hutton's spectacular
party in San Pedro to launch the Bundles for Bluejackets campaign,
designed to raise money for U.S. and foreign sailors in the Atlantic
and Pacific. On January 5, Cary and Randolph Scott, who still shared
the beach house, gave a large party to celebrate the opening of the
play *The Late Christopher Bean*, in which Cary's favorite stand-in,
Malcolm Gray, appeared in the leading role. There was word from
Douglas Fairbanks, serving aboard a destroyer in freezing waters off
Iceland. Jean Dalrymple was in town, full of memories of when she
had hired Cary for the Janis Company in 1925. Lord Beaverbrook
was also visiting from London, conferring with Korda and Goldwyn
on secret intelligence matters at the house of the Fox executive Joe
Schenck. In February, Cary, nominated for *Penny Serenade*, was
passed over as best actor at the Academy Awards, in favor of Gary
Cooper, who had made a splash in the title role of *Sergeant York*.
But the Oscars meant nothing to Cary; he had not attended the
ceremonies up to then and would not attend again for some years.
In March, Korda left for London on government business, and Cary
continued his intelligence activities with Samuel Goldwyn. On March
12, he and Barbara had a quarrel; apparently, she was determined
to pin him down to marriage and he was again proving skittish. She
flew suddenly to New York, where she took to her bed, and cried
almost constantly; she had a nervous breakdown. In Hollywood, Cary
also had a temporary rift with Randolph Scott, who took off for a
long stay in Virginia. It was clear that if Cary did marry Barbara,
Scott would finally have to move out.

During April, Cary was conferring with Leo McCarey and the writer Sheridan Gibney on a screenplay entitled *The New Order*, later to be renamed *Once Upon a Honeymoon*, an anti-Nazi adventure story about a couple traveling through occupied Europe before America's entry into the war. It was in many ways reminiscent of Cary's journey with Phyllis Brooks in the summer of 1939. Shooting was delayed for some rewrites. One disastrous sequence was retained, in which the couple posed as Jews to get into a concentration camp. How Cary could have lent his name to such a scene is beyond comprehension. As for McCarey, it reflected his incipient anti-Semitism and his failure to understand the real purpose of the war.

As always in Cary's life, events piled up, relationships became more complex, and he lived on several levels at once. Clifford Odets returned from New York and began writing a script based upon the life of George Gershwin, a project of Cary's original mentor, Jesse L. Lasky. Odets was determined that Cary should play Gershwin, who had been a friend of Cary's in the 1930s. Grant would have been ideally cast, but unfortunately, the director, Irving Rapper, who himself had been born in England felt that Cary was insufficiently American for the role and, in a decision he regrets today, ruled Cary out.

At the same time, Cary was meeting with Odets to discuss the Gershwin role, he met an attractive twenty-one-year-old tennis-court keeper named Milton Holmes and began to play tennis with him at the Beverly Hills Tennis Club. Holmes showed him an original story entitled *Bundles for Freedom*, the story of a gangster and draft dodger who is reformed by the love of a good woman. Cary was fascinated by the story and pulled a string at RKO that resulted in the fortunate young athlete getting the then colossal sum of thirty thousand dollars for his efforts, plus five hundred dollars a week on a ten-week guarantee. Just a few days earlier, Holmes had had to borrow ten dollars from George Cukor in order to buy food. Holmes worked on the script with Adrian Scott, a left-wing writer who would be blacklisted in 1952, while, simultaneously, Sheridan Gibney was at work on *Once Upon a Honeymoon*.

Cary and Barbara Hutton began investing heavily in land developments in Acapulco, correctly foreseeing a great resort area there. In 1942, Acapulco was little more than a fishing village in a magnificent setting—a huge crescent beach and flanking mountains. Perhaps annoyed by Cary's role in the hated British Secret Intelligence Service, with which he was supposed to be cooperating, J. Edgar Hoover sent a memorandum on April 6, 1942, to Adolf A. Berle:

> As of possible interest to you, information has been received from a reliable, confidential source to the effect that William Randolph Hearst, Cary Grant, the screen actor, and Barbara Hutton, the heiress, have all become interested in the potentialities of Acapulco, Mexico, as a tourist resort and have made investments in land developments at that place.
>
> It will be recalled that a large real estate allotment is presently being developed at Acapulco by an American named Glenn Pullen. Pullen has been associated in this enterprise with Wolf Schoenbrun, a naturalized American of German origin, and the firm is known as the Fraccionadora de Acapulco S.A.A.

This pointless report was also sent by Hoover to Nelson Rockefeller, Coordinator of Inter-American Affairs, as well as to the Coordinator of Information, the Board of Economic Warfare, the director of Naval Intelligence, and the chief of the Military Intelligence Service.

More seriously, Hoover and his Mexican staff were continuing to investigate Dorothy di Frasso and her association with Barbara Hutton, Cary Grant, and others. Frederick B. Lyons, assistant chief, Division of Foreign Activity Correlation, who worked directly under Berle in this Secret Intelligence branch, appointed Washington, D.C., lawyer Joseph B. Keenan to investigate the countess in Mexico City. Keenan was unable to leave until July 25, but in the meantime put feelers out in the Mexican capital.

That spring, the surveillance on Barbara Hutton was still unrelenting, and J. Edgar Hoover was keeping Berle informed about her activities, at the same time as she was seeing Cary almost every night. Her letters were intercepted and supplied to Hoover from what he described, in a memorandum to Berle dated March 20, 1942, as "a strictly confidential source." The memorandum read as follows:

This source is advised that the writer (Dr. Heinrich Klein-schroth), who was a famous German tennis star twenty-odd years ago, enclosed a letter to the addressee from one "G" (code name for Gottfried von Cramm), who seems to have been the addres-see's lover and with whom the addressee has been carrying on a correspondence for some time. The letter states as follows:

"Your letters and your love for him mean his only happiness and his whole life. If ever you should decide to change your life so that it would mean the end of G's dreams and hopes, don't let him know it before the end of the war, because it would make him too unhappy and he would suffer terribly."

In the enclosed note, "G" writes:

"During all the twelve months [referring to 1941–2] I have received the most lovely letters from you. Henry [referring to writer, whose first name is Henry] promised me to send you a cable as soon as possible, give you my love, and tell you the new address under which you can go on writing to me. Though I'll have to live in a more primitive way for a couple of weeks now, there will be no danger for me. If you should get a letter, written with a pencil, from me, don't think I have become lazy. I will then have no ink at my disposal."

The writer in his letter states:

"I have seen 'G' quite often. He left yesterday for a kind of inspection trip and will be back in a couple of weeks. Nothing to worry about, darling."

The confidential source has advised that in his opinion the writer is in some sort of confidential German Government service, inas-much as in his letter he states: "You can always write to me Palace Hotel, Madrid, or to the Hotel de Paris at Monte Carlo, or to a friend of mine, % Mr. Maro Bloch, 4 Rue de L'Andient Port, Geneva, Switzerland."

The confidential source has also advised that the Palace Hotel in Madrid has often been described by American correspondents as the chief hangout of secret and open German agents in Madrid. The fact that the writer travels a great deal in Europe and has permanent addresses in three cities indicates that he is secretly or openly in the service of the German Government.

Cary and Barbara's close friend and protégé Count Vejarano y Cassina continued to be under constant investigation by Berle and Foreign Activity Correlation. Memoranda flew to and fro in the State Department, many of them emanating from Visa Division chief Fletcher Warren. It was determined that Cassina was receiving a quantity of correspondence from his father via the New York shipping company of García and Díaz, which was believed to be the front organization for the extremist Fascist political movement known as Falangism. The theatrical producer Gilbert Miller (a friend of Barbara Hutton's through his wife, Kitty Bache), who had sponsored Cassina's visa, was being investigated for illegal currency transactions. Thus, while seeming to be leading a bland and comfortable life in the oasis of Hollywood in the middle of World War II, Cary Grant was hemmed in by every imaginable form of intrigue.

As all this was going on, he was filming additional scenes for the recently completed *The Talk of the Town*. He was also discussing with RKO the possibility of Rita Hayworth's appearing with him in *Bundles for Freedom*. She herself was embroiled in all manner of personal intrigue; her husband, Edward Judson, was involved in mysterious business activities that some considered criminal, while, according to the notorious "Red-Light Bandit," Caryl Chessman, she was indulging in an affair with him, thereby risking her career and perhaps her life. In June, Cary learned that Alexander Korda had been knighted for his special undercover war work, as well as for his propaganda films designed to assist the Anglo-American cause. Merle Oberon was granted the privilege of standing next to her husband at the ceremony at Buckingham Palace, a sure acknowledgment that she also had risked her life in the cause of freedom. It would be five years before Cary was honored for his war work.

While *Once Upon a Honeymoon* was still shooting, Cary, hoping for the Gershwin role, played the composer's works constantly on the piano and even studied rare recordings of Gershwin's speech, so that he could match his vocal patterns. Unbeknownst to the world, he also volunteered for service in the British Navy. The work he was doing as an intelligence agent evidently didn't satisfy him completely, and he wanted to see action. He was smarting from what Douglas Fairbanks, Jr., described (to Roy Moseley) as widespread criticism of his failure to serve in the war. The Admiralty in London was prepared to allow Cary to become a naval rating, subject to his being able to satisfy medical standards. However, a series of memoranda, now lodged in the files of the Public Record Office in London, makes clear that he was felt to be of more value where he was. The Foreign Office minutes referring to his activities say: "The position of BSS [British Security Service] in the U.S.A. has not been finally settled in detail." The same memorandum refers to Cary and the actors Richard Ainley and Ian Hunter, saying "[They] are very successful . . . and there seems no reason to alter our decision that they should stay." Another reason cited was that it was important for British characters to be represented by Englishmen on the screen; furthermore, British performers in American films helped to assure good dollar earnings. In addition, the men mentioned were virtually useless from a military point of view. The Foreign Office overruled the Admiralty in the matter, but as it turned out, both Ainley and Hunter returned to England the following year, and Ainley subsequently lost an arm in military service.

Cary Grant remained in Hollywood, to continue his liaison work with Korda, Coward, and the Goldwyns. It was clear that it would be necessary to secure him an unofficial position that would allow him to travel to Europe without attracting suspicion. Through Edith Gwynn, Wilkerson planted, in the *Hollywood Reporter* dated June 18, the statement that Cary would soon be "getting U.S. Army papers" but would be "given leave to finish *Once Upon a Honeymoon*." A further statement, on July 6, added: "Grant took a physical and as soon as he's finished *Once Upon a Honeymoon*, he will be a lieutenant in the U.S. Air Force." These two announcements of course struck nobody as contradictory, typical as they were of the random items to be found in Hollywood gossip columns. Cary was probably relieved when Edward Ashley, the British character actor, did not approach him to join a special investigative unit entitled Allied Artists, which operated up and down the California coast. Urged by Cary, Barbara Hutton was offering her Regent's Park mansion, Winfield House, to the British government. Because of the suspicion surrounding her, the offer was refused, whereupon, at Cary's suggestion, she gave the house to the antiaircraft defense brigades of London as a headquarters and dormitory combined.

Cary and Barbara were at last married on July 8, 1942, at Frank Vincent's Lake Arrowhead summer residence. Shortly before, Cary had legally changed his name from Archibald Leach and become an American citizen. He and Barbara signed documents waiving all interest in each other's property. (This was the agreement that had so greatly distressed Phyllis Brooks's mother.) The service lasted only six minutes. The U.S. Army Air Corps "Flying Parson," Reverend H. Paul Romeis, of the Lutheran Church of San Bernardino, read the wedding service. Frank Vincent was best man, Madeline Hazeltine, a friend of Barbara's, was matron of honor. Other witnesses were Cary's long-term secretary and former fellow vaudevillean Frank Horn, William Robertson, a friend of Barbara's, and Barbara's former governess, Mademoiselle Touquet. Ironically, because Cary had to report for work on *Once Upon a Honeymoon*, the couple did not have one themselves. Although columnist Sheila Graham wrote, two days later, that she had overheard Cary on the set saying that the wedding night was the best night of his life, some friends of Barbara insist that the marriage was not consummated.

As filming dragged on, Cary would come home late at night after a grueling shoot, almost too tired to speak. When Barbara had friends over, to keep her company, he would sometimes disappear upstairs, too exhausted for small talk and uninterested in the doings of the exiled European petty royalty who filled Barbara's living room. She in turn had little in common with his movie friends, who talked of nothing but contracts, deals, money, and movies. The couple found common ground only in the work they were doing for war relief.

Whether pricked by her reputation as a possible Nazi sympathizer or not, Barbara felt strongly, under Cary's influence, that she should give as much as she could to British War Relief, while he served with such figures as Binnie Barnes and Ronald Colman on the British War Relief Society committee. In one of her rare public appearances, Barbara joined Cary for the August 29 premiere of *The Talk of the Town*, to benefit the Hollywood Canteen, which was followed by a party given by Canteen president Bette Davis at Ciro's. In an attempt to improve their relationship, the couple flew to San Francisco in September.

Preparations for *Bundles for Freedom* began seriously that fall, as Cary and Barbara moved into Westridge House, the Douglas Fairbanks estate, at 1515 Amalfi Drive. Situated in the Pacific Palisades, with a sweeping view of the ocean, it had five bedroom suites, a massive hallway, a cavernous living room, tennis courts, a large swimming pool, and a sauna bath. There was an Oriental garden and a servants' cottage. So large was the household employed by the Grants—there were about twenty-eight servants, sometimes augmented to over thirty—that they had to rent adjoining houses to accommodate the staff. The Swedish butler, Erik Gosta, also acted as a bodyguard. There were footmen in livery, upstairs and downstairs maids, a valet, a masseur, and personal trainer for Cary, special security guards, two gardeners, and Barbara's live-in companion, Germaine (Ticki) Toquet.

On November 1, 1942, *Bundles for Freedom*, renamed *From Here to Victory*, (it was later retitled *Mr. Lucky*), began shooting. It was a fascinating movie, filled with echoes of Cary's life. The character of the gangster–draft dodger, who uses a dead man's 4-F card to escape enlistment, seems to reflect what his enemies thought of both Cary Grant and Bugsy Siegel. The gambling scenes evoked Bugsy's activities in Nevada, while the war relief organization on which the quintessentially English Gladys Cooper served as a major committee member was clearly modeled on the almost identical organization supported by Cary and Barbara in Hollywood. Moreover, there were curious parallels with the unfavorable gossip about Cary's private life. As if to convince those in Hollywood who cast aspersions on his masculinity, he was shown awkwardly learning to knit sweaters and socks for the army, instructed by an ebullient war relief committee member (Florence Bates). In one comic sequence, he knits away furiously, watched through a window by a row of highly suspicious men, his embarrassment increasing by the minute. "What will they think of you?" his henchman asks. In another sequence, a frosty committee girl, played by Laraine Day, kisses him. He responds by withdrawing awkwardly. Asked whether he enjoyed it, he replies that he isn't sure. Few male performers would have dared risk such a scene; much to the relief of his fans, he announced later, after a second kiss, that he did, this time, enjoy it.

Two further scenes he influenced can only strike chords in followers of Cary Grant's career. The first scene has him using rhyming slang, a typical cockney activity, much practiced in Bristol. At one stage, he refers to "a lady from Bristol," which means pistol, announcing that this is in his pocket. Could any "in" joke go further? In the movie's most remarkable episode, he is discovered in the Maryland country estate of Laraine Day's grandfather, played by Henry Stephenson (who would later repeat the role almost identically in *Night and Day*). Cary talks of his miserable, poverty-stricken childhood with a greater intensity and passion than he had ever displayed on the screen before. Cary's face grows gaunt and drawn, his eyes sharp with pain. He mentions running away from home, altering the age to nine. Then he launches upon a speech condemning the very rich and their follies, a speech he could have delivered to Barbara Hutton, and probably did deliver, repeatedly. Unfortunately, the purport of the speech became a prime factor in the condemnation of co-writer Adrian Scott during the blacklist era: it was taken as Communist propaganda, and Cary seems to have done nothing to quell this false judgment. By 1952, he would be committed to the cold war against Communism.

Mr. Lucky ran into trouble with industry censors. From the beginning, it had been disliked by Ulric Bell, former executive director of the Fight for Freedom group, who was now representative of the Office of War Information's Overseas Branch. Bell felt that the movie would be damaging to U.S. prestige overseas and that it failed to show that every sector of the American public was playing its part in the war. He hated the draft-dodging theme, quite misunderstanding it, and sought the banning of the film abroad.

Warm reviews for the picture the following year deactivated Bell, and the Motion Picture Production Code Administration under Joseph Green made arrangements for an export license to be granted. But the movie remained controversial. It was argued over for years to come.

During the shooting, on November 17, Barbara Hutton took her son, Lance, to the studio to see Cary work. Barbara had never seen him make a picture. She seemed bored by the long hours of preparation for a shot that lasted only a few minutes, and left quickly in the early afternoon, never to return. When she and Cary attended the wedding of Reginald and Nadia Gardiner on December 6, Barbara looked drawn and tired, suggesting late-night quarrels, or at least insomnia. At Christmas, columnists were told by Cary's press agent that he would soon be leaving to entertain the troops.

That fall and winter of 1942, Cary became a true father to Lance Reventlow. His frustrated need to be a parent, constantly eating away at him, was at least partially fulfilled in this happy stepfather-child relationship. Lance had name tags reading "Lance Grant" sewn into his clothing; Cary gave him several thousand dollars, stuffed into one of the suitcases in his bedroom. Cary and Barbara gave the boy Cartier cufflinks, tie clips, and jeweled tuxedo studs. Lance was not an easy child. He was a restless, miserable pupil at school; he was torn between Barbara and his father, who was living at the Huntington Hotel in Pasadena. He shocked everyone with his profanities; he was spoiled rotten. According to C. David Heymann, in his biography *Poor Little Rich Girl*, there were odd events at the Huntington when Lance was there with the Count and his wife, Peggy. A Miss Grant [sic] was engaged as a governess for the boy; she had a habit of stripping him bare, standing him in the bathtub, and beating him when he couldn't remember the Lord's Prayer. Barbara herself was changeable in her attitude toward her son, and this was troublesome to Cary. As if imitating his stepfather's involvement in secret intelligence, Lance devised a code, possibly with Cary's help, in which he would talk with his mother from the Huntington Hotel to foil Reventlow, who eavesdropped on an extension phone. At one point, according to Heymann, Peggy Reventlow discovered a written code and showed it to her husband. It consisted of dots, dashes, and circles. Reventlow steamed open a letter Lance sent to Barbara. The first line read: "To hell with my father. I hope he dies." In reply to this deeply felt message, Barbara wrote: "You must write me some more like that." And she added, almost giving her husband's game away: "General sends his best love."

More serious matters were afoot. Cary made some unfortunate mistakes. He hired Count Vejarano y Cassina to teach him and Barbara Spanish, a language Cary would need for intelligence activities in Mexico. He also arranged a screen test for Cassina. This was a failure, but soon afterward Cary got him a translator's job with Columbia Pictures. Cassina supplied Spanish sound tracks for films distributed south of the border that parodied or attacked the Nazis for whom he worked. Among these movies was *Once Upon a Honeymoon*. Even then, Cary was not alerted by J. Edgar Hoover or the FBI to the fact that he was aiding and abetting a Nazi agent.

How can one explain this? According to Ernest Cuneo, who was the special liaison between Roosevelt, Hoover, and Berle in matters of secret intelligence:

Hoover hated Stephenson. He detested having his territory invaded by a foreign intelligence organization. It would please him if one of Stephenson's people such as Cary Grant (I didn't know about the Grant matter personally) should be in any way embarrassed.

This statement is confirmed by Curt Gentry, author of a book in progress on J. Edgar Hoover (Norton, forthcoming). He says:

The fact that Grant was with British Security Coordination would be sufficient reason for Hoover to want to embarrass him.

Hoover did embarrass Grant. But not for another year.

NINE

Cary Grant's marriage to Barbara Hutton was in every way unsatisfactory. The British actress Binnie Barnes, who had known Cary since England in the 1920s, observes:

> It wasn't a very happy union. I don't know why they got married at all. He was an impetuous man; he sort of went into hibernation with all of his wives. I think he had a terrible time with most of them, to tell you the truth. I think they all found out after they were married that he was gay.

Cary's extreme parsimony emerged very strongly during this period. As early as the 1930s, he had begun putting a red mark around the milk bottles in the refrigerator to keep a check on the household staff. He counted the eggs and even counted the logs in the garage (a habit learned from Rosalind Russell), and he kept an eye on every item in every closet of the house. He was worried that the gasoline in his automobile tank might be syphoned off. He hated sending out furniture covers or drapes to the cleaners. He would not allow his clothes to go to even the cheapest Chinese laundry in downtown Los Angeles and, distrusting his staff, would roll up his sleeves and wash them himself. If a shirt or jacket finally wore out, he would clip off the buttons with a pair of nail scissors and save them. Every time he played a phonograph record, he meticulously dusted it, and he checked the needle almost every day of the week. He would invite people out to dinner in a fashionable restaurant and then insist that the check be divided among his guests, according to the exact amount each one owed.

If he saw an electric light burning in the daytime or unnecessarily at night or in a closet, he would not only turn it off but would determine who was responsible and dock the culprit's pay. Barbara Hutton paid black market prices for rationed shoes or foods that were in short supply. Cary refused to deal with black marketeers. In a conversation with C. David Heymann, Dudley Walker, Cary's valet, added details to the litany of stinginess. Cary restricted the household to one delivered copy of the newspaper a day; if any member of the staff wanted to read the paper, they would have to go out and buy it. At Christmas, Barbara would be lavishly generous, giving the help gifts of four-hundred-dollar watches, presenting the maids with designer jewelry. She handed over her used dresses, sometimes worn only once, to a maid she particularly liked. Once, Barbara gave Dudley Walker a set of expensive cufflinks; Cary grabbed them and put them in his pocket and handed Walker a cheap pair, which had been given to Cary by Bugsy Siegel. Walker added:

> He would sit at dinner and eat and put his fingers in his mouth and suck his fingers. He would eat very heavily, and Barbara would barely touch her food. And he was a bad drinker. He would really get nasty and cold. He would become sadistic. He could be a terrible bastard, that one.

Barbara Hutton's headaches worsened; she plunged deeper and deeper into depression and began drinking heavily. When Cary locked the liquor away, she was so desperate for something to drink that she once downed half a bottle of white vinegar. She was also on drugs. Separately housed in her own bedroom, she would not sleep with Cary, and there was no indication that he was eager to remedy the situation.

Cary broke the monotony of his personal life by appearing with the comedian Alan Carney in January 1943, doing impromptu skits at the Hollywood Canteen that convulsed audiences of servicemen. Noël Coward was in town again, on his way to special assignments in Latin America (Cary probably reaped the benefit of his lessons with Count Cassina when Coward sent messages in Spanish from Mexico and south of Panama). In early February, Cary renewed an earlier friendship with the vaudevillian Don Barclay, who had urged him to leave the crumbling world of vaudeville in the mid-1920s and make his debut on a legitimate stage. Cary now put together an army camp show, which included Barclay and Nöel Coward. The intention was to break off the tour in an obscure part of America, Louisiana's bayou country, to make a secret trip to England. Unfortunately, the *Hollywood Reporter* yet again exposed his intention, in an item dated February 8; as a result, he apparently had to be extremely careful to conceal the precise date on which he would leave for London by bomber. His movements at the time are still classified under the British Official Secrets Act, but Ray Austin, his personal assistant for many years in the 1960s, remembers Cary's references to the trip:

> He told me about the spy thing. Cloak-and-dagger stuff. Cary went to Switzerland, I think, he and another actor.* They went and brought back a lot of information in their personal clothing. Maybe they brought back film; he never went into great detail. Goldwyn sent him to Switzerland. Goldwyn was the head of the spy ring [in Hollywood]. Cary went into Europe under Nazi domination, and he could have been put away for it. He said it paid its dividends . . . that he was rather like Raffles in the old book and movie about the safecracker. He had to learn to crack safes, to get information. The government owed him so much that strings were pulled for him in an incident involving a sailor. . . .

The "incident," confirmed by other close associates of Grant, involved his arrest, at some stage just before his trip to Europe, for a sexual act with a young man in a men's room. Somewhere between

---

This must have been Don Barclay.

the department store where the incident took place and the police precinct, a response from headquarters to the radioed message from the police car caused the two arresting officers to make a diversion to a certain address. Grant was dropped off, and another actor, who was paid a substantial sum, was arrested in his place. Fingerprinted and docketed, the man was released soon afterward, on the understandable ground that there was insufficient evidence to convict him. (An almost identical episode would involve Howard Hughes nine years later.)

Cary was back in Hollywood in May, to appear on a radio broadcast of "The Talk of the Town" for the *Lux Radio Theatre*, no doubt combining his appearance with a report to DeMille. A recorded War Bond speech he apparently made in Europe had been broadcast on April 26. On May 24, he appeared in the patriotic air force broadcast "Island in the Sky," as Major Robert Scott, and on May 31 he was on "Where From Here?" another important patriotic program. With Cary's encouragement, Barbara gave several hundred thousand dollars to the Free French, a sum that greatly assisted members of the resistance in both Vichy and occupied France. He himself contributed heavily to the Free French, while continuing to cut corners at home.

Having managed, after considerable nagging, to free himself temporarily of his binding Columbia contract—using his own Frank Vincent Agency to twist the arm of boss Harry Cohn—he decided to make *Destination Tokyo* for Warner Bros., from an excellent script by Delmer Daves and Albert Maltz, another of the writers doomed to be blacklisted in the 1950s. The producer was pushy, energetic, manically productive Jerry Wald; Daves would direct. Daves was a fascinating individual—scientist, geologist, crystallographer, photographer of ancient American settlements and townships, an authority on the history of the West, and an expert in dozens of other fields unrelated to the movies. Huge, with a massive head and giant shoulders, he was equipped with a booming speaking voice and a genial but domineering manner that fascinated everyone who met him. He was a master film technician and he personally supervised the submarine sets for this story of a sub captain and crew heading for Japan through dangerous, enemy-haunted waters in the midst of the Pacific war. John Garfield, then at the height of his career, Alan Hale, and Dane Clark were among the co-stars.

According to Ray Austin, Cary left for the Pacific at about this time, his appearances with Don Barclay on the war front used as a cover to pick up information. The tour, plus his publicity for *Destination Tokyo* could have been used as an excuse by some diligent reporter to get onto him. But his covert movements were never made public, not even in the pages of the *Reporter*. Apparently, William R. Wilkerson and his wife had finally learned their lesson in the matter of secrecy.

Destination Tokyo began shooting on June 21, 1943. The Grants had just returned from a week at Lake Arrowhead, presumably in an effort to save their already crumbling marriage. At the studio, Cary predictably inspected every inch of the submarine, and for once he did not find the set wanting. Compulsively punctual, he was very annoyed when an actor was late a couple of times, and he and the rest of the crew banged loudly on gongs and on submarine piping when the actor turned up; the man proved unable to appreciate the humor of the gag. It was a grueling shoot. Cary's nerves began to fray; the extreme authenticity of the set proved to be a burden after all. It was done almost to the exact scale of a real submarine, cramped, filled with equipment, and made of steel, not painted wood. The cubicles used for cabins, the engine room, battery room, and cramped officer quarters of the U.S.S. *Copperfin* were stiflingly hot under the burning studio arc lights, trained relentlessly on the cast by cinematographer Bert Glennon. Cary and John Garfield sweated so much that thirty changes of uniform were kept ready for them; there was always the fear that the makeup would run down their faces and ruin their carefully starched navy shirts. In scenes in which the submarine was swamped, water bursting through the hatch and sweeping through the machinery of the conning tower, Cary and the rest of the cast were drenched to the skin. The submarine interior was mounted on rockers, which imitated the movement of a heavy ocean swell. Some cast members got seasick; Garfield complained of vertigo. Utterly professional always, Cary fought his way through the work, only occasionally breaking into an uncontrollable rage when he could take the strain no longer. He told the studio publicist for the wire services, "We spend most of our time in this show a hundred and fifty feet or more under water and there are no women. Take seventy-five men out on a 300-foot craft for two months without women and you can bet it's serious."

Dane Clark recalls:

> Working with Grant was a great pleasure. He was the most knowledgeable man I have ever met in this business. He was aware of every value, every detail on the set. I recall one day when we were shooting on Stage 21, shots of the submarine about to leave San Francisco Bay on its perilous journey to Japan. We were all aboard the sub. It seemed that there were about a thousand lights overhead, flooding us. As Cary got into the shot, he suddenly said to Delmer Daves, "There's a light missing up there. I'm not getting it!" Some members of the crew laughed: how could anyone see an arc light from that position when there were so many hundreds of others. "We'll try to find out," Daves said. Members of the crew went up into the flies and were amazed to discover that one small light was not functioning. We all applauded and continued with the work. Amazing!

Despite protestations from Jack Warner, shooting was broken off for a couple of hours on June 26 when Cary celebrated the first anniversary of his U.S. citizenship. He delivered a speech on the set, saying it was his gravest disappointment that the British government, followed by the U.S. Navy Department, would not allow him to be in the real man's navy. He received a round of applause.

The excellent *Destination Tokyo* provided Cary with one of his best parts. And, during the shooting, there was talk of his making another movie for Warners, the life of Cole Porter, which Hal Wallis had bought as an independent production for $300,000. Cary knew Porter well; he was fond of his music and would sing such Porter songs as "You're the Top" "Miss Otis Regrets," and "I've Got You Under My Skin" at parties. Grant was also friendly with Porter's talented boon companion, the bearded actor Monty Woolley. He was very interested in playing the part, but correctly apprehensive that the film would have to be almost totally fabricated, since Porter's homosexuality could not even be suggested on the screen.

With paradoxical generosity, Cary attempted to cheer Barbara with an eighteen-carat diamond ring on July 12. She responded joyfully, but soon afterward sank again into one of her depressions. Count Reventlow was still contesting her access to Lance, and she was bored and restless during the long weeks of shooting *Destination Tokyo*. Cary would come home with even his great strength depleted after the devastating, seemingly endless hours of work, which continued at times beyond midnight. Convinced she was unattractive, Barbara would stare moodily into mirrors, savagely upset when someone would compare her unthinkingly with an actress whose looks she disliked. When the critic would compound the felony by saying such words as, "You'd know I was lying if I said you looked like Lana Turner," she would plunge into an abnormal depression and begin to hate herself. Anyone else would have shaken off the harmless insult with a shrug. Her fragile ego made her virtually inaccessible. Her insecurity was in its different way as deep as Cary's; they were uniquely ill-suited to give each other peace of mind. No matter how often people would tell her she was pretty, she refused to believe it, just as he, incredibly would refuse to believe those who called him handsome. He fussed endlessly over his hair and teeth, and was disturbed beyond measure by the slightest flaw he detected in his face in the mirror.

On July 17, Cary appeared at a special gala for the men of the Army Air Corps at the Masquer Club in Hollywood. As a gag, Frank Vincent walked in with him disguised as Barbara Hutton in a wedding dress; he carried an exact replica of the bridal bouquet. Barbara was not amused: she hated allusions to Cary's bisexuality. Just three days earlier, her own wedding anniversary had been drab, uncelebrated, not even mentioned by her husband.

On rare occasions, Barbara would go out to nightclubs, but always without Cary now. On August 1, she turned up with Randolph Scott at the Mocambo. As if deliberately to annoy Barbara, Cary turned up in drag as part of a gag routine on Orson Welles's Magic Show on August 5.

The long-drawn-out shooting of *Destination Tokyo* finally ended in September. An odd episode occurred shortly afterward, in which a woman in New York who had the walls of her house lined with photographs of Grant claimed to be his sister. He angrily rejected this assertion, and there the matter should have rested, except for the fact that the gossip columnists tried to make something of the story. He threatened a legal action, and at last the matter was closed.

Cary and Barbara made their first appearance together in months at Ciro's, with Bugsy Siegel and his new mistress, Virginia Hill. This seemed to be a direct snub of Dorothy di Frasso, whom Bugsy had brutally jilted a few months earlier. Virginia and Bugsy made a striking team; both were attractive, charismatic, exciting, and dangerous. Moving from one location to another as they pursued their fiercely intense relationship, they would see Cary constantly. Virginia's jewelry, furs, and gowns cost over $400,000 a year. She had a hundred pairs of shoes, a dozen mink coats, chinchillas, ermines, sables, and furs. Even in the middle of the war, her sportswear was flown in by some mysterious influence from London. Her bright red Cadillac convertible was one of the sights of Hollywood. Siegel's ill-gotten gains also bought her a Miami Beach mansion formerly owned by William Randolph Hearst.

The price she paid for luxury was constant fear. She and Bugsy were certain that sooner or later they would be in grave danger from mob members they had crossed. They had twenty-four-hour guards on all their properties, and hidden cameras in their houses recorded the arrival of guests. According to Siegel's biographer Dean Jennings, the pair accumulated as much as five million dollars from illegal gambling, paid killings, and fixed races during a two-year period. Yet their activities seemed not in the least to faze their circle of friends, headed by Cary and Barbara Grant, George Raft, and Mark Hellinger, the fast-talking, roughneck producer and former writer. Cary spent more time with this remarkable pair than with almost anyone else. He also saw a great deal of Don Barclay, and on October 11 saw Barclay off to the South Seas with actor Joel McCrea.

Cary began work that fall on a film entitled *Curly* (later renamed *Once Upon a Time*), in which he played a theatrical producer who becomes interested in a young boy's caterpillar. The creature dances to the tune of "Yes Sir, That's My Baby" and the producer decides that this remarkable insect should be a major star. Alexander Hall, whom Cary remembered with pleasure from Paramount at the start of his career, was assigned to direct.

Cary was unhappy about the choice of the attractive and talented Janet Blair as his co-star, despite the fact that she was a close friend of his partner Frank Vincent, and, as a Vincent client, was in fact his own, but Vincent had overruled him. She recalls that he was charming at first; she confesses, "I felt almost faint when I saw him as we started work," but adds:

He had fought Harry Cohn over my being cast because I was so much younger. There would be too much contrast. There was a kissing scene between us he insisted be cut out. Sometimes he wouldn't communicate with me at all, just stare into space. He would be cold and distant and then even rude; he would walk past me without saying a word. He was deeply preoccupied with his problems with Barbara Hutton.

Sometimes he was skittish, jolly, happy, and cute, and he would do all sorts of funny things at the piano. He was incredibly limber. Then at the end he gave bottles of brandy to the cast and crew, and I wasn't included. . . . I didn't like brandy, but it was hurtful. He didn't even shake my hand or say goodbye. I thought of barging into his dressing room to talk to him, but finally I just slipped away. It was painful.

Ted Donaldson was the touching, winsome boy in the movie; he was discovered by the agent Edith Van Cleve, who later found Marlon Brando. In one of his rare gentle moods, the studio chief Harry Cohn himself supervised Donaldson's test and, despite the fact that the boy, sick with flu, was coughing and sneezing, gave him the role.

Then Donaldson had his dramatic test with Cary. He remembers that Cary spoke to him warmly, introducing himself and talking to Donaldson as though he were an adult:

He made everything easy for me. He had an innate graciousness. When we started shooting, he greeted me cheerily every day, always saying something amusing to put me at ease. He loved games and riddles. I loved them too, and we would have so much fun together. He loved the current hit of that time, "Mairzy Doats," with the line "and dozy doats and liddle lambzy divey." He loved it because it was so silly. It appealed to that wonderful, boyish side of him, which of course was part of his great charm.

He was so effusive and outgoing that I seldom saw the more reflective, private, withdrawn, and serious Cary Grant. But I do remember once we were sitting waiting while the cameraman, Franz Planer, who was very, very meticulous, was taking his usual two hours to light the set. Suddenly, Grant leaned forward on his forearms and began to talk about Lance. "You know, I have a son," he said. And he added that he didn't see the boy very much and regretted it. I could *see* the regret in his face. He wasn't joking now. He didn't deal with that regret in a humorous way. I was very moved. It was a loving moment, his talking like this to a ten-year-old boy. I think he had developed an affection for me. I certainly developed enormous affection and love for him. I wanted to help him. But how could a ten-year-old boy help Cary Grant?

Donaldson remembers that Barbara Hutton came to the set one day and sat on a couch. She was polite but cold, or so she seemed to Donaldson. He didn't understand her shyness. He had no rapport with her; but his rapport with Cary deepened every day. Donaldson was having difficulties with his father during the making of the film. They had an argument during the shooting. At one stage, his father raised his hand to him in a threatening gesture. This unpleasant situation drew him even closer to Cary, who, by contrast, was never anything but kind.

A difficult sequence in the film came toward the end of shooting. Flynn, played by Cary, had become desperate and had to sell Curly the caterpillar for a trivial sum in order to rescue himself from bankruptcy. Donaldson was to struggle with Cary, and Cary was to slap him. The child lost his sense of being in a movie and felt the terror he had experienced when his own father raised his hand to strike him. As Cary advanced for the blow across the face, Donaldson ignored the director's instructions and shrank, turning away so that Cary's hand descended on his neck. Although naturally Cary did not deliver the blow in full, he was afraid, given his extraordinary strength and the size and power of his hands, that he might kill the boy. The director became more and more frustrated as, even after eleven takes, the scene could not be concluded. Finally, Donaldson forced himself to hold his head in position, and Cary struck it, just hard enough to cause the boy to burst into tears. For years afterward, Donaldson was haunted by that moment, agonizing over the reason he had been unable to play the scene.

The relationship between the thirty-nine-year-old man and this talented child was perhaps one of the most remarkable in Cary's life. As a result, the film was moving and disturbing far beyond what its somewhat absurd theme would suggest.

One evening, when Cary returned home from the studio too exhausted to have dinner and was sharing a plate of scrambled eggs with Barbara in an upstairs drawing room, the doorbell rang unexpectedly. The butler, Erik Gosta, informed Cary that Captain Rand of the U.S. Army, who was involved in intelligence work and acted as a liaison for Cary in the European war theater, had arrived with two other army men. Cary walked downstairs with Barbara, to see Rand and his companion officers standing at attention and saluting. The three men took out a rolled Stars-and-Stripes flag and unfurled it, presenting it to Cary. He burst into tears. It was the army's way of thanking him for his work as a special agent, provider of funds for the war effort, and champion entertainer of the troops.

Cary was coming to realize how deeply American soldiers loved and respected him for his war efforts. GI's in the Aleutians sent him a needlepoint map of Alaska they had made, showing every small village in relief. On October 27, the incorrigible *Hollywood Reporter* had printed the following words: "Cary Grant is doing a wonderful constructive job in connection with the war effort on which he wants no publicity—and about which we wish we could shout here."

In November, Cary turned up at a farewell party for Phyllis Brooks, who was on her way to Australia to entertain the troops. He himself had plans to make another trip overseas after Christmas. He appeared with Laraine Day at a meeting of the Victory Committee to raise funds for improved food for the troops and, on December 10, bought a block of seats for the premiere of the film *Madame Curie,* a benefit for the same committee.

The same day, Jacob L. Fuller, a special agent of the FBI, arrested Count Cassina at Barbara's Sutton Place apartment in New York City, charging him with espionage. This was almost as great a shock to Cary as his own arrest almost exactly a year earlier. He and Barbara were panic-stricken. Informed by local FBI agent Richard B. Hood that Cassina was a suspected Nazi agent, they called Barbara's uncle Joseph E. Davies, the former Ambassador to the Soviet Union and one of the most prominent attorneys in the United States. Davies refused Cassina's case, which could damage his career as a patriotic diplomat. Cary and Barbara turned to an upcoming young lawyer, Milton S. Gould, today one of the leading Manhattan figures of the bar.

Gould, who was still building his reputation, took the case, despite his commitment to the anti-Nazi cause. He still remembers Cary's frantic telephone call from Los Angeles, as he begged him to protect the Grants' reputation. By skillful negotiation, Gould managed to reduce the charge from espionage, which would mean death by execution, to the lesser offense of being an unregistered agent for Germany. This was possible because Cassina was a citizen of Spain and thus technically neutral. Gould remembers that he advised his terrified young client to plead guilty five days before Christmas. The Grants were not present at the brief New York hearing, and by considerable effort, their publicists managed to keep their names out of the press. Among those who testified to Cassina's employment at Columbia Pictures through Cary Grant's influence was Columbia attorney Irving Morass. Two of Cassina's fellow workers also provided depositions. The story of Cassina's involvement with the enemy came out in his confession: his being hired by German agents in Biarritz, his attempts to determine pro- or anti-Nazi activities on the east and west coasts of the United States, and the circle of friends whom he milked for information. However, in his testimony he did not indicate that he had in any way guessed that Cary Grant was a British secret agent, nor was there any evidence that he had given away Cary's movements or put him in any danger.

It was fortunate for the Grants that the forces of protection for the rich and powerful were as strong as they were in 1943. Had it been known that they, however innocently, befriended a Nazi spy in time of war, and that they were paying a substantial sum to defend that spy, Cary's reputation could have been severely damaged, and Barbara might well have been ruined socially.

The Grants were forced to continue their social activities as though nothing had happened. Two days before Christmas, Cary was among the first to congratulate Randolph Scott, who had finally moved out of the Santa Monica beach house and announced his engagement to the heiress Patricia Stillman at a party at his house next to the Los Angeles Country Club. Scott and Miss Stillman were present when the Grants threw an open house on Christmas Day and Barbara gave Cary a painting by Diego Rivera.

On December 27, Cassina entered a guilty plea in New York Federal Court and was sentenced by Federal Judge John W. Clancy to a year and a day at Danbury, Connecticut Prison Farm. Three months later, he swore out a statement to the FBI. Cassina maintained that while in Berlin, in June 1937, reporting on his activities in the Spanish Civil War, he had been to the Spanish Embassy to pay his respects to his friend Antonio Vargas, the diplomatic attaché of General Franco. Vargas introduced Cassina to Errol Flynn's German associate Dr. Herman Erben. On Vargas's desk was a tall pile of photographs that Erben had just brought in. They showed the gun emplacements and other installations of the anti-Franco loyalist troops; Flynn was standing next to the guns. Erben had already taken one set of the pictures to the Berlin headquarters of the *Abwehr* Military Intelligence. Subsequently, the Austrian journalist Rudolph Stoiber discovered, from internal evidence of Erben's diaries and letters, that Flynn had personally taken thirteen reels of film of the loyalist installations and given them to the Franco spy, Bradish Johnson, at a meeting at the Plaza Athenée Hotel in Paris. (Cassina would spend less than the term of his sentence in jail and was deported to Portugal in March 1945.)

The fact that Cassina knew about Flynn's Nazi connections indicates that he may well have told Cary Grant about them. Hence the fact that Grant was able to discuss the matter with Joseph Longstreth at the party in Hollywood in 1941.

It was a painful way to start the year 1944. Cary was depressed, and canceled plans for another trip to Europe, possibly because he was deactivated and disciplined by M.I.6 at the time. Meanwhile, Brian Donlevy, a client of Cary's Frank Vincent Agency, had joined such figures as Eddie Albert and Rochelle Hudson as a secret agent. Cary was testy, uncomfortable, and hard to get on with that winter. He was also vexed by the many problems of Howard Hughes, who was in touch with him constantly on the matter of his latest obsession: a new flying boat, the HK-1—later known as the "Spruce Goose." Opposition by the government to various of his projects, plus a concussion he had suffered in the crash of an experimental plane being tested by the CAA, made him more eccentric and unstable than ever. He besieged everyone he knew with phone calls at all hours of the night, emitting a stream of anguished invective in his unique, high-pitched bat's squeak of a voice.

Cary, perhaps because of the stress he was under, had a violent quarrel with his old friend Jack Kelly, who left Warner Bros., apparently because Cary used his influence with Jack Warner to make sure that Kelly did not design the clothes for the Cole Porter film, which was now being discussed with Grant as its star. At the same time, Cary was deep in meetings with Clifford Odets to discuss a new picture, *None But the Lonely Heart;* Odets had written the script—based on a novel written in cockney slang by Richard Llewellyn—and would direct.

It was the story of a young man in London during the Depression. Odets and Cary worked together on the dialogue, ensuring the accuracy of the cockney dialect, which the Welsh author of *How Green Was My Valley* had sometimes misrepresented. Ernie Mott, the anti-hero, is a ne'er-do-well, an unemployed nobody who long ago deserted his mother. He returns reluctantly to her cramped house in the slums since he has nowhere else to live. His discovery that she has cancer draws him closer to her.

It goes without saying that the story was close to Cary's heart. He saw much of himself in the character as developed by Odets: a man obstreperous, cocky, and self-confident on the surface but, underneath, tense, angry, tortured by his inadequacies, filled with hidden guilts, and ambivalent about everything, at once attracted to and repelled by people and experiences. Odets cast Ethel Barrymore as Mrs. Mott. Cary had not seen her since the 1920s, when Jack Kelly had been her leading designer. With her huge, dark, liquid eyes, beautifully formed features, and deep, throbbing voice with a catch in it, she was ideally chosen for the role. She had not made a movie in eleven years, not since the controversial *Rasputin and the Empress,* in which she had played the Czarina of Russia. She felt more comfortable in the theater, and had made a tremendous impression in *The Corn Is Green,* which later became a vehicle for Bette Davis. George Coulouris, a member of Orson Welles's Mercury Theater company, was chosen to play the slimy East End villain who threatens the well-being of the Motts. He had come directly from a triumph in Lillian Hellman's *Watch on the Rhine.*

Odets and Cary continued the rapport that had marked their friendship from the beginning. As they began work on the film at RKO in March, the work was never less than pleasing for both men. At last Cary felt he had broken with the antic comedies of which he had grown tired. He would now be taken seriously as an actor, in a deeply tragic role. Jane Wyatt, who appeared in the movie as a struggling cellist, remembers the intensity and concentration that existed on the set, but she also recalls that after a sequence, Cary would do handstands and cartwheels, recalling his old vaudeville days, using this athletic, acrobatic form of release to break the excruciating tension of acting out so much of his early life.

On March 16, Odets wrote to a friend: "Directing a picture is really a labor [but it] is lightened by a talented actor like Cary Grant, not to mention Miss Barrymore." In a separate, undated note, he wrote: "Cary Grant is the hero of a Conrad novel: Lord Jim, etc." He was referring to Cary's capacity to detach himself from his surroundings, to find an island in himself away from the pain of existence. Like Lord Jim, he had managed to commandeer his own special territory, and no matter how vulnerable he might be (and he was especially vulnerable during the making of *None But the Lonely Heart*), he could set up defenses and push back the jungle.

He had other ways to relax. He turned up at the Show-Shop Theater to do a magic act with actor John Calvert. Cary performed a Houdini trunk trick, climbing into a large locked metal box after being tied hand and foot, and escaping within seconds, to loud applause.

But this was only a brief break in the tortured if rewarding job of making *None But the Lonely Heart*. And he had another cross to bear: In March, after obtaining a divorce under mysterious circumstances, and at a never-disclosed location, from Marion duPont, who was now living with a member of her horse-breeding staff, Randolph Scott married Patricia Stillman.

Filming of *None But the Lonely Heart* continued daily and nightly, including Sundays. The atmosphere created by the director began to weigh on Cary. He advised Odets on the sets, ensuring that the dimensions matched exactly those of sitting rooms and bedrooms he had inhabited. He asked for ceilings, made of muslin, to emphasize the claustrophobic character of life in the East End. The narrow street, with its semidetached houses and its railway bridge in the background, crossed by steam trains, was a marvel of the designer's art. In the ugly, cluttered dining area where Ernie eats with his stricken mother, the decor is so authentic that the viewer has the illusion of eavesdropping on the characters. The most remarkable sequence, shot on the last day, proved to be an endurance test for both Grant and Miss Barrymore. Mrs. Mott is dying in a prison hospital; the pain of the cancer is now unendurable and she is sustained only by her love for her son. Penniless, deceived by gangsters, Mott, finding his mother in this horrifying predicament, is desolate. He embraces her, and they burst into helpless tears. It was Cary Grant's finest moment on the screen. And it was also Miss Barrymore's. Neither performer would ever match that moment of transcendent beauty and terror. It was cathartic and shattering, and Odets's direction had a sensitivity, tenderness, and delicacy seldom matched in the American cinema.

By a coincidence that may have contributed to the intensity of the scene, a close friend of the two stars had died that same week. Myron Selznick, David's brother, had been the most important agent in Hollywood. Shooting was broken off while director and principals attended a funeral that drew virtually every prominent figure of the industry. A columnist noted: "Now that Myron is gone, Cary Grant is the best agent in Hollywood." Most people, including Cary's own clients, thought it was a gag.

The Grants turned up with Garbo at a huge party on May 4, 1944, given by Lady Mendl in honor of the celebrated clothing designer Mainbocher. For Cary it was a brief respite, followed by radio appearances, several of them with Don Barclay, who had returned from his South Pacific tour with Joel McCrea. Cary rejoiced in Barclay's company, reminiscing and laughing as they talked about the old days.

Barbara was frequently ill that spring, her relationship with Cary in serious trouble. Even the persuasive and charming Clifton Webb could not induce her to come to one of his famous parties. Suddenly, in June, a crisis arose, binding the unhappy Grants temporarily together. Count Reventlow, claiming that Barbara had used coarse and vulgar language in Lance's presence and had sought to undermine his affection for his father, refused to yield up Lance, and Barbara began fighting him in court. She lost a round of the custody battle that followed and was compelled to pay one million dollars to Reventlow to retrieve her son. Cary himself delivered the money and picked up the boy in Pasadena.

The reconciliation effected by Barbara's appreciation of Cary's faithfulness and encouragement during the long-drawn-out battle for Lance was short-lived. In the early part of August, Cary disappeared to an apartment in Beverly Hills, only returning to Barbara's house on August 22 to attend a party for the producer David Hempstead. He was encouraged by the Allied victories against the Germans in Europe and had temporarily reconciled with Barbara, only to break the relationship off again later the same month—his moods changed almost from day to day. But the first preview of *None But the Lonely Heart* helped take his mind off his marriage. "Cary Grant is actually off his handsome head with delight," Odets wrote to his secretary in New York on August 7. He would be nominated for an Academy Award for the film the following year and would reap some of his best reviews. Yet the picture's bleak realism ensured it a choppy passage at the box office. It was not what audiences were looking for in time of war, and not even the Grant name could save it.

Plans for a biographical film of Cole Porter began to accelerate in September, but Cary kept edging away from the project, uncertain if he could commit himself to it. He wanted to escape from the constrictions of Columbia, a studio he now detested, yet he was uneasy about portraying dishonestly an artist he knew and admired. The first-draft screenplay he was asked to consider was so contrived that it did not even adhere to the available public record of the rise and triumph of a genius of the American musical theater. The almost incomparable galaxy of songs and stars that made up Porter's life would of course lend itself ideally to the deluxe Hollywood treatment. But fresh from his experience with Odets, Cary wanted depth and richness and moving intensity in the treatment of Cole Porter's character, even though its most essential ingredient, his homosexuality, would have to be omitted.

On November 7, columnists were saying that Cary Grant might not make *Night and Day*, now the official title for the movie. Interviewed on November 15, he declined to discuss it. That same day, the Grants left Westridge House, so that the Fairbankses, who had returned to Los Angeles, could resume residence there. Mary Lee Fairbanks recalls that the beautiful Japanese garden she had helped to design had been replaced with a potato patch, Mrs. Grant's gesture for the war effort. Although the house was immaculately neat (she attributes this to Cary's influence), she was appalled to discover that Mrs. Grant's obsession with keeping the house temperature at eighty degrees summer and winter had caused some warping and cracking of the painted and enameled surfaces.

The new house the Grants occupied, 10615 Bellagio Road, Bel Air, was a white elephant of a place, huge, daunting, and lacking in warmth. With its structural problems and its colossal size, it seemed to come between the couple as they struggled to save their relationship. Their reconciliation was torturous and short-lived. Barbara would fling herself into extensive redecoration and then lose interest completely, becoming morose and distant. On November 30, Cary gave an extraordinarily convincing performance as a tormented, haunted near-psychopath in Cornell Woolrich's "The Black Curtain," for the CBS radio series *Suspense*. He played the role with brooding force, suggesting a spirit in purgatory. His thin, gaunt, and depressed appearance was noticed wherever he went, whether it was at a loan drive, an Elsa Maxwell party, or a Purple Heart veterans' get-together at the Bel Air Hotel. Always a determined achiever, Cary hated to admit that he had botched his marriage. He felt he had failed Barbara, though it would probably be more accurate to say that she had failed him.

On November 26, Steve Trilling, the Warners production chief, who had taken over the reigns of *Night and Day* from the recently departed Hal Wallis, called Frank Vincent to urge him to have Cary sign the film contract. Vincent told Trilling that because of Cary's mental condition, he would not be able to make any picture for an indefinite time. It might be six months before he could even consider working. Vincent knew that the Hungarian director Michael Curtiz and his writers were at the Waldorf Towers in New York, toiling with Cole Porter on the script and that aspects of the screenplay were specifically tailored to Cary's personality. But he also felt that Jack Warner should look elsewhere for his casting, that before the matter was entertained any further, Cary's "mind should be straightened out," because he was "so low."

There is no question that, as Frank Vincent's secret partner, Cary was the true author of this refusal. But Jack Warner stood firm. And so did Cole Porter, who would have nobody else play him.

That week, Barbara had gone to San Francisco with Gene Tierney. He begged her to return, and Miss Tierney interceded on his behalf. Although Barbara did return to Bellagio Road, she stayed only a few days before she moved out. Frederick Brisson and Rosalind Russell tried to patch together the broken relationship one more time. Miss Russell wrote in her memoirs:

[The Grants] wound up sleeping in Freddie's room at our house, and Freddie moved in with me. Next morning Freddie went back to his own room to get a pair of socks and saw Barbara alone in the bed. When he went into his bathroom, there was Cary asleep on the floor. Stepping over him, Freddie picked up a toothbrush and came back to me. "I think we've got trouble again," he said.

On February 26, the couple announced their official separation to the press.

Cary's Academy Award nomination for *None But the Lonely Heart* came two weeks later. He lost to Bing Crosby, who had achieved a great success in *Going My Way*. Ethel Barrymore received the award as best supporting actress. Cary still did not take the Academy Awards seriously (he did not attend the ceremony), yet he felt that he should not have been overlooked.

In April, Cary forced himself to sign the contract for *Night and Day*. He went in for color photo tests; he had never appeared in Technicolor before. The makeup irritated his skin and made him edgier than ever. He was difficult with the makeup staff and felt no rapport with Hungarian director, Michael Curtiz. He fussed over every line of dialogue and insisted that he be allowed to supervise both male and female costumes, sets, and even the selection of the cast. He was determined to have Porter's best friend, Monty Woolley, play himself in the picture, and he succeeded in overriding Jack Warner's puerile objections to the casting. He firmly approved the beautiful Canadian actress Alexis Smith as Linda Porter, Cole's wife. Tall and imposing, Miss Smith had been born lucky: she was discovered while at Los Angeles City College by a Warner Bros. talent agent, and after only two pictures she co-starred with Errol Flynn in the patriotic air force movie *Dive Bomber*. She had been outstanding in *The Constant Nymph*, in *Conflict*, and as a patroness of George Gershwin in *Rhapsody in Blue*. Although she achieved almost immediate stardom, by virtue of her flawless looks, charm, and perfect elocution, she today regards herself as having been no more than a Warner Bros. contract player, with little position and no influence.

The picture at last began shooting on June 14, 1945, on a replica of the New Haven, Connecticut, railway station built on the Warner Bros. back lot. Grant complained all day long about the dialogue, which he had already approved—how bad it was, how poorly written, and what a "lousy characterization" it gave him. Jane Wyman was unsettled by his behavior during the scene. It had to be completely redone, with new dialogue; again and again, in her heavy period dress in record heat, Miss Wyman had to climb onto the train, until she was exhausted. Ironically, it was a snow scene, and the ice machine and generators broke down. Everyone went home in a bad temper, most notably Cary Grant.

There followed some sequences in Cole Porter's Indiana home. Cary had cast Henry Stephenson, whom he had so much liked during *Mr. Lucky,* in an almost identical role, as a crusty grandfather; he enjoyed playing these scenes. Selena Royle, acting as his mother, was ill during the sequences, with a kidney infection and a 101-degree fever; she had to be virtually written out of the script, and scenes endlessly reconstructed around her. During one of those sequences, Alexis Smith had the pleasant assignment of kissing Cary Grant under the mistletoe. She says:

> Just a short time before, I had been seeing Cary at Saturday matinees in Hollywood with my girlfriends. Now all of a sudden I was actually kissing him! I completely forgot all my lines and didn't know what I was doing for several minutes. Can anyone blame me? I've never been so flustered in my life!

"[Cary] was a perfectionist; he agonized many times over something I might consider incidental," Miss Smith recalls. It didn't help that he kept changing the dialogue, and that she and the other performers had to memorize different-colored pages of script every day. There would be meetings in dressing rooms; Michael Curtiz would pull out cardboard boxes filled with red, yellow, pink, blue, and green pages, sifting through them in an effort to find a version that would work.

Cary was especially fretful over a sequence set in Kensington Gardens, London, where Cole Porter reencounters his future wife, who is taking care of a bunch of children. Porter assumes the children are hers. The gag was excessively overdone, and Cary repeatedly rewrote it, while the actors returned to their dressing rooms, to await a call for another stab at the action. For a sequence in a theater where one of Porter's musical shows is in progress, the director told Miss Smith to link arms with Cary to express her pleasure at the performance. She followed the instruction; her arms were bare. Suddenly, Cary drew back as though stung, saying, "Do you have body makeup on?" She replied that she did. And he said, rather sharply, "This is a Savile Row suit, and it's the war, and I can't replace it. If it gets covered in body makeup, it will be ruined." Exasperated, Curtiz scrapped the arm-linking. Then Cary shouted at Curtiz, "Do you see these cuffs? There's a quarter of an inch showing. It should be an eighth of an inch!" In despair, Curtiz summoned the wardrobe staff, as Cary returned to his dressing room, irritably removing his shirt and refusing to continue until it had been adjusted. "At the time, I thought it was silly," Miss Smith says. But she adds:

> That kind of attitude . . . was indicative of his work. I would rather have him be fussy about a quarter of an inch on a cuff and give the performance he did, because it was that care and attention that carried him through everything he did. His acting wasn't an eighth of an inch off.

Alexis Smith was intimidated by Cary in many ways. She felt paranoid about the constant reshooting, wondering if it was her fault and knowing that she wasn't on a par with him as a performer. She points out that one of the reasons Cary was unhappy with the film was that he had just been working with Clifford Odets, and suddenly he had to deal with lines that were virtually meaningless, delivered on colored pages out of cardboard boxes.

There were more problems on the picture. Monty Woolley, whose comic acting was so crucial to the overall success of the work, was suffering from a severe bladder problem. He had to be filled with drugs, and sometimes he failed to turn up at rehearsals. Cary warned Curtiz that if he continued pushing Woolley, the actor would very possibly die. Some of Woolley's scenes had to be rushed through so that he could get to the hospital for a very serious operation.

The cameraman, Bert Glennon, walked off the movie when he overheard Curtiz criticizing his daily rushes. He was replaced by William V. Skall, also experienced in color cinematography; Skall took ill and was replaced in turn, by Peverell Marley. The scene of Porter's grandfather's death was reshot again and again. Cary disliked the way he was photographed, complaining that he looked more deathly ill than Henry Stephenson was supposed to look. Cary hated the appearance of the frosted window in the scene, grumbling that the frost should be on the outside and not the inside. Curtiz tried to explain that the only way to photograph the window was to fake this effect, but Cary insisted there would have been central heating

in the Porter family home in Indiana, so that frost could not possibly have formed on the inside of a pane. He at last won the
argument.

On July 2, Monty Woolley was in the hospital, in great pain, and
Cary twice insisted that the shooting end early so that he could visit
him. There was another row in July 11, during the filming of an
outdoor musical scene at Yale. Curtiz lined up the young men playing students with Cary's stand-in, Mel Merrihugh. Cary was to
conduct the students in song, but he suddenly announced that he
detested the whole setup and did not feel that Cole Porter should
be portrayed on the screen as a cheerleader. Curtiz reminded him
that he had already agreed to the sequence, as written in the script.
Cary then announced he would play the entire scene with his back
to the camera, and he did.

On July 13, Curtiz was depressed and irritable, screaming at his
favorite propman, the British World War I veteran "Limey" Plews,
because he dared not scream at Cary. So desperate was the situation
by mid-July that Cary, studio boss Steve Trilling, Michael Curtiz,
and the writers would meet at the Brown Derby restaurant on Vine
Street and sit there until the early hours of the morning, trying to
pull the project together. On July 18, a hospital scene in France
had to be changed from beginning to end because Cary hated the
set and insisted—over the protests of the art director, John Hughes—
that it was inaccurate. On July 21, he suddenly declared that over
130 soldiers in the hospital were incorrectly uniformed. Milo Anderson, the experienced costume designer, was furious when he was
told to re-dress every single extra from head to foot. Alexis Smith
remembers that there were aspects of the World War I scenes that
also struck her as absurd. She says:

> Cary was composing the song "Night and Day." He was sitting at
> the piano in the hospital, and rain was dripping down, inspiring
> a line in the verse. I had to stand there as an ideal [woman],
> looking at him lovingly. It was so funny, because there I was as
> his romantic inspiration, and I was wearing this terrible nurse's
> uniform and heavy white regulation army shoes! I couldn't stop
> laughing. Cary didn't see the joke.

1 6 7

By August 3, Eric Stacey, the production manager, was writing in his daily memorandum, "It's a wonder some of us don't go nuts!"

On August 21, Cary walked onto the set of a five-and-dime store music counter, at which he and Ginny Sims were supposed to be selling sheet music. The moment he looked around, he flew into a rage and announced that he couldn't possibly work on the set, because he was married to the Woolworth heiress and everyone would think he was trying to promote her family business. Moreover, he said, everything on the set was wrong, including the clothes worn by the people in the store, which were totally out of period; the store itself looked contemporary. Michael Curtiz had to close down shooting for the day while Cary instructed John Hughes in the correct appearance of a cheap store between the wars.

On September 1, Cary complained loudly that the public address system used to summon people to the telephone, and the exhaust fans, which droned and whirred, made it impossible for him to work; he walked off the set. He was even more cantankerous on September 5, when he played a sequence in a theater box with eight-year-old Wayne, the son of Dorothy Malone and Donald Woods in the story. He objected to the child's lines and suddenly announced that the little boy must be dropped from the story completely and sent home. The child burst into tears and ran off the set. Cary seemed unaware of the cruelty of his action.

The same day, Eric Stacey wrote: "I don't think there is a set in this picture that hasn't been changed by Cary, and it has cost this studio a terrific amount of money." Six days later, a truss was mysteriously loosened on a large arc lamp, which crashed onto the stage, missing Cary by inches. Perhaps somebody was trying to tell him something.

A summit meeting was called in Jack Warner's office that day, to discuss the remaining scenes. Cary refused to appear. He was called repeatedly until ten o'clock that night, and still did not turn up. He refused to postrecord a scene in a New York taxicab, which had been ruined by noise. He was on edge again on September 9, when Jane Wyman, who was worn down from all the pressure, announced that some scenes would have to be rearranged to allow her to begin work on *The Yearling* at M-G-M. On September 29, he had a head-on collision with Curtiz; Cary had decided at the last minute to introduce his favorite studio hot-dog wagon into a London scene where it had no business to be. Curtiz protested against this, probably on the ground that after all Cary's emphasis on realism, it was absurd to have a hot-dog wagon in 1930s England. But Cary was adamant that the wagon's owner, Willy King, appear on the screen. Curtiz screamed furiously at the mixer and the boom boy, with words intended for Cary. At that moment, the entire crew and cast booed the director, an unprecedented episode in Hollywood filmmaking. Curtiz said he was going home and that Cary could direct the picture. It was only when Jack Warner turned up in the middle of this crisis that Curtiz was persuaded to continue, now some twenty days behind schedule.

T E N

Barbara filed suit for divorce on July 11. She told reporters that their last reconciliation had proved she and Cary could not live together as man and wife. She had moved out. Louella Parsons quoted Grant as saying:

> I feel badly that we couldn't make a go of our marriage. I honestly tried and I believe Barbara did too. Her ideas and mine were different. She was brought up in Europe and, well, I like [going to] prize fights [with] my gang. Barbara's friends were mostly continental titled people. She is a wonderful woman, kind and sweet, and I have only the best thoughts and wishes for her happiness.

On July 13, Cary learned that Count Reventlow, having failed to obtain full custody of Lance, had absconded with the boy, now nine, to Canada. Cary shared Barbara's extreme distress at the news, and despite the disintegration of their relationship, he promised to help her yet again with this disagreeable struggle for Lance. Grant was furious when, instead of standing firm with him in the fight, Barbara moved to New York, where she became involved with an infamous adventurer, crook, and Nazi collaborator, Freddie McEvoy. This lean and handsome athlete was Errol Flynn's closest friend and his spiritual twin, already involved with Flynn in gun, drug, and tungsten smuggling. He ran a "stud farm," where he sold handsome and virile young men to wealthy women in marriage.

Cary, already overburdened emotionally, was scheduled to make *Notorious*, with shooting to begin less than two weeks after *Night and Day* was completed. Again he was starring in a film with intriguing parallels to his own life. He had succeeded in turning the script of *Night and Day* into what was virtually his autobiography; in its final form, it would be the vibrantly directed story of an emotionally cold, utterly detached genius whose wife was a permanent grass widow, isolated from him by his obsessive pursuit of a career. Similarly, Cary had exerted influence upon Clifford Odets and Ben Hecht, both of whom had worked on the script of the new movie, to be directed by Alfred Hitchcock. The picture, a project of David O. Selznick, had been under discussion for just over a year. It was based remotely on a short story entitled "The Song of the Dragon," by John Taintor Foote, which appeared in the *Saturday Evening Post* in 1921. As adapted, it involved a German-American girl, Alicia Huberman, whose father had been apprehended as a Nazi agent. She is used by an FBI spy to infiltrate a circle of German industrialists in exile in Rio, who are planning to develop uranium from mines in the nearby mountains in order to start a third world war. Because of the recent American bombing of Hiroshima and Nagasaki, uranium was very much in the news. When it was discovered that Cary was to star as the spy, the FBI began to take a special interest in the film. J. Edgar Hoover had not forgiven him for his role with British Security Coordination on FBI territory; now the fact that he would be playing an FBI agent must have annoyed Hoover. For a time, the project hung in the balance; Hitchcock thought that the reason for the problem and for his constant surveillance by an FBI agent was that the allusion to uranium was a breach of security. It was only through the efforts of Selznick—who sold the property to RKO but maintained an interest in it—that the FBI finally permitted Motion Picture Production Code chief Joseph Breen to approve the script.

Cary wanted Ethel Barrymore to play the mother of the Nazi, Alexander Sebastian, whom Alicia Huberman has to seduce into marriage. But Miss Barrymore was back on the stage, capitalizing on her recent Academy Award, and declined the part. Instead, Leopoldine Konstantin was chosen. She had been the star of Max Reinhardt's productions of *Sumurun* in Berlin, and she had been acting in New York when Cary appeared there as a seven-year-old child. Claude Rains was the ideal choice for Sebastian. Ingrid Bergman was cast as Alicia Huberman. There were parallels in her own life as well: a Nazi sympathizer before World War II, she had been observed heiling Hitler; then she had repudiated the Nazi philosophy and had become a patriot in the Allied cause. Like Alicia, she was promiscuous, despite the fact that she had a husband and a child. During the shooting, she had a liaison with Larry Adler, the harmonica virtuoso. She would commute between Adler's home and her own, turning up, in defiance of the columnists, at Hitchcock's dinner parties with her lover. At the same time, tortured by her inability to stick to one man, she somehow contrived to date the eminent young photographer Robert Capa. She felt no attraction to Cary, nor he to her. Even though the movie contained some of the most intense love scenes yet seen on the screen, there was no sexual chemistry between these stars.

It was extraordinary for Cary to be acting out his real-life role as a spy on the screen. There was a close parallel to his friend Reginald Gardiner's affair with the suspected German agent Hilda Krueger in order to observe her activities. (Gardiner had painted a blood-dripping swastika on Miss Krueger's front door, to indicate what he thought of her.) Early in the movie, Devlin, the FBI man played by Cary, tells Alicia that her father has committed suicide in prison. This reflected the recent death of the prominent Nazi collaborator Charles Bedaux, a friend of Barbara Hutton's, who took his life after his arrest for treason. Like Bedaux, Huberman kills himself in a Miami prison.

Notorious also illuminated an aspect of Cary's sexual character. At the beginning, he says, "I've always been scared of women." When Devlin kisses Alicia, it is either to inveigle her into a plot that would involve her sexual betrayal of him or as a cover when they are discovered by her husband in an act of espionage. Having scarcely protested, and indeed aided, the FBI's manipulation of a beautiful woman into bed and marriage with a man she detests, Devlin criticizes her for what is in fact his own moral failure. His possessiveness, sexual ambiguity, and deep-seated guilt and fear are from beginning to end Cary Grant.

As for Hitchcock, he was virtually a sexual neuter, who once bragged to the Italian journalist Oriana Falaci that he had experienced sex only once, and that was because his wife, Alma, said she wanted a child. The film, in his own words to Charles Higham, was "a voyeur experience. The audience became one person, sharing a room with Cary Grant and Ingrid Bergman in a *ménage à trois*." The director dwelt on the couple's long, clinging kisses as they discussed such banalities as cooking and washing up. Nothing could be less erotic than the famous scene in which Grant and Bergman embrace on a balcony overlooking Copacabana Beach and then, pressed close to each other and whispering, move through shadows and light into the softly glowing apartment. In an additional joke, Hitchcock makes sure this protracted love-making is not followed by any suggestion of intercourse; the audience is left frustrated along with the characters as Devlin, in what can only be described as a direct jibe at Cary's private life, walks out on Alicia at the crucial moment, leaving her with the sole consolation of a wine bottle.

Unlike that of *Night and Day,* the filming of *Notorious* went smoothly, the director's habit of planning every sequence down to the tiniest detail resulting in a film that resembled the inside of a Rolex watch. It was the most perfectly formed and exquisitely timed of movies, expressing Hitchcock's talent at its peak. The scenes between Alex Sebastian and his mother could easily have been expositions of conventional villainy, but the strong hint of incest, the mother, fiercely jealous of Alicia, wearing a pierced-heart brooch during a critical confrontation with her son, carried a powerful charge. Rains and Konstantin were excellent, extracting every last drop of subtle menace from the cunningly written roles. *Notorious* was destined to be one of Cary Grant's greatest successes, and it remains arguably his most enjoyable dramatic film. And in another tiny touch, Sir Charles Mendl, mentor of Count Cassina and British special agent, turned up at the beginning as a wealthy old yachtsman, who tries to lure Alicia into accompanying him to Cuba.

During the shooting of *Notorious,* Cary was dating the beautiful, blonde, and ambitious Betty Hensel, whose parents had been sponsors of the St. Louis Municipal Opera, in which Cary appeared in 1931. The twenty-two-year-old Miss Hensel, who strongly resembled Phyllis Brooks, was well-to-do, undemanding, but delighted to be accepted in the highest levels of Hollywood society as Cary Grant's girlfriend. In March, she had been about to get married to Lieutenant Henry William Dodge, Jr., in San Francisco, but canceled the wedding at the last minute, following a nervous collapse during which she announced feebly to her parents in their suite at the Beverly Wilshire Hotel in Los Angeles that she couldn't proceed because she loved Cary Grant.

Possibly in order to irritate Cary and Betty Hensel, Barbara suddenly turned up in Hollywood with the handsome actor Philip Reed. Cary hated Barbara's interest in Reed and, quite irrationally, charged him with breaking up a marriage that had in fact long since ended. As it turned out, Barbara's inability to sustain any sort of relationship doomed her affair with Reed from the beginning. And besides, she was even more obsessed with Baron Gottfried von Cramm now that the war was over. To ensure that he did not have any trouble in Germany, she wanted the occupying forces to take full note of the fact that he had been in prison and forced to serve in the army on the Russian front. She succeeded in using her influence on his behalf. At the same time, at Cary's suggestion, she had given Winfield House, her home in Regent's Park, London, to the British government. Arrangements were concluded late that fall, and in December letters of gratitude were pouring in from dozens, including President Harry S Truman and Acting Secretary of State Dean Acheson. The transfer of title was completed at Christmas.

After *Notorious* was completed, Cary and Betty Hensel flew to Las Vegas, where Bugsy Siegel—who had just secretly married Virginia Hill in Mexico—was opening the Flamingo Hotel, in league with his mob connections. Cary returned to Los Angeles without attending the opening; there had probably been warnings of violence, and Cary didn't want to expose Betty to danger. Instead, the couple turned up at a party given by Edith Gwynn in Hollywood.

They didn't like it and walked out; neither was mentioned in the *Reporter* for a month.

In the meantime, Cary's association with Howard Hughes was scrutinized by the FBI. By now, the Bureau had a voluminous file on Hughes, in which Cary was frequently mentioned as the closest of his innermost circle. Agents checked on Hughes's assignations in hotels and apartments with the actresses Yvonne De Carlo, Faith Domergue, and others, trying unsuccessfully to determine anything untoward that might result from these harmless affairs.

J. Edgar Hoover was also concerned that Hughes had obtained large quantities of raw film stock for *The Outlaw* through the black market, and more important, he focused upon Hughes's special relationship with Bugsy Siegel. Hughes was in partnership with Siegel in establishing Las Vegas as a crime and gambling center, and had an interest in the Flamingo Hotel. At the same time, William R. Wilkerson, another partner in the hotel and one of Cary's friends and supporters, was being investigated for his association with Siegel.

Hughes was busy that December drumming up a salacious publicity campaign for *The Outlaw,* in which Jane Russell displayed her heroic breasts in camera shots that gave considerable pause to the Breen office. He was also continuing to work night and day on his "Spruce Goose," which Cary was invited to see in its vast hangar. Hughes invited a large number of stars and producers to accompany him on the inaugural flight to New York in his masterpiece: the Constellation aircraft on which he had been working through much of World War II. Several executives, including Louis B. Mayer, Darryl F. Zanuck, and Jack Warner, declined the invitation because they knew that Hughes was in trouble with Washington and that his aide and pimp Johnny Meyer was also under intensive investigation. However, quite rashly, Cary Grant accepted the invitation, probably because of the exciting idea of the trip and because (no small consideration in his case) it was free of charge. Siegel declined to go because he was tied up with severe problems in Las Vegas. He was bothered by threats from rival mobsters who resented his activities; he had opened the Flamingo Hotel too early and had overextended his budget so severely that he could not sustain initial losses of over $300,000 at the gambling tables. He was hard put to pay the four million dollars in architects' and builders' bills he owed. Dorothy di Frasso, though jilted by him, turned up and offered whatever help she could. But her wealth had been dissipated and she was unable to even begin to bail him out.

The Constellation flight left Los Angeles Airport on its historic journey at midnight on February 14, 1946. Forty of Hughes's best friends were able to make the trip, including Johnny Maschio and Constance Moore, Edward G. Robinson, Alfred Hitchcock, Linda Darnell, William Powell, Paulette Goddard, Janet Blair, and Celeste Holm. Cary had had a major quarrel with Betty Hensel and had decided to use the trip as an opportunity to get away from her for a time. Maschio was the genial host, plying the passengers with food and liquor. The atmosphere was uproarious, and at one stage, when the windshield misted over, Hughes wiped off the condensation with a cloth soaked in vodka. Cary was the only passenger Hughes allowed to share the trip with him in the cockpit. In New York, the guests checked into the Sherry Netherland Hotel, and the elaborate wining and dining went on. FBI agents kept a constant watch on the hotel, observing the comings and goings of Hughes's party, all of whom returned to Los Angeles two weeks later, with Cary's friend Count Bernadotte of Sweden and Governor M. C. Wallgren of Washington added to the passenger list. Upon the return, Cary joined with Jimmy Stewart to throw a party at the Clover Club for Hughes and Johnny Meyer at which Bugsy Siegel was present. Among the guests were the Cornel Wildes, Linda Darnell, Connie Moore, Johnny Maschio and Teresa Wright.

In April, Cary flew to London and met with Alexander Korda— ostensibly to discuss a company they would be forming to produce films of quality, including *The Third Man*. It is more likely that London Films was being used as a cover for the Secret Intelligence Service, still under the control of Sir Stewart Menzies and his special deputy, Major General John Alexander Sinclair. As Anthony Cave Brown wrote in his book *C: The Secret Life of Sir Stewart Menzies*:

> By early 1946, "C" had reformed the Service to reflect his belief that the only potential enemy was Russia. Nazism was so dead that it seemed it had never existed.

In view of the continued classification of the Grant files in London, there is no proof that Cary continued his work for British Security Coordination at home and abroad under Sir William Stephenson, but there is circumstantial evidence to suggest that he did. Korda certainly continued his activities, transposing his whole organization into an anti-Soviet network. Cary's reasons for being in London at this crucial time included his acceptance that May of the King's Medal for Service in the Cause of Freedom, an award that, according to the historian of M.I.6, Nigel West, was given to individuals who had performed special intelligence services for the Allied governments. The important award was never made public because its announcement could expose Grant's wartime activities and leave him open to danger from still-active Nazis.

When Cary returned to New York, his reservation at the Sherry Netherland was arranged by Johnny Meyer on behalf of Howard Hughes. Hughes had been living with Lana Turner in a suite at the hotel. Cary arrived on May 5. Two days later, Hughes and Meyer returned from Louisville, where they had been attending the Kentucky Derby; Miss Turner joined them and Cary for several dinners and small parties. The FBI was following them every minute, bugging their suites. At the same time, the well-publicized Senate investigations continued. A motley collection of actresses, clerks, and small-time hangers-on was interrogated, while Hughes and his entourage stayed on in New York. Cary spent a good deal of time that week with Virginia Cherrill, still Countess of Jersey, who was on her way to Hollywood.

Cary returned home to see the finished cut of *Night and Day*. He disliked the film but was naïvely surprised to find that Cole and Linda Porter thoroughly enjoyed the whitewashed version of their lives. In the third week of May, Cary agreed to make *The Bishop's Wife,* to be produced by Sam Goldwyn. He would play a bishop who, much troubled over the building of a new cathedral in a small American town, is visited by a polished gentleman stranger who turns out to be an angel. While Cary waited for revisions to the screenplay, Count Bernadotte stayed with him at his home on Beverly Grove Drive for the second time in less than a year. Bernadotte, who had played a part through the Red Cross in the negotiations that terminated the war between Britain, the United States, and

Germany, had a special role in the international Allied Intelligence Network against the Soviets. He had no interest in the film industry or in film people; it is interesting to speculate on the possibility that his purpose in coming to Los Angeles was to confer with Cary on problems that would arise in that postwar period.

Cary spent the summer of 1946 on Beverly Grove Drive. His relationship with Betty Hensel was unstable, a succession of arguments and reconciliations. He remained close to Randolph Scott and fond of Barbara Hutton. She had moved to Tangier and was embroiled in an increasingly complicated relationship not only with Freddie McEvoy but with his protégé, Prince Igor Troubetzkoy.

On June 17, Cary refused the leading role in *The Hucksters,* a story of the advertising business in Manhattan, and encouraged his friend Clark Gable to play the part; Gable did. At the same time, with *The Bishop's Wife* still not satisfactorily scripted, Grant somehow got talked into working out his old RKO contract with *The Bachelor and the Bobby-Soxer,* written by Sidney Sheldon. He would play a painter, involved in violent incidents in which he is wrongly suspected of criminal tendencies; a teenager, to be played by Shirley Temple, falls in love with him. He was not happy with the selection of a contract director, Irving Reis, a favorite of studio chief Dore Schary, to handle the project; he would have preferred Leo Mc-Carey or even H. C. Potter.

The Bachelor and the Bobby-Soxer began shooting on July 15. Characteristically, Cary introduced into it elements of his own childhood which included the mention of his old art teacher and the incident of alleged stealing.

The shooting of *The Bachelor and the Bobby-Soxer* was uncomfortable. Although Cary had always admired Miss Temple, especially in the films in which she appeared with Phyllis Brooks, and although he was glad to be working with the cool Myrna Loy again after more than a decade (she played a judge), he could not tolerate Irving Reis. Miss Loy recalled:

When I asked Irving to redo my first scene twice, Cary got his back up and left the set to phone Dore (Schary). "What's going on here?" he said. "You've got a director down here who doesn't know what he's doing, and Myrna's getting away with murder!" Dore came down to the set and Irving walked out.

Writing in his memoirs, *Heyday*, Schary commented:

Irving Reis . . . was a mercurial young man who did not respond too well under pressure, and one day he blew up and left the stage. I took over for him and directed some scenes with Cary, and Myrna. After a few days Irving returned, permitting us to establish a modus vivendi in which I could work closely with the actors while he worked on camera set-ups and movement. This arrangement satisfied Cary, who had found Irving too complicated a director.

Sidney Sheldon confirms the misery of making what was supposed to be a lighthearted comedy. Miss Loy recalls that Cary was in a stage of "jitters," nervous and uncomfortable during much of the shooting—which coincided with his interrogation by the FBI's Richard Hood on the Hughes-Meyer-Siegel activities in Las Vegas. Only the presence of Don Barclay on the set seemed to soothe him. Then he received an unpleasant shock. Frank Vincent, his beloved partner and friend for over twenty years, died suddenly of a heart attack, at the age of sixty-one. Furthermore, Howard Hughes was involved in a near-fatal accident during the shooting, which greatly distressed Cary. Flustered by his problems with the authorities, Hughes had poured himself into the final construction and test flight of his XF-II airplane. On July 7, he invited his new girlfriend, Jean Peters, to watch his pioneer journey. Taking off from Culver City, he circled around Hughes Field. But at five thousand feet, he began losing altitude and realized he could not maintain the XF-II in the air. Beverly Hills was suddenly looming underneath him, and he began to plunge toward the Los Angeles Country Club. Instead of hitting the club grounds, he crashed into 803 North Linden Drive, plowing into the second floor; the right wing of his plane smashed into the neighboring house. Finally, his craft skidded to a halt at 808 North Whittier. The plane and the house burst into flames. Fortunately, the owner Lieutenant Colonel Charles E. Meyer (no relation to Johnny), was in Europe; but Hughes was severely injured. Seven ribs were broken, his nose was fractured, his scalp was cut open, he was burned on his left buttock, his chest, and his hands. His left lung collapsed, and his right lung was damaged. His heart had been thrust aside in the chest cavity.

Cary rushed from the soundstage to his beloved friend's bedside; only Cary, Jean Peters, Lana Turner, and Errol Flynn of the Hollywood community were admitted. Investigations showed that the plane's right rear propeller had, according to Hughes's biographers Donald L. Barlett and James B. Steele, "lost oil, reversed pitch, and created a drag on the right side of the airplane." The investigating board also determined that Hughes was in error. He had not used a radio frequency authorized for the XF-II, had not understood the emergency operating procedures for the propellers, and had not properly retracted the landing gear. Hughes's recovery late that July and early August of 1946 was painfully slow. The visits to his sickbed during the convalescent period were harrowing to Cary. Hughes was screaming with pain, and his doctor had to fill him with morphine to appease him. Cary loaned him his house to recover in. While Hughes stayed at Beverly Grove Drive, Cary moved into a small house nearby, constantly calling Hughes to see how he was getting on. The millionaire talked to Cary of their taking a trip to Mexico together when he was better. Of all the people he knew, Cary was still the closest to him.

It is not surprising that Cary found it almost impossible, given even his professionalism, to act his way through the mindless situations of *The Bachelor and the Bobby-Soxer*. Moreover, he and Betty Hensel were still in trouble. Cary was more restless than ever, tortured over Hughes's condition, worried about the danger posed by Bugsy Siegel, harassed by Dorothy di Frasso's appearances at his door to complain of the situation with Siegel, on edge because of the FBI's pursuit of him, and vexed by the fact that the sudden decision to make *The Bishop's Wife* that winter removed all hope he might have had of going to Europe to work with Korda and Sir Stewart Menzies.

ELEVEN

After an uninspiring Christmas, relieved only by visits to nightclubs to see Jimmy Durante and Don Barclay in performance, Cary took off on a much-delayed flight with Howard Hughes. Hughes was now almost fully recovered from his accident, but his mind had been affected and from now on his behavior would become increasingly erratic and strange. He developed his manic notorious fear of being touched and wore white gloves everywhere; he had his food tested as though he were an occupant of the court of the Borgias. In January, while last-minute adjustments were being made to the script of *The Bishop's Wife,* he flew Cary, without a crew, in a B-23 bomber to New York. Hughes had to appear before representatives of the still-extant investigative committee; then he and Grant flew on to Washington, where Hughes would plead his case to Lieutenant General Ira C. Eaker, Deputy Commanding General of the Air Force. Commanding General Carl Spaatz listened to Hughes and authorized him to make another test flight of the XF-II. However, there was nothing the two leaders of the Air Force could do about the still highly adverse position the special committee was taking on Hughes's activities.

On their flight back to Los Angeles, Cary and Hughes were reported missing. They had made radio contact with the Indianapolis Airport, but no further word had been heard from them for several hours. Announcements flashed over the radio and wire services said that the two men were believed to be dead. The truth was that they had decided to slip away to Nogales, Arizona, and then to Mexico City, apparently using their influence with the local air controllers not to report their whereabouts. Walking into the lobby of the Reforma Hotel in Mexico City, Cary read the headline SENORS GRANT AND HUGHES BELIEVED DEAD. He called Betty Hensel and his friends in Hollywood and laughingly assured them that, as with Mark Twain, reports of his death were greatly exaggerated.

The two men returned to Hollywood. Hughes left for Washington yet again, to testify before the committee, while Cary began work on *The Bishop's Wife*. His friend David Niven played the angel in the story, to Cary's befuddled, irritable bishop. Niven had been devastated the previous May by the death of his beautiful young British wife, Primula, who had opened the wrong door during a game of hide-and-seek at the home of Tyrone Power and plunged to her death down steps that led to the stone floor of a cellar. She was only twenty-six. Niven had not recovered from the shock. Still depressed, he was out of sorts during the shooting; Cary was not happy with the director, William Seiter, who was working at a sluggish pace; and Goldwyn was disappointed with the daily work. After three weeks of desultory shooting, Goldwyn decided to scrap the existing footage. He called up the trusted, good-natured German-American director Henry Koster, who had made his name with the charming, *gemütlich* Deanna Durbin pictures. Goldwyn showed Koster the scenes that had been shot and told him that he was going to have Robert Sherwood's screenplay rewritten by Leonardo Bercovici. Cary would now play the angel and David Niven the bishop. Koster saw at once that this decision should have been made from the beginning. He remembered:

> I met with Cary Grant, whom I admired all my life, and who was the best comedy leading man in the world. He was very upset. He thought the part of the bishop, which he had been playing, was much better than the part of the angel, because the angel was simply a straightforward, very self-assured man, while the bishop would be comically befuddled, one of Cary's specialties.

He was annoyed because Goldwyn was forcing him to play this other part. Cary wanted to resign; he told Goldwyn he wanted the part for which he was signed. Goldwyn told him that only Goldwyn could decide what Cary would play. This created great friction.

Koster met the actors each morning before they were made up; he sat with them on the set, with the cameraman, Gregg Toland, next to him, and rehearsed the sequences so that everyone was prepared. Then he had the actors go into makeup and costume and return with a clear idea of how the scene was going to be played. Cary did not mind this approach, even though by now he was bored with the whole project. He liked Koster, but he still felt at odds with the material. He was so irritated by a scene involving an ancient Roman coin that he simply picked up the coin and began to walk off the set. Koster asked him where he was going. He replied that he couldn't play the scene. He was sweating; his face moist; he was very tense. Koster tried repeatedly to have him do the scene. Cary insisted that the angel would not do what the script made him do. It took a whole day to reach a compromise.

There were other problems. There was a scene in which Cary and Loretta Young, who played the bishop's wife, were supposed to be gazing at each other with a sense of communion without physical passion that was essential to the mood of the film. Neither actor had ever objected to being shot in profile. But now Cary said he looked better from his left side, and Loretta said that she also looked better from that side. In despair, Koster said, "How can I direct what is, in essence, a love scene if both of you are looking the same way?" The two stars shrugged and looked at Koster. Finally, Koster reworked the whole sequence so that Miss Young walked to the window and looked out, and Cary stepped up behind her and put his hands on her shoulders and looked out past her head.

Koster remembered:

Sam Goldwyn used to come in early to see the rushes. He called me to his office. He said, "What is this, Cary and Loretta looking out the window? That isn't the way the scene was scripted. They're supposed to be gazing into each other's eyes." I told him what had happened. He came down to the set. He was very annoyed with Cary and Loretta, but he let the scene go in as I had shot it. And he told them as he walked back to his office, "From now on, both of you guys get only half your salary if I can only use half your faces."

The truth was, of course, that both stars photographed perfectly from any angle. There was difficulty with a scene in which the angel and the bishop's wife go skating together. Although both performers could skate a little, the sequence called for great expertise on the rink. After searching for every possible solution, Koster put masks on doubles; seeing the picture today, it is impossible to tell the difference. Cary was annoyed about this, feeling that he could easily have mastered the technique of figure skating in no time at all. But Goldwyn was adamant that he must not risk an injury, and Cary continued sulking.

Koster added:

When Cary did a scene, any scene, I knew he was miserable, that he didn't want to play the character at all. This is the worst thing that can happen to a director, to work with an actor who doesn't want to play a part and is contractually forced to do it. David Niven was no more pleased than Cary.

During the shooting in the winter months of early 1947, Cary did his best to break up the tension and monotony of the work. He turned up at a party given by his old friends and fellow special agents Ralph and Carmel Myers Blum for the newlyweds Van Johnson and Evie (formerly Mrs. Keenan) Wynn. He delighted the guests by playing a record he had made at home, "One for My Baby," in which, grinding out the lines in nasal cockney, he entertainingly imitated a heavyweight torch singer, until everyone was convulsed with laughter.

On February 18, Cary let slip to the *Hollywood Reporter* for the first time that he was his own agent. He was also representing Edward G. Robinson, Rosalind Russell, and Joel McCrea until all three were able to find other representation. For some reason, the general public* never found this out. On February 21, the Blums gave yet another party, at which Cary was seen tenderly playing what one columnist described as "a right good, soft, hot piano for the benefit of Virginia Cherrill Jersey" and others, including his old friends George Burns and Gracie Allen, as well as Joan Crawford and Virginia Mayo. The party was in honor of Cary's friend Gardner (Mike) Cowles, publisher of *Look* magazine, and his bride, Fleur. At a soiree given by the writer Leonard Spigelgass, in honor of the British playwright Ronald Millar, Loretta Young was there along with producer Hal Wallis, who was dating the Australian actress Ann Richards. Miss Young was already telling people that she wasn't happy working with Cary, because of his fussiness over the sets in *The Bishop's Wife.* In an interview, she complained that he had held up a day's work, grumbling over the absence of frost on a window, an incident reminiscent of *Night and Day.*

Cary was seen with the actress Peggy Cummins, partying at the singer Ginny Simms's house with Howard Hughes on April Fool's Day (he again played piano), and only very occasionally, accompanying Betty Hensel. He was without her at a soirée given by Hughes on May 6. A few days later, they had a violent quarrel and broke up for the last time. Edith Gwynn reported in her column: "We've observed that they sure seem to have a deadening effect on each other." The British Foreign Office indexes show that Cary received at the time written notice of another award for distinguished services to the Allies, and a medal in France.

The Bishop's Wife finally wound up shooting in early June. On June 20, Cary received a phone call: Bugsy Siegel had been shot at his Beverly Hills house on North Linden Drive. The circumstances were dramatic and gruesome. Siegel and his friend Al Smiley were sitting in the living room in the early-morning hours, discussing the new edition of the Los Angeles *Times,* which in those days could be bought at midnight. A car drove up and parked at the curb next to Smiley's Cadillac. A man got out. He took a .30-30 carbine with a silencer and, fixing the back of Bugsy's head in the sights, he fired

---

*Outside Hollywood; the Reporter *was strictly a trade publication.*

directly through the glass window past the drawn curtain. The bullet smashed into Bugsy's skull and blew his right eye fifteen feet into the dining room. The second bullet struck Siegel in the back of the neck and exited, burning its way through Al Smiley's coat sleeve. A third bullet, which also ripped through Siegel's neck, struck the painting of an English duchess on the wall. Yet another slug crashed into a nude figure of Bacchus on the piano.

Virginia Hill was in Paris. Her brother Chick ran down the stairs, and Al Smiley turned out the lights. When Chick turned them on again, Smiley was cowering in the fireplace. Chick ran to the safe and took out Virginia's jewelry, while his girlfriend called the police. Chick dropped the jewels in the laundry chute, where they lay in the dirty laundry, until the police were gone.

Cary was among the handful of friends whom Chick Hill called. Wisely, Cary did not turn up at North Linden Drive; he stayed out of the publicity, as did Howard Hughes, whose refusal to help Siegel out of his financial predicament had undoubtedly played a major role in his death. Siegel had been unable to meet his heavy debts to the mob; a few days later, gangster Lucky Luciano, from the safety of Rome (Italy had no extradition treaty with the United States), took credit for the killing.

Virginia Hill returned to the United States, following a suicide attempt at the Ritz in Paris. She attempted suicide again at a Miami Beach hotel, but recovered, to spend the rest of her life in terror.

Perhaps wisely, Cary left for London in July, after a cross-country automobile journey, his first since 1932. While in London, he again conferred with Alexander Korda, on a picture to be entitled *The Devil's Delight,* which Carol Reed would direct. Cary would appear as Lucifer in modern clothing. He told a London reporter, "I wasn't happy as an angel. I think I'll be much more at home playing the devil."

Cary visited Elsie, who gave one of her rare interviews to the press, saying, "Archie always was restless, even as a child. He never likes to feel he's tied in any way."

During the stay in the British capital, Cary went to see an American play, *Deep Are the Roots,* in which a young American actress, Betsy Drake, was appearing. She was coltish, leggy, with a somewhat irregular but not unattractive face and an exceptionally well modulated, cultivated, and expressive speaking voice. She was tomboyish, determined but paradoxically pliant; she walked with a swinging, almost masculine stride. In late September, when Cary returned to New York on the *Queen Mary,* he was intrigued to learn that Miss Drake was on board. She was even more intrigued to learn that he was a passenger. For years, she had been deeply attracted to his screen persona. She was very eager to meet him.

Betsy Drake was born in Paris on September 11, 1923. Her parents separated when she was in her teens, and the broken home had made her wary, hypersensitive, and nervous. While living in a Manhattan slum neighborhood, she had become obsessed with the idea of escaping from her environment in the only way she thought possible, as an actress. She was not very well suited for her chosen profession. She was awkward and shy, and her habit of standing splay-footed was not particularly appealing. Somehow, she contrived to get obscure jobs as a model with the Conover Agency and for the Montgomery Ward catalog. She was hired as stage manager for a production of *Only the Heart,* but ran down the curtain by accident in the middle of a scene and was dismissed in tears. Director Herman Shumlin took pity on her and introduced her to Hal Wallis, who gave her a screen test. He was interested in her playing a blind English girl in the movie *I Walk Alone,* which would introduce Lizabeth Scott and Kirk Douglas. Wallis was pleased with her convincing impersonation of blindness and put her under contract. But when she came to Hollywood, he wrote her character out of the script and left her idle for months. When he offered to renew her contract, she declined. She did a cold reading for *Deep Are the Roots* and was cast over several well-known actresses for the London production.

Cary's fellow British secret agent Merle Oberon was aboard the *Queen Mary,* accompanied by Dorothy di Frasso. Merle, divorced from Alexander Korda in 1945, had just finished shooting *Berlin Express,* which Cary had turned down, and was recovering from an unsatisfactory romantic liaison with Robert Ryan. She was accompanied by her new lover (and future husband), Lucien Ballard. Cary was having tea with Elizabeth Taylor in the ship's lounge when he noticed Betsy Drake going to the telephone. He followed her, pretending to be making a call in the adjoining booth. As she came out, the ship was caught by a heavy wave and she stumbled; Cary grasped her before she fell. Commenting on this later, Cary said, "I think Betsy was using a bit of coquetry." In any case, she blushed and pulled away and ran out of the lounge.

Next day, Cary was walking with Merle Oberon on the boat deck and saw Betsy. He asked Merle to arrange an introduction. Astonished that Cary would require one, the romantic Miss Oberon invited the two of them to join her for a buffet lunch. Cary and Betsy became strongly attracted to each other. He was impressed with her intelligence, her knowledge of many subjects, especially psychology, and her interest in hypnotism, which he shared. He assumed the role of authoritative movie star, deciding that he could help Betsy in her career and using this to intrigue her. But from the beginning, it was noted by friends that their relationship seemed more like that of brother and sister than of lovers.

In New York, Cary announced that he would speak to Dore Schary about obtaining a contract for Miss Drake. He would also introduce her to David O. Selznick. They traveled to Los Angeles together. Cary was as good as his word: Selznick put Betsy under contract immediately. Whether this was a favor to Cary or he saw actual merit in Miss Drake is uncertain, but almost at once he began discussing the idea of loaning her out to RKO. He was already negotiating the possibility of buying RKO outright. Cary did not at first introduce Betsy at parties: he may have been too insecure about their relationship and uncertain whether this bookish, well-informed, and fiercely determined young woman would fit in with his more lighthearted, not particularly learned, and superficially cheerful circle of friends.

He was also preoccupied, for he was starting work at RKO on his next picture. *Mr. Blandings Builds His Dream House* concerned a New Yorker seized with a vision of a fancy weekend residence, who plunges into a series of comical and grotesque mishaps. Myrna Loy was once again his co-star. Betsy would turn up on the set to watch Cary work, her quizzical, intense stare somewhat irritating Dore Schary and the director, H. C. Potter. In the rather bland film,

Cary, as the harassed advertising executive faced with the problems of a bucolic existence, was certainly at his most accomplished. He concocted some business that alluded to his hidden preoccupations. In an early sequence, he drags his wife's underwear from a drawer while looking for his missing socks; the jokes he makes about the suitability of such garments for himself were improvised on the spot, in order to avoid censorship by the ever-vigilant Joe Breen.

While the picture was shooting, Cary made arrangements to appear on radio with George Burns and Gracie Allen, on *Maxwell House Coffee Time*. Gracie played his secretary in an episode on October 16, in which the amusing Bea Benaderet was a movie columnist interviewing Cary for a magazine. She was based wittily on Louella Parsons. Hedda Hopper was jealous. On October 30, he appeared with Hans Conried and Gale Gordon, both of whom he had worked with in his early stage career in New York. In a third appearance, on November 13, he was in a show called "Uplift Society," a parody of social life in Hollywood that he undertook in very high spirits.

During the shooting of *Mr. Blandings,* the early days of the witch hunts against alleged Communists in Hollywood were marked by dramatic conflicts within the industry. The directors John Huston and William Wyler turned up on the film's set and asked for support from the cast in order to establish a First Amendment committee, which would allow those who had been named in the initial investigations to fight against potential or actual blacklisting. Melvyn Douglas, who, along with his wife, the politician Helen Gahagan Douglas, was considerably left of center, agreed to cooperate with the committee. Miss Loy, who was above reproach politically, was at heart a liberal and was happy to join Melvyn Douglas in opposition to what she felt was a grave threat to freedom of speech. But Cary refused to have anything to do with the Committee for the First Amendment. Still a staunch Republican, he was committed to the secret war against the Soviet Union. Although he was opposed to any interference with personal freedom, he knew that many members of the film industry were, whatever their protests to the contrary, members of the Communist Party. According to the late Noah Dietrich, years later he named names in secret session before the House Committee on Un-American Activities. But the hearings' minutes remain closed to this day, suggesting that whatever he said was under special privilege; he was not exposed—as were Elia Kazan, Clifford Odets, and Lee J. Cobb, for example—to future calumny for informing on his fellow employees in the film industry.

In the winter of 1947, Howard Hughes, who was still suffering from the barrage of the Senate committees in Washington, took over RKO. Cary talked Hughes into buying the other half of Betsy Drake's contract, and then he talked Dore Schary into agreeing with Hughes that Betsy would be perfect for a comedy that Cary would make for the studio, *Every Girl Should Be Married.* She herself had aspirations to be a dramatic actress, but Cary felt that, with her awkward, appealingly gauche manner and crinkly smile, she would be far better suited to farcical material. By now, she was in his thrall—or seemed to be. She said later that he controlled everything she did, from the food she ate to the type of car she drove; from the clothes she wore to the way her hair was styled. He was molding her, slowly but surely, into his image of a desirable and sophisticated woman.

In *Every Girl Should Be Married*—co-written by the director Don Hartman (a specialist in visual and oral gags, who had written for Bob Hope and Bing Crosby) and Stephen Morehouse Avery, head of U.S. Military Intelligence in Los Angeles in World War II—Betsy Drake was cast as a department store clerk in a children's wear department who sets her sights on Cary, as the pediatrician Dr. Madison Brown. She researches him thoroughly, finding out about his college background, his favorite foods, even the color of his underwear. Despite a series of mishaps and roadblocks, she of course captures her prey. The story was a reversal of the real-life situation in which Cary investigated Betsy Drake.

This picture of single-minded female aggressiveness troubled several critics later on, and since Cary is known to have had a hand in the script, the movie may have reflected a deep-seated hostility and fear of women. For all the strenuous efforts of the director to make the character of Anabel Sims appealing, the result was a movie that could scarcely have been more misogynistic. Cary watched every move Betsy made on the set, endlessly checking her out, imitating her cruelly in scenes, and at times encouraging her—mistakenly— to imitate Katharine Hepburn's mannered playing. Betsy seemed to take on Cary's own fussiness, and soon studio publicists would be complaining that she was excessively concerned over her appearance on the screen. Self-conscious over her thinness, she refused to pose in a bathing suit.

Once again, Cary was drawn to an extremely sensitive, self-conscious girl with an inferiority complex; Betsy Drake even looked a little like Barbara Hutton. In March 1948, Cary was offered the leading role in A *Double Life,* the story of a Shakespearean actor who confuses his part in *Othello* with reality and strangles the actress cast as Desdemona. He turned the role down for two reasons: he was nervous about having to recite Shakespeare in his nasal accent and seemed unwilling to train with a voice coach; George Cukor, who was assigned to direct the movie for Universal, also made it clear that Betsy Drake could not possibly play Desdemona, for which role he had the Swedish Signe Hasso in mind. There was some tension between Cary and Betsy for the first time in April, when he was seen at the Café Gala with, of all people, Betty Hensel. It took much of his diplomacy and skill to overcome Betsy's concern. In April, he announced to the press that he was determined to appear in thé role of Morris Townsend, the shallow and heartless seducer who pursues the unattractive heiress in William Wyler's proposed version of Henry James's *Washington Square.* At forty-four, he was far too old for the part, which went to Montgomery Clift. He was disappointed; he had always wanted to work with Wyler, whose 1946 masterpiece, *The Best Years of Our Lives,* he had admired.

On April 12, Virginia Cherrill married the former World War II airman Florian Martini. She had obtained her divorce from the Earl of Jersey three weeks before. Her ardent Polish husband had met her in Liverpool in 1947 and had pursued her all the way to Los Angeles, where she had come to visit her mother. Cary did not attend the wedding or send a gift.

The situation at RKO was chaotic. Howard Hughes never appeared at the studio; he seemed to regard running RKO as a hobby, a secondary occupation. Schary wished to make a film called *Battleground,** for which he wanted Cary, but Hughes was totally opposed, hating the idea of a war picture and convinced that no one

---

* *Later transferred to M-G-M.*

would go to see it. He was still lingering on at Cary's house on Beverly Grove Drive, living without furnishings, except for two chairs and a sofa, and a mattress on the floor of the master bedroom. Schary would come for long conferences with Hughes on studio policy, and "there wasn't a paper, a cigarette, a flower, a match, a picture, a magazine . . ." Hughes blocked Schary at every turn.

Schary was also making painful trips to Washington to appear before the House Un-American Activities Committee. Every effort was made by committee chairman J. Parnell Thomas to discredit Schary, who by 1948 was under a cloud. Yet Schary was able to continue functioning because the committee was unable to prove anything concrete against him. Hughes shared Cary's right-wing position in the matter, and Schary was let go from RKO that summer of 1948. The situation was extremely difficult, and Cary was aware that Hughes was daily becoming more eccentric and impossible to deal with. Cary decided to break his contract with Hughes—it was an amicable rupture—and signed with 20th Century–Fox. As we know, he showed his devotion to his Jewish origins by giving a check for ten thousand dollars to the United Jewish Appeal on June 8, in the name of his "dead Jewish mother." Nobody picked up the fact that Elsie Leach, the mother the world accepted in that role, was both alive and a gentile.

On August 26, Cary and Betsy Drake left for Europe, where he would make *I Was a Male War Bride* for Howard Hawks. He would play a French army captain, Henri Rochard, who wishes to obtain entry to the United States after World War II but can do so only in the category "war bride." According to Hawks, he was apparently pleased to note that much of the performance would be spent in drag, with a large, dark brown wig cut in pageboy style.

En route to Germany, Cary stopped in London and had lengthy discussions with Howard Hawks at Shepperton Studios. Cary acted out a scene in a WAC uniform, but Hawks, always cold, hard, and detached, though with a wry, sharp sense of humor, was not amused. He told Cary to set aside his effeminate gestures; he must not pretend to be a woman but must walk and talk like a man. Cary protested that this was ridiculous: no one could possibly mistake an aggressively male figure in a skirt; much of the comedy sprang from the misunderstanding, and this approach would destroy the movie. Hawks won. His macho hang-up about homosexuality was such that he would not tolerate even an inkling of gay behavior on any of his sets, even when, as in this instance, the script unquestionably called for it. As for Cary, he knew that his large female audience so completely worshipped him as a sex symbol that nothing he did would risk his reputation.

England was suffering from postwar austerity, although Cary and Betsy were scarcely aware of it, housed as they were at an apartment in Grosvenor Square. They had many pleasant dinners and lunches with Ann Sheridan, Cary's co-star, immediately drawn to her outgoing good nature. The three of them needed to keep their spirits up: the weather was depressingly dreary and rainswept. When they reached Heidelberg, the weather was even worse. Ann Sheridan's luggage had been removed by customs officials at the French-German border while Miss Sheridan was asleep in her compartment. She was accused of smuggling, and it took considerable effort for 20th Century–Fox to prove that she had been mistaken for another passenger. In one of the first days of shooting, Miss Sheridan had to drive a motorcycle in a downpour, with Cary sitting in the sidecar. She had assumed a double would be used, but Howard Hawks, tough as always, told her she must master the eight-hundred-pound contraption herself. She was petrified, and to put her at ease, Cary helped the former German paratrooper engaged to train her. On her first rehearsal drive, she was hysterical, shaken badly by the jolting and vibration, and then to her horror she ran over a goose. Upset by the blood, she broke into tears. But finally, the sight of Cary bumping up and down in the sidecar turned her tears to laughter. She began to relax and enjoy the experience.

Working in Germany was difficult. Not only was the weather cold and depressing, the hotel in Heidelberg was inferior, and it was almost impossible to get a decent meal. Conditions were no better in Zuzenhausen, a fifteenth-century village with tiny, winding cobbled streets and stone houses. The cast, Cary included, had to eat meals off tin plates, and when the makeup man suddenly disappeared, they had to paint their own faces. Betsy tried to cook for Cary on a hot plate in their room, but the result was hopeless; she burned the food, and her attempts at omelets were disastrous. On weekends, in desperation, Cary and Betsy took local planes across the border into Switzerland or to Strasbourg, France, where they could indulge in good, expensive food, especially Cary's favorite, *pâté de foie gras.* It was difficult to return on Mondays to recommence the making of the picture, the rigors of which were intensified by the populace's bitter resentment against Americans. Ann Sheridan was Cary's chief consolation; no matter how unpleasant the conditions, she was eternally joyful, spunky, and full of life.

Late in October, about a month into shooting, Cary began to experience symptoms of infectious hepatitis. He felt ill, lost much of his energy, and was frequently nauseous. When the doctor pressed the area of the liver, he felt pain. He began to have attacks of vomiting and diarrhea, and when he went in for a series of laboratory tests, his lymph nodes were found to be enlarged and he had developed antibodies. Shooting persisted. There was a scene in which he had to ride into a haystack. It was suffocating in there, and Cary began to feel faint. When the crew pulled them out, he was breathing with difficulty, and his skin had a yellowish tinge. He asked feebly to be rushed to London, where he could get the best care. Hawks agreed; Cary was flown there for tests by a Harley Street specialist and the picture closed down. Then Hawks fell ill, breaking out in hives all over his body, probably in response to nervous stress.

Betsy nursed Cary through several weeks of illness. An old friend, Pamela Churchill, who had been married to Winston Churchill's son Randolph, insisted that Cary move into her apartment where, with the aid of day and night nurses, she could take care of him. Betsy was supposed to return to Hollywood before Christmas, to appear in a movie that Cary had more or less forced on 20th Century–Fox. He had insisted the studio buy *The Bandwagon,* a 1931 stage success by Howard Dietz and Arthur Schwartz, and that she star in it. From it, a script was adapted, about a fallen movie star who finds an obscure young woman and pushes her into success on the stage. The story had resemblances to *A Star Is Born* and *Citizen Kane.* William Powell would play the fallen movie idol (a part originally written for Clifton Webb) and Betsy Drake the ambitious girl, who turns out to be his daughter.

Betsy had not wanted to make the film. She had hated herself in *Every Girl Should Be Married;* she was so shocked by her appearance on the screen, and what she felt to be her terrible acting, that after the first private preview, she had told Cary she wanted only to return to New York and the stage. She was convinced she wasn't photogenic and now she was going to play in a picture that called for her to sing and dance. She could do neither; she was very bright, and she knew instinctively that the result of the film would be public humiliation. But she was so anxious to please Cary, and perhaps so afraid of his extraordinary will and his temper if crossed, that she fell victim to his ambitions for her and agreed to go ahead with the project.

She returned to Los Angeles with a heavy spirit, not at all happy about leaving Cary behind, still seriously unwell, in London. He made his way on a Dutch ship, the *Volendam*, through the Panama Canal to join her. Meanwhile, at the outset of 1949, she began shooting *The Bandwagon*, retitled *Dancing in the Dark*. Incredibly, in view of Cary's dislike of him and the unfortunate circumstances of *The Bachelor and the Bobby-Soxer*, the producer, ex-vaudevillian George Jessel, chose Irving Reis to direct the movie. It takes no feat of the imagination to visualize Cary's anger and Betsy's despair at this selection. Moreover, Jessel, an old friend of studio boss Darryl F. Zanuck's, had wanted either June Haver or Carole Landis to star in the film; both were capable of singing and dancing and were gorgeous, voluptuous women of the kind Jessel favored.

Furious at being forced to use Betsy Drake, Jessel set about humiliating her. He ordered the dance director, Seymour Felix, to push her relentlessly through various dance routines, which she finally broke off, in tears of hopeless disappointment. There was no way she could reach Cary on his ship to tell him what she was going through; for long periods, he was incommunicado. There was a line in the script, "I walk like a duck," which she would not speak because so many people had told her that was one of her problems. Jessel came on the set and insisted she say the line. She still refused. That night, she appeared with Jessel on Louella Parsons's radio show. Jessel turned on her in fury and told her she was acting unprofessionally and disgracefully by not following the script. To Louella's astonishment, Betsy reciprocated and, in an unprecedented burst of rage, condemned him out of hand. There had never been an incident like this, in which two guests on a radio show tore at each other while the host made a futile attempt to referee. Those who heard the broadcast were amazed to discover that the mousy Betsy Drake could be dangerous when crossed. She had a steel will underneath all her seeming weakness and subservience, and the horrible experience of making *Dancing in the Dark* slowly but inexorably hardened her.

After weeks of monotonous voyaging, Cary arrived in Los Angeles on April 7. He was some thirty pounds lighter, his skin still a yellowish shade under the heavy tan acquired from hours on the boat deck in the tropical sun. Betsy, worn out by the long and depressing filming of *Dancing in the Dark*, told him of her ordeal, but there was little he could do anymore. Later that year, and early the next, the punishing reviews poured in, with critics repeatedly saying that it was shocking to think that 20th Century – Fox, which had Betty Grable and June Haver under contract, would choose to cast in a musical an actress who was uniquely incapable of performing in one. The critiques only confirmed what Betsy thought about herself.

Understandably, Cary and Betsy withdrew from the Hollywood scene for most of the year. Declining all invitations to parties, they tried to make a life together at her apartment and his house. Betsy in some ways grated on his nerves. She was untidy and clumsy, and Cary fanatically neat. She was an obsessive reader, who would pile books up everywhere, even on her bed, in the back of the car, on chairs and tables. Books meant nothing to him; his interests remained chiefly in the field of old-time vaudeville, and his friends from the old days aggravated Betsy as much as they had aggravated Barbara Hutton. It was almost willfully perverse of him to have entered into a relationship with a woman with whom he had almost nothing in common. What could they talk about in the evenings? Virtually nothing. The pairing of a tortured, neurotic, but elegant and graceful matinee idol and an introspective bluestocking seemed doomed to failure from the beginning.

The year 1949 was a dreary one for Cary. The filming of *I Was a Male War Bride* recommenced that summer, and scenes that had been shot in Germany were more or less efficiently matched up with new studio work. But Cary had lost interest in the picture, and the well-known weakening effects of hepatitis weighed him down. He tried to cheer himself up by appearing in the radio series version of *Mr. Blandings Builds His Dream House*, starting July 1. His friend and director H. C. Potter turned up as a guest on the program to discuss the theme with Cary before the studio audience. Frances Robinson played the Myrna Loy role of Jim Blandings's wife; later, Betsy took it over and, surprisingly, contributed several scripts. In the second half of 1949, following a week of tests at Johns Hopkins Hospital in Baltimore, Cary began to improve. He gave up trying to run the remnants of the Frank Vincent Agency and his own career, and signed with MCA on August 5. That relieved him of much pressure, and his enthusiasms returned. From complaining about Betsy's obsession with books, he even started to examine them, discovering that her serendipitous mind had its own appeal. He would pick up a volume on spiders or on astronomy or mysticism and dip into it, expertly seizing on elements in it without having to read the entire book. He began storing up all kinds of odd, entertaining information, and instead of resenting Betsy's superior intelligence, his appreciation of her wide-ranging interests grew. Bit by bit, she started to gain, if not an upper hand, certainly an almost equal one. She was at last earning his respect.

A new friendship was formed in 1949. The couple got to know the handsome and dashing, fiery and opinionated young British star Stewart Granger, who had made a great success in such entertaining films as *The Man in Grey*, *Caesar and Cleopatra*, and *Saraband for Dead Lovers*. He had just come to the United States to make *King Solomon's Mines*, a romantic story of adventure set in Africa.

Granger says:

I was fitting clothes for *King Solomon's Mines* and was testing for the leading role in *Quo Vadis*, a part which later went to Robert Taylor. As I entered the M-G-M commissary, Cary was paying his bill. He gave me a warm smile. He said, without any preamble, "Would you like to come and have lunch with me?" I knew he was sexually attracted to me. He never laid a hand on me. But I knew.

Instead of lunch in the commissary, Granger was surprised to find himself enjoying midday meals at Beverly Grove Drive. He mentioned the severe rationing of postwar England, of which, of course, Cary was aware. He asked, naïvely, how much butter, sugar, beef, lamb, bacon, and eggs he would be allowed in the United States. Cary laughingly informed him there was no such thing as rationing in America, and hadn't been, except in a very minimal sense, during the war. Cary drove the bedazzled Granger to the Farmer's Market, where the produce was piled up, and stood by grinning while Granger snapped up ten pounds of butter, ten pounds of sugar, and the same amount of beef, lamb, and bacon, as well as four dozen eggs. Despite the fact that the Beverly Hills Hotel offered lavish meals, Granger stored these newly acquired treasures in the refrigerator in his suite as though they were diamonds from Tiffany's.

Granger remembers how Betsy Drake was always concocting extremely complex dinners from a variety of gourmet cookbooks.* When all three went out to dinner, sometimes with Granger's girlfriend, Jean Simmons, and with another friend, the twenty-three-year-old actor Richard Anderson, Cary displayed his niggardliness to an astonishing degree. Granger recalls:

> One evening, as we finished dinner, I called for the check. Cary demurred. I insisted; but he wouldn't take no for an answer. He took up the check himself. I thought, These stories about him are wrong. He's going to pay. He examined the check carefully. And then, instead of taking out the money, he said to me, "Well, you had the wine and such-and-such a dish," trying to figure what my separate payment would be. I was furious, and I dragged the check out of his hand and paid for everyone. He was very upset indeed.

---

* *Hitchcock told Charles Higham that he utilized Betsy's culinary mishaps in his film* Frenzy *(1972).*

Later, when Granger became engaged to Jean Simmons, he told Cary he was looking for a diamond engagement ring. Cary took him to the safe in his house. Granger was astonished to find that the safe was "full of the damnedest things you've ever seen in your life: diamond cufflinks, diamond rings, gold cigarette cases . . . all sorts of things." Granger continued:

> He had one diamond ring which he was prepared to sell me himself. It was a four-carat ring, and I wanted a six-to-eight-carat. He would have sold it to me for what he paid for it. He wasn't trying to make money off it. As it turned out, he introduced me to the diamond merchant who sold me the ring I wanted. But it had a big flaw, or rather a chasm. I should have bought Cary's ring. It was beautiful.

Late in 1949, Betsy Drake appeared in the movie *The Second Woman* for United Artists. It was a thriller about an architect, played by Robert Young, whose Rebecca-like first wife has died and whose presence haunts the second wife, played by Miss Drake. The architect's life is threatened, his favorite horse is killed, his rosebushes are poisoned, his favorite painting is defaced. It was not a satisfactory movie; Young was struggling with a drinking problem and Betsy was disturbed by the sequence involving a horse: she was petrified of them. Yet at the same time, Cary suddenly discovered a long-lost interest in riding and began trying, without success, to help Betsy overcome her fears.

The couple decided after much discussion and argument that they should be married that December. Together they had a tendency to overintellectualize and discuss things too much. And this in itself complicated their feelings for each other and delayed the wedding. They were both so insecure, and then there was Betsy's disastrous first marriage—which she had managed to conceal from the press—to a poor and struggling young actor, with whom she had shared a cold-water apartment in Manhattan. She was afraid of being hurt again. It took much effort for her to make another attempt.

TWELVE

Even before *The Second Woman* was completed, Betsy began shooting a comedy, *Pretty Baby*, at Warners. She was cast as a young woman in an advertising agency who, in order to get ahead, pretends to have a child which she names after her boss, played by Edmund Gwenn. The comedy sprang from her attempts to conceal the fact that the infant she carried around with her in the streets and subways and offices of New York was a doll.

She broke off shooting for two days at Christmas to fly with Cary, in a plane piloted by Howard Hughes, to Phoenix, Arizona, where the simple wedding ceremony took place at the desert home of Sterling Hebbard, an old friend of Cary's lawyer Will Hinckle, rich in Arizona real estate. The Reverend Stanley M. Smith presided. Hughes was best man. Betsy had no bridesmaid—an indication of how remote the couple had become from all Cary's friends in Hollywood. Test pilot C. A. Shoop and Phoenix attorney Richard Mason were witnesses. As with the marriage to Barbara Hutton, there was no honeymoon. Hughes flew them back to Los Angeles, and the next day Betsy Drake appeared with her fake baby in a scene shot on a subway train at the rush hour.

Ten days later, Cary began work at M-G-M on Richard Brooks's *Crisis*. The tough, skillful Brooks, who would soon become a close friend, had made his mark with the admirable screenplay of *Cross-*

fire, based upon his novel *The Brick Foxhole*. The story had been altered from a homosexual theme to the more acceptable one of anti-Semitism in the army. Brooks had written a fine script for John Huston's *Key Largo* and had signed a contract with Metro as writer-director. However, his first two scripts were handled by other people, and he was about to quit because the terms of his contract had not been satisfied. He was at work on *Crisis* when he went to the Santa Anita racetrack on a Saturday and was introduced to Cary. Cary said he was enjoying reading the *Crisis* screenplay. He was thinking about making the picture. Brooks asserted his determination to direct the script himself. Cary asked him, "How do you get along with people?" Brooks replied, "I don't know." And Cary said, characteristically, "Well, I guess what you don't know about directing, I do."

Cary liked Brooks at once: the man was honest, straightforward, and decent, and he had the look of someone who could direct a picture well. Going to Dore Schary, the M-G-M boss, Cary said that he wouldn't make the picture unless Brooks directed it. That settled the matter. Cary was cast as Dr. Eugene Ferguson, a brain surgeon who is kidnapped while on vacation in an unnamed South American country and forced to perform a dangerous and difficult operation on a Juan Perón—like dictator, Raoul Ferrago, played by José Ferrer. Ferguson is told by a rival junta to kill the dictator; instead, he saves his life. The story of medical versus political ethics was an interesting one, and was intelligently rendered by Brooks. Nancy Davis, later Mrs. Ronald Reagan, was supposed to play the role of the doctor's wife. But Dore Schary was not pleased with the choice and decided to cast Paula Raymond instead. In a letter to Roy Moseley, ex-president Ronald Reagan has stated how grateful he was to Cary for his kindness and support to Nancy, wanting her to have the part and soothing her spirits when she lost it. The former president writes:

Cary took her to lunch at the studio cafeteria and very kindly talked away her disappointment and complimented her on her acting. He told her she did something [on the screen] many actors didn't know how to do. She *listened* to the other actor.

The shooting was marred by violent arguments. According to Richard Brooks, the cameraman, Ray June, who had for years wanted to be a director, insisted on usurping Brooks's powers. Several quarrels ensued. On the first day of shooting, there was a cumbersome, difficult shot, with the camera mounted on a wheeled crane traveling on metal tracks. Brooks was nervous that June would defy him in the composition of the shot, and he walked beside the crane, monitoring its every movement. Whether accidentally or deliberately, someone pushed the crane over Brooks's feet. Cary came running over, shouting, "You ran over his foot! Take him to a hospital." Brooks said, "The hospital is next to the funeral parlor on the lot. If I leave this stage for five minutes, there'll be another director on this movie." Cary replied, "There is not going to be another director. I want you to go there, because first of all, the insurance people will require it. Second, you probably broke some toes, and you'd better get them attended to. And thirdly, if they throw you off the movie, I'll walk." All through the conversation, Brooks was hopping on one foot, and there was blood all over his shoe. But amazingly, nothing was broken. His foot was bandaged, it was dunked in an ice bucket back on the soundstage, and he continued till the end of the day.

Cary was in a nervous mood as *Crisis* began. Perhaps because of the strain of a new marriage, perhaps because Betsy was having problems at Warners, he started drinking, more heavily than he had in years, and he twice smashed his car in collisions in Beverly Hills. Apparently, strings were pulled so he wouldn't lose his license. Paula Raymond, his leading lady, reports that shooting *Crisis* was an ordeal for all concerned.

This was Richard Brooks's first assignment as a director, and he knew nothing about the camera. He was having people go off-screen to the right and coming back on the right, and this wasn't the correct way to direct. He was so frustrated—and I could understand why—he screamed at everyone; he even screamed at me. I would tell him to calm down. He screamed at the grips, the cameraman, the electricians. He might have been forgiven, except that he never screamed at Cary Grant. That was much resented. Brooks was a darling guy; I understood that with all that massive responsibility, he had to react the way he did.

Cary celebrated his forty-sixth birthday on the set. He was shown cutting the cake with Paula Raymond. The caption in one magazine read: "Paula: When you invited me up for a piece, I thought . . ." Cary wanted to sue the magazine, because he felt that the caption suggested that an affair was going on, and that Betsy would be upset. Paula Raymond refused to join him in the suit. She said, "Cary, how can you sue a sense of humor?" Cary did not forgive her, and much of the remaining time of shooting was tense and difficult for her.

Cary had little political rapport with José Ferrer, who would soon name names to the House Un-American Activities Committee, but he enjoyed working with him. Richard Brooks remembers: "Cary and José would often improvise, come up with touches to enhance the scenes. They were inventive actors. They managed to create the impression of normal or haphazard dialogue through their skillful handling of my lines."

Betsy's difficulties at Warners continued. She was much disliked there: as early as December 5, twenty days before her wedding, studio legal chief Roy Obringer and production chief Steve Trilling were discussing in memoranda her difficult behavior. Trilling noted that Betsy was "trying to throw her weight around, possibly supported by Grant," and later there were some troublesome days of shooting, in which she was unfairly blamed for the problems. She hated picturemaking more and more. And the contrived humor of *Pretty Baby*, the humdrum directing of Bretaigne Windust, and the uninspiring presence of her fellow actors Jack Carson and Dennis Morgan left her frustrated and irritable. The truth was that not only did she lack the timing, skill, and coloring necessary for high-comedy acting, but the sort of routine movies she was appearing in insulted her intelligence. The hard-working troupers who played with her sensed her feeling of superiority and resented it. It seemed that in every sense, both as Mrs. Cary Grant and as a would-be star, she was miscast.

Toward the end of the filming of *Crisis*, Cary's hepatitis flared up—not surprisingly, since abstinence from alcohol is prescribed to prevent a recurrence—and he was briefly hospitalized. The shooting ended on June 15. It had been strenuous; Cary had had to learn the techniques of surgical procedure in the grim operating room sequences. He had studied with a surgeon at night, attended operations, and interviewed nursing staff. The result was one of his most authentic and carefully molded performances.

On August 1, Howard Hughes offered Cary a property he had recently bought, the Terence Rattigan play *O Mistress Mine*, which had been an excellent stage vehicle for Alfred Lunt and Lynn Fontanne. Hughes wanted Cary to play the part of a British cabinet minister in charge of munitions during the London Blitz. Sick, bored, fatigued, Cary was not anxious to work; Hughes was unable to talk him into proceeding. At the same time, Cary's plans to work with Alexander Korda finally and irrevocably were called off. He and Betsy remained in almost complete isolation. "We never saw them," his close friend Johnny Maschio says. "They gave no parties. And she just never went out. We never knew why. But certainly, none of us in Cary's circle ever really got to know Betsy Drake."

During that period, Cary deepened his friendship with Richard Brooks—a friendship that continued for many years. Brooks would often visit Cary and Betsy at home. When Brooks made his film *Elmer Gantry*, ten years later, Cary would prove to be extremely helpful on the subject of evangelism and Brooks to this day remains grateful to him.

That August, the seemingly interminable matter of the investigations of Howard Hughes continued in Washington. Hughes would overreact to the charges and call Cary at all hours to discuss them. Hughes had established a code name, Kato, which members of his immediate circle were to use if they wished to reach him urgently and much of Cary's time was spent trying to soothe Hughes's nerves.

In December 1950, Hughes flew Cary, Stewart Granger, and Jean Simmons to Tucson, where Granger and Simmons would be married; depressed by the reviews of her first two movies, Betsy Drake continued to talk about leaving the screen. Meantime, Cary began work on his second movie for 20th Century–Fox, *People Will Talk*— an appropriate title, since the script, by the director Joseph L. Mankiewicz, was among the most prolix on record. Cary played Noah

Praetorius, an obstetrician who falls in love with an unmarried woman who is about to have a baby; she has tried to commit suicide. It is easy to see how Cary would be drawn to such a story in view of his own history. The premise provided a springboard for a comedy-drama in which the crusading doctor fights against the repressive attitudes, prejudices, and traditions of a university medical school. The implicit critique of the establishment appealed to Cary, who fought hard against the complacency and inefficiency of conventional medicine and was an exponent of health foods long before they became fashionable.

There was another parallel between the story and real life. Although Cary had shied away from any involvement in critiques of Senator Joseph McCarthy and the House Un-American Activities Committee, and although he remained opposed to Communism and apparently named names, he had become disturbed by HUAC's invasions of privacy, prejudicial charges, and disruption of family life. Mankiewicz used the movie as a platform to criticize these matters; Howard Hughes approved of the project: the subject matter reflected his own David vs. Goliath attacks on the Brewster Committee. Betsy Drake, with her intellectual interests, also liked the script, and it was a disappointment to her that she herself was not cast as the pregnant woman in the story.

Betsy filled her spare time writing scripts for the radio version of *Mr. Blandings Builds His Dream House*, and she now took over as costar. It says much for her determination that she had mastered the specialized craft of radio drama; her shortcomings as a screen actress were not so evident in her radio performances. Her greatest asset, her resonant and expressive speaking voice, was notably revealed in a fine and harrowing version of Alfred Hitchcock's thriller about a mass murderer, "Shadow of a Doubt." She spoke the part with considerably more expertise than the rather shallow and uninteresting (and vocally thin) Teresa Wright had done in the movie version. By contrast, Cary was unsatisfactory in the central role of Uncle Charlie; his vocal inadequacies were always sharply exposed by radio. His limited range of voice and his habit of gabbling his lines in strangely exaggerated cockney ruined the authenticity of his performances in the nonvisual medium.

Cary was now among the highest-paid movie stars, earning

$300,000 for *People Will Talk*. Betsy, meanwhile, who remained unemployed and unbankable in films, was simultaneously pleased with her freedom and disappointed that she had been shelved by the industry. The only way to save her film career was for Cary to co-star with her in a film.

Betsy was concerned with the problems of homeless children (she would one day become a child psychotherapist, as well as write a novel about the unhappy offspring of divided parents). She was interested in appearing with Cary in *Room for One More*, adapted from a book she liked by Anna Perrott Rose. The deal was struck. She would play Anna Rose, a naive, outgoing girl who, along with various animal waifs and strays, adopts the unwanted daughter of divorced parents, gradually weaning her away from her mistrustfulness. Later, she adopts a handicapped boy. Cary would play "Poppy" Rose, Anna's much-embattled husband. In view of the character of the movie, and the evident sincerity with which the Grants embarked on it, it is curious to reflect that they themselves did not adopt children, since they had none of their own. Such an adoption would have cemented their marriage, and perhaps given them the fulfillment they failed to find in each other. Whatever the reasons, which may only have been dislike of responsibility and fear of being tied down, the Grants remained childless.

Room for One More started shooting on August 16, 1951, and was finished October 18. At the wrap-up party, Cary said to Melville Shavelson, the co-author of the script, "So this picture cost four mil. It's not much of a movie, but it's something I wanted to do for me and Betsy." Shavelson comments: "He wanted to change the image of Cary Grant, from the ultra-sophisticated, too-rich whatever, to a family man, which he always wanted to be." Years later, Shavelson would renew his working relationship with Cary under very different, and quite disturbing, circumstances.

In November, the magazine *Motion Picture* published damaging statements against several stars. These were unfounded: Cesar Romero, Joseph Cotten, and Dinah Shore were charged with having black ancestry; Scott Brady and Dan Dailey were accused of being drunks. It was said, absurdly, that "Jimmy Stewart didn't get married for so long because he was the type of male with no great interest in the opposite sex." Nothing could have been further from the truth. The article went on, referring to certain stars' lack of interest in women: "Cary Grant heard this one about himself, too, although no one who knows Cary can exactly figure out why." Surprisingly, none of the victims of this piece sued the magazine. And Mike Connolly of the *Hollywood Reporter* compounded the felony by reprinting the article in a condensed form.

At the end of 1951, Cary once again joined forces with Howard Hawks, to film the entertaining *Monkey Business*. The screenplay was written by Ben Hecht—whose impassioned support of the recently formed state of Israel had drawn Cary's financial and personal backing—Cary's old friend Charles Lederer, and I.A.L. Diamond, later Billy Wilder's collaborator. (Diamond would cruelly parody Grant in *Some Like It Hot*: in a scene set on a yacht, Tony Curtis, doing his Cary Grant imitation, pretends to be sexually impotent in order to seduce Marilyn Monroe.)

Monkey Business was a daring farce, made in defiance of the Motion Picture Code. Cary played Professor Barnaby Fulton, a research chemist working on a formula to revitalize exhausted tissues of the human body. Applying the formula, he renders himself young again, along with his wife, played by Ginger Rogers, and several other individuals in his clinic. (Grant's performance foreshadowed his preoccupation with rejuvenation during the last decades of his life.) He had seldom been better; his manic playing of a now "teenaged" academic, jazzing around, contained more than a hint of his own middle-aged distaste at the mindless enthusiasms of adolescents. The script exposed the foolishness of 1950s American popular culture, which was sweeping postwar Europe. The film satirized the American obsession with youthfulness, showing the absurdity of trying to preserve the impossible. Grant's acting was effortlessly assured, carefully stylized and timed.

Neither *People Will Talk*, *Room for One More*, nor *Monkey Business* succeeded at the box office, and Cary Grant began to feel that his time in movies had passed. He was out of step with the 1950s; he had no rapport with such new idols of the screen as James Dean and Marlon Brando. Years later, he said to an interviewer, "That was the period of blue jeans, dope addicts, and Method, and nobody cared about comedy at all." It wasn't true, of course: several comedies of the period were successful, but *Monkey Business* was altogether too sophisticated and satirical a work to appeal to the general public. It exposed too much; it didn't pander to mass tastes.

Cary poured much of his frustration into a renewed foster fatherhood: Lance Reventlow, now a good-looking sixteen-year-old, returned to Hollywood with his mother. Cary found a home for them in Beverly Hills; the house had belonged to Irene Mayer Selznick, who had settled in New York, following the great success of her production of *A Streetcar Named Desire.* Cary loved the boy, and the feeling was returned. He helped him with his schooling, assisted him in problems with his fellow pupils, sat up late at night tutoring him for exams, and encouraged him to develop his athletic skills. If he could not be a father himself, he could certainly be a surrogate father to Lance.

In a last-ditch effort to find a popular comedy, Cary embarked on *Dream Wife,* for M-G-M, with Dore Schary as producer and Sidney Sheldon as director, from a script by Sheldon and two other writers. Cary would play Clemson Reade, a businessman married to a State Department official whose concerns over an oil crisis threaten her marriage. The comedy springs from Reade's interest in an attractive Bukistan princess, Tarji, who is a specialist in the techniques of pleasing men.

Cary was not well when he began making the picture. Sheldon recalls that he was yet again suffering from a bout of hepatitis, and was thin, drawn, and pale, with a yellowish cast to his skin. He refused to wear makeup. He fought with Sheldon from morning to night. When he saw the elaborate set of a Bukistan palace, he snapped at the writer-director, "If I had known that that set was going to look like this, I never would have agreed to make the picture." The same statement greeted a change in a tiny scene. He was angry when Sheldon forbade him to kick a little boy in an airport who was bothering him. "I told Cary, 'You can't do that,' " Sheldon says. " 'The audience will hate you.' He replied, 'Well, I want to do it.' And he did it. I wasn't even watching him, because I knew I wouldn't use the scene. And then we got into an argument because I wasn't watching him do it."

In another sequence, in which Cary was discussing the oil crisis with Deborah Kerr, playing his wife, he spoke the lines with such excessive solemnity that both Miss Kerr and Sheldon burst out laughing. Time and again, the scene was attempted, with the same result. A love scene with Deborah Kerr bored Cary so much that he raised and lowered his eyebrows like Groucho Marx. Sheldon begged him not to. He promised he would cooperate and then repeated the mannerism. When Sheldon laughed uncontrollably, Cary turned around and said, "Sidney, if you're going to laugh, I can't go on with the scene." It had to be dropped.

His fussiness was displayed repeatedly. He objected to such details as the type of collar he wore; when Walter Pidgeon appeared in a suit of the same cut and color as his own, he announced that he would change into another, holding up shooting for hours. He had, of course, arranged for Pidgeon to wear the duplicate suit.

During the making of *Dream Wife*, Betsy Drake began hypnotizing Cary, to cure him of smoking and of other habits she disliked. Melville Shavelson remembered that Betsy made a recording on tape in which she said, "Cary Grant, you are the greatest actor in the world. Cary Grant, you are the greatest actor in the world. Cary Grant, you are the greatest actor in the world. Cary Grant, you have nothing to worry about. Cary Grant, stop worrying," over and over again. She played it during the day and while he slept. By building his ego, Betsy obtained at last a degree of power in the relationship. Cary said later:

Betsy planted a post-hypnotic suggestion that I would stop smoking. We went to sleep, and the next morning when I reached for a cigarette, just as I always did, I instantly felt nauseated. I didn't take another one that day, and I haven't since.

At the end of 1952, weary of Hollywood and feeling dubious about the future (Betsy for her part left the motion picture industry), Cary accompanied his wife on a long freighter trip to the Orient. In Japan, where he visited U.S. military hospitals, he took the opportunity to announce at a press conference on February 2, 1953, that he was annoyed by the ill-treatment of Charlie Chaplin, who had been accused of being a Communist and was forbidden by the U.S. Department of Justice to return to America.

On the Grants' return to Hollywood, Cary was offered the role of Norman Maine, the failing actor who adopts a young and struggling singer, in George Cukor's remake of *A Star Is Born* with July Garland. The script was written by Cary's old friend from his New York days, Moss Hart, who had had Cary in mind. As we know, Hart had tried to persuade him in 1946 to appear in his version of Laura Z. Hobson's best-selling novel *Gentleman's Agreement*, but Cary had refused the role of a magazine reporter who poses as a Jew to expose anti-Semitism in American society; he claimed that he not only was Jewish himself but looked Jewish, and that therefore the audience would not accept him in the part. Hart had understood, and the role had gone to Gregory Peck.

In rewriting the original Alan Campbell–Dorothy Parker script of *A Star Is Born*, Hart had incorporated many of Cary's characteristics: Maine's drinking was counterbalanced by Cary's; the polished matinee idol played in the original version by Fredric March had become more complex: a moody, introspective man, filled with anger and seized by fits of depression. Cary may have recognized too much of himself in the character. George Cukor invited Cary to his house several times to discuss the part; Cary read the part aloud in the ornamental garden, while both Katharine Hepburn and Greta Garbo swam in the pool. Cary was characteristically skittish, changing his mind almost from hour to hour, making excessive financial demands, dining and going to the races with Judy Garland and her producer husband, Sid Luft, but it is doubtful that he ever seriously entertained the idea of playing in the picture. The movie emerged as Cukor's masterpiece, with James Mason ideal as Norman Maine and Judy Garland in the performance of her career as the up-and-coming Vicki Lester.

During the Grants' Far Eastern journey, while they were in Hong Kong in February, Alfred Hitchcock had flown a script to them, with an urgent request that Cary respond quickly. The screenplay, by John Michael Hayes, was based on a novel by David Dodge. The title was *To Catch a Thief.* In view of Cary's dismissal from Fairfield School for theft, this was possibly one of Hitchcock's sadistic little jokes. *To Catch a Thief* was the story of John Robie, known as The Cat, a reformed jewel thief who is living in comfortable retirement on the Riviera. A series of burglaries takes place in Cannes, many of them carrying the Cat trademark. While attempting to clear his name by capturing the real criminal, Robie meets and falls in love with a wealthy heiress.

This slight plot was enlivened by Hayes with witty and provocative dialogue, and it would provide Grant with an ideal role as a debonair, sophisticated crook who, untroubled by moral considerations, enjoys a hedonistic existence in the south of France. But Cary did not respond at once to Hitchcock's invitation to appear in the film. When he returned to Hollywood, he discussed it with Paramount executives and with Hitchcock himself; he seemed to lean more toward a musical with Vera-Ellen.

Cary had been troubled for some time by the declining health of Dorothy di Frasso. Her extravagance had finally consumed her personal fortune—from an inheritance of twelve million dollars, she was now worth less than twenty thousand—and she was afraid she might have to sell her jewelry in order to live. She had never fully recovered from the death of Bugsy Siegel. Now she developed a coronary condition that made her painfully aware of her mortality, and she was warned that she must forgo alcohol, rich foods, and love affairs. She complained that she was forced to live like "a turnip." But nothing would stop the ebullient countess, who continued to go to parties night after night. When her close friend Marlene Dietrich opened in her one-woman show in Las Vegas at the outset of 1954, Dorothy insisted upon going. Cary talked her out of taking the plane; she took the eight-hour train journey instead. He saw her off at the depot, then flew, without Betsy, to Las Vegas, to keep watch over her.

She vigorously led the applause at Marlene's first night at the Sands Hotel. She, Cary, Clifton Webb, and other friends were guests at the home of Tom Douglas, show producer for El Rancho Vegas, where Cary always stayed over the years. The group attended a big party at El Rancho and the next night another at the Sands. Dorothy suddenly collapsed after leaving the ladies' room at the Sands, and Marlene and Cary rushed to her side. As Marlene found nitroglycerin tablets and gave them to her, Dorothy said, "You know, darlings, I am going to die." Cary insisted that she return to Los Angeles immediately; he had already called her doctor in Encino, to arrange a chiropractic treatment. According to some reports, he drove her to the train; according to others, he accompanied her on the journey, along with Clifton Webb, the three taking adjoining compartments. The countess boarded the train with luggage that contained two pearl necklaces, two emerald hatpins, a pair of diamond earrings, ruby clips, and gold compacts, the whole valued at almost a quarter of a million dollars. She hugged her mink coat about her, telling Clifton Webb she felt unnaturally cold, as though death were creeping up on her already. She lay down in her compartment under an expensive ermine wrap. As the train rolled through Pomona, on its way to Los Angeles, Webb came in to wake her up. She was dead.

Cary insisted on accompanying the coffin to New York for burial in the Taylor family plot, and he and Betsy sat up all night, as Dorothy had wished, with other friends on the eve of the coffin's departure, paying tribute, in laughter and tears, to Dorothy's much-beloved memory. Asked the reason for the wake, Cary and Betsy told the *Hollywood Reporter*'s Mike Connolly: "We did it because we remembered how much Dorothy hated being alone."

Perhaps to quell his grief, to find escape in an attractive and undemanding project, Cary finally accepted Hitchcock's long-standing invitation to make *To Catch a Thief*. The picture would start shooting on May 1 in Cannes; he and Betsy, who had now reached a watershed in a troubled relationship marked by quarrels, would welcome the chance to spend spring and summer in the south of France. Cary's vanity was touched when Hitchcock told him he would be doing many of his own stunts, including running across rooftops, and would be displaying his physique in swimming trunks in several scenes. Although he told reporters he did nothing to maintain his fitness, this was typical of his cavalier attitude to the press. In fact, he now began each day with push-ups (he could still manage twenty at a clip), swam laps in his pool, did fast walking, and exercised with a personal trainer. The result was that he rapidly lost a burgeoning double chin and suspicious signs of extra flesh at his waistline, the dread of all leading men past fifty. Even his hair was merely touched with attractive hints of gray and showed not an inkling of thinning.

While he was looking forward to this new Hitchcock film, Cary suffered a second bereavement in two months. He learned in late February of the sudden death of the former Mrs. Clifford Odets. He had grown very fond of Bette and had much regretted that she and Odets had divorced. Beautiful, talented, she had had an abortive career as an actress, handicapped by her easily unsettled nerves. Someone had given her children, Walt and Norma, a pair of parrakeets, and she had grown fond of the birds. Suddenly, she came down with severe fever and stomach upset, and within a matter of days she was dead. Her condition was diagnosed as psittacosis, a rare malady contracted from parrot feathers. Cary wrote to Odets on February 26, 1954:

There's an unreality, delusion of disbelief, an incredulity that affects—perhaps even protects—the feelings of each of us when we lose, and miss, someone who has shared our emotions and thoughts, yet none of us can know the extent of another's inconsolability or the degree of his sadness.

He added that he was sending the note "as I would reach out a hand, to bring you sympathy and affection, dear friend." This heartfelt communication posed the more sensitive and considerate side of the actor's complex nature.

Cary and Betsy left for New York, then sailed on May 15, two weeks later than originally planned, for Cherbourg. In Paris, on the 25th, they met the Hitchcocks at the Ritz, and all four flew to Nice, then transferred to the Hotel Carlton at Cannes. They were joined ten days later by Grace Kelly, who was cast as the wealthy and attractive Frances Stevens. Cary had enthusiastically agreed to Grace Kelly's selection as his leading lady. Impressed by her discipline, looks and poise, he had admired her in *Fourteen Hours* and in *High Noon*. When M-G-M proved reluctant to lend her out to Hitchcock, he is believed to have pulled strings behind the scenes to influence the studio to relent.

Cary and Betsy were delighted with Grace. Although she was exhausted from shooting a film about emerald mining, *Green Fire*, she was unfailingly charming, lacking in star temperament, and letter perfect. Hitchcock, often testy, was greatly mollified by her and Cary, by the Carlton cuisine, and by visits to the Moulin des Mougins, a three-star restaurant only a short drive from the city. Food, good company, and fine wine were among the few palliatives to Hitchcock's savage nature. A sure sign that he was happy was when he would run his hands over his ample stomach and his face would flush deeply and he would blink heavily from his fleshy eye sockets.

Making *To Catch a Thief* was one of the most pleasant experiences of Cary Grant's life. James Spada, Grace Kelly's biographer, recalled that the Grants, the Hitchcocks, Grace and her lover Oleg Cassini would dine together in a variety of excellent small restaurants or would have a flutter at the local casinos. Grace became fascinated by Monaco, and in one scene with Cary, Prince Rainier's palace is shown in the background. Again and again, Cary was impressed by her professionalism. In one sequence, the script had John Robie grappling with Frances Stevens and pushing her up against a wall. Cary's hands were so powerful that Grace had to massage her wrists, her face twisted in pain, between takes. But she returned uncomplainingly to play the scene repeatedly.

Grace was a notoriously bad driver, and the tortuous roads of the three Corniches were hazardous to all but the most expert of motorists. There was no way to fake or double her at the wheel; Hitchcock took a deep breath and instructed her to drive rapidly around the bends, with a sheer drop below and Cary in the passenger seat. In no time at all, Cary began to panic. He begged her to be more careful, but twice she nearly carried him over the edge. The second unit director screamed to her to stop, and she did, with a grinding of brakes, on the edge of a precipice—a foreshadowing of her death in 1982 at the wheel of her car.

To Cary, who exceedingly admired control and excellence, Grace personified both. Her gentle, considerate nature endeared her to the Grants, and they became lifelong friends.

To Catch a Thief was much liked by audiences; reviews were quite good; the combination of the stars was irresistible: neither had ever looked as glamorous or performed with greater polish or more perfect timing. The director handled the superficial material with impeccable skill.

In the wake of the disastrous *Room for One More, Monkey Business* and *Dream Wife,* Cary had felt his career was at an end. *To Catch a Thief* restored his confidence in himself and made him feel he could continue as an actor. But ironically, as so often happens in major careers, he followed this shrewd choice of subject with a blunder. He elected to appear in *The Pride and the Passion,* for the producer-director Stanley Kramer, the script of which had been written by Edna and Edward Anhalt, based upon the novel *The Gun,* by C. S. Forester.

THIRTEEN

The Pride and the Passion would be ready for shooting in April 1956. The producer-director, Stanley Kramer, who had made his name as Hollywood's foremost liberal producer, had spent many weeks in Spain laying the groundwork for this top-heavy epic. Cary had agreed to play the role of a British naval officer during the Napoleonic Wars who has to protect an enormous Spanish cannon from French seizure. Peaceable by nature, the officer wants only to obtain possession of the cannon and transport it to a safe place. But he encounters the passionate and committed Miguel, a Spanish guerrilla leader who is determined to have the cannon dragged across many miles of difficult terrain, then aimed at the French garrison at Ávila. Much of the story involved a grueling cross-country journey, followed by a spectacular siege.

It had taken considerable powers of persuasion for the determined Kramer to convince Cary that he should undertake the movie. Cary decided to go ahead when C. S. Forester told him he would be perfect as the hero. In Hollywood, he had several meetings with Clifford Odets to discuss doing Thomas Mann's *Joseph and His Brethren* for Jerry Wald at Columbia (Odets commented in his diary on Cary's "evasive, non-committal commitment . . . strange 'flirting' ") but nothing came of this. Cary was juggling with another Odets project. He had seen in the newspapers the story of Edgar Fassberg, of Brooklyn, who had been found dead, by his own hand, in a hotel room in Baltimore. When police questioned his widow, she told them that she had known him as Edward James Phillips and had thought him to be a brigadier general in the Army Reserve, assigned as a pathologist at Governors Island. She was horrified to learn that he had had at least eighteen aliases and lived several lives at once. Cary sent a note to Odets on March 1, saying: "Was it HIS body that was found? Perhaps he hid behind someone else even then . . . his final triumph." It is not surprising that Cary was drawn to the idea of a life lived in deception.

At the same time, he was talking more seriously with his friend, the writer-director Melville Shavelson, about a story Betsy Drake had written, recounting the adventures of a couple living on a houseboat. Yet again, the material concerned adopting children. Cary was delighted with it, seeing an opportunity for him to co-star once more with his wife. One of the reasons he wanted Shavelson, and his partner, Jack Rose, to film the story was that he had liked their recent comedy, *The Seven Little Foys*, starring Bob Hope. Based on Eddie Foy's memoirs, that film dealt with the adventures of the celebrated vaudeville family of the first two decades of the century, who had, as we know, appeared with the young Archie Leach in more than one theater in the provinces.

Shavelson recalls that neither he nor his partner thought much of the scenario, finding it dull and lightweight. However, knowing that Betsy Drake was the author, they felt compelled to say they loved it. The truth was that they would have been quite happy to work with Cary Grant on any project, even the story of the world's last flea-circus proprietor, or of someone who built the Empire State Building out of matchsticks. At a second meeting with Cary, they asked him how much money Betsy would want to co-star. The question was accompanied by a sinking feeling: much as they liked her personally, they knew that she had no pull at the box office. He told them she would want thirty thousand dollars, a not inconsiderable sum at the time. They agreed, provided that Paramount, their studio, concurred.*

Cary told Shavelson and Rose: "You must understand this: I will

---

* *Cary had resumed his original role as agent, and in fact was handling Betsy as his only client.*

not commit to make the picture until the studio buys the story, because I don't want Betsy to know that they didn't buy it because they wanted it for itself, but only because I would agree to star in it." This put the two men in an impossible position. After all, the truth was that no one would buy the story unless Cary Grant went with it. But in order to preserve a cordial relationship with Cary, they went to see Paramount boss D. A. Duran, whom they dubbed the Tower of Jello because of his alleged dislike of making decisions. He told them, "Okay. *Houseboat* isn't very good. How can we commit to this project and agree to buy the story and hire Betsy Drake to appear in it without knowing whether we'll get Cary Grant?" Shavelson reassured Duran that Cary would definitely do the picture; he just didn't want Betsy to know how the project had been put together. But Duran had his doubts.

Just as Cary was about to leave for Spain to make *The Pride and the Passion*, Duran turned up at the airport and cornered him, saying, without any beating about the bush, "Cary, unless you sign the contract and make a commitment, we're going to tell Betsy everything." Cary panicked; reluctantly, he was forced to agree. As he flushed with irritation and anger, Duran, who was certainly not the Tower of Jello on this occasion, took the contract out of his pocket and handed it to Cary, who signed it in desperate haste before Betsy turned up to see him off.

Sophia Loren had been cast as a passionate girl, Joanna, who falls in love with the British naval officer played by Cary. Cary had not wanted her for the part; he would have preferred Ava Gardner. However, Stanley Kramer believed that this virtually unknown Italian actress, whom he had admired in *Woman of the River*, was the only possible choice for the part. Cary remained skeptical; he had the typical star's reaction to being cast opposite a newcomer. Miss Loren, who was sensitive and vulnerable despite her headlong ambition and drive, was all too aware of his attitude toward her when she appeared at the cocktail party that inaugurated the production. It was a big affair, crowded with paparazzi and attended by many of the society figures of Madrid.

Perhaps because of his lack of interest in meeting Miss Loren, Cary broke his usual rule of punctuality and arrived over an hour late. Frank Sinatra, cast as the guerrilla fighter Miguel, upstaged him by turning up after an hour and a half. Cary greeted the actress with "How do you do, Miss Lolloloren, or is it Lorenigida? I can never get these Italian actresses' names straight." But he didn't talk to her in a condescending or deliberately wounding manner. He spoke to her teasingly, lightheartedly, as he explored her eyes. She was scarcely able to absorb the fact that she was actually talking to Cary Grant, so swift had been her rise from obscurity and poverty, her encounters with fame and money and power.

The shooting began. It was arduous for all concerned. The first scenes were of the retreat of the Spanish army, shot not far from Madrid; April 20–24 were spent in Segovia. Cary suddenly experienced another recurrence of hepatitis; he seemed to have been stricken by another virus, probably because of his weakened liver, and he was laid low. Scenes had to be shot around him. Yet he failed to send for Betsy; who was concerned when she heard of his condition. According to Melville Shavelson, Cary had become romantically interested in a young male Spaniard; their relationship continued throughout the shooting. He recovered gradually, joining the grueling cross-country trek in his heavy period uniform. He was reliable as always, uncomplaining and supportive of Stanley Kramer. But he had little rapport with Frank Sinatra.

Sinatra was at his worst at the time, his nervous, volatile temperament annoying to everyone. He insisted on calling Cary "Mother Cary"; he refused to drive in a chauffeured Mercedes but insisted that his Thunderbird be flown in from Hollywood, a request that was finally refused; he threatened to urinate on Kramer if the director would not get him back to his hotel before midnight. He also charged hundreds of dollars to the company for calls to his bookie in Chicago and allowed his girlfriend, Peggy Connolly, to charge all her clothing and jewelry to the studio.

Stanley Kramer remembers that Sinatra "had an eye on Sophia, maybe not actually, but jokingly." Kramer adds:

Frank always said, in the vernacular, which Sophia didn't understand, "Sophia, you're going to get yours." It was pretty obvious what he meant. He meant she was going to get Frank Sinatra.

Finally, Sophia asked someone, "What means this, 'get yours'?" and they explained to her. We were shooting at night and called a dinner break at midnight. I remember tables were set out under a big tent because it had begun to rain. Sinatra had had a few drinks, and he yelled out, "Sophia, you're going to get yours!" Now she was ready for him, and she stood up and said, "Not from you, you Italian son of a bitch!"

Sinatra screamed constantly about the primitive conditions of work, threatened to walk off the picture, refused to rehearse, wouldn't wait around while shots were being set up, and created so much tension that several people were ready to beat him up. Cary hated this unprofessional behavior. He tended to ignore the temperamental star, and instead he focused upon Sophia Loren. Betsy, reading the gossip items in Hollywood, must have suffered intensely. Despite the fact that Sophia was dating the producer Carlo Ponti and was close to becoming engaged to him, she couldn't resist Cary Grant. He began using her as a kind of psychiatrist, talking of the fact that, in her words, "he had never had a really sustained relationship in his life." He displayed his self-doubts, probably revealing to her his sexual problems. She knew that he wanted to be open and honest with her, and yet "not make himself vulnerable. Of course, one cannot have it both ways." She reported in her memoirs that as he grew to trust her, he no longer bothered wearing his mask; she was referring to his false image, so carefully sustained, of unequivocal masculinity and strong emotional security. They compared notes on their unhappy childhoods and they visited romantic restaurants in the hills, listening to the guitars and the high, piercing sounds of the flamenco singers. And, Miss Loren declared, they fell in love.

It wasn't easy for him to be involved with a woman who was already seemingly committed to another man. But Carlo Ponti was married, with children. Miss Loren's mother had warned her that if she waited for Carlo to be free, in a Roman Catholic country which didn't recognize divorce, she would wind up "an old maid lighting candles." Cary assured her (fortunately, Betsy didn't hear about this) that he would obtain a divorce and marry her immediately if she was ready.

Yet there is no evidence that the relationship between Cary and Sophia Loren was physically consummated. The candles and the flamenco and the flower-scented evenings in obscure hideaways went on and on, the discussions focusing on Cary's emotional problems, but there seem to have been no elements of a profound personal liaison. However, he offered her the starring role in *Houseboat*, thus ruthlessly ditching Betsy. She accepted, not knowing Betsy had been cast. Stanley Kramer comments:

I have no idea whether Cary and Sophia had a [physical] affair. It is true he was taken with her, but she, of course, already was tied to Carlo Ponti. She was pretty matter-of-fact about it. I guess she'd been approached by many men in her time, God knows. There was something almost boyish about him in his attitude toward her—in his insecurities, whatever they were, vis-à-vis this sex symbol. Certainly, they were friendly; he was wonderfully courteous and gallant, as he always tried to be. I don't think anyone took the situation between Cary and Sophia seriously. Ponti always loomed on the horizon; he visited us often. I never heard him make any objection about Cary. He was an older man, was kind of Sophia's mentor, discoverer, sponsor. Love can be many things, and who can say whether one person loves another? . . .

Cary wined and dined Sophia often on balconied overhanging restaurants all over Spain. She had a sense of humor, and she treated the whole thing lightly. And I suppose she must have known he was a married man. Of course, she had a lot of pride. Anybody from bare beginnings who raised herself to her position would have pride.

In his novel *Lualda*, Melville Shavelson is anxious to point out that the central character, an ambitious Italian actress, is not based on Miss Loren. Yet Shavelson confirms that the portrait of Bart Howard —described as "America's Number One screen lover, who offered to make Lualda an international superstar in return for her making him a man"—was based upon Cary Grant. Bart Howard, the handsome idol of millions of women, is a secret homosexual who is privately insecure and nervous, and feels forced to "make love to women when the whole sex repulsed him." Howard confesses to Lualda that he is gay, and that his emotional condition is at the root of his mental stress and temper tantrums. At one stage, Howard explains to Lualda how easily anything can be learned while one is asleep. Lualda snaps at him, "Then why don't you learn how to fuck girls?" He replies, "I've tried. You'd think being able to have such complete control over my body would be enough. But you see, that's where the God you mentioned has been able to laugh at me. He put the control of *that* function not in the body, but in the mind. Sex is a mental process." Later he goes to bed with Lualda.

Shavelson believes that if there were in fact any physical union between Miss Loren and Grant, it did not take place until considerably later, when Cary had begun experimenting with lysergic acid.

The laborious shooting continued. Betsy finally did come to Spain, only to find everyone talking about the situation between Cary and his female co-star. She felt humiliated, a not unfamiliar sensation for this young woman. Whatever her physical relationship with Cary was, she can only have been chagrined by his seeming indifference to her happiness in continuing to see Miss Loren after she had arrived.

Stanley Kramer recalls that Frank Sinatra's behavior grew more outrageous as shooting continued. To this day, Kramer remembers Cary's extraordinary skill in dealing with the situation.

I think Grant felt that what Sinatra [was doing] was unreasonable and not professional. Sinatra left the picture. It was six weeks before completion. He simply told me, "I have a lawyer and you have a lawyer," and that he had to go. I pleaded with him, because the six weeks concerned revolved around him, but to no avail. Finally, I made a deal with his attorney, Martin Gang, to finish the film in California on a stage with fake palm trees.

Cary made superb efforts to fill the gap. Nothing was too difficult: he played close-ups that were supposed to be with Frank with coats on hangers, put himself out no end, and acted as a professional from beginning to end, for which I was everlastingly grateful. I've never forgotten him for it. But he couldn't save the picture.

Kramer recalls that some of Cary's work in the film was physically dangerous: Once, he was helping to push the cannon on a steep hill, when it rolled down, dragging him on a cable. But he took the risk in his stride.

Cary grew tired of the interminable production. He said to Kramer, "Let's give up and go home." And Kramer remembered that he was tempted. Although doubles were used for some shots, in others Cary had to fall into mud, wade through a swirling river, and struggle up the side of a flint-strewn hill. At the end of the day's work, he would ignore Betsy and take off to a rendezvous with Sophia Loren. Toward the end of shooting, they were in Ávila. He proposed marriage at a restaurant one night, romantically accompanied by a half-moon shining through a window and the echo of flamenco music from the valley below. Miss Loren was dumbstruck. She told him (she wrote) that she "still needed time . . . to go back to [her] own environment and to be able to make up [her] mind away from the magic of those Spanish nights."

Cary accepted her hesitation. By now, Betsy had understandably had enough. She joined the *Andrea Doria*, a vessel that had taken her and Cary to England in happier days. With her she had almost a quarter of a million dollars' worth of jewelry Cary had given her, and the manuscript of a semi-autobiographical novel, which were locked in the ship's safe. She was seen by few passengers on the Atlantic crossing.

On July 25, 1956, the ship was on the last leg of the voyage, sailing toward New York harbor. A dance was in progress in the first-class saloon. Never particularly fond of social life, Betsy had gone to bed early in her boat-deck cabin, to enjoy a book. She was packed for arrival, and her luggage was ready to be placed in the corridor outside.

At shortly after 11:00 P.M., she heard a disturbing, grinding sound; the ship shuddered from stem to stern. The *Andrea Doria* lurched, and as Betsy looked out of the porthole, she saw a burst of multicolored lights in the dense ocean fog. There was a scream of torn steel and the cry of someone in pain. The lights of another vessel gleamed through the darkness. There was no alarm, and Betsy couldn't determine what had happened. No one answered the telephone when she picked it up.

Throwing on a life jacket, she ran out into the corridor. The vessel was listing badly. People were running about, panic-stricken, screaming. There was smoke, and the smell of oil. The vessel shuddered again. No one, crew or passenger, seemed to have the slightest idea what had taken place. Betsy followed instructions and made her way to a lifeboat station, assigned at the boat drill on the first day at sea.

As she struggled along the sloping deck, she was surrounded by hysterical passengers. At last, she found the boats, but it had been impossible to launch them with the passengers aboard, and they were dropped, empty, into the water. She had to slide down a rope to one of the small craft, which was then rowed out into the turbulent sea. The ordeal ended when the rescued passengers were taken abroad another ship, the *Île de France*, and transported to New York.

It was not until the early morning hours that Betsy learned what had happened. The *Andrea Doria* had collided with the Swedish ship *Stockholm*, whose heavy steel bow had ripped the Italian vessel apart. Many died; one survivor, a small girl, was flung from the tortured metal of what had been her cabin onto the *Stockholm* itself, surviving this astonishing transition. She was found clinging to an autograph book—which, by coincidence, contained Cary Grant's.

News of the mishap reached Cary in Madrid. He waited through a day and night of anxiety for word of Betsy; she was unable to get through to him on the *Île de France*'s overcrowded ship-to-shore telephone system. When at last she spoke to him from New York, following a cablegram she had managed to transmit, he cried out with relief and gratitude. Sophia Loren had just turned down his marriage proposal; Betsy must have seemed his only hope.

The Pride and the Passion turned out to be a disaster. Stanley Kramer is the first to admit this. He continued to feel deep admiration for Cary and regarded him as the finest of his professional associates. When he made the picture *Ship of Fools*, he wanted Cary to play the difficult role of the ship's physician, a tortured alcoholic; it would have been a complete change of course in Grant's career, but Cary, despite Kramer's promise to rewrite the role for him, decided against playing it.

Betsy had a consolation prize for her ordeal at sea: the co-starring role in *Houseboat*. Cary had told Melville Shavelson that he wanted Sophia Loren to appear in the film, and Shavelson had assured Paramount that Miss Loren would be the co-star. Now Cary vengefully rejected Sophia for rejecting him.

Before *Houseboat*, Cary was to make another film, under a long-standing arrangement with 20th Century–Fox. *An Affair to Remember*, with Deborah Kerr, would start shooting in early 1957. Cary's old friend and colleague Leo McCarey was signed to direct this remake of McCarey's own *Love Affair*, made for Columbia in 1938, when Cary was under contract there. It was the poignant romantic fairytale of a couple—Charles Boyer and Irene Dunne in the early version—who meet aboard a ship and fall in love, but are unable to consummate their relationship because of difficulties involving their separate backgrounds. The ebullient Jerry Wald was the producer. His decision to make the picture reflected Cary's own desire to return to the make-believe world of 1930s romantic comedy-dramas.

On the first day of shooting, Cary made a scene, objecting to the buttons on the officers' uniforms, and refused to continue work until they were corrected. He continued making trouble throughout the filming, doubtless still reacting to Sophia Loren's rejection of him.

Meanwhile, Paramount, behind Cary's back, had contracted Sophia Loren to make *Houseboat*. The contract he had signed so hastily at the airport when he was on his way to make *The Pride and the Passion* had been ingeniously worded so that he had no right of choice of co-star. Melville Shavelson had the unpleasant task of telling Cary that Sophia had been cast. Once again the unfortunate Betsy Drake was out of a job and humiliated. She would have to face the ordeal of seeing her husband's former lover playing the part she herself had created, speaking lines that were based on her own.

She was distraught. Cary was hysterically angry. Shavelson recalls: "He offered Paramount two pictures free if they would pay off Sophia's contract. They refused." Cary fumed, screamed, but it was useless. He was forced to appear in a movie with a woman who had rejected him; Miss Loren had signed to co-star in a film with a man she now no longer wanted to see. *

---

* She had signed the contract before they broke up in Spain.

When Sophia Loren and Carlo Ponti arrived in Los Angeles and checked into the Bel Air Hotel, Ponti was annoyed. He realized that as a fat and unattractive man, he could not possibly compete with the idol of millions of women. There was always the danger that Sophia's futile, probably sexless but still threatening romance with Grant might resume. In a desperate effort to soothe everyone, to try to begin the picture in some kind of harmony, Shavelson invited Loren and Ponti and the Grants to his house for a discussion. The conversation was understandably strained. The only thing that was made clear was that Loren and Ponti were obtaining the necessary papers to get married in Mexico following Ponti's Mexican divorce.

The shooting of *Houseboat* began on August 8, 1957. The same day, Cary irritably turned down an offer to appear with Frank Sinatra and Shirley MacLaine in *Can-Can*. At first, Cary was so edgy that it was almost impossible for him to play the light comedy scenes. Then Sophia's magic reasserted its power, and he decided once more that only she could unlock his sexual problems and make a complete man of him. He went to her dressing room to make peace. She shook hands with him, and would have been happy to leave the matter there. But to her horror, Cary proposed that she leave Ponti once and for all and marry him. She was utterly committed to Ponti. She must have known that Cary's sexual insecurity would make her life a torment, and that his challenge to her to cure him was no basis for a proposal. As she told more than one reporter, she felt much safer with an ugly man (she seemed unaware of her brutal insult of Ponti, her inference being that most women would want Cary Grant, but how many would want Carlo Ponti?).

In this ghastly circumstance, *Houseboat* continued. Cary refused to take no for an answer. Shavelson recalls that Sophia would come to him in tears, crying, "This man is married. Now he's starting again with me. He doesn't know that Italian girls are different and I am looking for a proper husband, not a glamour man." Shavelson did his best to soothe her. Cary was by now completely out of control. He went to see Carlo Ponti and offered to do four movies for him for virtually nothing (an assurance of several million dollars in profits) if Ponti would give Sophia up. Disgusted, feeling that Cary was less than a man, Ponti refused.

After that, Shavelson says, "It was murder on the set. Cary made things very, very difficult for everybody, because he was in such a bad temper, having to kiss, to hold, to play love scenes with a woman who not only had turned him down but was living with her lover." Cary complained about the daily rushes. He hated the very good camera work of veteran Harry Stradling. Charging Stradling with making him look as though he had a double chin, he forced the out of shape cameraman to climb up ladders to shoot him from above, so that a shadow would conceal the fleshiness under his jaw. For all his careful exercise and his dietary regimen, middle age was catching up with him.

The cinematographer Charles Rosher heard about the needless cruelty to his close friend Stradling, who risked a heart attack by making perilous ascents to the top of the soundstage to satisfy a star's vanity. As Cary came out of his dressing room one morning, the powerfully built Rosher blocked his path, grabbed his jowls in both hands, and screamed into his face, "Why don't you get rid of this shit so Harry can photograph you?" Cary flushed, turned on his heel, and slammed into his dressing room. He didn't come out for the rest of the day.

He exploded during a sequence in which he was dancing with the actress Martha Hyer. As had happened with Alexis Smith when *Night and Day* was being made, the heavy tan foundation on Miss Hyer's arms stained his tuxedo. He screamed and walked off the set, refusing to continue until it had been removed. He was even angrier when Sophia Loren used body makeup. She was already dark-skinned, her exquisite olive coloring the result of her Italian origins, but she held to the lower-class Italian canard that a deep suntan bespoke great wealth. Her character—the daughter of a famous conductor—was supposed to be rich, so she kept adding more and more makeup, until she looked virtually black.

Cary took over the direction, giving orders to both Miss Loren and the children in the cast. He screamed at Martha Hyer persistently. Determined to destroy Sophia Loren, he accused her of having an affair with the virile and handsome Harry Guardino, a member of the cast, and sent a detective to spy on the actor's house. There was no basis for his suspicion; Miss Loren was incapable of being unfaithful to Ponti. But even when the detective reported that Guardino was having an affair with another woman, Cary wasn't satisfied. He called the man a liar, fired him and hired another detective, who issued an identical report. Guardino, who had been a fan of Cary Grant, learned that Cary was having him followed. Now he had to go on the set and play scenes with Cary, concealing his fury.

All through the shooting of *Houseboat*, Betsy Drake seemed to accept what would have driven most women from a man for good. Possibly, the glamour of being Mrs. Cary Grant and a residual fondness for him that persisted through every conceivable kind of humiliation, held her to him. In her eagerness to alleviate emotional turmoil, she encouraged him to try a new treatment. Together they began to experiment with LSD.

It is possible that Cary may have been aware of LSD, as the so-called truth drug used by both British and American intelligence organizations to obtain information from prisoners. LSD removed inhibitions and released the unconscious mind, and the drug was particularly used by men who suffered from sexual problems. Emphasizing every aspect of the human mind to an extraordinary degree, it had a deeper and more lasting effect than hypnosis. The good and bad elements in the psyche were unleashed, and the memory chain was opened up, often with painful consequences. LSD freed the mind to confront itself.

This was a severe challenge and, on top of it, the LSD patient had to deal with hallucinations. Acid, as LSD became popularly known, could cause an individual to walk into his own bathroom and suddenly see violent streaks of color in the basin, a flushing toilet like Niagara Falls, a face in a mirror turned into that of a gila monster, a vision of oneself as a baby or an old, dying human being, a magnificently formed athlete or a cripple. The patient could become violently hysterical or rigidly catatonic. For some people, the experience of LSD produced nausea, terror, and despair. For others, it brought exhilaration, visions of transcendent beauty, and the confidence to deal with anything. Cary Grant went into LSD treatments to overcome his constant self-doubts, the identity problems characteristic of actors, the painfulness of his human relationships, and the tormenting memories of his childhood.

He wanted to be the impossible: an average, "normal," uncomplicated human being who could experience simple happiness. But the fairy godmothers who had bestowed upon him his many gifts exacted the familiar price of depriving him of the very things he wanted most. His actor's egomania would not tolerate such misjudgment on the part of the guardians and fates. He wanted it all: money, success, looks, and, more than that, the ability to enjoy day-to-day living without complications and without conflicting thoughts, the ability to relax, the ability to love and be loved, which of course starts with loving oneself. And for all his efforts, for all the roller-coaster rides of acid treatments, there were no signs that his earnest wishes were to be fulfilled.

He underwent carefully guided treatments with two of the leading proselytizers of the new cure-all: Dr. Mortimer Hartmann and Dr. Oscar Janiger. He met with Aldous Huxley, one of the self-appointed shamans of mescaline, and he soon encountered Timothy Leary, who was not yet well known.

Leary recalls that Cary had been involved with LSD for five years before Leary became the chief glorifier of the drug. He met Cary through a mutual friend, Virginia Dennison, of the Rama Krishna Vedanta group, of which Huxley and Christopher Isherwood were adherents. Miss Dennison had taught Cary yoga. Leary was in San Francisco at the time, with his friend Peggy Hitchcock. Cary invited the couple to lunch. Leary says:

> It was a thrill, because it was the first time I'd been in a movie studio. Cary Grant was always my idol. When I was young I modeled myself on him. I'm very pleased; I think I made a wise choice. Cary was eager to meet me.

Later, Cary told Leary how he discovered love for Elsie Leach for the first time because of LSD; the drug enabled him to knit up some raveled threads of his life. Over the years, Cary saw a good deal of Leary; he was helpful to the younger man, advising him on many things including film making, in which Leary wanted to be involved. Leary started a training center for the use of psychedelic drugs in Mexico, and Cary wanted to attend, but the Mexican government closed down the center. Leary insists:

The joke of all this is that, in a sense, Cary Grant got me into psychedelic experiences.* I was a psychologist, from Harvard, when I heard about Cary Grant getting into [LSD]. That struck me very much; that attracted my attention. I had been very much against the use of drugs before that; I had written books on the subject, because I felt that doctors shooting patients up and giving them pills was making them into an assembly-line cure. I knew that truth drugs were being used by the CIA and the KGB, and that LSD was being used in chemical warfare, so I was much against it. Cary changed my views. He converted me.

Cary began telling anyone who would listen that he was gaining strength through his treatments; he was finding happiness for the first time in his life. He would turn up on Saturday afternoons at the offices of Dr. Hartmann and Dr. Arthur Chandler, stretch out on a couch with an eye shield, block his ears with wax, and revisit his past in the near darkness. He wrote later: "I passed through changing seas of horrifying and happy thoughts, through a montage of intense love and hate, reassembling, through terrifying depths of dark despair replaced by heaven-like religious symbolism." He would also write: "I had to forgive my parents for what they didn't know and love them for what they did pass down—how to brush my teeth, how to comb my hair, how to be polite, that sort of thing. Things were being discharged. The experience was just like being born for the first time; I imagined all the blood and urine, and I emerged with the first flush of birth. It was absolute release. You are still able to feed yourself, of course, drive your car, that kind of thing, but you've lost a lot of the tension."

He added that all human beings were "unconsciously holding their anuses." In one LSD dream, he defecated all over the psychiatrist's office rug. In another dream, he became an enormous penis, shooting off from earth like a spaceship. He realized that in his earlier days he had despised himself. Betsy Drake later commented upon LSD: "You learn to die under [it]. You face up to all the urges in you—love, sex, jealousy, the wish to kill. Freud is the road map."

---

* *It was generally claimed that the reverse was true.*

Cary had several further discussions with Timothy Leary. Leary
says:

He took me aside and started pouring out things to me. . . . The
LSD experience is a life-changing experience. Today people are
cool, they don't talk about it. But in the sixties, with everyone
running around taking off their clothes and saying they'd found
God, and John Lennon eating LSD like popcorn, people talked
about it a lot. Actors are insatiable neurotics. Actors depend upon
getting love all the time. And after all, Cary was the focus of a
hundred million women lusting after him. You couldn't expect
him to be like the guy next door; he was carrying the weight and
freight of the world's fantasies. LSD helped him with his burdens. And he was always charming, professional, courteous, open
and helpful. I remember he said, referring to his Universal cottage, "What do you think of this bungalow? Would it be a good
place to have LSD?" I replied, "Well, I always like to have a
fireplace [during the experience]." He said, "I'm going to call the
studio right now and have them put a fireplace in." That was
typical of him.

Leary comments upon other reasons why Cary needed LSD:

All actors are impossibly sensitive and impossibly questioning. If
the phone doesn't ring every minute, they're worried nobody loves
them anymore. This is not a neurosis that normal people have. I
don't mean to say that you can equate this neurosis with the kind
of self-questioning of a man like Cary.

In the midst of meetings with Leary, the psychedelic nightmares
and happy dreams, the visions of defecation and masturbation, Cary
Grant continued to act out the bland, meaningless comedy of *House-
boat*. Toward the end of shooting, Sophia Loren married Carlo
Ponti by proxy in Mexico; two men stood in for them before a judge.
The day Cary received word of this, he had to appear in the wed-
ding scene in the picture, walking up to the altar with Sophia Loren.
The sequence was tormenting for both of them—and for Betsy.

Much to everyone's relief, *Houseboat* was at last finished. Cary had accepted the leading role in *Indiscreet*, a romantic comedy to be made by Warner Bros. in London. The screenplay was by Norman Krasna, based on his play *Kind Sir*. Stanley Donen would produce, and Cary's co-star would be Ingrid Bergman.

Before shooting began, Cary and Betsy flew to England to spend a few days with Cary's old friend the author Fleur Cowles, who had remarried and lived on an estate in Sussex. Fleur had wanted Cary and Betsy to spend Christmas there, but they had accepted an invitation from Aristotle Onassis to join him on his yacht off the south of France.

In November, Cary acquired a new assistant, the burly, twenty-one-year-old Ray Austin, who doubled as chauffeur and secretary. Betsy was shooting the picture *Next to No Time*, with Kenneth More, in London, and Austin drove her from her hotel to the studio each day. One evening, Cary, Ray, and some friends were sitting at the back of a coffee bar on Park Lane, enjoying cappuccinos. Two men and a young woman appeared in the doorway and, spotting Cary, came over to the table. The girl asked for his autograph. Cary scorned the custom of autograph hunting; like so many stars, he failed to realize that it was such fans who made up the bulk of his audience. He refused, saying, as politely as he could, "Please, if you start doing this, everybody in here will want my autograph." One of the two men accompanying the girl insulted Cary because of his lack of cooperation. Cary, Ray, and their party stood up to leave. The man blocked Cary's way, and Ray, telling Cary to step back, struck the offender across the face. When Cary and Austin reached the street, Cary immediately offered the young man a job.

Ray was intelligent, charming, and reliable; he was not homosexual, and thus provided a good cover for Cary: a gay assistant would have drawn untoward gossip. A cockney, with an accent similar to Cary's, Austin also liked pantomimes and the music hall tradition. Cary again assumed a Professor Higgins role. He began training Austin to modify his accent, to talk more slowly, and not to swallow his words as so many English people do. Austin says:

I told him I was proud of my accent. He said that no one in America would understand me. So I gradually began to adapt my speaking until I finally sounded exactly like him! When were alone together in the car, we would sing old cockney songs. We would enjoy such things as sausage and mash, fish and chips, and kippers.

Ray, then and later, would drive Cary to Bristol to see Elsie. Cary would never say, "It's time we went to see my mother." He would just announce, "Let's go to Bristol." Austin would leave Cary at the door of Elsie's house, with instructions to return two hours later. Austin knew Cary would never stay in the house for the full two hours, even though he had the best intentions. The visits were those of a loving son, but it was difficult to stretch out conversation, when Elsie had no interest in show business and had nothing else in common with Cary.

On one occasion, Cary and Ray carried a portable television set into the house, but Elsie said she had no interest in owning it. Disappointed, Cary was startled when a few days later Elsie decided she wanted the set after all. This unpredictability was difficult for him.

Once or twice, Austin stayed with Cary during the visit and witnessed the halting, painful communion between them. There were a few introductory remarks, empty and of no consequence, and then Cary would ask Elsie if she needed anything. She would shake her head, and there was nothing left for them to say. Austin adds: "He desperately wanted to say more to her, but there was no conversation possible. She would just answer yes or no, and that was it. She wouldn't even go out with us, nor did she really like Cary's fame. She could never think of him or call him anything but Archie. She didn't even want to see any of his films."

Austin soon found out that Cary was bisexual. He says: "Cary was gay, but nothing that would ever disturb anyone at all. Cary would purposely *play* being gay, way over the top." At a party, there would be some attractive women with their husbands, and Cary, according to Austin, would deliberately make a great fuss over the husbands until they were uncomfortable. Later, he would phone a husband and invite himself over; the man would suggest that he visit the wife instead. When people would say to the husband, "How could you leave Cary Grant with that gorgeous wife of yours?" he would reply, "Don't worry; he's gay. Didn't you know?" The man was quite unaware that, according to Austin, his wife would in fact be sleeping with Cary.

Ray Austin was attracted to Betsy Drake from the start. He found her wistful, delicate charm appealing. Because of his respect for her, and for Cary, he didn't at first reveal his feelings, which later turned into love. He always called her Mrs. Grant.

FOURTEEN

Indiscreet began shooting in October. Donen's direction was polished; Cary's role of Philip Adams was another in his gallery of romantic deceivers: Adams tells Anna Kalman, the woman he dates, that he is married to a Roman Catholic who will not grant him a divorce. Though Kalman is in love with Adams, he becomes jealous of a butler-chauffeur when he sees him with Anna in her bedroom. (It would not be very long before Cary became equally suspicious of his own assistant-chauffeur, Ray Austin, vis-à-vis Betsy Drake.)

Ingrid Bergman, cast as Kalman, flew into London in icy November weather to begin wardrobe fittings and photographic tests. She was already in the headlines because of the deterioration of her widely publicized, and scandalous, marriage to Roberto Rossellini. She was suspicious of Rossellini's relationship with another woman, and he, in turn, was consumed with jealousy because of her interest in another man, Lars Schmidt. Both husband and wife were financially troubled, and Ingrid's five-year-old daughter Isabella had just undergone surgery.

When the unhappy Miss Bergman arrived, Cary and Stanley Donen were at the airport to meet her. The press was there too, demanding to know what was going on between her and Rossellini, and seeking details of her children. Cary interjected, "Why don't you talk to me? My troubles are far more interesting!" Generously—

for her nature was generous—Miss Bergman assumed that Cary's interruption was not a display of egotism but was aimed at protecting her from the importunities of the press. But when they got into the limousine that was to convey her to the Connaught Hotel, where Cary and Betsy were staying, Cary, instead of expressing his solicitude, talked nonstop about his LSD treatments and his inner conflicts. Ingrid tried not to sigh with boredom.

The weather worsened. Betsy kept hypnotizing Cary so that he would not catch influenza; he believed that if the mind was sufficiently positive and composed, viruses would have no chance to strike. Absurd though this was, he was almost the only member of the cast who remained healthy from the beginning to the end of the shooting.

The temperature fell close to freezing; the rain was cold and persistent and accompanied by a bitter wind. Stanley Donen contracted a severe case of Asian flu. Fighting his symptoms, Donen courageously returned to work, but others caught the virus and were sent to bed. Margaret Johnston, an admired Australian actress who played a major supporting role in the movie, turned out to be opinionated and aggressive, and failed to agree with Donen on anything. She did the unthinkable and actually left the picture. It had to be started all over again, with the charming Phyllis Calvert. Then, on the day she signed the contract, Miss Calvert's husband died suddenly. This delayed things further, but with great professionalism and courage, Miss Calvert, to save Warner Bros. enormous costs, went to work. No trace of her distress is visible on the screen; she gave an expertly light and graceful performance.

A heavy yellow sulfur fog descended on London at the beginning of December. Day after day, Ray Austin had to drive Cary to the studio through its swirling, toxic clouds. Betsy remained marooned at the Connaught.

The film's cameraman, Frederick A. Young, fell ill, also from Asian flu on December 18. Max Greene (Mutz Grünbaum) took over. Then the editor, the assistant cameraman, and the wardrobe mistress took sick. Heavy snow often delayed the work.

During the shooting, Cary formed a closer friendship with Ingrid Bergman and grew to appreciate her extraordinary qualities as an

Grant with *Indiscreet* co-star, Ingrid Bergman, at a press conference launching the film (AP/Wide World Photos)

Grant with director Delbert Mann on the set of *That Touch of Mink,* 1961 (Delbert Mann collection)

Ray Austin with Grant on location for *North by Northwest,* 1959 (Ray Austin collection)

Rock Hudson, Cary Grant, Marlon Brando, and Gregory Peck pose for a photo while talking shop at Universal Studios, 1962 (AP/Wide World Photos)

Judy Garland visits Grant and Richard Brooks (Richard Brooks collection)

Berri Lee, magician and close friend, arriving with Grant in Las Vegas for Lee's debut (Berri Lee collection)

Grant with date Dyan Cannon at wedding of
Lance Reventlow and Cheryl Holdridge, 1964
(AP/Wide World Photos)

Jennifer Grant with her father, 1966
(Mrs. Reginald Gardiner collection)

Cary Grant with fourth wife, Dyan Cannon,
and daughter, Jennifer, returning to U.S.
from a visit to his mother in England, 1966
(AP/Wide World Photos)

Cary escorting estranged wife Dyan Cannon,
after her performance in *The 90-Day Mistress*
(AP/Wide World Photos)

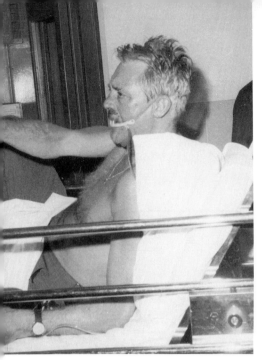

Grant being admitted to St. John's hospital in Queens, following an auto accident on Long Island Expressway, 1968 (AP/Wide World Photos)

George Barrie of Fabergé with Grant in the 1970s (Roy Moseley collection)

Cary Grant watches baseball as his fifth wife, Barbara Harris, watches him, 1985 (AP/Wide World Photos)

Grant in harness for hang gliding in his seventies (Roy Moseley collection)

Barbara Harris with Grant and friend Charlton Heston (Picture by Marc Courtland, 1986, Marc Courtland collection)

One of the last photographs of Cary Grant, taken in Hollywood, 1986 (Marc Courtland collection)

Commemorative plaque at 15 Hughenden Road, Bristol, Cary Grant's birthplace, unveiled in 1987 (Courtesy Bristol United Press, Ltd.)

actress. He was not in tune with her lover, the imposing Lars Schmidt, a Swedish producer, who seemed always to be present. Though at times he was testy over Schmidt's visits to the set, preferring to work without an audience, Cary did not provide his usual number of problems on the production. He was impressed by the impeccable design and by Donen's tasteful, elegant, and accomplished handling of the action. And he felt confidence in the British film craftsmen, knowing they had superior standards of taste and authenticity in designing and building sets.

Ray Austin recalls the curious behavior of Cary during the shooting. He and Betsy moved from the Connaught Hotel to 9 Brompton Square, to escape the unwanted attention of press and fans alike. Cary would go to newspaper libraries, public libraries, and anywhere else where publications were stored, even in Bristol on the weekends, to explore the indexes for any references to Archie Leach, and then, with a razor blade, cut out the appropriate articles and destroy them. He couldn't bear anything in print that referred to his former persona.

Austin adds:

Sometimes he would go off walking on his own in London. My instructions were that, if I dropped him at the corner of the embankment, I would wait by the telephone, and then, after a period of one or two hours, according to what we set, pick him up again. Often, this was on the Thames embankment. I had to sit by the phone because I never knew when he would call me. As it turned out, he never did. And I never found out where he went.

At that time, Roy Moseley, a young admirer of Cary's, approached him, for an autograph. Cary flew into a temper and, in front of Ray Austin, violently clutched at Moseley's hair, with so much strength that he succeeded in taking out a tuft of it.

Seeing Moseley's discomfort, Cary realized the seriousness of what he had done and yelled at the young man to come into the Brompton Square house. There, he lectured him furiously for fifteen minutes on the foolishness of seeking stars' autographs, and advised him to do something better with his life, including learning languages, and in particular Hebrew. By now, Cary had calmed down and realized that Moseley would "let him off" once he had supplied the requested signature. He willingly gave him the autograph. Later, Moseley laughed uproariously with Austin over the incident.

The picture stopped production for Christmas week to allow everyone a break. This was a custom almost never followed in Hollywood at the time, where only Christmas Day itself would be taken off. Ingrid Bergman flew to Rome to spend a week with her family. Cary and Betsy paid a quick visit to Fleur Cowles and her husband in Sussex, and then flew via Nice to Cannes to spend the rest of the holiday with Aristotle Onassis on his yacht. They both ate far too much of the superb food served aboard, and even Cary gained weight. Members of the international set arrived in droves, bitching, as Betsy Drake later reported in a letter to Clifford Odets, in several languages, a habit which irritated her intensely. She complained about the constant vicious gossip, neither joining in, nor entirely able to ignore it.

Everyone reassembled after New Year's Day. Betsy wrote a long, graphically picturesque letter to Odets on January 9, to which Cary added some handwritten comments. Betsy thanked Odets for his letters; she described how she and Cary would read them together and apart, and then out loud to each other. She expressed her gratitude to Odets for arranging that his friend, the actress Claire Bloom, visit them. She talked of London lying at the bottom of a "yellow black gray, dirty green dead blue fog funnel," how the rain was dirty, making her and Cary sneeze, and how the cold was like that of an old wet cave, but London was "still beautiful," with its parks and squares and crescents, and friendly doors and inviting windows and trees and Rolls-Royces. She wrote of the coziness of the suite despite its shortcomings in decor, of how a brass coal box reflected "what looks like sunlight on the wall."

Jack Warner was in London to see forty-five minutes of *Indiscreet*. Dapper and suntanned, with slicked-down dyed black hair and a well-tailored blue yachting blazer, Warner was his usual self, alive with mischievous humor, self-confidently delivering himself of witless remarks, and behaving very much as he had done as a young man on the vaudeville stage. Cary and he always got along well. Warner had been annoyed with Cary for not accepting the role of Norman Maine in *A Star is Born*, but, in the wake of James Mason's excellent performance, had forgiven him, and they were good friends again. The studio chief was on his way to the South of France, to win and lose several fortunes at the gambling tables.

To console himself for the weather and the long drawn-out days of shooting, Cary exchanged the dove gray Rolls-Royce he owned for a black-and-tan Silver Wraith, with CG1 on the license plates; it was put on the production account and would be sold when his services were concluded. However, he decided to keep the car, transfering the title in it to a third party to save taxes. He could afford it: apart from his existing wealth, he was being paid $25,000 a week for twelve weeks work on *Indiscreet*.

When shooting ended, Cary and Betsy flew to Moscow for a week's vacation; Betsy returned to England to make a movie entitled *Intent to Kill*, directed by Jack Cardiff. It was a thriller, set in Montreal, about a murder in a city hospital; Betsy played a member of the medical staff. Cary flew back to Hollywood with Ray Austin, who had never been there before. Clifford Odets wrote in his diary on March 8:

> My mysterious friend, Cary Grant, back from Europe. He wants and says we must meet immediately. But it will be weeks before it happens. I wonder what he is so busy with all the time? . . . You never know where he has come from or where he is going, as if he had no home, like a fish in the oceanic night.

During the making of *Indiscreet*, Alfred Hitchcock had completed plans for a new thriller, *North by Northwest*. Cary and Sophia Loren—with whom he had become friendly again, apparently resigned to her marriage to Carlo Ponti—were to co-star. Cary would play an advertising executive who is kidnapped by a Soviet-controlled espionage ring when he is mistaken for someone else. It was yet another in his gallery of people who were of confused identity, or whose identities were confused with others'. The plot in many ways paralleled that of *The Man Who Never Was*, about an invented character concocted as a decoy by British Intelligence in World War II. It was the kind of story that was calculated to appeal immediately to Cary Grant. The picture would be shot at Bakersfield, California; Rapid City, South Dakota; New York City, and Long Island, starting in the fall.

Betsy was back in Hollywood in June. She and Cary joined Clifford Odets for dinner at Chasen's on June 24. Cary's friendship with the playwright was troubled. Odets had become embittered because Cary would constantly promise to do a picture and then go cold on it; Cary's name would enable Odets to obtain a commitment by a studio to allow him to direct one of his own subjects.

By late summer, Betsy and Cary, who were arguing over everything, had separated. So paradoxical was their relationship, however, that even as they discussed property settlements, he still acted as her agent, attempting to get her motion picture roles. He did not succeed: she had made very little impression in *Next to No Time* and *Intent to Kill*, which were released within a few days of each other in July.

Odets tellingly summed up much about the Grants when he learned of their separation in November. He wrote in his diary:

They made . . . an unwritten and unspoken (indeed unconscious!) pact of invalidism, of not living fully together and not really disarranging or disturbing each other inwardly, or making demands in true depth or dimension. This was living by a negative, by default. Their common life was oiled by good manners and politeness, by a style of breeding, true affection, by reticence and even some diffidence, not to say characteristic embarrassments and unease. Candor was not present and real relatedness was bypassed for small common enthusiasms and fads. Also by commonly held prejudices. What each wanted was supposed to be understood by *RADAR*, never directly.

Odets summed up Betsy Drake with great perception:

She was early rigidly held up to standards of behavior and affection. She stammers, feels deficient and inadequate, and she marries Cary Grant, who has so many empty standards. She believes, finally, only in manners and good taste and makes *no human* demands. She goes to nostrums.

No sooner had Betsy left than Cary fretted at her departure. He was in that not uncommon position of human beings who cannot live with or without their emotional partner. Cary began discussing Betsy obsessively with friends like Melville Shavelson, whom he told, during one tête-à-tête, "If you want to know why I married Betsy, she was the only woman who could hypnotize me." He relied very heavily on Ray Austin for friendship and psychological support.

By now, Cary was happily settled at MCA Universal. He became very friendly with the studio chief, Edward R. Muhl, who recalls:

We all liked Cary very much. But most of the time we had a devil of a time coming to terms with him, getting him to say yes to anything. He was very cautious, very thoughtful, he wanted to review everything, and, of course, one would go mildly mad wondering why he wouldn't say yes.

Muhl reports that there was no official contract with Cary at the studio. Each deal for a picture was made separately, and each had different terms. Cary enjoyed the campus-like atmosphere of Universal, with the executives housed in bungalows, one of which was given to Cary as his office. Rabbits and cats ran around wild in the grass and bushes outside the bungalows, and, Muhl says:

When Cary saw the bunnies grazing on the grass and nobody chasing them or rounding them up and sending them off the lot, I think he must have felt: These people can't be all bad. We liked him resident there, because one could go by and say, "Morning, Cary," or one could just drop into his bungalow with the words, "I have a script here; I just wish you'd give me your expert advice as a comedy man," and he'd say, "Well, yes, if you'd give me a little time I'd be glad to read it." He always responded, even on scripts of films other than his own. Sometimes he lived in the bungalow at night.

Muhl had made a unique arrangement, whereby Cary would get three quarters of the profits of a picture, in return for taking a fairly modest $100,000 up front. After a certain number of years, the picture's rights would revert to him. Cary soon set up a separate production unit with Stanley Donen, as an effective tax shelter, and they would make more than one good film together. Muhl says: "It was still a very good deal for us. Cary's name ensured very high grosses, and while he made an enormous amount of money from the arrangement, so did we." However, several members of the Universal executive board gave Muhl an extremely hard time over the deal, which remains historic.

Shooting of *North by Northwest* began. Eva Marie Saint replaced Sophia Loren; there had been alleged contractual problems. Miss Saint, all too clearly aware that she was a substitute, acted, very intelligently, the part of an American double agent who becomes romantically involved with Cary Grant's Roger Thornhill. In a reversal of the situation in *Notorious*, she has been forced to put patriotism before personal loyalty and affection, and sends her lover into a situation of mortal danger. One can scarcely doubt that Cary, with his intelligence background, had encountered similar situations.

The filming started in Manhattan, in the lobby of the Plaza Hotel. Cary had to get out of an elevator crowded mostly with women, as two men were following him. Ray Austin was present during the scene. Hitchcock was heard to observe rudely as Cary walked across the lobby with Austin, "Here comes Mr. Grant and his man." Austin says:

> Twenty years later, I was at Universal Studios. I called Hitchcock's name when I saw him filming a sequence. He ignored me. So I went to his office, and he said, "Lord love a duck. What are you doing here?" He added that he had been watching my career (I was a director by then). And as we sat down and talked, he said, right out of the blue, "I owe you an apology. I always thought you and Cary were . . . you know."

A famous sequence was shot at Bakersfield in the first week of October 1958. Roger Thornhill has been lured to an obscure destination in the middle of nowhere. Cars pass; a bus stops and goes. The sky is a hard, blank blue. The road is dusty and endless. Suddenly, Thornhill becomes aware of the buzz of a crop-dusting plane. An observer points out that the plane is dusting crops where there are none. Moments later, Thornhill realizes that the mysterious group determined to kill him has armed the crop duster with a machine gun. He narrowly escapes death when the pilot slams his plane into a truck.

The sequence had been carefully planned on the drawing board. There was nothing Hitchcock liked better than to see perfectly groomed stars disheveled, and he looked pleased when Cary was forced to crawl on his hands and knees in the dust, ruining his beautifully tailored pale gray suit. But Cary didn't quite achieve the look of absolute terror Hitchcock required. Suddenly, as he crouched down, Cary saw a tarantula crawling across his hand. He screamed like a frightened child. Hitchcock made sure the cameras were turning. The scream was not recorded, but the expression of horror was. It would have been typical of Hitchcock to have planted the spider: every inch of the ground had been checked, on Cary's nervous instructions, for signs of insect life.

During the shooting, Cary became friendly with Martin Landau, who played Leonard, the homosexual sidekick of the villain, acted by James Mason. Landau recalls a curious incident during the shooting. Hitchcock wanted him to be better dressed than Cary—a tall order—and took him to Cary's tailor on Wilshire Boulevard, ordering several suits made for him, sometimes in duplicate because they would be damaged in a scene of violent struggle, and they must always look elegant. It is clear that Hitchcock was using Landau's clothing symbolically, to show him as menacing and dominant.

For a sequence that was being shot at Chicago's railroad station, Hitchcock wanted Landau to turn up ahead of time so that the director could make sure his suit was perfect. Arriving, Landau hung back, concerned that he might be visible in a large crowd scene that he was not supposed to appear in. Suddenly, somebody tapped him on the shoulder—Ray Austin, as it turned out.

"Excuse me," Austin said. "Mr. Grant would like to know where you got that suit." Landau, astonished by this question, delivered in a cockney accent by somebody he had never met, replied, "Why does Mr. Grant want to know?" Austin answered, "Only two tailors in the world could make a suit like that: one's in Hong Kong and one's in Beverly Hills." Landau said, "I would suggest that Mr. Grant discuss the matter with Mr. Hitchcock."

It is possible that Cary finally acquired the very suits, because they were assigned to the wardrobe department. The men were similarly built, although Cary was broader; both were somewhat round-shouldered, though Cary's problem was less obvious on the screen. Landau says, "Grant actually did have curvature. The suits compensated for it." He remembers that during the shooting, Cary would look at Landau's clothes and say, "We're about the same size, aren't we? Let me try your suit on," or "You don't have anything in your contract about keeping these, do you?" Despite his wealth and his already extensive wardrobe, Cary coveted the beautiful free clothes.

At a later date, Landau asked the tailor, Quintino, about Cary and was told that Quintino had never had so fussy a customer. Cary measured his lapels with a ruler to be sure the angle of the cut was precise to the millimeter.

Landau recalls an occurrence during filming at Mount Rushmore:

The tourists were there to see the famous carved heads of the presidents on the mountain face. They found us shooting and besieged Cary for autographs. He charged twenty-five cents for each autographed picture! He would give the money to the Actors Fund. He collected something like forty or fifty dollars that day. We were lunching in the cafeteria, all of us, when an old woman with blue hair appeared. She said, "Mr. Grant, I've been a fan of yours for years." And she asked him for his autograph. Cary replied, "For twenty-five cents you can have it. And for fifty cents I'll bite it in your neck." Eva Marie Saint exploded, coughing out a mouthful of coffee. Hitchcock didn't bat an eyelash. The woman was shocked out of her mind!

One day, Landau walked on the set and Cary Grant was missing. He had been there earlier, discussing evangelism with Richard Brooks, who was preparing *Elmer Gantry*. A call was put through to Cary.

Asked why he was not present for the day's work, he replied, "If you look at the appropriate clause in my contract, it says that my mobile dressing room has to be a precise number of feet from the set, and it isn't." The position of the mountainside home that played a crucial role in the narrative made it impossible to avoid including the trailer in wide-angle shots of the living room. Not until the production manager found a solution, and the dressing room was wheeled into place just inches out of camera range, was Cary satisfied.

In a fight scene on Mount Rushmore, Landau had been instructed by Hitchcock to press his foot hard on Cary's hand as Cary clung to one of the monumental faces. Landau says:

Cary was anxious. Nervous. He said, very politely, "I'll be indebted to you if you don't actually step on my hand, but instead fake it, Martin." I decided to pull his leg. I told him, "Oh, I'm from the Actors Studio. I'm a Method actor. I have to actually step on your hand, very hard. I hope you'll forgive me." Now he was really nervous. He said to me, "Oh, no, you won't." I replied, "Yes, I will. You'll never play the piano again. You'll never play the guitar again." Of course, when it came to it, I faked the pressure on the hand, and nobody knew the difference.

Cary, who fretted over Landau's constant smoking during the production, told him he could rid himself of the habit through self-hypnosis. This fussy man could be remarkably relaxed. Landau remembers standing in a small airport as they waited to take off over the Black Hills. As they looked at the plane, somebody was heard to say, "Do you think we'll make it?" And Landau replied, "Jesus, is there any doubt?" He went over to Cary anxiously, saying, "They're talking about whether this bloody thing can get off the ground." Cary was utterly calm: "It'll be all right. The pilot has a wife and family." They boarded the airplane, and Cary, saying, "I'll wake up when I get to Los Angeles," fell asleep. Reassured, Landau was no longer afraid.

Landau remembers that Cary consulted with Hitchcock through much of the shooting. There was a sequence in which Roger

Thornhill creates a commotion in an auction room. Cary helped Hitchcock choreograph all the movements of the complicated scene, which had already been prepared on the drawing board.

Cary was on his best behavior during the making of *North by Northwest.* His respect for Hitchcock was so complete that he knew every set was perfect and that sequences such as the auction scene would become classics. Now fifty-five years old, he proved to be as athletic as ever. Since the final Mount Rushmore sequence could not be done on the actual site (Hitchcock told Charles Higham, "They objected to a chase sequence up the nostrils of Lincoln's nose. Maybe they were afraid he would sneeze at this desecration of the shrine of democracy?"), enormous replicas of Gutzon Borglum's presidential heads were built on the soundstage. Still, a good deal of hazardous clambering about was involved, in which Cary could easily have sustained an injury that could hold up production for days. He went through the experience unscathed.

Cary played scene after scene with wit, charm, and energy. He conspired with Hitchcock to introduce all kinds of personal touches into the picture; at one stage, he uses his favorite motto "Think thin." In one scene, Roger Thornhill produces a matchbox bearing the initials "R.O.T." Asked by Miss Saint's Eve Kendall what the "O" stands for, Thornhill replies, "Nothing." This was a dig at David O. Selznick. Hitchcock had cast as Thornhill's mother Jessie Royce Landis, an actress almost the same age as Cary. The director loved to play this kind of joke on an audience; here he relied on Grant's athletic youthfulness to carry it off. There is a strong homosexual subtext in the film, most overtly in the relationship between the Soviet agent Phillip VanDamm and his evil familiar, Leonard. Leonard tells VanDamm that his suspicions of Eve Kendall are based upon "a woman's intuition." VanDamm replies, "I believe you're jealous. I'm very touched." One wouldn't put it past Hitchcock to have inserted these sly references as a secret joke against his star.

Both *Indiscreet* and *North by Northwest* were enormous and deserved successes at the box office and were almost uniformly admired by critics. At the end of shooting, Cary took a vacation in Key West. When he returned to Hollywood, he and Betsy patched things up, and she moved back into his house. It was a kind of truce rather than a restored marriage, because each was essentially alone and lost.

There was talk, at the outset of the year, of Cary filming *Beloved Infidel*, from Sheila Graham's autobiographical account of her relationship with F. Scott Fitzgerald. But nothing came of this, and Gregory Peck assumed the role. Instead, Cary agreed to make *Operation Petticoat*, to be directed by Blake Edwards, its screenplay by Stanley Shapiro and Maurice Richlin. A quarter century after *Destination Tokyo*, he would be back in a submarine, playing a skipper determined to raise a sub that has been sunk by Japanese planes off the Philippines during World War II. Cary was attracted to the role of Captain Sherman, which gave him an opportunity to play the kind of deadpan, befuddled, punchbag character he had played in *Arsenic and Old Lace*, combined with the looks and manner of Captain Cassidy in *Destination Tokyo*. He was delighted when the studio agreed to shoot the movie in pleasant winter weather in his now beloved Key West.

Cary was troubled at the time by the many personal and professional problems of Howard Hughes. Although Hughes's biographers Donald L. Barlett and James B. Steele claim that Hughes was without a single friend at the time, that is not true. Not only was Noah Dietrich still close to him, but he also had the constant support of Cary, as well as half a dozen other associates. He was living at the Beverly Hills Hotel, in Bungalow 4, while his wife, Jean Peters, occupied Bungalow 19. Barlett and Steele reported that he had leased several other bungalows to house his personal staff, including one for cooks and waiters, one for messengers, doormen, and gofers (known as the "third man detail"), and one for storing Poland Water, the only kind he would drink, and cartons of Kleenex. Cary, visiting Hughes, found that he had reached an extraordinary degree of eccentricity, living on a diet that consisted largely of milk, Hershey bars with almonds, pecans, and his inevitable Poland Water.

Suddenly, Hughes left the Beverly Hills Hotel and moved into a private screening room on Sunset Boulevard, where he lived like an animal. He would urinate on the expensively carpeted floor or all over the bathroom, and when the janitors tried to enter to clean up, he would lock the door on them, pushing them out with violent imprecations. He would not allow anyone else to use the bathroom and, according to his associate Ron Kistler, told visiting Los Angeles police, "Piss in your milk cartons!" Then, without warning, he moved back to the hotel. He had kept Bungalow 4 fully paid up.

Hughes cut Jean Peters out of his life completely. He would squat naked in the living room, staring blankly as countless movies were unreeled on a screen. He was surrounded by enormous piles of newspapers, through which Cary and other visitors had to pick their way as through a labyrinth. Fastidious Cary, who hated even a flake of dandruff on a shoulder, must have been appalled, but ever loyal, he put up with everything.

In February, Cary flew to Key West to make *Operation Petticoat*. He had just had a strong difference of opinion with Clifford Odets. An entry in Odets's diary, dated February 23, 1959, states cryptically: "Dinner—Cary Grant—6:30. Went to Cary's house. Angry. He euphoric."

Odets's secretary of the time writes:

I believe it was on this occasion that Mr. Odets told me he was really angry with Cary Grant's attitude. Cary Grant was in bed (where, I'm sure you know, he often transacted his business, ate his meals, etc.), and Mr. Odets had expected to firm up plans for a movie. As I understood it, Grant had been vague and evasive and simply wouldn't commit himself. Mr. Odets finally told Mr. Grant he was tired of his pussyfooting around.

While shooting proceeded aboard a borrowed U.S. Navy submarine in March, Cary had an interesting visitor at Key West. Joe Hyams—former lover of Ava Gardner, close friend of Humphrey Bogart—was a tough, skillful Hollywood insider reporter, a doyen in the field and a power broker through his widely admired column. With his hooded eyes, piercingly observant stare, tense, watchful manner and lean, whipcord physique, he was something to behold. People either loved him or hated him; and very few had the temerity to refuse him an interview.

Cary agreed to see him, to discuss his career for a series of articles that would appear in the New York *Herald Tribune*. Seemingly hypnotized, Cary, who was accustomed to talking skillful balderdash to most journalists, for whom he had little time, opened himself up to Hyams as he never had before. He described his experience with LSD, saying, according to Hyams:

> Now I know that I hurt every woman I loved. I was an utter fake, a self-opinionated bore, a know-all who knew very little. Once you realize that you have all things inside you, love and hate alike, and you learn to accept them, then you can use your love to exhaust your hate. That power is inside you, but it can be assimilated into your power to love. You can relax. And you can do more than you ever dreamed you could do. I found I was hiding behind all kinds of defenses, hypocrisies and vanities. I had to get rid of them layer by layer. That moment when your conscious meets your subconscious is a hell of a wrench. You feel the whole top of your head is lifting off. . . . There was one day, after weeks of treatment, that I did see the light. Now, for the first time in my life, I am truly, deeply and honestly happy.

He told Hyams that in his early days he had despised himself; but only when he admitted that fact to himself did he begin to change. He said he was a bad-tempered man but hid it—a barefaced lie Hyams had no way of seeing through. Ignoring his physical cruelty to Virginia Cherrill, he said, "I was very aggressive, but without the courage to be physically aggressive." He said he did not intend to foul up any more lives; he could be a good husband now; his attitude toward women had changed. Yet he failed to explain why he had, just two weeks before, left Betsy Drake high and dry again and, despite her loyalty to him, was already preparing the groundwork for a divorce. He added as a footnote the curious fact that he wore women's nylon panties: they were easy to drip dry when one was traveling, he said.

Hyams was excited by these revelations, but Cary asked him not to publish them, at least for the time being. Yet, mischievously, Cary gave a comparable interview to the London *Daily Mirror*'s Lionel Crane, and Crane published it.

Cary returned to Hollywood, fit and relaxed, from the pleasant, uncomplicated shooting of *Operation Petticoat*. One night, he went to the theater, and by coincidence, Joe Hyams was seated next to him. Betsy Drake sat not far away, with another man. Cary remarked on Betsy's good looks. Hyams asked him how he felt about her dating another man. Cary remarked with a smile, "Betsy would be incapable of being unfaithful. None of my wives have been unfaithful; neither have I. This has never been a problem."

Hyams wrote his articles on Cary for the *Herald Tribune*. The editor was delighted with these revealing pieces, and a splashy announcement in the paper told of their appearance. Despite the fact that he had already given much of the material to Lionel Crane, Cary took this as a breach of his arrangement with Hyams, and demanded that he instantly cancel the series. Hyams told him it was out of the question; there was no way he could interfere with the newspaper's plans. Still angrier, Cary told him he would have to find a way. Hyams repeated that he could not stop the articles. Cary threatened that unless the articles were withdrawn, he would discredit Hyams by saying he had never seen him. Hyams told Cary that was absurd, but Cary snapped, "It's your word against mine! And you know who they'll believe!"

Cary immediately called his lawyer, Stanley Fox, who demanded Hyams's cooperation. Hyams refused. Fox charged him with making the series up or pirating it and told Hyams that Cary had declared he hadn't seen him in two years.

Hyams reminded Fox that he had met with Cary in Key West, and that they had just run into each other at the theater. Cary phoned Louella Parsons and even his old enemy Hedda Hopper, claiming he had not seen Hyams in months. Louella said in her column that Hyams had made the whole series of interviews up. Hyams reported in his memoirs:

I was a nervous wreck . . . running between the bathroom and the office. My stomach was churning and I couldn't keep my food down. Most of the people who called me were well-meaning friends. They sounded amused at the controversy and impressed with the articles, but I felt that they too thought I made them up. Cary had been right; when it was his word against mine, no one would believe me, not even my friends.

Cary's influence spread. Stars who had promised to see Hyams for interviews backed away. Hyams's son Jay was bullied at school, where his friends called him "a liar's kid." The matter blew up into a giant controversy. Newspaper after newspaper, magazine after magazine, influenced by Cary's continuing hysterical phone calls, refused to believe Hyams. Proud and stubborn, Hyams was so angry at their disbelief that he wouldn't even condescend to arrange a press conference and play his taped interviews with Grant.

Determined to obtain revenge, Hyams began to do some detective work. He discovered that Cary had a reason for canceling the series, a reason that had little nothing to do with his love of privacy. He had signed a contract with *Look* magazine to write a piece about LSD and its effects on him. Hyams, furious, filed suit against Cary for slander, asking $500,000 in damages. He threatened Louella Parsons with a lawsuit if she didn't retract her statements against him. Universal Studios yielded up a photograph of him with Cary on the deck of the submarine during the shooting of *Operation Petticoat*.

This surely was sufficient evidence that Cary was lying. But even when Hyams's lawyer, Arthur Crowley, advised Stanley Fox that this piece of crucial evidence had surfaced, Cary rashly refused to drop the case. Fox subjected Hyams to twenty-four hours of deposition testimony and the following curious exchange took place:

HYAMS: I chose not to say that Cary wore women's panties.
Fox: Why?
HYAMS: If I wrote it, some people might think it unmasculine.

Hyams produced the Key West tapes; Fox did not respond to this conclusive evidence.

When it was time for Cary to give his deposition to Crowley, he panicked. Although Hyams insists that he never found an inkling of Grant's bisexuality, and although it is doubtful that Hyams would have been ruthless enough to bare Cary's mental disturbances and constant addiction to lying, Cary could not have known this degree of blindness and tact in his shrewd and hard-bitten opponent. Up to the last minute, hardly able to sleep, his alleged happiness as described to Hyams totally dissolved in a daze of anziety, terror and self-hatred, he still seemed to want to risk the ultimate exposure. But then he finally realized he dared not. Fox offered Hyams a compromise: Cary would drop the lawsuit and would work with Hyams on an autobiographical series. Hyams could keep all the money.

Hyams was uncertain whether anything would come of this, but he wanted to avoid a protracted lawsuit. It is unfortunate in many ways that he did not have the nerve, and perhaps the capital resources, to proceed with this case. By doing so, he would have removed every last vestige of suspicion about his motives and actions; although he saw himself as vindicated, in fact Cary's fans probably would not agree.

Hyams was not particularly impressed by the so-called settlement. He knew Cary Grant well enough by now to know that he might dodge his responsibility and give a meaningless interview. When he arrived at Cary's office at Universal, Cary, with expertly disarming stage management, did not greet the embattled journalist in a business suit, neatly bespectacled in horn rims behind a massive desk, the manner in which most guests were received, but instead, covered only by a towel over his loins, lay flat on his back on a massage table. He announced, with total falsehood, that he did no exercise, thought thin, and willed his teeth not to decay. Certainly, he was in excellent condition, thanks to countless massages and male beauty treatments, a meticulously watched diet, and frequent swims in his pool. These, and stretching exercises learned long ago in vaudeville, he kept from Hyams, so that he would seem to be a miracle man, his firm muscles and flat stomach evidence of some kind of mystical self-control rather than of the grueling effort necessary for their preservation.

Hyams began to make a series of taped interviews. Gradually, his feelings of bitterness and resentment faded, swept away by Cary's carefully applied charm. Cary skillfully reworked the truth, omitting his childhood journey to New York, rearranging facts very much as he had done for the last forty years, carefully avoiding any discussion of Virginia Cherrill, not mentioning his war work, skating past Barbara Hutton, and saying little of consequence about his marriage to Betsy Drake. Hyams did his usual expert job on the series and, by prearrangement, handed them to Cary to check. Characteristically, Cary rewrote them, and, with extraordinary modesty, Hyams accepted his version as an improvement.

For months, into 1960, Cary devoted many spare moments to working on the series. It was his skillful way of getting the best of the bargain, and it is surprising that Hyams did not realize he had been duped. Finally, Cary messengered the finished product to Hyams, and it was sent to the *Ladies' Home Journal* under the byline "By Cary Grant as told to Joe Hyams." Hyams was paid $125,000. Heavily in debt, he needed cash to support his wife and son, and accepted what some writers might have thought was a humiliating arrangement: the publication of a piece that was unchecked for accuracy, suffused with its real author's self-protective fantasies, and, though ably written, quite lacking in self-analysis or incisiveness. The *Ladies' Home Journal* was of course delighted to have Cary's own story. They fixed up the erratic punctuation and spelling, and Hyams sent the final edited draft to Cary, who again, with shocking unpredictability, reversed his stand and demanded that the articles not be run. Hyams was appalled. He saw $125,000 going down the drain.

At the last minute, Cary relented. He turned up at the magazine's offices for lunch with the editors. The executive dining room and the corridor outside were crowded with almost every female member of the staff. He announced that he wanted the grammar, spelling, and punctuation restored to their original form, no matter how clumsy they might seem. The magazine must run the piece exactly as it was written or not at all. Laughing, the editors agreed.

Hyams was advised of Grant's latest demand. Then came another catch. Hyams had neglected to mention to Cary that he had been paid $125,000. When Cary found out, he was very upset. He wanted a share of the money. Hyams asked Stanley Fox how much. Fox replied that Cary wanted a new Rolls-Royce. A Rolls-Royce in 1960 cost $22,000. Hyams's lawyer said he would be insane to give Grant any money at all, but with astonishing generosity, Hyams, who needed every penny for his family, gave the millionaire movie star $22,000. And there the matter ended, except that the editors of the *Journal* corrected the spelling and grammar after all. Cary was furious.

In the meantime, Cary was in trouble with another prominent columnist. Hedda Hopper had disliked him for years, and now she conducted a secret campaign against him. Since she could not state her suspicions about his sexuality in print, she began attacking magazine editors when they wrote of his romantic affairs with women. In an extraordinary letter to Mike Cowles of *Look* magazine, dated August 31, 1959, she had written:

> The article you ran on Cary Grant was the damnedest mish-mash I have ever read. Whom does he think he is fooling? This will probably surprise you: he started with the boys and now he has gone back to them.

Referring to a man who was very close to Cary, Miss Hopper added:

> Grant introduced him to his social friends, and now Cary is using a lot of pretty girls to cover up. I used to like him, but no more.

FIFTEEN

Ray Austin recalls a memorable encounter he experienced that year. He and Cary flew to Las Vegas, intending to see several shows. Cary received a message, and he told Austin to hire a car. Austin picked up an expensive vehicle, but Cary told him to return it and rent a Chevrolet instead.

Cary refused to say where they were going, but when they neared the Desert Inn, he told Austin to park at the rear laundry exit. As they drew up, Cary said, "Stay out of the way. I'm meeting Howard Hughes." The exit door opened, and a figure appeared. Cary got out of the car and walked over to Hughes, who stood there holding the door open. They looked at each other for a few minutes, saying nothing. Austin couldn't help watching them, deeply fascinated by this silent communion.

After a few minutes, Cary beckoned Austin over and introduced him to the billionaire. Forgetting that Hughes refused to shake hands with anyone, Austin reached out with his own. Hughes withdrew; then Austin remembered.

Hughes said, "You look after Cary, do you?" Austin replied, "Yes, as much as I can," and Hughes said, "Good. Look after him. I had to see him."

Ray returned to the Chevrolet* and, looking back, saw that Cary

---

* Hughes always drove Chevrolets.

255

had already finished his brief meeting with Hughes and was approaching the car. Hughes slipped back into the hotel, the emergency door closing behind him. Today Austin realizes that Cary only went to Las Vegas for the one meeting: "It was touching; I think Howard Hughes just wanted to look at Cary one more time."

It was not long before Cary's friendship with Austin ended. Betsy Drake was living alone, separated from Cary, at the time. Cary would visit her, not necessarily seeking a reconciliation but perhaps worried that if she divorced him, she would make excessive demands on his finances. He was paying her a fairly modest separation income. Austin found himself becoming more and more drawn to Betsy. Ashamed and embarrassed because of her marital status, but still fascinated by her. He says:

I fell in love with her. We would walk and talk together. I wanted to get rid of all the other silly things in my life. I used to lie to her as well when I was with other women. But she really liked me. In the end, she found out that I was a Romeo. That upset her, and she dropped me.

Cary became convinced the couple were having an affair. With the jealous possessiveness he had demonstrated repeatedly in his life, he flew into a violent temper and dismissed Austin from his service. He never forgave him, and never spoke to him again. Austin was, he said, so depressed he was driven to attempt suicide.

Soon after, Cary received an offer to go to England, and Betsy accompanied him, allaying any stories of adultery in the press. The project that took Cary there was *The Grass Is Greener*, to be made under his new Universal Studios agreement (he never had a formal contract), which granted him a percentage of the profits (the considerable success of *Operation Petticoat* added substantially to his personal fortune). Stanley Donen would produce and direct, from a screenplay by Hugh and Margaret Williams, based upon their successful West End comedy. Noel Coward would supply the music and lyrics, and—another link with the past—the setting was Osterley Park, ancestral home of the Earl of Jersey, Virginia Cherrill's former husband. Studio work would be done at Shepperton.

Originally, the British actress Kay Kendall, who had made a strong impression in the comedy *Genevieve*, was supposed to act the leading role of the Countess Hilary, wife of Victor, Earl of Rhyall—to be played by Rex Harrison, Miss Kendall's husband. But she died of leukemia before she could start filming. Harrison naturally withdrew, leaving the part clear for Cary, who had originally been selected to play Charles Delacro, an American millionaire who falls in love with the countess (Robert Mitchum assumed the part). Ingrid Bergman wanted the role of countess, but Deborah Kerr called Cary and said, "What about me?" He decided at once to accept her instead.

The film was shot in the summer of 1960. All except two days of work were hampered by rain. Cary walked through the role, acting easily but without much enthusiasm; the material was quite artificial and uninspiring. Jean Simmons's presence in the cast was awkward, because she was involved in a messy separation from Stewart Granger, Cary's old friend. However, the cast tried to make the best of a bad job, meeting in the evenings to discuss such intriguing trivia as the fact that the house was supposedly haunted by a Lady Caroline Woods, who was said to have thrown herself from a window to her death in a wedding gown because King William IV had rejected her. This spooky nonsense at least kept the cast reasonably entertained.

During the filming, Cary met Alma Cogan. She was one of England's most successful recording artists, a variety performer who had been a joint headliner at the London Palladium. About thirty at the time, she was busty, tall, and sturdy, with masses of dark hair and warm, intense eyes. She shared with Cary a love of music halls and pantomimes and she had a broad, down-to-earth, brassy sense of humor, combined with an odd aloofness toward most people that exactly matched his own. Their relationship developed quickly, despite the fact that Betsy was in London, staying with Cary at the Connaught. Suzy, the society reporter, wrote in her column:

Cary, . . . holding hands with Alma Cogan, is quoted as saying, "She's the sweetest girl in the world. She has brains, talent, a sense of humor and a wonderful sense of understanding. She's such wonderful company." Cary has neglected to mention whether his third wife Betsy thinks Alma is wonderful, too.

At the same time, Louella Parsons mentioned that Cary had been seeing Jackie Chan, former girlfriend of Anthony Armstrong-Jones, who married Princess Margaret. ("Cary, my informant tells me, is completely fascinated with the tiny Oriental beauty, and they make quite a picture.")

During the shooting of *The Grass Is Greener*, Cary became friendly with Moray Watson, a talented young actor in the cast. He told Watson of his Jewishness. He complained about the dialogue, feeling that he was called upon to deliver too many long speeches and confessing that he had great difficulty in learning chunks of indigestible dialogue. He also opened his heart on the subject of his marriage. Watson recalls:

One day, Cary said Betsy was coming over. I said, "Oh, good; are you looking forward to seeing her?" He replied, "Yes, I'm looking forward to seeing her, very much indeed. But as soon as she gets here, I shall look forward to her going away again." That was typical of him. He did need her, and yet he didn't; he had too much independence. He was obviously not a happy man, nor was he relaxed. He could never make up his mind about anything.

Watson asked Cary whether he was at all happy. Cary replied, unconvincingly, "Oh, yes, I suppose I've had quite a good life, looking back." Watson went on, "Are you at your happiest like this, when you're making a film?" Cary replied, "No, no, no. I'm at my happiest when I am perhaps with one other person, maybe two other people, and I'm in the hills in California."

Watson remembers some of the problems during the production. Cary was restless over the numerous takes called for by Donen, sometimes as many as thirty. Deborah Kerr failed to communicate with Cary, and at times, Watson observes, they were rude to each other. Cary was exceptionally fretful when visitors to the set, or even crew members, got into his line of vision, and he used to insist that the rehearsals be conducted in a studio from which all personnel except the actors and the director were banished. At times, Cary would usurp Donen's role and announce after, say, a twenty-seventh take, "Let's print that one." According to Watson, he wasn't concerned whether Deborah Kerr was at her best in the take. Neither he nor Donen ever consulted with her when they selected the take they would use.

Jean Simmons found Cary distant throughout the shooting, never referring to their friendship when she had been married to Stewart Granger. Cary had nothing in common with Robert Mitchum, who ambled about the set, his eyes baggy after a late night, but gave an effortless performance, his professionalism concealed in the appearance of total casualness. Cary, as ever, worked with grueling intensity on perfecting his scenes and, anxiously, was always first on the set. Mitchum, arriving at the exact moment a scene began, would appear to do absolutely nothing in the way of acting, and upstage everyone in the process.

Cary invited Watson to lunch one day, and Cary ate nothing but eggs and bacon, the eggs poached, not fried—a light diet to keep him thin. Typically, despite the cheap fare on the menu, Cary asked for separate checks. Once, he asked Watson what films he had done. Watson replied that he appeared mainly in the theater, and Cary commented, "God, that's brave of you. I wouldn't have the nerve. You can face a thousand people a night, live? I would never dare do that." Cary confessed that he was winding down his career. When the characters he played could no longer get the girl without looking embarrassing because of age, he would quit. Nor would he dream of becoming a supporting actor like the grizzled old Britisher C. Aubrey Smith. "I'll always want to be the hero," Cary said.

Watson, who hated going to the day's rushes to see himself walking and talking on the screen, told Cary he was convinced he overacted. What was Cary's technical approach? Cary replied, "My idea of film acting is that if you and I are having a conversation, and the camera's peeping through the keyhole at us, it's just natural; it's just you and me, and there happens to be a camera somewhere, hiding."

Deborah Kerr called Watson aside one day and said, "Cary's different. He's just not the man he was when I knew him before. He was fun then, and amusing, and fast, and funny, and professional, and always knew his lines, and was cooperative, and there was total give-and-take. That all seems gone now. It's very sad." The truth was that Cary no longer felt a rapport with Miss Kerr; she had become a part of his entire feeling of dissatisfaction with *The Grass Is Greener*.

Cary lingered in London, continuing his affair with Alma Cogan.* Betsy returned to Hollywood, but greeted Cary at the airport when he returned in October. (She told a reporter: "My marriage was lived on Cary's terms, really. It was terribly frustrating to be married to him.") During November, Cary was mentioned frequently in the columns because of his alleged relationship with the actress Ziva Rodann. He was supposed to have given Miss Rodann a bracelet, inscribed; "To Ziva, the only one who really knew. Love, Cary." Knew what? Several reporters asked Miss Rodann. She replied: "It's an inside joke, strictly between Cary and me. It wouldn't make sense to anyone else." Asked about Betsy Drake, Miss Rodann replied to a *Photoplay* magazine writer: "Cary and I never talk about Betsy. I know she is very much in love with him, and I admire her intelligence although I have never met her. No one will ever hear any details from me, even if Cary should stop dating me tomorrow."

That December, he and Betsy, living together again in Hollywood, heard appalling news. They had always been close to Patricia Neal and her husband, the author Roald Dahl. Betsy received a phone call. She was told of a ghastly accident that had occurred to the Dahls' baby son. The nursemaid had been wheeling the child across a New York street when a taxi crashed into the pram and carried it forty feet, crushing the child's head against a truck. Cary and Betsy flew to New York to be at Patricia's side, then returned to Hollywood.

On December 21, Ziva Rodann, wearing the bracelet Cary had given her, drove him to Los Angeles Airport for a flight to London. Betsy, who had gone ahead, picked him up at Heathrow and a chauffeur drove them to the Connaught. Almost immediately, Cary

---

* *She died of cancer at age thirty-three.*

again began dating Alma Cogan. He accompanied her to a performance of *Humpty-Dumpty*, a popular pantomime that year, in which
the title role was played by tiny Sammy Curtis, Cary's old friend
from the Pender Troupe. Since Humpty-Dumpty fell off the wall at
the end of the first act, Sammy Curtis would go home, a stand-in
bowing at the end inside the oversized egg. Cary ran into Roy Moseley after the show and asked him where Sammy was; he wanted
to renew their friendship. He told Moseley how delighted he was
that Humpty-Dumpty, throwing snowballs at the audience, had aimed
most of them at Cary and Alma. In the Pender Troupe, Cary said,
Sammy and he were known as "The Long and the Short of It."
Mosely told Curtis afterward that Cary had come backstage to see
him, and Sammy was delighted, reminiscing happily about the old
days.

Back in Hollywood, Cary yet again assumed the role of surrogate
father to Clifford Odets's son Walt and daughter Nora. Walt Odets
writes:

> Cary regularly gave us Christmas and birthday presents, and
> treated us with that generous charm which he seems famous for.
> He would take me clothes shopping several times at Carroll's on
> Santa Monica Boulevard in Beverly Hills. I recall his expressing
> some disapproval of my father's rather intellectual, New York style
> of dress—baggy woolens mostly—and wanted to provide a better
> influence. He told me that he knew about clothes because his
> father had been a tailor [*sic*]. And I also recall his saying, en
> route to Carroll's in his Rolls-Royce, that the car and the clothes
> were important to him because he had grown up in such poverty.
> I remember him as quite honest and direct about such things.
>   He arrived at our house once during the day, quite elegantly
> dressed, but with bare feet in his black, tasseled loafers. I asked
> him why he was not wearing socks. He said he was more com-
> fortable without them, and took one shoe off, showing me how
> they were specially lined in soft leather and constructed with hid-
> den stitching so that he could wear them without abrading his
> feet.

Walt Odets remembers feeling with Cary an easiness and acceptance which his very critical father never gave him. On one occasion, Cary gave Walt an expensive telescope, and Clifford Odets
made what Walt describes as "a stink" about it. Odets, Sr., felt
that to deserve such an instrument the recipient should be seriously
interested in astronomy. He gave Walt a serious lecture about that.
Walt Odets adds:

> Later, when Cary was at the house, I mentioned this rebuke to
> him in front of my father. Cary said, "But really, Clifford, why
> can't the boy just have fun with it?" My father didn't argue the
> point. This was a relatively common event in my childhood, for
> my father was filled with a lot of serious expectations and didn't
> like other people intervening when he was trying to communicate
> them to me.

Early one night in 1961, Cary sat alone in his house in Beverly
Hills, watching television, as he would do before retiring, sometime
around ten. In an episode of an uninspired television series, he noted
a striking girl in her early twenties. She had a mass of honey-blond
hair tumbling over her eyes, a button nose, staring eyes, and thick
lips. She was fleshy and needed to lose a little weight. She wasn't
conventionally beautiful, but Cary was aware at once of her sexuality, the warmth of her laughter, the sensual way she moved her
body. Her habit of throwing back her head and tossing her mane of
hair must have reminded him of Phyllis Brooks. He quickly found
out who she was. Although very young, she was already a veteran
of television. Her name was Dyan Cannon.

Born Samille Diane Freisen in Tacoma, Washington, on February 4, 1936, she was the part-Jewish daughter of an insurance executive. She had made her way to Hollywood on a combination of
chutzpah, driving energy, brash good humor, and down-to-earth
common sense. A good, sincere but not great actress, she had an
earthiness with which many women identified. A streak of coarse-
ness added to her appeal for some men: she seemed to promise them
a sort of slangy companionship that they seldom found in women.
Her face, for all its irregularity, its lack of classical prettiness, was

made for the camera. She toiled through almost two hundred fifty TV shows, including *Playhouse 90, Gunsmoke, 77 Sunset Strip, Bat Masterson, Highway Patrol,* and *Have Gun–Will Travel.* She had just finished shooting a gangster picture, *The Rise and Fall of Legs Diamond.*

Obsessive as ever, Cary, like Alfred Hitchcock, who behaved similarly in the matter of Tippi Hedren, called everyone imaginable to find out where Dyan Cannon was. He discovered to his annoyance that she was in Rome and made it known to her agent that he wanted her to test for a part in a picture, which in fact didn't exist. When she received word that the great Cary Grant wanted her for a part, she showed common sense, asking whether the fare would be paid. Told that it would not—Cary's legendary miserliness emerging again—she stayed where she was.

When she had completed work on an obscure film, she returned to America and went to see Cary at Universal. She made the screen test, suspecting the real reason she had been asked there. Perhaps sensing that for all his charm, Cary was essentially self-absorbed, and that to become involved with him might lead to disaster, she shied away. Again and again, she would break their dinner dates. Sometimes she would just not turn up, which exasperated the punctilious Grant. But of course, her behavior augmented his interest. She told the author Henry Gris (*Coronet,* March 1971):

Ours was a Pygmalion-Galatea relationship. I was like a sponge. I soaked up everything. I did anything he said, but then Cary has an incredible mind and I was very, very naive. He wanted me to accept his beliefs, and I came to accept them as gospel truth. Until the rebel in me finally began to say, Oh, no, that doesn't make sense. That's not good for me.

In the meantime, Cary continued to date Betsy—who was again living apart from him—as though deliberately shunning commitment to Dyan. This must have irritated both women considerably.

He began preparations for a new picture, *That Touch of Mink,* to be directed by Delbert Mann. Early in the filming, Cary wandered into the office of Stanley Shapiro, the film's co-producer and co-writer; he wished to talk about Miss Cannon. Shapiro recalls saying, "Cary, why don't you get married and have a baby? Look, you've got all this. What are you going to do with the rest of your life? Have your lawyer drive you to the studio every day? Father a child. What the heck; why not? It's a great joy, I imagine."

As it happened, Cary had become determined to be a parent. He told the Los Angeles movie critic Kevin Thomas many years later, "Be sure you have a child. No matter how, have a child." He had even decided he would have a Jewish baby, and for a while dated Susan Strasberg, actress-daughter of Method teacher Lee Strasberg, and offered her marriage and security if she would give him a Jewish baby. Now it was clear that he wanted the part-Jewish Dyan Cannon to be the mother of his child. But first, like the obsessed central figure he might have played in Alfred Hitchcock's *Vertigo*, he had to remold her, changing her hairstyle, her makeup, her clothing, even her behavior, until she satisfied his requirements and became the woman he wanted for his wife. How soon their physical relationship began is uncertain, but what is clear is that, despite his frequent cruelty and his domination, Miss Cannon was unable to break with him. He had a hypnotic influence over her, and even compelled her against her will to get into two LSD treatments, which made her ill and severely affected her sense of well-being.

That Touch of Mink was a foolish, superficial affair about a millionaire bachelor whose Rolls-Royce splashes a small-town girl—Doris Day—on a rainy afternoon in Manhattan. A romance ensues, the situations predictable and uninspired. There were, as usual, reflections of Cary's own life. In one sequence, he takes Doris Day to what she assumes is a romantic assignation in his apartment. She finds that the place isn't completed; the pair spend an antiseptic evening in an unfinished, unfurnished habitation. Later, all manner of meaningless events occur to prevent them from marrying and going off for their honeymoon in Bermuda. The peculiar sexlessness of the film, the plastic central performances, were all too typical of Universal movies at the time.

Delbert Mann recalls:

I found Cary rather strange. He was always charming: always smiling, warm, and witty, and very likable. But I think he knew he was quite close to the end of his career. He was rather bored with acting by now; he was looking forward to not doing it anymore, and it just did not challenge him or excite him. Maybe it was the role; he was playing someone, I think, essentially rather close to himself; therefore, the role itself didn't offer the kind of stimulation another part might have. His concern seemed more with the physical aspects of the production than with his performance, though in every way he was always totally professional, on time, never caused any problems, knew his lines.

Mann feels that Cary's chief concern was with the paintings that decorated the set, the clothes and shoes Doris Day wore. Though grateful for Cary's warmth and friendliness, Mann kept asking himself:

How can a man be this cheerful all the time? What is it that's going on behind that? There was a wall there that I never could get through and come away saying, "Yes, I really know Cary Grant."

Stanley Shapiro remembers Cary's fanatical emphasis on detail during the making of the film. Convinced that the rather cheesy office set supplied by the Universal art department scarcely suggested the opulence of a multimillionaire, he brought in some paintings he had owned since the Barbara Hutton period and hung them on the walls. The doorknobs looked cheap to him, and day after day he put a spot of black paint in the middle of each, thinking that made them appear more elegant. At night, Shapiro would wipe off the dots with paint remover. Next morning, Cary would arrive, note that the color had been erased, take a tiny paintbrush from his pocket, dip it in paint from another pocket, and replace the dots. Once again, Shapiro would erase them. Finally, Shapiro said, "Cary, if you and Doris are on the screen and someone looks past you into the back of the set and sees a dot in the middle of a doorknob, we're paying you too much money." Cary laughed, but the dots went back again.

Delbert Mann remembers the story somewhat differently; he recalls that there were two ornate brass handles on the office double door, each handle with a jade-colored stone in the center, about three-quarters of an inch in diameter. It would barely be seen in a long-distance shot. Cary felt the color was inappropriate. Shooting stopped for two hours while the art director came down to discuss the matter. Cary insisted the doorknobs be replaced. Alexander Golitzen, chief studio art director, announced that he was unable to find anything similar. Meanwhile, the company was kept waiting, at very considerable cost. Finally, Golitzen had the jade green painted white. Mann adds:

> I made sure in photographing the picture that we never saw the goddamned door handles, that they were never visible on the screen. That did annoy me. It was such a foolish waste of time and money. I never said anything about it to Cary; I wanted to maintain as comfortable a relationship with him as possible.

An incident recalled the making of *The Bishop's Wife*. In a scene in a fake taxicab supposedly traveling through the streets of New York, both Cary and Doris Day insisted their faces be photographed on the right side—a difficult proposition in the circumstances. Mann remembers that Cary came on the set first and said very quietly that he wanted his right side shown. The director shrugged, saying that this could be arranged without any trouble. He reversed the two stand-ins in the taxi seat. Satisfied, Cary returned to his dressing room. But when Doris Day emerged and saw that the stand-ins had been switched, she went back to her dressing room and angrily called her husband, Marty Melcher, who was one of the co-producers. Melcher called and Mann explained the problem to him, then Cary and Melcher joined Miss Day in her dressing room for a prolonged discussion. Mann had all the stage lights turned off and sat in near darkness, waiting for a decision. At last, Melcher emerged and requested that Mann join the discussion. Mann refused. "Doris is crying," Melcher told Mann. Mann replied, "I can't help it. It's your problem." After two hours of further discussion, Cary walked out of the dressing room and returned to his own. Melcher told Mann, "Put the stand-ins back in position." Doris Day had won.

This difficult decision was painful for Cary, but he proved to be both a gentleman and a professional in the matter. Mann remarks succinctly: "It took another couple of hours for Doris's tears to be dried and for her makeup to be repaired." He adds:

> Cary never mentioned the matter, nor did she. They were quite cheerful and at ease with each other in the doing of the scene. She won the battle. She was the lady, and she was firm-willed. And there is some distinction between her right and left pro-files—more so than Cary's.

Mann had been accustomed in other pictures to a certain amount of relaxed badinage between himself and the players. On *Lover Come Back*, with Doris Day, Rock Hudson, and Tony Randall, he had had a wonderful time. But working with Cary was different:

> With Cary, there was not that kind of ease and teasing each other and joking back and forth. Our relationship was pleasant but for-mal. The toughness I saw in Doris was expressed in her extreme attention to how she looked, which led to that sort of overgauzed, soft-focus sort of close-up. She was aware of the fact that lines were starting to show, and one can understand that concern, but beyond that she was marvelously witty and gay and fun, and highly professional. I would say she was more popular with the crew than Cary was—not that Cary was in any way disliked. He was jovial and easy, but he didn't bring the kind of totally relaxed sense of fun that Rock brought to the set.

According to Alexander Golitzen, soon after the shooting began, Cary decided he was bored with the view from his bungalow, which showed nothing more interesting than some bushes. He ordered the art department to make him a trompe l'oeil painting of a pinewood door opening onto a typical English scene of a path going up through a garden to a cloudy gray skyline with patches of pale blue, and lambs gamboling on distant hills. There would be a white wicker gate. The scene was painted perfectly—or so it seemed. But Cary summoned the whole art department and demanded to know why they had made a serious mistake. They protested they had not. He pointed to the door. "Don't you *see?*" Cary said. "You can't see the sky through that knothole in the door!"

One of the friendships Cary preserved at the time was with his former director Richard Brooks. Brooks was shooting *Elmer Gantry*, with Burt Lancaster as the star. Cary had sent Brooks clippings about various evangelists, with notes suggesting an appropriate approach to the story. Brooks would drop over to the house on Beverly Grove Drive, and Cary would provide all kinds of valuable ideas. After *Gantry* was released, they would have close discussions on religion. Brooks says:

Cary was of the opinion that everybody should have his own religion and not interfere with anybody else's. My impression is he was not sure about the existence of a God, a formal God as described in the Bible. Yet despite that, he felt there was a power on earth which made things cohesive, made everything hang together, and if that was God, he understood it. He could not believe in a personalized God because of the injustices he saw around the world. He hated the fact that formal religion caused anger and hatred among people, which annoyed him and hurt him deeply. He took these matters very seriously.

After *That Touch of Mink* was completed, Delbert Mann received no feedback from Cary. He says that there was "a sense of relief that the picture was finally over, even though it was a comedy, and right to the end I had felt I should have been having a better time doing it than I did."

That season, Cary enjoyed a much-publicized liaison with Greta Thyssen, the former Miss Denmark. He first noticed her when she walked by his table in a restaurant; he had word sent to her the following day that he would like her to have dinner with him in his office. Beautiful, with masses of gold hair, a wide smile, brilliantly intense eyes, and high cheekbones, Miss Thyssen was seen with him everywhere. She made a telling statement to the fan magazine *TV Movie Screen* in August 1963:

One of the first things he explained to me was his unique philosophy of life. According to him—and this is a viewpoint he expressed over and over again—he has a full right to love all the attractive people he meets. He believes that many people feel this way, but that most are afraid to admit it. . . . Maybe he's right. Maybe the only thing different about him is the fact that he dares to admit his feelings. At any rate, that is his theory, and it carries over even to marriage: if people are married, he says, they can still have an attraction to others. What I suppose he actually means is that you can love more than one person at a time.

Continuing in the same vein, Miss Thyssen remarked that Cary told her often, "I might love you today, but I can make no promises if I find someone as pretty as you tomorrow." She added that one of the reasons they were happy together was because she never made any demands on Cary; he was used to having his own way and did not appreciate anyone disagreeing with him. Once again, he applied Professor Higgins tactics: he told her how to dress and apply makeup; on their second date, he criticized her use of cosmetics (an echo of his rudeness to Alexis Smith on *Night and Day*, and to Martha Hyer on *Houseboat*). She described, accurately or not, romantic evenings in charming restaurants with strolling violinists, dinners in his huge circular bed, served by a butler on individual trays, followed by cognac and coffee. Evenings were spent eating and watching television on an enormous set built into the wall near the bed. Miss Thyssen went a step further: "[Cary] can teach younger men quite a few tricks when it comes to the romance department!" She described aimless drives in the Rolls-Royce through the Hollywood Hills. Sometimes, she insisted, he would utter such words as "You have the sexiest-looking body I have ever seen."

Whether this relationship was as romantic as Miss Thyssen claimed is uncertain. Certainly, it did not last more than a short time. Simultaneously, Cary was seeing Dyan Cannon and was still married to Betsy Drake.

The rest of 1961 passed without incident. There were still no signs that Betsy would divorce Cary. On Thanksgiving Day, Clifford Odets wrote in his diary:

At night I went alone out to Betsy's for . . . dinner. A nice, small group there, an older couple and a younger, both men writers. And Cary with his usual unease—where to put the feet down. His relationship with B seems a very strange and tangled one. They live apart and are on the verge of legal divorce, but he spends as much time with her as possible, as if she were home for him. As for her, she seems to be forging ahead from weak member to the stronger, with him somewhat abject and apologetic.

Odets added the following note:

In one way or another, [Cary] is always trying to *disarm* you. He feels threatened—you may lose your regard, affection or whatnot. He is always disarming everyone. . . . Later he may take it out on you.

For some time in 1962, studio boss Edward Muhl tried to convince Cary to make a comedy thriller, *Charade*, in which he would play opposite Audrey Hepburn. Cary was very reluctant to agree, Muhl says, because the script called for him to chase a much younger woman.

He was fifty-eight years old at the time, as charming and handsome as ever, but for some reason he thought the screenplay was unseemly. So it was changed, and in the new version the girl was coquettish, leading him on, and he was playing hard-to-get.

Cary went ahead, with one of his favorite actresses, Audrey Hepburn, as co-star. *Charade*, based upon a script by the accomplished Peter Stone, was to be shot in Paris. Cary would portray Peter Joshua, an American agent living in France, who helps Regina Lambert solve the mystery of her husband's murder. Walter Matthau would play the villain. The director would once again be Stanley Donen.

Cary decided not to stay in a hotel but instead, rather surprisingly, moved into Barbara Hutton's Paris apartment. Mona Eldridge, Miss Hutton's secretary at the time, recalled Cary walking down the long central hall of the apartment, with its glass-fronted display cabinets, containing priceless antique figurines, pieces of jade, and snuff-boxes. He did not examine the contents but instead glanced from right to left to observe his reflection in the mirrored cabinet doors, fussing over his hair, and fretting over his wrinkles.

Miss Eldridge recorded that he was the despair of the cook, Herminie, who planned elaborate meals for him; he would wind up eating nothing much more substantial than a poached egg, served on a flawless china dish. His frugal diet fulfilled his most often repeated personal slogan, "Think Thin."

Miss Eldridge noted that Cary would ask her to make complicated travel reservations all over the world, and then would suddenly cancel. He swore daily that he would autograph a portrait photograph for Herminie, dazzling her with his smile, but finally failed to fulfill his promise. Although he fascinated both Mona Eldridge and Herminie with a constant display of high-powered charm, he failed to send a thank-you note when he left.

In her memoir, *In Search of a Prince: My Life with Barbara Hutton*, Miss Eldridge commented: "It would appear that [Grant's] bisexuality took the form of alternate preferences. One period of his life it would be men, then he would be heterosexual for several years. I often wondered if he was capable of real, genuine feelings, so obsessed was he with his own public image." At this time, he was constantly getting in touch with very young women, expressing his love enthusiastically, then dropping them with startling swiftness. His quirkiness intrigued Miss Hutton's secretary. Although he allegedly disliked the press, he would, she noted, stare out of his bedroom window to see if reporters were waiting there, and he would express great pleasure when he found that their number had increased. Noting a very pretty dark girl among them, he summoned her to the apartment and gave an exclusive interview, as she stared at him with rapture.

Although Audrey Hepburn and her husband, Mel Ferrer, got along well with Cary, there were differences. Herbert Sterne, who was in charge of publicity for the movie, says:

It was normal for contact sheets of stills, prepared for approval by stars, to include both the male and female lead in a picture.

However, both Cary and Audrey wanted separate sheets, in which neither one would appear with the other. This was absurd. Cary didn't want Audrey to look as good as he did in the photographs, and Audrey didn't want Cary to look as good as she did. So I said to Stanley Donen, "Let us have two sheets, so each star can kill a still and the other will not know which still they have killed." This went great until my secretary, who was busy kissing Audrey's ass, sneaked out a print that Cary had killed and made sure it was published. Cary came in, very gentlemanly, showed me the newspaper picture, and asked me how did it get out? I said, "I haven't the fuckingest idea." "Well," Cary asked, "how are we going to stop this happening again?" I told him that each negative would go to him and to Audrey, and both would be given a punch to kill what they didn't like. We couldn't find a punch in Paris, so somebody went down and paid all kinds of money and bought punches from the people in the Metro, the Paris subway.

Cary and Audrey worked well together. There was a sequence shot among the pillars of the Comédie Française, in which Audrey had to decide whether Cary Grant or Walter Matthau was telling her the truth. Cary and Audrey worked out a series of movements similar to those that would be performed in a ballet, giving what could have been a tiresome episode a good deal of visual charm.

One night, in Paris, a member of the movie company staff went to a famous gay bar and restaurant. He recalls: "The atmosphere was very highly charged, as it tends to be in such places. It was even more so that night because, to the astonishment of many people there, Cary Grant appeared with a very handsome young man, sat down at a table, and had dinner, with every eye in the room on him and his companion! He didn't seem to care."

Despite the grueling Parisian winter, Cary had good reason to be in high spirits during the shooting of *Charade*. *Operation Petticoat* had earned him at least three million dollars, and the picture would be his property after eight years. It was one of the most commercially successful comedies ever made. *The Grass Is Greener* had done slightly less well, but he still benefited from substantial profits from its release, and *That Touch of Mink* earned him a fortune. *Charade* would enhance his bank balance still more. It was a pleasant, undemanding movie, fairly well directed and well played, especially by the principals.

On August 14, 1962, Betsy Drake obtained her divorce from Cary. In a Los Angeles courthouse, she told Judge Edward R. Brand that Cary had left her for long periods, appeared bored with her, preferred watching TV to talking to her, and "told me he didn't want to be married." She said, looking tense for a moment, "I still love him very much. I was always in love with him, and I still am." The divorce was granted without demur; the ground was mental cruelty. There was a reasonable property settlement; Grant did not attend the hearing.

In 1963, Clifford Odets was found to have terminal cancer. His career had declined, and his health with it; he was not yet sixty. His disaffection with Cary had increased; he blamed Cary for not helping to advance his scripts either by guaranteeing an appearance in certain of them or by finding a place for them at MCA Universal. In August, Odets lay dying at Cedars of Lebanon Hospital. Cary arrived with a large bouquet of carnations, but Odets refused to see him. Odets was convinced Cary was phony and false: he told the nurse to give the flowers to another patient. It was a painful and unpleasant ending to a friendship that had lasted over twenty years.

In December, *Charade* had a triumphant opening at Radio City Music Hall in New York; despite mixed reviews, the film was an instant hit, and Cary enjoyed standing at the back of the auditorium on opening night to drink in the audience's laughter. He was already planning another movie, *Father Goose*, from a script by Peter Stone.

At Christmas, he put through his customary phone call to Elsie Leach, now eighty-six years old. In the previous twelve months, he had made three trips to Bristol to see her. Reporter Henry Gris dropped in for an interview with him at his Beverly Hills house right after the holidays. Gris asked how he looked so young. That unhappy, anxious, and fanatically obsessive man fibbed cheerfully:

It's because I am permanently relaxed. I don't like to call this the secret of keeping young, but that's what it amounts to. And I have accomplished this by various means over the years.

He revealed that he was still taking LSD regularly. Commenting on the drug's healing properties, he said:

You have to overcome fears. One fear that lives in every heart, including mine, is the fear of death, but I have conditioned my- self to accept it and so reduce even this fear to a minimum. There should be no limit to one's desire to stay alive . . . for a hundred years. And longer. You reassure yourself of that and go on from there. And as long as a man remains a man with an ability to love, he should feel secure.

Cary did not, according to statements made later by Dyan Can- non, live up to these precepts in real life. She was living with him at the time at 9966 Beverly Grove Drive. It was scarcely an accom- modating establishment. His miserliness showed in the lack of lux- ury in his personal environment. There was very little furniture, and some rooms were virtually bare. Venetian blinds were poorly dusted, odd in view of his fanaticism over cleanliness, and, when broken, remained unrepaired for months. Carpets were worn and threadbare. There was no sense of warmth and comfort in the home, which seemed austere and even unpleasant, and few people were entertained there.

As Dyan would charge in their divorce hearing in 1967, Cary would "beat me with his fists" and "laugh when I cringed in fear." On one occasion, he locked her in her room. On another, he struck her to the ground because he didn't like her wearing a miniskirt. His relationship with her resembled that with Virginia Cherrill in its brutality and harshness. Yet, perhaps because she loved him, perhaps because he was Cary Grant, and perhaps because the cou- ple had many happy times together, Dyan forgave everything.

She took up health foods, homeopathic medicine, hypnotism— almost anything that might possibly help her depression. Yet the pain remained, and to this day she is unable to talk about Cary Grant. She once told her friend Corinne Introtter, "My life with

Cary was hell. It was like *The Diary of a Mad Housewife*." In that novel, the heroine was made to suffer from the insupportably priggish and domineering behavior of her husband, who constantly and rudely criticized her hair, her makeup, her clothes, her figure, her deportment, her ability to reason, and her common sense.

Cary was determined to have a child with Dyan Cannon, yet time passed without her becoming pregnant. He became absorbed in *Father Goose*. It was a change of pace for him: the story of a beachcomber, Walter Eckland, living on New Britain during World War II, who is enlisted as a coast watcher, one of the courageous Australian spies who radioed their reports on Japanese fleet and troop movements. The story contained a distorted echo of the past: Errol Flynn had begun his association with Dr. Hermann Erben of German Naval Intelligence in New Britain in 1933 and had volunteered to be a coast watcher during the 1940s. Fortunately for Australian and American security, he was turned down.

Cary worked on the script with Peter Stone and Frank Tarloff. At that time, David Miller, a good director who had handled one of Joan Crawford's best pictures, *Sudden Fear*, was to have made the movie. Charles Higham visited Cary Grant in Hollywood one morning, following a production meeting. He noticed the cleanliness and order of the Grant bungalow. When he arrived, Grant was wearing a gray suit and tie, while everyone around him was in jeans and open shirts. Grant had just finished dictating his correspondence to his secretary, Dorothy Palmer.

Grant explained how the company was working long hours on *Father Goose*, breaking off in the evenings for dinner at Storey's, a nearby restaurant. He spoke of his involvement in casting the picture, running endless film clips in order to make selections. The day before, he had chosen Trevor Howard, whom he had seen in *Outcast of the Islands*, to play the taciturn Australian naval commander Frank Houghton. When Audrey Hepburn proved to be too busy with another picture, he had decided to use Leslie Caron as the coast watcher's girlfriend. He said he had no immediate plans to marry. He found it hard to believe he·was sixty. He was looking forward to being the bearded, grizzled, and unkempt beachcomber in the new picture.

The conversation was bland and superficial, designed to conceal his personality. His glasses seemed like props, almost like stage glasses, while the eyes—which had the curious staring blankness of a ventriloquist's doll—appeared to be equipped with contact lenses. There was something too perfect about the razor-cut hair. The face was steely, hard, secretive. The charm was dodgy. One glanced off the surface of it.

As his secretary and an assistant disappeared, Grant showed Higham into an inner office, and pointed to a Mexican table painted bright yellow and decorated with a circle of flowers. "Kind of gays things up a little," Grant said, with a frank and knowing wink. It was hard to miss the point.

When Higham had to interrupt Grant to say that he had to leave for a lunch appointment with the director George Cukor at his house, Grant's face froze for a moment. It was clear that he was displeased. But he recovered himself and said, with a flashing smile, "It's your loss." Then, perhaps fearing that his remark might be misinterpreted, he added, "Of course, George Cukor is much more important than I am!"

David Miller dropped out of *Father Goose* after many script discussions. Ralph Nelson, a capable middle-of-the-road director, took over. Shooting took place in Ocho Rios, Jamaica, in early 1964. After Cary's return, Dyan Cannon, who had unwisely given up her screen career for him (he had asked her not to make pictures during their relationship), was touring in the musical *How to Succeed in Business Without Really Trying*. He became lonely at Beverly Grove Drive and had her fly from the various cities on her tour to spend Sundays with him. This was exhausting and difficult, but apparently she had lost her willpower.

Cary's life assumed a dull monotony. He arrived very early each day at the studio, where the popular gatemen Chester and Scotty greeted him. Once in his office, he would have a cup of tea; he attended to his correspondence, conferred with his assistant Fred Clasel, and granted the occasional interview. After a light lunch of salad, he always consulted with his attorney, Stanley Fox. Then he would go out on the sun deck of his bungalow and tan himself, wearing a metal face frame. On weekends, he went to the hacienda he had bought ten years earlier in Palm Springs. He took a close interest in all his investments and knew to the last penny where his money was.

In June of 1965, Dyan at last became pregnant. She was overjoyed. At the same time, she came from a conventional family and couldn't face the idea of bearing a child outside marriage. According to Cary's friend Binnie Barnes, "When Dyan knew she was pregnant, Cary had to marry her." Delighted though he was, even thrilled at this long-delayed proof of his virility, Cary became characteristically skittish again in the wake of the discovery, and it was only after a protracted delay that he decided to marry Dyan. Meanwhile, she underwent a good deal of mental anguish. She told Henry Gris:

I remember my finding out that I was pregnant, and my being so nervous about telling him. I came home and made four tuna-fish sandwiches and ate them all while figuring how to break the news to him. And then he walked into the house, and he knew by the look on my face. . . . We celebrated that night by going to a ballgame. . . . He was so frightened, even if he didn't want to show it, and concerned, you know, suddenly, my God, it's happened!

You know, he didn't want to get married because, he thought, if we did it would ruin our relationship. "I can't be married," he said. "I've tried. I ought to know." But I couldn't understand that, and of course I wanted a child, his child. So, after that he asked me three times. The first time he was so nervous he came down to my house and cracked up his car in the garage.

I said, "Okay, I'll marry you," then nothing happened. So after a while I said to him, "It doesn't look like we are getting married, so I'd better check out." He didn't like that, so he asked me again.

Cary wanted her to meet Elsie, and they flew to Bristol. The first time they drove to the nursing home where the old woman now lived, he panicked and decided not to introduce Dyan to her after all. However, she did meet his cousin Eric* and Eric's wife, Mag-

---

* Not to be confused with Cary's half-brother, Eric Leslie, whom he did not acknowledge at the time.

gie. She loved them. While he visited Elsie, Dyan told Henry Gris, "I did the town and read books and walked through churches and spent a lot of time with his cousins, who are marvelous."

At last, Dyan did meet Elsie. The old woman called Dyan "Betsy" all the time, but she didn't mind. Dyan said later, "Elsie's incredible, with a psyche that has the strength of a 20-mule team. We had good times with her, we had fish and chips and drank beer with her. A remarkable woman."

Cary was apprehensive about too much attention before the wedding, so he and Dyan decided to have a secret ceremony in Las Vegas. The marriage took place on July 22, 1965, at Howard Hughes's Desert Inn. According to some versions, Hughes was present, but this is unlikely, since he had become a horrifying spectral figure and was living in almost total seclusion. The newlyweds flew to London to honeymoon and to do some advance promotion for *Father Goose*. They traveled on to Bristol for another visit with Elsie. The paparazzi swarmed into the city, besieging the Grants at their hotel, asking such rude questions as why they had not invited her parents to the wedding. Cary became red-faced and angry at this intrusion into his life. When reporters tried to worm their way into the nursing home and talk to Elsie, he had them thrown out.

Cary had always been very careful not to provoke the press, but on this occasion he antagonized them, and for once some of the reports on him were less than flattering. Yet few took the occasion to attack Dyan, and many remarked on her strong, sexy attractiveness. When they returned to Hollywood, the first announcements that the couple were expecting a child appeared on the wire services.

SIXTEEN

Soon after the wedding, Cary embarked on plans for another picture, *Walk Don't Run*, a remake of *The More the Merrier*, which had been directed by his old friend George Stevens. The breezy comedy was set in Tokyo during the 1964 Olympic Games; unfortunately, the new script, by Sol Saks, was a pale echo of the original, the whimsical humors of which were drawn from the bundling that was necessary in similarly overcrowded World War II Washington.

Cary decided to leave for Japan alone. The official reason given was that Dyan was not feeling well enough to make the journey across the Pacific, but in fact she was seen in public, glowing vibrantly, with all the apparent cheerfulness of an expectant mother; the couple apparently felt they needed to separate for a while to try to iron out differences. Barely two months after the marriage, in the last week of September 1965, Cary flew with the director Charles Walters to Tokyo, where he joined his co-stars, Samantha Eggar and Jim Hutton. The Columbia movie was fully backed by Grant's own production company.

Cast and crew were housed at the vast and excessively modern Okura Hotel, with Cary occuping the Imperial Suite. The weather was bad that fall, and as in so many other pictures Cary had made, day after day was washed out by rain. Cary seldom emerged from his hotel during the breaks in shooting. He attended only one major social function, at the American embassy, a cocktail party in honor of Senator Ted Kennedy and his wife, Joan. He saw a good deal of them during their stay.

He spent much of his time training with Toshio Hosokawa, the Japanese Olympic walking-race coach. Cary kept up remarkably well with the athletic young Jim Hutton, who had spent three months at Terry Hunt's Gymnasium in Hollywood, mastering heel-and-toe walking. Scenes were shot at the Olympic Stadium, in the narrow, winding streets of the Shinjuku district, on the Ginza, with its dazzle of electric signs, in the Happo-En Gardens, and at the Shimbashi railroad station. Despite the black clouds that filled the sky, and the sudden bursts of rain, the gifted cinematographer Harry Stradling, of *Suspicion* and *Houseboat*, overcame every technical problem, shooting in the midst of dense crowds in all areas, never allowing anyone to suspect the presence of his hidden cameras. He used food trucks, vans, boarded-up buildings, and telephone booths, and even had cameras tucked into the overcoats of the crew, or (for stills) carried by Japanese messenger boys in their bicycle baskets. Cary was in a somber, detached mood during most of the work. Attempts to lure him to a geisha house failed. He apparently needed time to reflect, to be alone, to feel peace of mind in a foreign environment. Few journalists penetrated his privacy in the tour bus used as his dressing room.

The other actors were equally preoccupied. Jim Hutton—according to his son, the actor Timothy Hutton—was overwhelmed by the idea of working with Cary, hero-worshiping him unabashedly. Samantha Eggar was caught up in her marriage (to the producer, Tom Stern) and in her newborn son.

Cary took a paternal interest in his fellow actors, monitoring Hutton's drinking, helping to supervise his physical training; making Samantha Eggar alter her hairstyle and change her wardrobe. On the occasional evenings when he went out, it was only to visit with senior Japanese company executives, who gave official, rather dull dinner parties in his honor. The head of Sony was a fan of his and invited him several times to his home.

Dyan, her warm and sentimental feelings for Cary overcoming her misgivings, turned up to surprise him on his sixty-second birthday, January 18, 1966. She stayed only briefly; the film publicity department, in an attempt to build up the importance of the quick stopover, pretended that she had come to see Cary for several weeks. Shooting ended at the end of January, with Cary in a dejected mood. Jim Hutton recalled that Cary would talk to him for hours about what he wanted for his child and how he hoped to have many more children; becoming a father, he said, was more important to him than anything he had ever done.

When he returned to Los Angeles, Dyan was eight months pregnant. She had found a bigger house for them, in Benedict Canyon. Now that the baby was about to be born, Cary seemed to be in a better mood; but he was aware that *Walk Don't Run* was not going to be a success. He was also aware that his marriage was not successful. His moods kept switching from exhilaration and excitement to considerable gloom, and he began taking LSD again. These were not happy times, and neither Cary nor Dyan felt inclined to discuss them later.

On February 26, 1966, Cary drove Dyan to St. Joseph's Hospital in Burbank—which he had settled on after going, with his usual obsessiveness, from hospital to hospital to decide which one should be favored. He had gone through ward after ward checking rooms, inspecting entrance halls, examining diet sheets. If he could have built a hospital for the occasion himself, he would have done so. Once Dyan was installed, he fussed over the decor of the room, the flowers and how they were arranged, the food Dyan was getting, and the cleanliness of furniture and of the floor. No one would have been surprised if he had taken out a scrub brush, soap and a pail, and got down on all fours. Yet along with his numerous interferences with hospital administration, he was so irresistibly charming in his persistence, and the nurses were so overcome by his presence, that he conquered everyone. Female members of the staff would line up outside Dyan's private room just to catch a glimpse of him.

He gave an almost comic performance of an expectant father, pacing up and down outside the delivery room and peeking in every few minutes. He was not present at the actual birth, a custom that did not come into general effect until later. But he was under so much stress he might as well have given birth to the baby himself.

It was not an easy delivery, but Dyan finally gave birth to a girl, Jennifer. She weighed only four and a half pounds and was placed in an incubator, but after she left it, she exhibited a winsome and adorable personality. Cary had never been more jubilant. And yet, such was his nature, he couldn't relax in his new role as father, but became consumed with what turned out to be his greatest obsession. From now on, Jennifer would constitute virtually his entire life. Since she supplied proof of his manhood, he felt that she was part of him—not just his child but his raison d'être, an extension of his physical being. According to Henry Gris:

> He went to his daughter's room at 7:30 each morning to gaze down at her; he supervised the warming of her bottle and the food she would be weaned on; he made certain that he would always be back from working on the editing of *Walk Don't Run* for her 7:00 feeding time.

Her every sound was tape-recorded, her every move photographed, either by himself or by photographers he hired. He sent picture after picture to Elsie, not merely showing off his offspring but, quite clearly, telling her in effect, "You see, I'm a normal man after all." There was something verging on the psychotic about his monomaniacal interest in the baby. The more practical and down-to-earth Dyan, passionately though she loved Jennifer, found his behavior grating and extreme. And then there were other problems. Dyan's father objected severely to his grandchild's mother taking LSD, and he arrived at the house unexpectedly one day, insisting that she stop at once. Cary shouted, "You may be her father, but I'm her husband, and I'm the one she answers to now!" Cary infuriated Dyan by refusing to allow her to take the baby to Tacoma to visit with her grandparents. The arguments went on and on. Although Jennifer brought her great happiness, Dyan was utterly miserable with Cary at a time when they should have been bound together by their parenthood. His fanaticism over the child slowly but surely ground her down. Years later, she told a reporter: "I'm telling you, if I'd stayed in that marriage I'd be dead today. Dead. Dead. Dead.

Dead. Really *dead!* In a grave! Dead! I don't want to talk about him. He's a real pain."

As for Cary's behavior at this time, so hypertensive a personality, needing to control everything in his life, would be bound to become consumed with fatherhood. He fussed and fretted over Jennifer's slightest sign of discomfort, and a cough or a sneeze brought him to the verge of hysteria. He would snap at Dyan if he felt she was doing something wrong. Sometimes, so extreme was his tension, he would, with gross unfairness, accuse her of being an unfit mother. As the spring of 1966 dragged on, only one relief was offered: Cary found a valuable and likable new employee, who became one of his most trusted aides and friends.

William D. Weaver was a good-looking, somewhat scholarly twenty-five-year-old Kansan with glasses and thinning, fair hair, who had devoted his younger years to assisting his mother with his five brothers and sisters; he had toiled at night school for an English degree and finally obtained a job with the Atomic Energy Commission. Cary advertised for a secretary through an employment agency, and Weaver applied. In his book, *The Private Cary Grant*, written with Cary's later close friend, the multimillionaire industrialist William Currie McIntosh, Weaver remembered the circumstances of his interview. Cary asked him to sit down in a large armchair, placed so that his eye level was below that of Cary, at the desk. According to McIntosh, Cary liked the fact that Weaver had been with the Atomic Energy Commission, because that indicated he would have the capacity to keep secrets. The existing secretary, Dorothy, was dismissed, and Weaver took her place. Warned that Cary would not tolerate the slightest degree of unpunctuality, Weaver reported to work every day at exactly 9:00 A.M. He found himself making reservations for Cary at the Polo Lounge of the Beverly Hills Hotel or the Swedish restaurant Scandia; the studio bungalow became a second home to him, with its brown leather chairs, spinet, Argentine rug, and trompe l'oeil paintings, its wedding pictures of Elsie and Elias Leach, and the sun deck where Cary tanned himself.

Often, Weaver would come to the house in Benedict Canyon, with its swimming pool and rich plantings of trees. According to Weaver and McIntosh, Cary would sometimes greet the secretary in his pajamas, ill-tempered, darkly brooding, shouting or screaming at some real or imaginary slight. They wrote: "There would be an air of dither and oppression over the entire household." The atmosphere was cheerless, the recently engaged English butler-chauffeur, Tony Faramus, resembling, Weaver claims, a figure in a Charles Addams drawing and the maid, also English, stealing around silently, almost invisibly, as though afraid to be seen. So irritated was Cary by his beloved Jennifer's screams that the nanny would become greatly distressed if the child even whimpered.

Cary proved to be as cruel to Weaver as he was to Dyan. He constantly bitched over his secretary's punctuation and spelling, his style of writing, his clothes, the food he liked. Walking up and down, tense, in his white pajamas, Grant grumbled like a fishwife.

Although Cary had given some support to Dyan in her career when she went on the stage in *How to Succeed*, he now assumed the Victorian attitude that, as a mother, she was never to leave the house. Once, when she announced she was going to an acting class, he ran after her down the entrance hall, demanding that she not leave. She broke free from his grasp and drove off. On more than one occasion, he hid her car keys, and she was forced to walk to the acting school. Weaver and McIntosh wrote: "On one momentous occasion, the entire household was galvanized into appalled silence, when, after a row had broken out, Grant pursued his wife into the bathroom, locked the door, and could be heard to be spanking her. A few minutes later, the bathroom window was flung open and Dyan scrambled through to make her way back down the canyon and into the city."

Despite Cary's many statements that LSD had relaxed him, changed him from a tormented and tormenting person into a sunny persona not unlike the man whom millions saw on the screen, it had in fact done nothing of the sort. Friends like Binnie Barnes and Johnny Maschio and Constance Moore were appalled by Cary's cruelty to Dyan.

Dyan made two trips to New York in 1966. One of them was recalled by Tom Stout, then a TWA representative at Los Angeles airport. Dyan had decided to take Jennifer to Manhattan. She told Stout that only she and her baby would be traveling. No sooner had

Stout seen mother and daughter to the VIP lounge than he got a message to go to the curbside, where Cary sat in his chauffeur-driven car. Cary told Stout that he would be going to New York with Dyan and Jennifer. Stout said the flight was full. Cary jumped out of the car and ran to the airport and, locating the gate number from the monitor screen, dashed to the gate as the passengers boarded. Stout was just behind him. Despite the fact that he didn't have a ticket, Cary pushed past the checker and forced his way through the plane door, joining the silent and embarrassed Dyan. Challenged, he shouted, "I will not leave this plane! I am traveling to New York with my wife and baby!" Passengers and attendants were stupefied. A woman who knew Cary spoiled everything for Dyan by offering to give up her seat and take another flight. The last thing Stout saw was Cary flopping into the vacated first-class seat, arguing vigorously with Dyan.

On another occasion, Constance Moore accompanied Dyan on a trip. They returned a few days before the first anniversary of the Grants' wedding. Cary came to Constance and Johnny Maschio's boat, moored in Marina del Rey, begging them to help him repair the marriage. Anxious to help, they invited Dyan, without telling her Cary would be there. Maschio stocked the bar with Dom Perignon, and the food was the best available, but despite the sailing and swimming and sunning, nothing could break the severe tension that existed between the Grants. "It was terribly sad," Constance Moore says.

In a last-ditch effort to save the marriage, the Grants decided to sail to England in August of 1966. They boarded the British supership *Oriana*, which would take them via the Panama Canal and the Caribbean to Southampton. It should have been a happy occasion, with brass band and streamers, but Cary made the boarding procedure a torment for all concerned. Among the entourage who saw them off were the Maschios and William Weaver. Constance Moore remembers:

It was very tense when they left. They suddenly fired the nanny at the last minute. And hired another one. Cary had booked four cabins by mistake, one for himself, one for Dyan, one for the nanny, and one for Jennifer, who of course would have to be in with the nanny. So one cabin went to waste.

Dyan didn't make things any easier. Cary had sensibly insisted on having very few suitcases, realizing how restricted the cabin space was. But Dyan was nervous about the numerous parties that would be taking place on board, from the Captain's soirees to the various festive nights commemorating different countries. As a result, much to Cary's fury, she took with her thirty-six suitcases, like a traveling princess, and thus compelled Grant to enlist not only the Rolls driven by Tony Faramus, but two station wagons, one driven by Bill Weaver, and the other by a second chauffeur.

When the couple arrived at the dock, a horde of paparazzi appeared. Cary screamed at Weaver when the secretary dropped Dyan's jewel case and it was almost trampled by the reporters and photographers. Up in the main deck cabin, Cary, in front of Weaver, lashed out at Dyan with another of his increasingly frequent outbursts. Charging her with ruining the trip with her excessive possessions, he ripped open suitcases, hurling clothes and shoes all over the cabin. As Dyan burst into tears, Cary ordered Tony Faramus to pile all but two suitcases full of clothes into one of the cars and take them home. The wretched voyage did not improve for the Grants. The streak of cruelty that had disfigured Cary's relationships with others now emerged most dangerously, and it was clear by the time the couple reached London that there was no hope for the marriage.

Cary turned on the charm for the press in London. In Bristol, following his usual visit to Elsie, Cary acceded to persistent requests by his half-brother's family to meet him. Although from time to time he had sent gifts to Eric Leslie's wife and children, he had shown little interest in them. He had in a sense disowned Eric, only yielding to the family's entreaties when they addressed him through his solicitor in London. He probably blamed him for Elsie's years in the asylum.

He met the children at the Clifton Gorge Hotel in Bristol. Dyan was with him, if only for appearances. When Eric's daughter Betsy went to touch Jennifer's toe, Dyan pushed her away with a gruff warning. The children sat virtually silent, gazing at Cary's almost too immaculately groomed hair, his perfectly tanned and still-handsome face, his impeccable figure and suede shoes. They were overcome and said almost nothing. At the end of what must have been a very strange encounter, Cary, with one of those odd bursts of naturalness and generosity that paradoxically marked his character, offered to drive the family home. Embarrassed because they lived in a council house—a government-financed dwelling—they told him they had some shopping to do and asked him to drop them off next to a favorite store. They were amazed to see he did not drive a Rolls-Royce but rather an old Austin automobile.

The Grants returned to Los Angeles. Dyan moved into a guesthouse on their property. At last, she could endure the situation no longer. She took Jennifer with her and rented a house at Malibu. Even a last-ditch effort to repair matters through counseling failed. Dyan Cannon said later:

> The decision to go through with the divorce was the most difficult . . . of my entire life. It took a great deal out of me. I had been hurt and I couldn't understand why. But in order to get myself out of it, I knew I would have to take myself apart and put myself together again, understanding what life is all about. I went to Esalen.

The Esalen Institute was located in northern California, near Carmel. There, in carefully controlled conditions, people with emotional problems were taught to release their nervous tension and distress in primal therapy techniques, which included wailing and screaming like newborn babies or socializing nude and sharing hot tubs. The intention was to tear away the layers of tortured civilization that encumbered most individuals and revert to primitive, uncomplicated feelings. It took Dyan some time to feel comfortable with the Esalen method. She wasn't happy with her body and, she said later, felt painfully self-conscious of displaying its flaws.

Gradually, she did gain strength. Meanwhile, Cary was in an appalling state of nerves. Losing Jennifer even for a day was unbearable for him. He would break down and sob over the loss of the child. As much as anything else, his ego was wounded. He was forced to realize that even he, with all his wealth and fame, could not control everything and everyone in his life. Dyan agreed to allow him visiting rights, so long as they were within reason. Only when he could play with Jennifer, talk to her, and dangle her on his knee was Cary able to deal with life. He tried to woo Dyan back with promises; he even encouraged her to appear in a play. But the inconsistency of his behavior warned her off. Sometimes she fled to her parents in Seattle, trying to introduce Jennifer to a normal family environment.

Cary, unpredictable as ever, suddenly flew to England for yet another visit with Elsie. On his return, he had meetings with an old friend, producer-director Mervyn LeRoy, to discuss a film about the life of Buffalo Bill. He said to a *New York Times* writer on June 18: "I've thought about Buffalo Bill for a good many years—I saw him perform in person as a kid—and I think his story as William F. Cody, the post–Civil War Indian scout, and, later, was the Wild West performer in circuses—he was an all-around romantic figure—would make a truly great spectacle film." He overlooked the fact that Buffalo Bill's last appearance in England was before Archie Leach was born. Nothing came of this.

On August 22, 1967, Dyan sued Cary for divorce, stating that he had treated her in "an inhuman manner." In the suit, Dyan estimated Cary's worth at more than $10 million, and his annual income as $500,000. She asked for reasonable support for her and for Jennifer, citing her monthly expenses as $5,470.

There were numerous delays before the next hearing. Cary's state of mind was appalling. He was terrified he would lost his child completely to her mother. Visits to Jennifer in the wake of Dyan's statements were, of course, severely strained. Cary tried to break the tension that October by making his first record, at Columbia Studios in New York. One side was a New Year greeting, "Here's to You," by Dick Hazard and Peggy Lee, and the other side was "A Christmas Lullaby." As Dyan grew more and more extroverted and happy to be free, Cary became almost suicidally morose. He spent several weeks in New York, partly to be near Jennifer when Dyan took her there. He stayed with an old friend, the former Warner Bros. publicist Bob Taplinger, whom he had remembered with pleasure from the old days. Taplinger was a warm and charming companion, and to some extent he was able to assuage Cary's unhappiness. Taplinger recalled to a journalist that Cary "used to wait at the house all day for word from the nurse as to when he could see [Jennifer] for an hour or two. He wouldn't make plans for doing anything if there was a chance of seeing her." When Dyan opened in what proved to be a short-lived play in Manhattan, Cary turned up at her first night, then hung on and on in the city. Cary was still in New York in March of 1968, leaving only briefly to attend the World's Fair in Montreal.

Dyan's play closed, and she went to Los Angeles for the next divorce hearing, at which details of the settlement would be set forth. Cary tried to halt the divorce by helping her to reactivate her movie career. He successfully persuaded the producer Mike Frankovich who was married to his old friend Binnie Barnes, to cast Dyan in the film comedy *Bob and Carol and Ted and Alice*. She would prove to be a great success and be nominated for an Oscar.

On March 12, Cary set out from New York to see Jennifer in Los Angeles. It was a rain-swept, icy night, with a howling wind. Accompanied by a friend, Baroness Gratia von Furstenberg, Cary, in an especially restless mood, urged the driver of his limousine to step on it along the Long Island Expressway. It was intensely dark, and the visibility was virtually nonexistent. A tractor trailer pulling a wheeled metal platform was approaching from the opposite direction, when it was struck in the rear by a large truck. The platform broke loose, jumped the dividing yellow line, and smashed into Cary's limousine. Cary blacked out. When he woke, he found himself in St. John's Hospital. Two of his ribs were broken, and he was bruised from head to foot. Baroness von Furstenberg had broken a leg. The driver suffered a broken knee.

Cary, frantic that he could not continue to Los Angeles, struggled repeatedly out of bed, only to be told that he couldn't possibly leave. He called in his lawyers and began a damage suit against the owners of the truck. (The insurance companies fought the matter out for years.) He complained that he was in a hospital in Queens rather than Manhattan. But he acted the role of Cary Grant, dazzling the nurses, who, predictably, lined up just to catch a glimpse of him and used any excuse to attend him personally.

He was hospitalized for seventeen days, sharing a room through-

out with the chauffeur, Troy Lindahl, "so that I would have someone to talk to." A smiling Sister Thomas Francis assisted him to the
car. Through the whole of his stay, he had absurdly assumed the
name Count Bezok, even though everyone knew who he was.

It was at this time that Cary formed a very important new friendship. George Barrie, the president of Fabergé, the giant cosmetics
empire, was a frequent visitor to the hospital. Barrie was a charming, enormously energetic man whose obsessive concern with his
products had advanced the company to preeminence during the previous decade. Cary had met him just before the accident; Barrie was
staying with Taplinger, and had offered to take Cary to the airport.
Cary had refused, wishing to spare Barrie the unpleasantness of
driving in such severe weather.

Taplinger had been intent on bringing Cary and George Barrie
together. Knowing Cary's extraordinary power over millions of women,
Taplinger realized that if he joined the board of Fabergé, not only
would he benefit from a new interest, now that his movie career
was apparently over, but he could assist Barrie tremendously, making personal appearances worldwide on behalf of Fabergé products.
Over the next few months, discussions would take place between
Taplinger and Barrie, and between Taplinger and Cary; at last, Barrie brought them together for a discussion.

Meanwhile, the divorce hearing had taken place on March 20, as
Cary lay in his hospital bed. In her testimony, Dyan omitted a great
many of the more unpleasant details, but she stated that Cary had
driven her to the verge of a nervous breakdown, urged her to take
LSD, which she had done only twice, and had been in numerous
ways heartless and cruel. She described his spanking her, spoke of
his jumping up and down on the bed and screaming at the television
set during the Academy Awards, insulting the honorees. She repeated earlier charges:

> He started to hit me. He screamed. He was laughing as he hit
> me. He screamed for the help to come and see what he was doing.
> I was frightened because he was laughing, and I went to call the
> police. He stopped me by pointing out how damaging the publicity
> would be.

When we were planning our trip to Bristol, he would not let me take Jennifer's baby food. He said the English cows were as good as American ones.

Witnesses produced by Cary's attorneys included Dr. Judd Marmor, who said he had examined Cary psychiatrically and found no evidence of mental damage from LSD; in fact, he said, the drug had deepened Cary's sense of compassion for people and his understanding of himself, and had "helped cure his shyness and anxiety in dealing with other people." A second psychiatrist testified that he saw no evidence of irrationality, erratic behavior, or incoherence in Cary's behavior.

The settlement was to cause Cary acute distress. Although the alimony was a comparatively modest fifty thousand dollars a year, Cary was allowed only two months out of twelve with Jennifer. He would be permitted visitation by special request on birthdays and at Christmas. Moodily, Cary moved back into the Beverly Grove Drive house. William Weaver's brother David became the houseman. He later described the house's state of deterioration: a trelliswork breezeway connecting the garage to the main house had fallen apart; the screen door had collapsed; shingles were missing from the roof, which leaked badly; "water stains had pitted the ceiling, where entire patches of plaster sagged dangerously under the weight of water collecting in the eaves. In the bathroom, whenever it rained hard, a rivulet of water streamed down from the central overhead light fitting." In a bizarrely comic scene, Cary had Weaver place empty jam jars from the larder* and old paint tins from the garage under the ceiling holes. Local authorities insisted that Cary have the garden groomed—it was a veritable jungle of weeds—but he, begrudging the expense, did nothing. Because of his name, the Beverly Hills officials could only send out gardeners to cut away the vegetation. Cary was delighted: he wouldn't have to spend anything.

Then, much to his displeasure, he received a stern letter from City Hall, which informed him that he must have the house remod-

* He forbade the use of the expression "Butler's Pantry" in his house.

eled to avoid its being declared a condemned property. Cary was forced to hire an architect, but then he would change the plans from day to day. Like Mr. Blandings, he plunged in sudden pratfalls as he tripped over furniture, or he so clumsily hammered a nail that it penetrated his finger. He and Weaver spent days plowing through old storage boxes, piled in cardboard mountains everywhere. They were filled with damp and moldering books and documents. Among the few items that could be rescued were two valuable Tiepolo drawings, gifts from Barbara Hutton in the 1940s. A Boudin painting emerged virtually untouched by mildew. But many other items were ruined.

Weaver wrote that Cary became obsessed with the positioning of a light socket, changing it again and again until the electricians hired for the job were exasperated. In an unwonted fit of extravagance, he imported earthenware tiles for his new patio. The architects had personally supervised the packing of the tiles, each one numbered for positioning. On the drive to the house, the trucker accidentally set fire to the tiles' protective straw with his cigarette. The tiles were scorched beyond retrieval, and the whole order had to be duplicated. In a similar disaster, the plaster on one wall contained too much sand, so that it dried almost immediately and cracked from top to bottom. The new plumbing failed to work, because brand-new pipes were not properly matched to ancient ones, and there were many leaks. In his bedroom, Cary had a dressing room mirror surrounded by soft, slightly pink bulbs that would deemphasize the lines in his face. He hated and dreaded neon lighting because of its cruelty. Unfortunately, the brackets connecting the frame to the glass were incorrectly screwed in, and the summer heat caused the mirror to splinter and blow out.

Cary ordered a plate-glass window for the sitting room, to provide a fine 180-degree view of the city. First a U.S. company, then a French company, proved unequal to the task of making the window. After some months, an American contractor was found who would undertake the job, but only if the window could be supplied in three pieces. The glass was finally fitted expertly into place, with vertical metal dividers. Cary looked at the windows, at the view, and then exploded. Weaver couldn't understand what was wrong. Impatiently, Cary pointed out that the manufacturer's trademark was inscribed, almost imperceptibly, with a diamond drill at the bottom-left-hand corner of each pane. Cary had the entire window removed and sent back to be redone without the offending logo.

Cary remained reclusive in the late 1960s. He hated to go to parties and was irritated by the roasts or tributes to aging celebrities that seemed to turn a changing Hollywood into not much more than a mutual-admiration society. Like his friend Howard Hughes, he enjoyed, if that is the word, an empty life, devoid of intellectual or physical satisfaction, devoid even of luxury, of material pleasures.

He kept in touch with Hughes, who now resided almost entirely in Las Vegas, deprived of the healing presence of the brisk and attractive Jean Peters Hughes, who had moved back to California. His aide Noah Dietrich told Charles Higham that Hughes found Cary Grant supportive, as he called him from time to time to tell him of his grievous woes.

Cary found temporary release from his self-imprisonment in his restricted visits with his beloved Jennifer. Even with her he could not relax, but fretted endlessly over her diet, her health, measuring her, taking her blood pressure, fearful day and night that Dyan was not doing the best for her. And yet he failed to give Dyan sufficient sums of money for a substantial home for Jennifer. Despite successive court orders, Dyan was forced, by the time Jennifer was four years old, to live in a mediocre West Hollywood apartment house frequented by visiting New York actors, with a sprinkling of prostitutes and drug addicts.

Cary did escape occasionally to the Magic Castle, an eccentric, neo-Gothic structure above Franklin Avenue in the Hollywood Hills. There, for a fee of a mere fifty dollars a year, he could join the friendly brotherhood of magicians who made the castle their headquarters. (He had long since refused to become a member of certain country clubs because of their membership fees.) Cary befriended a young parking attendant at the castle, Berri Lee. As with Ted Donaldson some twenty-seven years earlier, and with Lance Reventlow, whom he still saw, this was an asexual friendship, disinterested, warm, fatherly, and considerate. Lee recalls that Cary encouraged him in his budding career as a magician. He would make a special point of coming to see Lee's magic act, and later helped him to get engagements on television shows. He paid for Lee to fly to New York, where Lee got an engagement at El Morocco and where, perhaps due to Cary's influence, Liza Minnelli and Pearl Bailey turned up. Cary encouraged Lee when the young magician appeared in Las Vegas. Berri Lee says:

> He was like a father to me. . . . I had never had a father. He was a guiding light. . . . He would give me advice, tell me what to do and how to deal with things. One time, he invited me to his house for Christmas. The biggest star in the world. I was overcome. He gave me a book called *Stick and Rudder*, which is one of the greatest books on flying. He encouraged me to learn to fly.

Lee attended a holiday dinner at Cary's house.

> We had Christmas dinner on a big table, with a sheet with a hole in it for a tablecloth, and dime-store knives and forks. Against the wall was a stack of paintings, six or eight feet deep, which may have been worth three, four, or five million dollars. He told me that he had been robbed. Everything in the house had been stolen—all his silverware, all his stuff. He pointed out that the reason the paintings had not been lost was that everytime the thieves went to pick up some silver, or a TV set, or some insignificant thing, they walked around those millions of dollars' worth of artwork because they didn't know what it was.

Cary had, apparently, been keeping questionable company. For example, in July 1969, a wire service report appeared on the desks of certain overseas newspapers. It stated that Cary Grant had been brought in for questioning when the mother of a young man accused Cary of picking up her underage son in his Rolls-Royce at a Los Angeles freeway entrance and making an improper suggestion to him. There was no implication that the young man had responded.

We come now to the most mysterious and puzzling aspect of his entire career, still unsolved and baffling to the biographer. Hard evidence is lacking, but—perhaps because of his persistent use of LSD, which was now illegal, or perhaps because of his penchant for curious nocturnal adventures—Cary had apparently befriended a young male.

According to the late Hollywood producer William Belasco, Cary was visiting the youth on the night of August 9 at a house at 10050 Cielo Drive, a short distance from Cary's own home. The two men were talking in the garden when screams were heard from the main house. Cary fled in the Rolls.

Next morning, Cary learned what he had narrowly escaped: Charles Manson had burst in and slaughtered the occupants of the main house, including actress Sharon Tate.

Manson said on a Los Angeles TV program in 1987, "The greatest thrill I ever knew was sleeping in the bed Cary Grant slept in." In his memoirs, published in 1988, Manson described spending several nights in Cary Grant's bungalow at Universal, apparently during Grant's absence. Manson claimed to have been having an affair with a male member of the studio staff.

Berri Lee describes Cary's terror following the crime. Perhaps he feared that because he was present on the grounds, he would subsequently be murdered. Lee says:

> The instant the telephone company and utility companies could be reached, he had his phone lines and utilities put underground, so that if somebody came to break into the house, they couldn't cut the power or the telephone. He hadn't forgotten the earlier burglary. He was very worried about Jennifer. He first disconnected his telephone, then had it put back on, with the number changed. He put $100,000 in a cash account in the bank.

Cary arranged for permanent bodyguards, day and night, for Jennifer. At this time, he appeared in court, and succeeded in preventing Dyan from taking Jennifer to Seattle. He got his visiting rights increased to ninety days a year.

As if he did not have sufficient trouble, Cary had begun an awkward affair with a beautiful showgirl named Cynthia Bouron. A close friend of Bouron's, the late Marilyn Hinton, alleged that Bouron had dated Jerry Lewis. According to Mrs. Hinton, Cynthia soon drew the attention of Frank Sinatra, who even considered marrying her, but then discovered that she had lied to him. She said that her real name was Bourbon and that she belonged to an American branch of the European royal family of Bourbon. According to Mrs. Hinton, Sinatra, understandably, dropped her immediately. Without the support of either Lewis or Sinatra, Marilyn Hinton recalled, Miss Bouron was unable to find work, and she claimed she was blacklisted. She was living in poverty when Mrs. Hinton discovered her and became her mentor. Mrs. Hinton introduced her to Cary Grant. Miss Bouron apparently shared several evenings with him in his suite at the Dunes in Las Vegas, but to her disappointment, nothing came of these romantic encounters featuring candlelight and champagne and sexy evening gowns.

Cynthia Bouron felt humiliated, and she went about obtaining vengeance in a manner that seems to contradict her sensitivity and gentleness as portrayed by Marilyn Hinton. (Mrs. Hinton insisted she knew nothing of Miss Bouron's plan.) She schemed to become pregnant by a man who somewhat resembled a younger Cary Grant and then announce that Cary was the father. In view of the fact that Grant was struggling with Dyan over visitation rights to Jennifer, and it was essential that he have an impeccable image, Miss Bouron knew that this vicious deceit could seriously damage him.

She conceived in June 1969, two months before the Manson murders. On March 12, 1970, she gave birth to a daughter at the Good Samaritan Hospital in Los Angeles, and named the child Stephanie Andrea Grant. The birth certificate carried the name Cary Grant as the father; birthplace: England; age: sixty-six; present occupation: actor; and, in a deliberate slap, industry or business: self.

While Cary was in the Bahamas, Joyce Haber, a Los Angeles *Times* columnist, obtained police records showing that Miss Bouron had been arrested for theft in April 1967 but had been found not guilty. She had been married twice and had had a child by each marriage. Miss Haber learned that Cynthia Bouron had for some time owned a collie called Cary, which some friends asserted the star had given her.

Cary had scarcely recovered from the horror of the Manson affair when he was dealt this new blow. The timing was appalling: the next month, he was due to receive an honorary Oscar for lifetime achievement. It was more essential than ever that his reputation be unblemished. He was terrified that not only would he lose face in the eyes of the public but the new visitation arrangement, whereby he was allowed Jennifer on alternate weekends, Monday afternoons, and one month of the summer vacation periods, would be suspended.

To keep out of Hollywood as much as possible, he traveled, visiting Noël Coward in Jamaica and Elsie in Bristol. Meanwhile, friends of his in Hollywood began investigating Cynthia Bouron further, and more was discovered about her murky past: her second husband had been a stuntman, who, in 1966, had murdered Mickey Rooney's wife Barbara. The man committed suicide. Determined to prove that the baby was not his, Cary sought a court order to obtain a blood test, but he had to wait for it to be carried out. It was an appalling burden to carry as he prepared for the important night at the Academy. He wondered whether he should cancel his appearance, then realized that if he did, it would be worse for him: people would say he was guilty and afraid. And in these excruciating weeks, he was tortured more than ever about the situation with Dyan and Jennifer.

Berri Lee says:

Cary would say, "Berri, I have a little place in Connecticut. If everything goes wrong, you and I will go there, and we'll get some girls and just make babies." I'll never forget that. Another of his quotes to me was: "The hand that rocks the cradle fucks the world." He accused Dyan of using her child as a tool, and talked about how mothers "fuck up your mind as a child" . . . screw you around, make you afraid of life, how a lot of men are ruined by their mothers. There was a direct reference to Elsie here.

We never talked about the gay situation. Just things that I saw . . . I think gayness was just another escape, a way out. This was a man who, all his life, had women chasing him, and he never knew whether somebody wanted him or Cary Grant, wanted him for himself, and he was hurt very much by women.

Even in the midst of his crisis over Cynthia Bouron, Cary's bitterness over Dyan was intense. To Lee, he damned women for "being the way they are." Lee shared his feelings: he also loved women, but was frustrated by them. "If things are broken up in a relationship, why can't you just say it's over and try to work it out, instead of a woman coming and just going at you," Lee says. "We were just two unhappy guys, we were going through these things together, and we'd try to give each other advice."

On April 7, 1970, Cary walked tearfully to the stage of the Dorothy Chandler Pavilion in Los Angeles to receive his honorary Oscar from his old friend Frank Sinatra.* There was a standing ovation as the now smiling star received the award. A montage of his career from the early Mae West vehicles to *Charade* dazzled and excited the audience. Sinatra said, accurately, "No one has brought more pleasure to more people for so many years . . . nobody has done so many things as well. Cary has so much skill that he makes it all look easy." Then he read the statuette inscription: "To Cary Grant, for his unique mastery of the art of screen acting, with the respect and affection of his colleagues." Deeply moved by the standing ovation, the tormented supercelebrity delivered a brief, expertly phrased speech, mentioning many of his directors and writers, and adding, "This is a collaborative medium. We all need each other. . . . Probably no greater honor can come to a man than the respect of his colleagues." If Cynthia Bouron had appeared at that moment, she would probably have been lynched. That same evening, Dyan Cannon narrowly lost the Academy Award as best supporting actress for her vivid comedic playing in *Bob and Carol and Ted and Alice*—the film in which she had been cast through Cary's efforts. They barely acknowledged each other in the crowd.

---

* *The differences between the two stars during the filming of* The Pride and the Passion *were long forgotten. They had become fast friends. In 1972, Sinatra would "give" Cary to his mother as a birthday gift.*

SEVENTEEN

By 1970, Cary was firmly established as a member of the board of Fabergé. He received a salary of only $25,000 a year, but the perquisites were extraordinary. Among them was use of the penthouse at the Hotel Warwick in New York, a magnificently furnished, oak-beamed suite, formerly occupied by Marion Davies, who had owned the hotel. In addition to the company DC-3 available for his private use, he had access to a G-2 jet—which had won an industrial prize for the best private jet plane in the nation. The aircraft was furnished with a daybed, comfortable seats and armchairs, and a bar. He was also able to use a Convair, a propeller plane, which had a proper bed. Cary, who hated traveling in commercial planes because of the cramped space and the attention he attracted, relished the privacy and comfort of these conveyances. He obtained permission to redecorate the DC-3, in a style Weaver described as "rather like a small bungalow, with an ash dining table and four chocolate-brown swiveling chairs, a collection of bright-yellow armchairs . . . and two sofas, in tomato red and green." There was a Lazy Susan bar, and a piano at which Cary could sit, playing and singing old music hall songs. The bulkheads were lined with pictures of Jennifer at play. He used the DC-3 for vacation trips, or to go to San Francisco for lunch or New York for dinner. He had reached that eminence at which almost nothing is paid for.

He flung himself into promoting Fabergé's inexpensive perfume lines with all the obsessive energy that had marked his life to date. He became a proselytizer, a supersalesman who was maddened by the thought that some other line might compete successfully with what he now regarded as his own. Boarding one of his private planes, he would turn up unannounced at drug and department stores across the country, throwing staff and management into a state of near hysteria because they had made no special arrangements. The instant he turned up at a cosmetics counter, an immense crowd formed, and virtually every other counter in the vicinity was deserted. By snatching up all the Fabergé items at the counter, his fans were able to get a close look at their idol. Cary would also have long conversations with store managers about what they felt were their needs. He discussed strategy with buyers. His meetings with salesmen were always popular and inspiring. He appears to have covered as many as three hundred stores between 1969 and 1971.

Cary remained concerned about the Cynthia Bouron affair. According to Marilyn Hinton, he engaged a private detective, who managed to make his way into Cynthia's apartment and, in a scene reminiscent of *Rosemary's Baby*, peered into the cradle; he found the infant did not resemble Cary. When Miss Bouron was summoned to undergo a blood test, she understandably failed to appear. Two years later, she was found dead in her car in a San Fernando Valley parking lot. Press reports said she was beaten to death; Marilyn Hinton said she was severed limb from limb. The murderer was never found.

The custody battles over Jennifer continued throughout 1971 and 1972, as Cary traveled ceaselessly throughout the world, vigorously selling Fabergé products, even in Iron Curtain countries. These trips effectively deprived him of visits with Jennifer at a time when he was struggling for added days with her and was alleging that he cancelled certain official engagements, including tributes to personal friends in show business, because he could not bear to be separated from his daughter. It would seem that he used Jennifer as an excuse to avoid social engagements.

Cary made frequent visits to Las Vegas to keep in touch with Howard Hughes, even though on many occasions he spoke to him only on the telephone there. When Hughes was living at the Britannia Beach Hotel on Paradise Island in the Bahamas, Cary could be found in that region more frequently than was called for by his normal schedule.

On December 7, 1971, the McGraw-Hill Publishing Company announced in the press that it had bought world rights to a book which was supposed to be a Hughes autobiography as told to the American writer Clifford Irving. A press release accompanying the announcement attributed to Hughes the statement: "I believe that more lies have been printed and told about me than about any living man—therefore it was my purpose to write a book which would set the record straight." Cary knew that Hughes could never have written his memoirs, nor could he have authorized a biography of any sort. The Hughes Tool Company issued a denunciation of the memoir as a hoax. McGraw-Hill and *Life* magazine, which had the serialization rights, stood firmly behind Clifford Irving. At the publisher's request, Irving supplied a document, confirmed by handwriting experts as having been written by Hughes, that affirmed the manuscript as genuine.

Cary, who had dreaded that something of the sort would happen to him, urged Hughes to come out of his cocoon of silence and obscurity and make a public denial. Since it would be difficult for Hughes to face the press, Cary (according to the late Noah Dietrich) suggested that he give a telephone interview to seven selected reporters—who would be gathered at the Sheraton-Universal Hotel in Burbank, California—from his suite at the Britannia Beach Hotel. All seven were known to him personally. Hughes agreed, and the telephone press conference was held on January 7, 1972. Surprisingly, except for one or two errors, Hughes responded well to the interview and proved that, despite his uncertain state of health and extreme eccentricity, his mind was in good shape. Cary suggested to Hughes that Clifford Irving's movements on the days he was supposed to have been interviewing Hughes be checked out; one method would be to examine library registers to ascertain Clifford's whereabouts on certain days. Hughes's aircraft designer Ted Carpentier remembers doing this and finding that Irving was in a library when he claimed to have been interviewing the tycoon. Within a month, Irving admitted his guilt.

In the early 1970s, Cary became involved with a British photojournalist named Maureen Donaldson. Small and blonde, with a round, cheerful, healthy face, a spunky manner, and a great deal of energetic charm, Miss Donaldson fascinated him. Normally, he was extremely wary of photojournalists, particularly those for magazines, as she was, but, like so many stars, he was susceptible to admiration, and she hung on his every word. By 1972, their relationship had deepened, according to her, into a serious love affair. When she told him that she had once been a nanny, he apparently thought her an eligible stepmother for Jennifer. They also had their nationality in common and a shared sense of humor; Maureen enjoyed Cary's performances of music hall songs.

Unlike Dyan Cannon, Maureen didn't fight Cary when he objected to her wearing shorts or jeans, T-shirts and sweaters. He worked hard on molding her into an elegant young woman. Once more, his paternal instincts were at work: Maureen was not yet thirty.

At first, he continued to see other young women. She was probably under the impression that he was devoting himself exclusively to her. She was sensitive enough to know that Jennifer came first in his life, that she must never try to usurp the child's place in his affections. He rewarded her for her thoughtfulness: he gave her, with uncharacteristic generosity, a Bill Blass wardrobe and a thousand-dollar Cartier Tank watch.

Their life during those periods when Cary was not traveling for Fabergé was unexciting. The couple spent most of their time at his house, sitting around and talking desultorily; in the evenings, they ate a gourmet TV dinner while watching vintage Hollywood movies on the outsize television set. Very occasionally, they would dine out. When Cary acquired a beach house near Dyan's in Malibu—so that he could be close to Jennifer—they would drop into the Polynesian restaurant Tonga Lei; during the winter months, they sometimes dined at Chasen's in Beverly Hills, where Cary had an account and didn't have to produce cash.

They saw very few people, and appeared to observers to be totally involved with each other. The relationship continued into 1976. According to Miss Donaldson's statements to journalists at the time,

Cary didn't treat her cruelly, as he had his wives; he exhibited the sensitivity he had shown to Phyllis Brooks in the 1930s. When Maureen had a jaw infection and had to undergo surgery, he checked into the hospital with her, as he had done with Dyan when Jennifer was born, and he nursed her at his house during her convalescence, attending to her day and night. When her parents arrived from London, he made sure they had a good time.

In 1970, Cary became close to William Currie McIntosh. Handsome, lean, dark, the wealthy McIntosh was a man possessed of youthful charm. He interested Cary in a promotional venture: Cary would lend his name and support to a residential development on the banks of the Shannon and Fergus rivers, close to Shannon Airport. This would be ideal for American retirees, who could obtain comfortable, not overlarge houses in a handsome rural setting. It was expected that these prospective purchasers would be largely of Irish descent, returning to their ancestors' native soil for their final years.

Cary, who had always had a fondness for Ireland and had visited it for Fabergé, saw considerable potential in this project, which became known as Shannonside. Surprisingly, he handed McIntosh a ten-thousand-dollar check as an initial investment. Then, following a visit to Elsie in Bristol, Cary met with McIntosh at London's Heathrow Airport and flew across the Irish Channel to Shannon. Cary surveyed the territory and was impressed: the scenery had a soft, dark-green Irish beauty, with splendid views of the gray-green Atlantic.

He became a director of the company in September 1971, and consulted constantly with McIntosh and the architects. They wished to build just over two thousand dwellings, to the tune of thirty million dollars. So proprietorial was he, so consumed, McIntosh reported in his book, with a conviction that he alone was the champion of Shannonside, that he objected violently when Jack Lemmon invested twenty thousand dollars in the scheme. McIntosh hung on to the Lemmon investment.

Cary, missing his visitations with Jennifer, absented himself from California repeatedly, to check out the new development with McIntosh. He fussed over the plumbing, the electricity; he took an inordinate amount of interest in roof tiling and insulation. He even allowed himself to walk around with members of the press and news photographers, showing them how wonderful everything was. He allowed a film to be made under McIntosh's supervision, in which Cary was seen boasting about Shannonside while walking the length and breadth of the property.

In 1973, he was granted a plot on which to build his own home. He consulted with an architect on the design, excluding a dining room because he loved to eat in the bedroom, allowing a special area for Jennifer to live in, and making sure that there was a colonial-style veranda overlooking the river and extending the full length of the house.

According to McIntosh, Cary thought of Jennifer constantly during these trips, buying her gifts and writing daily letters to her, containing jokes and puzzles. He always enjoyed going with McIntosh to London, where he stayed at the Connaught. He made a shrewd deal with Sir Charles Abrahams, jovial chairman of Aquascutum, a leading British clothing manufacturer, in which he would wear Aquascutum suits on well-photographed public occasions, in return for substantial discounts. He still freeloaded everywhere: Fabergé covered most of his hotel and meal bills, the Shannonside directors paid others, and very often managements would waive his restaurant charges because of the customers he attracted when it slipped out through the grapevine that he would be in a particular place on a particular night.

Cary was beginning to show his age. His once meticulous, carefully controlled behavior dissolved during travel. He was absentminded and would be excessively flustered as he searched for a pair of spectacles that were actually sitting on his nose, for documents that had slipped down the side of his seat, for articles of clothing he had forgotten he had hung in a closet, and for luggage checks that had mysteriously become detached from his ticket and couldn't be located—this on the rare occasions when he used commercial aircraft.

Cary had a brief relationship at the outset of the 1970s with the beautiful widow of a Hollywood agent turned producer. The widow, who had been born in France, first met Cary in 1969 in Palm Springs.

She shared his love of privacy and his dislike of social events and crowds. They made a trip to Paris, accompanied by William Weaver, in which Cary was at his best. But like so many women before her, the sensitive widow found that Cary was not as deeply committed to her as she was to him. She would cry often, sometimes walk out on Cary and then come back, complaining, unlike Maureen Donaldson, when he would leave her behind for his extended trips to London and Ireland. On one occasion, she became so distraught at the Benedict Canyon house that she collapsed; William and David Weaver, fearing that she had suffered a heart attack, tried to revive her, without success. They were forced to call the paramedics. Cary, meanwhile, had left for New York.

The ambulance drive was a nightmare, and the driver was so flustered that he approached a freeway by way of the off ramp, almost colliding with approaching traffic, by which time the widow appeared to be dying. At the hospital, only a tracheotomy saved her life. Perhaps mistaking her sudden illness for the sort of fake suicide he had attempted in the 1930s, Cary, according to William Weaver, adamantly refused to go near the hospital. He wouldn't even send her flowers, informing her with wicked humor on the phone that the flowers would deprive her of what little oxygen she had. She broke with Cary soon afterward, and finally achieved a happy marriage. By now, Cary's attitude to her was one of total and cruel contempt.

In July 1972, Lance Reventlow, whom Cary, still somewhat of a surrogate father, had continued to visit with over the years, crashed in his single-engine plane in a violent electrical storm. He did not survive. There was an unseemly squabble over the remains. Barbara Hutton wished Lance to be buried in the Woolworth crypt, but Cheryl Reventlow was determined that her husband be cremated, his ashes scattered at Aspen, Colorado. Grant supported Cheryl and managed to override Barbara Hutton's preference; with William Weaver, he attended an elaborate memorial service at Aspen.

Six months later, in January 1973, Weaver answered the phone at the Benedict Canyon house, to be told by Eric Leach's wife, Margaret, that Elsie was dead. Weaver beckoned Cary to the telephone, but Cary held back. He looked dazed but not grief-stricken. He seemed unable to deal with the questions Margaret raised. She naturally wanted to make preparations for a funeral, and asked whether he wanted to authorize a particular service or flower arrangement for the church. But according to Weaver, he only kept saying that her death was not to be made public, and he added the extraordinary statement: "No hearse. Can't we have a cart?" He ruled out any kind of service.

Understandably, Margaret preferred to ignore his requests, and she herself made the arrangements. Cary flew with Weaver to England to attend the funeral, making the slow walk through fog and drizzle to the cemetery. The plain pine coffin carried not a single flower. Apart from Cary and Weaver, only Margaret and Eric Leach were present. Weaver recalled: "As the coffin was lowered into the ground, Grant leaned over, took from Margaret's hands the single rose she was carrying, and laid it on the lid." At tea afterward, in the Leaches' sitting room, Cary did not appear to be grieving. He spoke of his father with affection, but said little or nothing about Elsie. William McIntosh comments:

> I have always felt that Cary's visits to Elsie were carried but, not so much from a deep sensitivity or love of her, but because he knew the world was watching him, and his image would be affected if he did not keep going to Bristol. There was no real rapport between them, none of the love of a son for his mother. Weaver and I knew there was something deep and dark in the relationship with her at the outside of his life, but not what it was. Elsie didn't know Cary was her son; sometimes she didn't recognize him; she was uncomfortable at being called his mother. I doubted if she really *was* his mother.

Elsie, who was always disinterested in money, died with pathetically little. She had steadfastly refused to let Cary bring her to Hollywood or make her wealthy. She remained stubbornly indifferent to his film career. And if truth be told, that hard, unyielding woman showed very little gratitude to him for his constant flights to Bristol. Perhaps, sharply observant, she sensed that his visits were dutiful rather than inspired by intense affection, and that very often he coordinated them with trips to England for other purposes. The absence of mourners at the funeral seems to indicate her inability to attract a circle of loving and devoted people. Nostalgia had softened Cary's memories of his father, whose philandering had made him neglectful and who had so casually handed him over to a vaudeville troupe at the age of six. Elsie Leach was not so fortunate. He seldom spoke of her again.

In the mid-1970s, Cary formed a friendship with the gifted vocal impressionist Rich Little. He was enchanted with the comedian's Las Vagas act, and one night invaded his dressing room after a show—astonishing Little's wife and sister, who did a double take when they saw him—and burst out with childlike enthusiasm: "Do you realize what you do? For just an hour you let people forget all their troubles, you let them remember all those great stars and great pictures! It's a wonderful gift to be able to do that! You don't realize how many people you have made happy. You should be proud of it!"

For several years, Cary closely followed Little's career. Sometimes they would fly together on one of Cary's Fabergé planes. Little, a committed movie buff, wanted to discuss movies, but Cary would reply, "Let's talk about the real things in life: nature, music, that kind of thing. I don't want to talk about my movies, because they aren't worth talking about." Little says:

And then about ten minutes later the conversation would swing around and we would be talking about one of his movies. And suddenly he'd stop and say, "I don't want to talk about my movies." The pictures he would talk the most about were the Hitchcocks. He had a great respect for Hitch.

Little would delight in pretending to be Cary Grant when booking various hotels. He would say that he had been in Africa; that he had picked up a couple of animals, an orangutan and a cheetah, and that the creatures were with him and would need a room each. He was testing Cary's fame and influence. Little adds:

There was always a long pause after I made the request in Cary's voice. One time, when I used the request at the M-G-M

Grand Hotel, I remember the clerk saying, "No problem at all, sir." Then I added, "Well, *we* have a little problem. How are we going to get the animals up to the rooms?" "Good point, sir," the clerk replied.

I said, as Cary, "We don't want to disrupt everyone in the casino. How about we dress the orangutan up as a woman and put her in a wheelchair, and just smuggle her in that way." And then I would go on and suggest how the cheetah might be smuggled in. I kept going. I said, "Maybe we could arrange for some bananas for the monkey. We could use the shower rail for a swing for him." And the man replied, "I don't know how many bananas we can get, but I'll check with the kitchen." It was a long time before I put the guy out of his misery and told him it was a put-on. Cary always came totally unglued when I told him the story. He just didn't realize how famous he was.

Little remembers that when he traveled, he would often use his Cary Grant voice to get food quickly:

The guy who brought the food was greeted by my manager, who would sign the check while I was in the bedroom, saying through the door in Cary's voice, "Thank you very much. I really appreciate it. I'm in a big, big hurry." The waiter would reply, "No problem, Mr. Grant. Anytime. Anything you want, sir." And "Cary" would say, "Really, it's very sweet of you." These sorts of scenes would go on into the 1980s.

Cary's relationship with Maureen Donaldson began to decline in the mid-1970s. Tim Barry, a popular tennis pro, witnessed the deterioration. He recalls that in late 1974, he was enjoying a drink at a bar in Malibu with a close friend, a South African tennis player, when an attractive girl in her twenties walked in. In an English accent, she spoke about how horribly her boyfriend, an older man, was treating her. Eventually announcing that her name was Maureen Donaldson, she told Barry that her lover's name was Cary Grant. Barry said rudely, "You've got to be joking. What would Cary Grant be doing with you?" She answered, "It's true. I live with him in

Beverly Hills, and he gives me an apartment of my own." She talked about their touch-and-go, clandestine relationship, and that they'd been together for a few years.

About three months after his meeting with Maureen Donaldson, Barry received a telephone call from Cary Grant's manager, Don Carey, who stated that Mr. Grant would like his daughter, Jennifer, to have some tennis lessons. At the time, Cary had Monday visitation rights. Barry still remembers the time, 4:00 P.M., when a large blue automobile stopped at the Malibu tennis court and five people stepped out: Don Carey; a black maid; Jennifer, now about eleven years old, and looking beautiful, a girlfriend Lisa Lennon; and finally Cary himself. Barry's knees were shaking—he was in his twenties and just out of UCLA—at the prospect of meeting "the idol of everybody's lifetime." Numbly, he shook Cary's hand, realizing that now he would be put to the test of making a good tennis player out of Jennifer. To add to his extreme nervousness and discomfort, Cary had brought a movie camera, to film Jennifer at her lesson.

Barry recalls:

I said to myself, "Oh, my God, there's enough pressure on me as it is. Here I'm going to be teaching Cary Grant's daughter, and on film!" It was too uncomfortable to think about. Jennifer was nervous herself. I could tell she wasn't comfortable at the thought of everybody in the world watching her learn tennis, and her father himself was making her nervous.

Barry began the process of whipping Jennifer into shape. He worked very hard on her backhand, her overhead drive, and the other strokes, painfully conscious of Cary's constant presence with the camera, supervising everything Barry did. As if he were not already sufficiently nervous already, he had to deal with Dyan's frequent visits to the court. Like Cary, she was just a short distance away, in her beach house. Dyan would turn up on the Mondays when Cary was allowed access to Jennifer, because she needed to ask something of her daughter. Both Barry and Jennifer would jump as Dyan would suddenly call out to her daughter to come off the court and talk to her. "She would not confront Cary face to face," Tim Barry says.

Barry remembers that Cary was delighted with Jennifer's progress. He confided that he had always wanted to play tennis but had never had the time, although he himself proved his statement false by batting balls around the court. Barry noticed that Cary muttered to himself and gazed transfixed at Jennifer in a manner that surpassed ordinary parental devotion.

Barry says that Jennifer was as devoted to Cary as he was to her. But then some embarrassing incidents took place. Cary would bring a friend onto the court, and they would carry on in an effeminate way which deeply embarrassed Jennifer. Lisa Lennon was equally embarrassed by Cary's "gay" clowning and did not warm to his companion.

Maureen Donaldson turned up for lessons later; Cary wanted her to be a tennis mate for Jennifer, joining her with Don Carey and a male partner in mixed doubles. Maureen remembered her having met Barry at the bar and, as her lessons continued, talked more and more about the difficulties in her relationship with Cary.

Barry says:

He had treated her so cruelly. It came out that he had been sleeping with men. I didn't want to get into the juicy details. I said, "Oh, poor Maureen, you've got to deal with this" and I would just kind of pat her on the shoulder. And I'd say, as I patted her on the shoulder, "Okay, let's get on with the tennis lesson, okay?" She said, "Sometimes he can be so nice, and other times a devil." She was very distressed. He would yell and call her terrible. He would get mad at her, she said. It was very painful.

Occasionally, Barry recalls, Jennifer and Maureen would train together, as Cary wished. The two liked each other tremendously. And both Cary and Maureen seemed to work hard to keep the stresses and miseries of their relationship from Jennifer.

Shortly before Christmas, 1974, Jennifer brought Tim Barry a package in Christmas paper. It was marked "From Cary to Tim." He opened it excitedly, only to find that it contained a Fabergé gift package with Brut cologne. Barry was tickled, quite overlooking the fact that Cary was giving out his own free samples as presents.

As time went on, Jennifer became very friendly with Tim Barry. She at last became proficient at tennis, and she began confiding in him. Barry says:

> She told me how uncomfortable it was when Cary and his friend were around and the two of them would be carrying on like a couple of girls. Even if she knew her father was gay, she still loved him.

Finally, Jennifer changed schools and couldn't get out to Malibu on Mondays. She wanted to train at night, but Barry didn't have a lighted court he could use, so he says, "We all just parted. And Maureen just faded into the woodwork. I always felt stupid, not having gotten an autographed picture."

As if his life was not complicated enough in the mid-1970s, Cary became embroiled in yet another love affair when he was seventy years old. This new relationship proved to be as ill-fated as the others. Victoria Morgan was a dark-haired girl with an exquisitely proportioned figure and a voluptuous face. Her sensual lips suggested all manner of erotic possibilities, and her expression was at once inviting, decadent, and suggestive of potential danger. She was born in 1952, the child of a disastrous marriage of a U.S. Air Force man turned Texas department store executive and a British war bride. In high school, the ravishingly beautiful Vicki was the target of passionate attention from virtually every boy in her class. She became pregnant and was abandoned by the child's father. Checking into a Los Angeles maternity home, she gave birth to her son, Todd, in January 1969; she was only sixteen. She struggled to obtain work as a model, but rapidly discovered the competition: Los Angeles was filled with beautiful girls. She married a clothing wholesaler and moved with him into a luxury apartment in West Hollywood. The marriage failed. While walking along Sunset Boulevard one day, she was picked up by the multimillionaire Alfred Bloomingdale, who said he wanted Vicki to work with his daughter to improve her tennis. According to Miss Morgan, Bloomingdale confirmed the invitation by putting a check for eight thousand dollars in her hand.

Besotted with the young woman, he began pursuing her relentlessly. Bloomingdale would force her to watch while he lashed two women's naked buttocks, then he spanked her violently. Soon she herself began to satisfy his sadistic impulses. In 1971, she became pregnant. Bloomingdale talked of divorcing his wife and marrying her, but in the end he demanded that she have an abortion. By now she was trapped in a potentially dangerous relationship.

In 1972, Bloomingdale discovered that he had cancer of the larynx and underwent extensive cobalt treatments. But despite his appalling condition of health, the result of years of neglect, he continued his cruel treatment of the unhappy girl. She plagued him with requests that she be helped toward a career as a Hollywood actress. Her magnificent looks, only slightly affected by her atrocious lifestyle, would have qualified her, but she had no acting ability. Bloomingdale did what he could. He introduced her to the producer-director Mervyn LeRoy, whom Cary visited one day when Vicki Morgan was there. The girl resembled Phyllis Brooks, with a touch of Dyan Cannon. Cary asked her if she was an actress and said he might be able to help her. Though he was still involved with Maureen Donaldson, he began to take Vicki out to various restaurants, and then at last, risking Bloomingdale's intense displeasure—he felt he owned her—she moved into Cary's Malibu beach house. She was excited at the thought of having an affair with Cary. Her friend Ann Louise Bardach, who later co-wrote her biography, recalls that Vicki knew of Cary's bisexuality, and her specialty was gays. "She loved to prove that there was no man that wasn't at least something of a man, and wouldn't respond to her physical beauty." But, like others before her with the same attitude, she was disappointed. Instead of taking her to bed, Cary suggested she sleep in the guest room. According to another friend, Vicki displayed herself in negligees or even walked nude through the house, trying to excite Cary; every effort failed. His motivation seems incomprehensible. He would have had to lie to Maureen Donaldson about his whereabouts on the weekends, and he would also have had to make sure that the press never got wind of the situation. Bloomingdale might easily find out and cause severe problems. It was as though Cary wanted to humiliate this captive bedroom bombshell, because she could not attract him, the most desirable of men.

The relationship, devoid of meaning or substance, dragged on for much of a year. Cary was as stern with her as with other women, refusing to allow her to dress casually on the occasions when they went to a private party or a restaurant. She had to put on heavy jewelry and magnificent gowns—usually bought by Bloomingdale—to satisfy him. Apart from her excitement at having a platonic relationship with Cary Grant, there was little or no advantage for Vicki Morgan in this empty liaison. Except, as Miss Bardach points out, in persisting in her attempt to overcome his sexual reluctance. Meanwhile, she continued her ugly relationship with Bloomingdale. Her attempts at being an actress, studying with Lee Strasberg, came to nothing.

Finally, and we have to take Vicki Morgan's word for this, Cary consummated their relationship, but only once. She, at last realizing that he would never pay her money, not even for costume jewelry, left him, extremely disillusioned. By 1976, he had also parted from Maureen Donaldson, who understandably had had enough. It was tragic that, at this time of his life, he had not found a woman of sufficient stature, background, position and intelligence whom he could marry and find happiness with in his last years.

On July 7, 1983, Marvin Pancoast, a thirty-three-year-old man with a police record, turned up at the North Hollywood police precinct and announced that he had shot Vicki Morgan in a Colfax Avenue apartment. Some reports stated she was beaten with a baseball bat; her death sparked off a scandalous story that involved alleged tapes of her lovemaking with prominent political figures and revealed a lifetime of sordid activities leading to near-terminal depression. Bloomingdale had died of cancer, his grave marked with Vicki's calling card and a newspaper photograph with a scrawled message from her. According to Joyce Milton and Ann Louise Bardach, co-authors of *Vicki*, their biography of Miss Morgan, "His family had buried [Bloomingdale] hastily in a wooden coffin, before the news of his death became public knowledge." There is one element missing in this unhappy story. Is it possible that Cary, who cruelly mistreated women when the darker side of his nature took over, simply took advantage of Vicki's willingness to be victimized, without his being required to make love to her? If that is true, perhaps it was a way of releasing his frustrated needs without hurting Maureen Donaldson physically.

In the midst of this squalid misadventure, Cary's public career continued. He gave interviews to the press commenting about the sweetness and loveliness of women; he pontificated about mother love and family unity. In May 1973, at the Fabergé Straw Hat Awards in New York, he appeared with the veteran actress Helen Hayes. When he asked her why they had never made a picture together, she replied, with a roguish wink, "I'm ready anytime you are, Cary!" At the June 1975 Straw Hat ceremony, which honored his old friend Rosalind Russell, he deliberately mixed up his introduction cards, dropped his glasses, bent down to pick them up off the floor, and did a drunk act. He quipped, as he read out the name of one of the performers, "It says here that Helen Gallagher was born dancing. Rough on her mother, wasn't it?" Handing Dortha Duckworth the best supporting actress award, he joked, "She should get another reward for resisting the efforts to get her to change her name." When Danny Aiello, voted most promising actor, thanked his wife and four children, Cary brought a gale of laughter as he said, "Everybody should have a hobby!"

Cary suffered a number of major and minor blows in the 1970s. The Shannonside project, into which he had poured so much passion and enthusiasm, foundered and finally collapsed. According to William Currie McIntosh, the first inklings of trouble appeared in early 1974, when the consortium backing the development ran into capitialization problems. McIntosh blames "a self-styled environmentalist" for some of the problems. Cary lost a mere ten thousand dollars, but typically, he would no longer consider living in Ireland, because the bargain town house he had been promised was no longer available.

Howard Hughes was experiencing a precipitous decline in health. Hughes's biographers Donald L. Barlett and James B. Steele, in their book *Empire*, described his appalling condition by 1975. A malignant tumor grew out of the left side of his scalp; his teeth were too loose to be able to chew food; many were eaten away by decay, he weighed only 100 pounds, and his limbs were covered in needle marks. He had a peptic ulcer, his urinary tract was partly blocked, his prostate gland was enormously enlarged and his kidneys were shrinking. Despite the existence of four physicians on his permanent payroll, none seemed able to help him.

It is not known whether Cary visited with Hughes at the time. It is probable that Hughes, given his atrocious appearance, kept him at a distance. McIntosh records two encounters between Cary and Hughes in the 1970s. The first was in Las Vegas, at the Desert Inn, just before Hughes's drastic final deterioration:

Howard had long, long gray hair and long, dirty fingernails and was unbearably thin. Cary was full of compassion for him. He didn't stay long. Just as we were leaving, the police arrived. Hughes was being accused of being responsible for a murder.

The other occasion—not a face-to-face meeting—was at the Inn on the Park in London. McIntosh reports:

Howard had hidden cameras monitoring the corridor outside his suite to see who was coming. Cary knew that Howard watched anxiously all the time. As we walked past, he waved to the camera, with great warmth and cheerfulness, so Howard would know he was in the hotel.

By the summer of 1975, Hughes was dying. He moved to Freeport in the Bahamas, and then, falsely informed that codeine was not available in the islands (and he was addicted to it), he was flown, in February 1976, to Acapulco and the garish excesses of the Princess Hotel. He stopped eating, and even refused water. Shifted to Houston, Texas, he at last passed away. He left Cary nothing in his will, which was fought over with great bitterness in the months to come. Cary received news of his death with great sadness. A part of his life was gone forever.

Randolph Scott, happily married, apparently had preserved a sentimental feeling for Cary. In the 1970s, Cary and Scott would turn up at the Beverly Hillcrest Hotel late at night, after the other diners had gone, and in the near darkness of their table at the back of the restaurant, the maître d' would see the two old men surreptitiously holding hands.

Virginia Cherrill recalls that she spoke to Cary in England, soon after his mother's death, to tell him that a mutual friend, a girl named Troy Sondheim, was dying of cancer and wanted to see him. Virginia had obtained Cary's number from the former agent Minna Wallis and left a message for him at the Inn on the Park. He called her back from Bristol, where he had been settling some of Elsie's affairs. She asked if he would be coming to New York, and he said he would. But when he got to the hospital to see Troy Sondheim, she panicked at the last minute and refused to let him in because she looked so terrible: she had lost her hair from the radiation treatments.

Back in California, Cary called Virginia at her home in Santa Barbara, where she lived with her third husband. He said he wanted to bring Jennifer, to show her off. Virginia said she would be delighted. Why didn't he drive up? He said he wanted to come in the Fabergé plane, and would she mind? She said she would, since she didn't want to have press photographers taking pictures of them together at the airport; it would get in the papers that he had brought his daughter by his fourth wife to see his first wife. He snapped at her, "You always were a bitch!" They didn't speak again.

Barbara Hutton was anorexic now, suffering from declining health in the wake of her beloved son's death. She would turn up, spectral, always dressed in black, at dinner parties, complaining about the food and charging that the host was poisoning her soup. There were those—Truman Capote among them—who said that she had once ingested a tapeworm in order to get thin, and it had finally eaten her away; she threatened them with lawsuits. She would call Cary at all hours, shouting bitterly that those around her were trying to kill her and were keeping her locked up in her suite at the Beverly Wilshire Hotel. In 1979, wasted away to a skeleton and no longer knowing her own name, she finally died of a heart attack.

Betsy Drake was made of sterner stuff. Her career as an actress long over, she became a psychotherapist, specializing in disturbed children and adolescents; she also led psychodrama groups at UCLA and published a novel. Occasionally, she spoke with Cary on the telephone. Phyllis Brooks was living comfortably in the Northeast, having married a close friend and associate of President John F. Kennedy; she was the mother of an attractive family that inherited her perfect looks and charm. Mary Brian had married the film editor George Tomasini, who had worked on many Hitchcock movies, including Cary's own *North by Northwest*. She saw Cary occasionally at social events. Sophia Loren and Cary were violently in conflict over her memoirs, written with A. E. Hotchner, in which she described her romantic relationship with him in terms appropriate to a fairy tale; he objected to her having written about their relationship at all, even though she was extraordinarily protective, sympathetic, and flattering. If she could be accused of anything, it was of giving the impression that the liaison meant a great deal more than in fact it really did.

As for Dyan Cannon, her struggles with Cary over Jennifer never abated. Both Cary and she constantly challenged the court order that Jennifer must be restricted to the United States, Canada, England, France, and Mexico, and that her parents must not harass or annoy each other. For example, in the summer of 1973, the child spent July with Cary in Westhampton, Long Island, after being in Montreal during the shooting of Dyan's first picture as a director, *Child Under a Leaf*. Cary managed to block Dyan from taking Jennifer to Tunisia that August. He showered his daughter with gifts. Some of her happiest days were spent with her father at the racetrack; Cary had become deeply obsessed with racing in his seventies.

Various court actions occupied Cary in the 1970s, including his suit for one million dollars against 20th Century–Fox for splicing scenes from *Monkey Business*, his co-starring vehicle with Ginger Rogers, into a semidocumentary account of the career of Marilyn Monroe. He was awarded ten dollars, a humiliating settlement, which he bravely described as "a moral victory." In 1975, Cary was elected to the board of Metro-Goldwyn-Mayer, where he had made one of his favorite pictures, *The Philadelphia Story*. He proved to be a skillful and dedicated board member, not merely a figurehead. For him, there was the irresistible attraction of the many perquisites, influences, and benefits that went with the position.

A final link with his childhood snapped when his half-brother, Eric, died of cancer in 1976. That year, Cary spent time in London, staying, for a change, at the Royal Lancaster Hotel in Bayswater. He liked the hotel, and he especially liked the public relations woman there, who assisted him during a Fabergé trade show. Her name was Barbara Harris. She was in her twenties, of medium height, dark, slender, and athletic, with beautifully chiseled features and intelligent, sharp eyes. She exuded efficiency, coolness, a degree of cultivation, and an open, uncomplicated friendliness. He was amused by the fact that she would drive him around town to interviews or meetings in a Mini Minor, which he had to almost bend double to enter, and he loved the fact that she didn't treat him like a movie star. Cary enjoyed driving with Barbara through small English villages and drinking glasses of beer in pubs. He liked visiting with her parents, retired Tanganyika public servants, at their Devon farm. Although Barbara was far removed from his usual physical type, Cary found in her a true, unambitious, and unchallenging friend. In his seventies, friendship was more important to him than anything else. He longed for a safe harbor.

Yet even now he was not destined to enjoy complete happiness. He had for some years failed to maintain his earlier and rigorous exercise routines. His well-developed physique, the result of years of acrobatics, had remained with him to an extraordinarily late age, provoking much envious admiration from friends. But he had forgotten that although it is difficult, given a careful diet, to lose the muscularity of a pure mesomorph, even athletes can succumb to age if they do not maintain aerobic activity. His heart had been weakened, and his cardiovascular problems became increasingly severe; he began to suffer from high blood pressure. At last, even his muscles began to soften.

In 1979, he was deeply saddened by the killing of his old friend, Lord Louis Mountbatten, by the Irish Republican Army. Cary attended the funeral service in Westminster Abbey and broke into tears. At a special reception following the funeral, he was greeted with enthusiasm by the Queen and the Duke of Edinburgh, admirers of his.

He was upset that NBC was going to film Sophia Loren's memoirs and sought an injunction against the network and the production company. Finally, he agreed to allow John Gavin—whom he much admired and liked, and had seen a good deal of in his years at MCA Universal—to portray him, in return for the sum of $250,000.

There was more serious trouble with NBC in November 1980. Chevy Chase appeared as a guest on Tom Snyder's popular *Tomorrow* show. Cary, who admired Chase, appreciating the style of his bumptious comedy routines, made a special point of watching that night. He was horrified when, after Snyder asked Chase what he felt about Cary Grant, Chase said, "He really was a great physical comic, and I understand he was a homo. What a gal!" Chase accompanied the statement, delivered in a lisping, effeminate voice, with a limp-wristed gesture.* Cary exploded, called his lawyer in the middle of the night, and slapped a ten-million-dollar slander suit on Chase. Chase's agent, Jasper Vance, said that Chase would not respond. And, sensibly, Cary failed to pursue the suit; it could have led him into a disastrous situation. More than one friend recommended that he present whatever money he might gain from a victory in court to gay liberation, and in a characteristic switch, he laughingly agreed. Chase finally commented, "I shouldn't have said that, because it's been such a pain in the neck."

By 1980, Barbara Harris was living with Cary at his homes in Benedict Canyon and Malibu. When she revealed that she was leaving London to join him, she had said to a colleague, "I only hope I can stop smoking!" Cary refused to have smokers in his presence. Jennifer adored Barbara, and the feeling was mutual. Barbara, with her English coolness, her lack of neuroses or strong emotionalism, and her dislike of theatricality, proved to be an ideal companion for Cary. Although at first he stated in more than one interview that he had failed at marriage and would never marry again, he at last began saying to journalists that he wanted Barbara to be "the lady of my manor."

She humored his desire to live to be over a hundred. When the much-traveled Henry Gris arrived from Russia, with a formula of

---

* In another version, friends called Cary the morning after the telecast to tell him about it; he had been asleep when it was aired.

fresh honey and walnuts to be eaten for longevity and sexual prowess, he happily devoured the concoction every morning. He longed for more children. In the wake of the fracas with Chevy Chase, he apparently had no homosexual inclinations. And it is reasonably certain that Barbara never accepted that aspect of his past history.

He now entered the only really happy time of his life. Dyan Cannon had grown more mellow, and now that Jennifer was well into her teens, with a strong and well-balanced personality of her own, the extreme tensions between her parents lessened. It seemed time to consolidate his joy at last. On April 15, 1981, Cary and Barbara were married in the living room of the Beverly Grove Drive house, with Jennifer, Mr. and Mrs. Stanley Fox, and two members of the domestic staff as witnesses. The newlyweds were guests ten days later at the twenty-fifth wedding anniversary party of Princess Grace and Prince Rainier, with Frank Sinatra as host.

On December 6, 1981, Cary joined Count Basie, Helen Hayes, Jerome Robbins, and Rudolf Serkin as a recipient of the Kennedy Center Award in Washington. Among those present at the gala reception at the White House were Cary's old friend Audrey Hepburn, James Stewart, and Victor Borge, whom Cary doted on. Art Buchwald brought the house down when he said to Ronald Reagan, "Mr. President, if you hadn't gone into politics you might be sitting in the seat where Cary Grant is now—and Al Haig would be sitting in yours."

In May 1982, Cary was honored as Man of the Year by the New York Friars Club at the Waldorf-Astoria Hotel; the event raised a quarter of a million dollars for charity. Although Cary disliked dinners honoring him—he wished he could simply spend his time in peace in Los Angeles—and was extremely tense over his speech, he was overjoyed by the presence there of George Burns, from whom, he felt, he had learned his comedy timing. Cary burst out laughing when Burns said, "I was introduced to Cary by Abraham Lincoln's widow." He broke up completely as Rich Little recreated Cary's cockney dialogue in *Gunga Din*. Tony Bennett sang "It Amazes Me," Cary's favorite song, and Peggy Lee delivered "Mr. Wonderful" directly to his face. Sinatra, in his best form, inimitably delivered "The Most Fabulous Man in the World," Sammy Cahn's reworking of a Rodgers and Hart number. Cary was so moved by the entire evening that tears streamed down his face as he walked to the podium. Saying ruefully, with a smile that would have melted lead, "To indulge in one's emotions is a privilege allowed to the elderly," he abandoned most of his prepared speech and talked simply and touchingly of his gratitude for the admiration of his peers.

There were two further bereavements. It was one of the burdens of old age that so many of the nearest and dearest passed away. He had long suffered the agonizing final illness of Ingrid Bergman who, with great courage, had battled against breast cancer. The growth had metasticized, and she had called to tell Cary the news. At an American Film Institute Life Achievement Award banquet for Alfred Hitchcock, which Cary had come to reluctantly because of a cold, she had moved him deeply by giving a Yale key, a souvenir of their film *Notorious,* to Hitchcock. An even greater loss was in store. In September 1982, Princess Grace, whom Cary had never ceased to admire and love, had set out to drive from her mountain residence to Monaco along the twisting Grand Corniche, when she suffered a stroke, lost control of her automobile, and crashed to her death. This second grief following Miss Bergman's death just a few weeks earlier was intolerable. Cary was in agony as he and Barbara flew to Monaco for the funeral and did their best to console the devastated Prince Ranier. As the service in the cathedral ended, Cary's face suddenly looked shockingly old. Barbara had to raise him from his seat, as he seemed unable to stand. But he never lost his dignity in the face of the crowd and the photographers. A trifle unsteadily, he made his way to the waiting car, and then he broke into helpless tears.

He himself had never been much of a driver; he was now drastically concerned for Jennifer. He begged her not to drive the Honda he had given her for her sixteenth birthday, and discussed his apprehensions with Dyan Cannon. Finally, he let Jennifer drive. This matter brought him closer to his former wife than he had been for years.

In 1983, he set off on a world cruise with Barbara aboard the Royal Viking Sky. *To Catch a Thief* and *Charade* were shown while the couple was on board. Crew members recall that the Grants were happy and relaxed, mingling not only with the passengers but with the crew, appearing at their table for two in the dining room with broad smiles, accepting questions from passengers, and enjoying the company of the Norwegian captain and officers. It was an ideal opportunity to get away from everything and everyone.

The experience of giving question-and-answer sessions on board, something Cary had long avoided (Joan Crawford and Bette Davis were among those stars who enjoyed such sessions in their later years), prompted him to start a new career as a one-man performer, with a presentation entitled "A Conversation with Cary Grant." It would be something to do—he was beginning to be bored and fretful and sensed that he was getting out of touch—and he would visit parts of America he had never seen. In Schenectady, New York, he delighted a large crowd at Proctor's Theater, giving quick and intelligent replies to questions while seated onstage on a backless stool for ninety minutes. Dressed with expected elegance in a black tuxedo, he was occasionally provocative. When somebody asked him about Mae West, he commented: "I don't have a fond memory of her. She did her own thing, to the detriment of everyone around her. I don't admire superficiality." For the most part, though, his comments were sweetly innocuous, and no one had the temerity to inquire about inconvenient matters. The ovation—from people of all ages—was prolonged.

It was always a strain for Cary to attend the Academy Awards, but as an elder statesman of the industry, he felt it was a social obligation to appear. Timothy Hutton recalls an incident at the 1984 awards:

> I had never met Cary Grant before, and I went up to him and introduced myself. I mentioned my dad, Jim Hutton. We started talking about how much he liked my dad, and he made me feel great. He didn't just say, "Oh, that's nice" and walk away. He sat down next to me, and we talked. Despite all the activity in the room, I remember how incredibly gracious and warm and interested in the memory of *Walk Don't Run* and of my father Cary Grant was. Here was this very, very electric atmosphere, with pages running up and giving last-minute script changes, and

countdowns, and loud noises—and there he was. I thought: If only my dad could hear this, hear the person that meant the most to him professionally, in his field, saying the things about [Dad] that he admired most and looked up to.

I asked him if he would ever want to make another movie, and he just dismissed it. He said, "Absolutely not. I'm having far too great a time doing what I'm doing these days to get back into that." He didn't need to have done what he did, talking to me. It was something I'll never forget. The last of the great gentlemen: Cary Grant.

At home in October 1984, Cary experienced a dizzy spell. Doctors at Cedars Sinai Medical Center in Los Angeles told him he had had a slight stroke. He was warned to ease up on his constant travels and his appearances at gala occasions. But Barbara loved to socialize, and he always enjoyed displaying his amazingly preserved looks. They continued their whirlwind activities, which still included work for Fabergé.

He was wearing himself out. On November 28, 1986, he arrived at Davenport, Iowa, for another of his question-and-answer sessions and checked into the Blackhawk Hotel. He was in the best of moods, buoyant, looking forward to the evening's event, holding hands with Barbara for the photographers. All passion spent, his tension and neuroses seemingly banished for good, he was a radiant presence, and everyone he met stared at him in disbelief, noting his glowing good health. But he was not feeling well. He had a wobbly, unsteady sense of discomfort, and at a run-through to set the microphones and lights in the correct positions, at which he was expert as always, he seemed forgetful and uneasy. Beads of perspiration started on his forehead as he moved around the Adler Theater, discussing with the coordinator, Lois Jecklin, how best he might handle two and a half hours of questioning. Toward the end of the session with Miss Jecklin, he suddenly went pale under his tan and almost fell into an armchair. Barbara anxiously asked him if he would like a physician. He refused, perhaps aware of the effect a doctor's attentions might have on his image of eternal health and youthfulness. He was determined not to disappoint the audience, and he sat very still in his dressing room, trying to summon up his energy. Again, Barbara asked him if he would accept medical attention and again he refused. Finally, Davenport businessman Douglas Miller called Dr. Duane Manlov, who arrived and, much to Cary's annoyance, took his pulse and temperature. Manlov realized Cary was having another stroke. Cardiologist Dr. James Gillson turned up and insisted that Cary go to the hospital. Cary refused. He wanted to return to Los Angeles at once.

Stubborn in the face of everyone's advice, he became impatient when Barbara, who was by now in a state of appalling anxiety, demanded that he go to the hospital. An ambulance arrived; Cary was suffering from chest pains. He was grumblingly taken to St. Luke's Hospital; he kept holding Barbara's hand and expressing his love. When he at last reached the intensive care unit, it was revealed that he had in fact suffered a major stroke. In a daze of confusion throughout, he probably didn't know the extent of his illness. At 11:22 P.M., he was dead.

There was no funeral; because Cary always hated Forest Lawn, the body was cremated. His eighty-million-dollar fortune was divided between Jennifer and Barbara, who have kept his memory alive.

He was, and is, mourned. He represents a vision of much that is lost to us. Though, until the last years, he found little happiness himself, he gave an unlimited amount to others. The timeless grace of his performances will never be forgotten. As for Archie Leach, he never left Cary Grant; and Grant never found himself. Someone asked him, "Who is Cary Grant?" and he replied, "When you find out, tell me. . ."

ACKNOWLEDGMENTS

The authors are deeply grateful to the following individuals who gave unstintingly of their time in order to assist us in our research for this biography: Ronald Reagan, Katharine Hepburn, Dr. Timothy Leary, Stewart Granger, Rich Little, Ralph Bellamy, Sidney Sheldon, Stanley Kramer, Alexis Smith, Richard Brooks, Timothy Hutton, George Burns, Ambassador John Gavin, Douglas Fairbanks, Jr., KBE, Marlene Dietrich, Margaret, Duchess of Argyll, Milton Goldman, Virginia Cherrill, Phyllis Brooks, Mary Brian, Binnie Barnes, Mike Frankovich, Martin Landau, Jane Wyatt, Johnny Maschio, Constance Moore Maschio, Melville Shavelson, Stanley Shapiro, Martha Scott, Joan Bennett, Janet Blair, Delbert Mann, Edward R. Muhl, Movita, Mrs. Reginald Gardiner, Phyllis Calvert, Frank Capra, Dane Clark, Rita Gam, Sammy Cahn, John Howard, Laraine Day, Richard Gully, Priscilla Lane, Pandro S. Berman, David Manners, Fritz Feld, Dean Jagger, Jane Wyman, Gene Raymond, Arthur Lubin, Richard Anderson, Ted Donaldson, Irving Fein, Owen Crump, Mrs. Owen Crump, Frances Drake, Craig Stevens, Fay Wray, Jean Rogers, Peggy Moran Koster, Miles Kreuger, William Currie McIntosh, Ernest Cuneo, Curt Gentry, Ted Carpentier, Peggy Shannon, Curtis Harrington, Vincent Sherman, Marvin Paige, Jack Martin, Mrs. Ernst Lubitsch, Nicola Lubitsch, Samuel Marx, Moray Watson, Jean Howard, Robert Cohn, Alexander D'Arcy, Peter

Pit, Billy McComb, Ann Doran, Jean Dalrymple, Michael Harris, Paula Raymond, Alister Hunter, Matthew Kennedy, Max Tishman, Mr. and Mrs. Geoff King, Sally Bulloch, Johnnie Riscoe, James E. McVeay, Keith Blackmore, Florian Martini, Robin Macdonald, Kendall Carly Browne, Ned Comstock, Seth Green, Madame Olga Celeste, Bert Granet, Berri Lee, Tim Barry, Demetrios Vilan, Geoffrey T. Roberts, J. P. Wearing, Guido Orlando, Henry Gris, Kevin Thomas, Walt Odets, and Virginia Rowe; and the following, who, sadly, are no longer living: Mary Lee Fairbanks, Henry Koster, Noah Dietrich, Marilyn Hinton, Johnny Meyer, Marion Gering, Elsa Lanchester Laughton, Brian Aherne, Howard Hawks, Joseph Ruttenberg, Casey Robinson, Mae West, George Stevens, Carmel Myers, Delmer Daves, Hal B. Wallis, and Sammy Curtis.

To the following, close personal friends, we are most deeply grateful. Without their kindness and generous help, this book could never have been written: Gavin Kern, Bruce Cohn Curtis, Richard Lamparski, Harold Schwab, Marc Courtland, Daniel Schott, Stephen Breimer, Stephen Ortloff, Patrick Thomas, Keith Hook, John Marven, Bijou Durden, Robert Uher, Pasquale and Veronica Pavone, Philip Masheter, John Leach, Nicholas Armstrong, Peter Moore, Stephen Rattey, Peter Seyderhelm, B.Sc. (Econ.) Hull, Martyn Shallcross, and Jane and Glen Kern.

Our agent, Mitch Douglas of ICM, proved magnificently supportive throughout. His assistant Jerry Thomas was a tower of strength. Ray Austin broke a long silence to tell us of his extraordinary friendship with Cary Grant, combining in great degree both honesty and a sincere and lasting respect and admiration for the great star. James P. Maloney III did a very good job of winkling out secret documents in Washington, D.C., which had never been declassified. Stuart Halperin did fine work in New York. Daniel Re'em in London helped us in the difficult pursuit of the matter of the King's Medal awarded to Cary Grant for valor in World War II. Nigel West and Tessa Perfect were also indispensable in tracing this important matter. Miles Kreuger was very helpful. Herbert Goldman did sterling work in New York, reading through thousands of pages of *Variety* and other show-business publications in order to trace the movements of young Archie Leach in the vaudeville theater in the

1920s. We would especially like to single out the very special help of Martin Masheter (who did superb research in obscure theater magazines in London), and Christian Roberts, and Mavis Hawkins, who made everything so clear.

We were greatly assisted by Cary Grant's family and friends in Bristol, who were kind, helpful, and proud of what had happened to Archie Leach: Valerie Bagnall, Vivian Selley, Nicola Leach England, Betsy Leach Shapland, "Ted Morley," Ellen Hallett, Francis Chivers, and Lillian Pearce.

Ann Splain and Richard Babcock of the Luxury Line in Beverly Hills made so much of this book possible. Thanks are due also to Anthony Slide and Richard Goetz.

We thank the staffs of the FBI, State Department, Military Intelligence, Naval Intelligence, U.S. Passport and Visa Divisions, USC Doheny Library, UCLA Research Library, New York Public Library at Lincoln Center, Library of Congress, St. Louis Opera Company, British Library, Bristol Public Library, Colindale Research Library of London (Periodicals Division), and all other British provincial libraries and theater collections. Bill Warren did much useful research, and the staff of the Academy of Motion Picture Arts and Sciences were especially helpful.

NOTES

CHAPTER ONE

The birth records of Archibald Alec Leach were obtained by Martin Masheter from St. Catherine's House, Central Record Office, London. Details of the birthplace were obtained from Bristol registers by genealogist Geoffrey T. Roberts. These included a floor plan and survey map of the house itself. Mr. Roberts secured the family tree back to 1842.

Stewart Granger and Ray Austin confirmed from firsthand knowledge that Cary Grant was circumcised. Mrs. Sam Jaffe is the source on Grant's declaration that he was Jewish, and this was confirmed by many others. An almost equal number stated that he failed to mention any Jewish origin. His autobiographical statements were published in the *Ladies' Home Journal* (January–April 1963), in the series he published to replace Joe Hyams's authorized work. Martin Masheter obtained detailed particulars of pantomimes and other theatrical shows in Bristol during Grant's childhood. Particulars of the Lomas Troupe emerged from period magazines of the early years of the century and from research done by J. P. Wearing for his *The London Stage* (Metuchen, N.J.: Scarecrow Press, 1976). An especially valuable piece was found in the *Pall Mall* magazine of January 1910, which had pictures of the troupe. A small boy watching in the background at a rehearsal may have been Archie Leach. The Bristol *Times and Mirror* and *Western Daily News* were valuable sources. *Variety* gave a full account of the Pender Troupe's European tours. The magazine's 1910, 1911, and 1912 annual editions had many articles on music hall conditions in England. *Popular Mechanics* supplied details of the construction of stilts at the time.

CHAPTER TWO

Shipping lists were obtained showing passenger manifests that accurately established the movements of the Pender Troupe. The *New York Times* gave a detailed account of the performances of the Folies Bergère, and *The Stage* and *Variety* filled out the picture. Jesse L. Lasky's memoir, *I Blow My Own Horn,* (Garden City, NY: Doubleday, 1956) was especially valuable. Again, J. P. Wearing, in *The London Stage,* supplied details of the troupe's performances in British pantomime. Mrs. Lillian Pearce, Ellen Hallett, and "Ted Morley" supplied much valuable information on his school days. Various histories of magic included accounts of David Devant. Again, research by Martin Masheter and Herbert Goldman pieced together the jigsaw puzzle of the Pender Troupe's further career, supplemented by Grant's *Ladies' Home Journal* memoir. John Marven obtained details of Charlie Spangles from the late performer's closest friend, James E. McVeay, interviewed in Liverpool. Various interviews with the late Jean Adair confirmed her friendship with Archie Leach. Sam Marx and Matthew Kennedy (among others) remembered Archie Leach on stilts.

CHAPTER THREE

Jean Dalrymple, doyenne of veteran Broadway producers, was a great source here. So was her former partner Max Tishman, now approaching ninety, who, despite illness, supplied vivid memories (she had not heard from him in forty years). The great George Burns was a major source. The Lester Sweyd and Phil Charig papers, the former housed at Lincoln Center, New York, were drawn from. So was *Act One,* (N.Y., Random House, 1957), Moss Hart's brilliant autobiography. Miles Kreuger and the staff of the Lincoln Center Library provided programs of the New York musical shows in which Archie Leach appeared. Reminiscences by Jeanette MacDonald were drawn from, and were found in several libraries; Gene Raymond provided more particulars. The Shubert archive was a great source. Many relatives of the late Orry-Kelly in Kiama, New South Wales, Australia, gave his background, and Joel Greenberg in Sydney obtained birth and baptismal records. The staff of the St. Louis Municipal Opera Company provided memorable photographs, programs, and clippings. The late Casey Robinson recalled details of Archie's screen test. Demetrios Vilan remembered the farewell party for Archie Leach and Phil Charig in New York.

CHAPTER FOUR

Files of the Los Angeles *Times* and *Examiner* were consulted for details of Hollywood in 1932. Files of the *Hollywood Reporter* were read from 1932 until 1986. In the 1930s, the publication, which is very different today, provided an extraordinary time capsule of a forgotten world. Studio files provided a detailed account. Ned Comstock of USC Doheny Library discovered the long-lost files of the store named Neale's Smart Men's Apparel. Arthur Lubin provided a personal anecdote. Mrs. Ernst Lubitsch added much personal data. Budd Schulberg's memoirs were a good source. Anthony Slide and Robert Gitt showed certain films. Roy Moseley interviewed Sam Jaffe (the former agent) in 1975 for Charles Higham's book on Marlene Dietrich, and Miss Dietrich gave long interviews to Charles Higham. Virginia Cherrill, in one of the most memorable and courageous interviews that Roy Moseley has ever conducted, gave the complete emotional history of her relationship with Cary Grant from the beginning. The Ben Maddox article was drawn from *Modern Screen.* The Mae West material was drawn from Charles Higham's several interviews with Miss West.

CHAPTER FIVE

David Manners, now aged 87, recalled the crossing on the *Paris.*
The *Hollywood Reporter* was the source on the splendid parties of
the era. Edith Gwynn Wilkerson was a social reporter with a Swiftian
eye for the peculiar behavior of the society in which she found herself. The sources on Howard Hughes's affair with Cary Grant were
the late Noah Dietrich, interviewed at his house above Sunset Strip
by Charles Higham many times in the mid-1970s, and the late Johnny
Meyer, whom Higham talked to at the Drake Hotel in New York
City on three occasions in the summer of 1978, in the course of
researching a book on Errol Flynn. Guido Orlando, a Hughes publicist, confirmed the relationship without hesitation, and so did a
leading Hughes aircraft designer, who prefers to be anonymous. That
same designer fully confirmed Hughes's bisexual activities then and
later. *Empire: The Life, Legend and Madness of Howard Hughes,* by
Donald L. Barlett and James B. Steele, (N.Y.; W. W. Norton, 1979)
is much the best biography of the late tycoon, and has been our
main source on particulars of his life as a great airman and aircraft
manufacturer. Seth Green in Orange, Virginia, former editor of the
Orange *Record,* reminisced on a rain-swept Sunday afternoon about
the extraordinary life of his intimate friend the late Marion duPont
Scott. Several other citizens of Orange confirmed the authenticity
of his description, and Mrs. Scott's memoirs were also used. The
late George Cukor and the late Brian Aherne told Charles Higham
of the particulars of *Sylvia Scarlett.* Mary Brian, in her first interview ever on the subject, told Roy Moseley of her love for the actor.
The late Noël Coward often discussed Grant with Roy Moseley.
Joan Bennett supplied some warm and affectionate comments.

CHAPTER SIX

The authors regard Phyllis Brooks's long interviews in Maine and
London with Roy Moseley as the high spot of the book's research.
Miss Brooks opened her heart for the first time with unstinting
warmth, decency, and generosity. It was not easy for her to re-

awaken the long-lost past, but for her it will always be present. She is in love with Cary Grant to this day. Kendall Carly Browne, Frank Vincent's secretary for several years, confirmed the statements of others that Grant was his own agent. Hal Roach supplied a unique interview on his association with Grant. Jean Rogers, memorable as the girlfriend of Flash Gordon, supplied clear memories. Alexander D'Arcy was a helpful source. CBS, NBC, and SPERDVAC, the well-known radio archive, gave details of Cary's wireless career. The Randolph Scott/Katharine Strother Scott files were found in Room 6E of the Diplomatic Archives. Higham interviewed Katharine Hepburn, Howard Hawks, and Fritz Feld on *Bringing Up Baby*. Mrs. Reginald Gardiner, Douglas Fairbanks, Jr., and the late George Stevens filled in particulars of *Gunga Din*.

CHAPTER SEVEN

Howard Hawks, in conversation with Charles Higham, was the main source on *Only Angels Have Wings*. SPERDVAC supplied useful cassettes of the Grant radio programs. Ralph Bellamy was entertaining on the subject of *The Awful Truth* and *His Girl Friday*. Rudolph Stoiber and the massive Errol Flynn files at USC, drawn from every branch of the government, supply the full record of Flynn's and Erben's treason to the United States. Sir William Stephenson, in a special cabled message to Roy Moseley, dated June 12, 1987, responded to his question as to whether Cary Grant was a British secret agent in World War II. The reply read: "Your letter, July 2, question, answer is: I assume so, as Cary was one of a group in constant [touch] and helpful to BSC [British Security Coordination] member Noël Coward. Others in group included Sam and Frances Goldwyn, Alex Korda, David Niven . . . all strongly anti-Nazi, pro-Semite. Greetings, good wishes, William Stephenson, inter[office] Bermuda." The late Carmel Myers told Charles Higham of the group of British agents in Hollywood. FBI files confirmed the roles of other agents, including June Duprez and Reginald Gardiner. For full details and documentation on Merle Oberon's role, read *Princess Merle: The Romantic Life of Merle Oberon,* by Higham and Moseley. Bert

Granet vividly recalled the shooting of *My Favorite Wife*. Sir Douglas and Lady Fairbanks were excellent on the leasing of their house to Cary Grant. The Hilda Krueger documents obtained by Charles Higham from the Diplomatic Archive are in public access and were later lent to Robert Lenzner for his biography of J. Paul Getty. The Cary Grant Special Agent travel documents were obtained by James P. Maloney through the passport office in Washington. The best sources on Hutton remain C. David Heymann's controversial *Poor Little Rich Girl* (Secaucus, N.J.: Lyle Stuart, 1984) and Mona Eldridge's interesting memoir, *In Search of a Prince*. Johnny Maschio and his wife, Constance Moore, told us much about Miss Hutton. Joseph Ruttenberg and John Howard filled out memories of *The Philadelphia Story* supplied by Katharine Hepburn to Charles Higham in 1975. The Noël Coward quotation appeared in *A Man Called Intrepid*, by William Stevenson, the authorized biography of Sir William Stephenson. The Clifford Odets documents were a good source and were provided by Virginia Rowe, Mr. Odets's secretary, with the written approval of Odets's son Walt, who also gave a fine interview.

CHAPTER EIGHT

The documents on Sir William Stephenson are to be found in Room 6E of the Diplomatic Archives. The activities of Bugsy Siegel were recorded in detail in the Los Angeles *Times* and *Examiner*, and in Dean Jennings's biography of the gangster. Numerous State Department documents covered the activities of Dorothy di Frasso in the United States, Mexico, and Italy. Joseph Longstreth, breaking a long silence, maintained during the publication of Charles Higham's Errol Flynn biography, at last agreed to confirm (in view of Cary Grant's death) the secret information that Grant had exposed Errol Flynn as a Nazi agent and collaborator. Longstreth had never forgotten his meeting with Grant at the 1941 party. The files on Count Cassina are still maintained at FBI headquarters in Washington, and in Room 6E. The Barbara Hutton correspondences with Nazi Germany are in Room 6E. So are the von Cramm documents.

Priscilla Lane talked about *Arsenic and Old Lace,* and Charles Higham interviewed Frank Capra several times in the early 1970s. Richard Anderson helped us to understand the relationship of Cary Grant and Lance Reventlow. Curt Gentry and Ernest Cuneo told us of J. Edgar Hoover's intense dislike of William Stephenson and, by extension, Cary Grant.

CHAPTER NINE

Binnie Barnes was extremely helpful in a memorable luncheon with Roy Moseley. Ray Austin described Grant's activities as an agent. Dane Clark and the late Delmer Daves were indispensable on *Destination Tokyo.* The Warner Bros. files preserved at USC, and examined by courtesy of the Doheny Library staff and Warners, gave day-to-day particulars. Janet Blair and especially Ted Donaldson were excellent on *Once Upon a Time.* Donaldson's touching account of Grant's fatherliness to him proved to be very moving. Jane Wyatt, the late Ethel Barrymore's memoirs, the papers of Clifford Odets, and Richard Brooks helped us very much in coming to grips with the extraordinary relationship between Grant and Miss Barrymore on *None But the Lonely Heart.* Alexis Smith was marvelous on *Night and Day;* the Warner Bros. studio files were a major resource. Jane Wyman and the late Hal Wallis told us more. Miss Smith's statement, "Cary Grant's acting was never an eighth of an inch off," surely said it all. Contemporary interviews with Monty Woolley were called on. Eric Stacy's production notes were helpful.

CHAPTER TEN

The Louella Parsons quotation is from her Hearst Newspapers column. Material on *Notorious* is drawn from interviews at various times between the two authors and Alfred Hitchcock. The Betty Hensel affair was widely reported in the press. The flight from Los Angeles to New York was described by Johnny Maschio, Constance Moore, and Janet Blair. Andre de Toth added a couple of details.

Myrna Loy wrote of *The Bachelor and the Bobby-Soxer* in her auto-biography *Myrna Loy, Being and Becoming* (N.Y.: Knopf, 1982). So did Dore Schary in his memoirs, *Heyday* (N.Y.: Little, Brown, 1980). Howard Hughes's plane crash was described by his associate Ted Carpentier, confirmed in *Empire*.

CHAPTER ELEVEN

Again, the FBI files on Hughes have been drawn from here. The late Henry Koster was the main source on *The Bishop's Wife*. The matter of the King's Medal was researched by the authors, based on an entry in the British Foreign Office Indexes. Nigel West, Daniel Re'em, and Tessa Perfect assisted in London. Douglas Fairbanks, Jr., was also consulted in the matter, and Antony Acland, the British ambassador to the United States, provided some comments. The award was never made public. Much of the material on Betsy Drake was drawn from the Warner Bros. files at USC Doheny Library. When she was signed to make *Pretty Baby,* both the David O. Selznick and the Leland Hayward files on her were copied and retained in the Warner collection. Myrna Loy's published comments on *Mr. Blandings Builds His Dream House* were drawn from. The shooting of *I Was a Male War Bride* was commented on to Charles Higham by the late Howard Hawks; Ann Sheridan gave several interviews on the subject over the years. George Jessel's memoirs were a most valuable source on *Dancing in the Dark;* his hatred of Betsy Drake was sustained many years after the event. Stewart Granger was fascinating on the subject of his friendship with Grant and his odd, superficial relationship with Howard Hughes.

CHAPTER TWELVE

Richard Brooks made possible the section on *Crisis,* and Paula Raymond supplied much detail, some of it contradicting the director's. We decided to run both of their accounts, side by side. President Reagan added his own indispensable touch in recounting Mrs. Reagan's disappointment in being replaced. Melville Shavelson was helpful on the subject of *Room for One More*. Sidney Sheldon was very good on *Dream Wife*. The death of Dorothy di Frasso was reported in the Los Angeles *Times*. Charles Higham had a long discussion with Princess Grace on the subject of *To Catch a Thief* at a Lincoln Center tribute to Hitchcock in the 1970s. Roy Moseley also interviewed the princess on the matter.

CHAPTER THIRTEEN

Stanley Kramer was, of course, the main source on *The Pride and the Passion*. Melville Shavelson learned much about the production and the personal circumstances surrounding it, and shared the details with Roy Moseley. Mr. Shavelson's novel *Lualda* gives a curious account of some of the matters with which we are concerned, the author is at pains to say that the heroine is not based on Sophia Loren. Sidney Sheldon's novel *Bloodline* also provides a thinly disguised portrait of Cary Grant. The account of the sinking of the *Andrea Doria* is drawn from contemporary newspaper accounts and from Alvin Moscow's definitive *Collision Course* (N.Y.: Putnam, 1959). Mr. Moscow was contacted at his home in Florida on some details. A few touches were supplied by A. E. Hotchner's ghosted memoirs of Loren. Dr. Timothy Leary supplied us with crucial information on the matter of Grant's involvement with LSD and the effect it had on the star. Ray Austin was a rich and varied source on his several years with Cary Grant. His vivid memory for detail helped us considerably.

CHAPTER FOURTEEN

Ingrid Bergman's memoirs, *Ingrid Bergman: My Story* (N.Y.: Delacorte Press, 1981) were a good source on *Indiscreet*. They were put together by Allan Burgess, with the assistance of Jeanne Bernkopf. Phyllis Calvert talked to Roy Moseley about making the film. Edward R. Muhl gave a unique interview, perhaps the first he has ever given, on his close association with Grant. Martin Landau was vivid on *North by Northwest*. Joe Hyams told Charles Higham of his experiences with Cary Grant and, as mentioned, the *Ladies' Home Journal* series and Hyams's memoirs were researched.

CHAPTER FIFTEEN

Ray Austin continued to be a great help in the matter of Howard Hughes. Moray Watson was the chief source on *The Grass Is Greener*. The late Sammy Curtis spoke fascinatingly to Roy Moseley about the past. Delbert Mann and Stanley Shapiro gave somewhat different accounts of the making of *That Touch of Mink*. Doris Day's memoirs, prepared by A. E. Hotchner, were again a good source. The account by Greta Thyssen appeared in *Photoplay* magazine. Mona Eldridge's story came from the aforementioned *In Search of a Prince* London: Sidgwick & Jackson, 1988). Herbert Sterne's interview on *Charade* was given to his friend Anthony Slide to convey to Charles Higham. Details of the divorce of Betsy Drake and Cary Grant were found in the Los Angeles *Times*. Henry Gris, veteran journalist, interviewed Cary Grant about his LSD involvement for a national tabloid. The quote from Corinne Introtter about Dyan Cannon's life with Cary Grant was supplied by Kevin Thomas.

CHAPTER SIXTEEN

The account of Cary Grant in Tokyo was drawn from the Los Angeles *Times* and the Japan *Times*, published in English. Timothy Hutton added some remarks on Jim Hutton's association with Grant. The description of Jennifer Grant's birth was very widely reported. The excellent book *The Private Cary Grant*, by William Currie McIntosh and William Weaver (London: Sidgwick and Jackson, 1983), provided a great deal of information that would otherwise not have been available. The late Tom Stout, former TWA representative, provided the colorful description in these pages. Constance Moore and William Weaver were the sources on the departure of the Grants for England. Nicola and Betsy Leach, Cary's nieces, daughters of his half-brother, Eric Leslie, gave an unprecedented interview on their meeting with the Grants. The Weaver-McIntosh book and the Barlett-Steele book supplied information in this chapter. Berri Lee gave an excellent interview on the many aspects of Cary Grant's life at the time. The late William Belasco, press reports (later withdrawn), and a statement made by Charles Manson on Bill Stout's CBS interview program formed the basis of the material on Grant on the grounds of the Melcher house during the infamous murders of Sharon Tate and her friends. The late Marilyn Hinton, with only six months to live, met with Charles Higham and told him of the long-concealed story of Cynthia Bouron.

CHAPTER SEVENTEEN

Weaver and McIntosh were the best source on the Fabergé association. Berri Lee and Tim Barry provided much detail on the Grant–Maureen Donaldson relationship. Several witnesses proved nervous on the subject of the producer's widow and asked not to be quoted. Their accounts have been supplemented by details in the Weaver-McIntosh book. Rich Little was his marvelous self in telling hilarious stories of his "becoming" Cary Grant. He also told us of Frank Sinatra's close friendship with Grant. Again, Tim Barry was indispensable on the subject of Maureen Donaldson. Joyce Milton and Ann Louise Bardach provided the only available account of Cary Grant's affair with Vicki Morgan in their sadly overlooked biography, *Vicki* (N.Y.: St. Martin's Press, 1986). Both were friends of the late Miss Morgan. William McIntosh was separately interviewed for a description of the final visits to Howard Hughes. He had not supplied these particulars in his and Weaver's book. The maître d' who saw Randolph Scott with Cary Grant at the Beverly Hillcrest Hotel does not wish to be identified. Virginia Cherrill once again proved intriguing as she recounted her renewed, very brief contact with Grant in the 1970s. Mary Brian also saw him again and talked about that. Sally Bulloch was our main source on the meeting of Grant and Barbara Harris. The Chevy Chase interview with Tom Snyder was, of course, widely reported at the time, as was the Grant-Harris marriage. The staff of the Royal Viking ships has described to Charles Higham the charm and considerateness of the Grants on their world cruise. Timothy Hutton provided the moving description of Grant's thoughtfulness toward him at the Academy Awards. Grant's death was best reported in the Los Angeles *Times*.

INDEX

341